Advanced Information Processing

T0138152

Hisao Ishibuchi · Tomoharu Nakashima
Manabu Nii

Classification and Modeling with Linguistic Information Granules

Advanced Approaches to Linguistic Data Mining

With 217 Figures and 72 Tables

 Springer

Hisao Ishibuchi
Department of Computer Science
and Intelligent Systems
Osaka Prefecture University
1-1 Gakuen-cho, Sakai
Osaka 599-8531, Japan
email: hisaoi@cs.osakafu-u.ac.jp

Tomoharu Nakashima
Department of Computer Science
and Intelligent Systems
Osaka Prefecture University
1-1 Gakuen-cho, Sakai
Osaka 599-8531, Japan
email: nakashi@cs.osakafu-u.ac.jp

Manabu Nii
Department of Electrical Engineering
and Computer Sciences
Graduate School of Engineering
University of Hyogo
2167 Shosha, Himeji
Hyogo 671-2201, Japan
e-mail: nii@eng.u-hyogo.ac.jp

ACM Subject Classification (1998): I.2

ISBN 978-3-642-05860-8   e-ISBN 978-3-540-26875-8

Springer is a part of Springer Science+Business Media

springeronline.com

© Springer-Verlag Berlin Heidelberg 2005
Softcover reprint of the hardcover 1st edition 2005

Cover design: KünkelLopka, Heidelberg

Printed on acid-free paper 45/3142/YL - 5 4 3 2 1 0

Preface

Many approaches have already been proposed for classification and modeling in the literature. These approaches are usually based on mathematical models. Computer systems can easily handle mathematical models even when they are complicated and nonlinear (e.g., neural networks). On the other hand, it is not always easy for human users to intuitively understand mathematical models even when they are simple and linear. This is because human information processing is based mainly on linguistic knowledge while computer systems are designed to handle symbolic and numerical information. A large part of our daily communication is based on words. We learn from various media such as books, newspapers, magazines, TV, and the Internet through words. We also communicate with others through words. While words play a central role in human information processing, linguistic models are not often used in the fields of classification and modeling. If there is no goal other than the maximization of accuracy in classification and modeling, mathematical models may always be preferred to linguistic models. On the other hand, linguistic models may be chosen if emphasis is placed on interpretability.

The main purpose in writing this book is to clearly explain how classification and modeling can be handled in a human understandable manner. In this book, we only use simple linguistic rules such as *"If the 1st input is large and the 2nd input is small then the output is large"* and *"If the 1st attribute is small and the 2nd attribute is medium then the pattern is Class 2"*. These linguistic rules are extracted from numerical data. In this sense, our approaches to classification and modeling can be viewed as linguistic knowledge extraction from numerical data (i.e., linguistic data mining). There are many issues to be discussed in linguistic approaches to classification and modeling. The first issue is how to determine the linguistic terms used in linguistic rules. For example, we have some linguistic terms such as *young*, *middle-aged*, and *old* for describing our ages. In the case of weight, we might use *light*, *middle*, and *heavy*. Two problems are involved in the determination of linguistic terms. One is to choose linguistic terms for each variable, and the other is to define the meaning of each linguistic term. The choice of linguistic terms is related to linguistic discretization (i.e., granulation) of each variable. The definition of the meaning of each linguistic term is performed using fuzzy logic. That is, the meaning of each linguistic term is specified by its membership function. Linguistic rules can be viewed as combinations of linguistic terms for each variable. The main focus of this book is to find good combinations of linguistic terms for generating linguistic rules. Interpretability as well as accuracy are taken into account when we extract linguistic rules from numerical data. Various aspects are related to the interpretability of linguistic models. In this book, the following aspects are discussed:

- Granulation of each variable (i.e., the number of linguistic terms).
- Overlap between adjacent linguistic terms.
- Length of each linguistic rule (i.e., the number of antecedent conditions).
- Number of linguistic rules.

The first two aspects are related to the determination of linguistic terms. We examine the effect of these aspects on the performance of linguistic models. The other two aspects are related to the complexity of linguistic models. We examine a tradeoff between the accuracy and the complexity of linguistic models. We mainly use genetic algorithms for designing linguistic models. Genetic algorithms are used as machine learning tools as well as optimization tools. We also describe the handling of linguistic rules in neural networks. Linguistic rules and numerical data are simultaneously used as training data in the learning of neural networks. Trained neural networks are used to extract linguistic rules.

While this book includes many state-of-the-art techniques in soft computing such as multi-objective genetic algorithms, genetics-based machine learning, and fuzzified neural networks, undergraduate students in computer science and related fields may be able to understand almost all parts of this book without any particular background knowledge. We make the book as simple as possible by using many examples and figures. We explain fuzzy logic, genetic algorithms, and neural networks in an easily understandable manner when they are used in the book. This book can be used as a textbook in a one-semester course. In this case, the last four chapters can be omitted because they include somewhat advanced topics on fuzzified neural networks. The first ten chapters clearly explain linguistic models for classification and modeling.

I would like to thank Prof. Lakhmi C. Jain for giving me the opportunity to write this book. We would also like to thank Prof. Witold Pedrycz and Prof. Francisco Herrera for their useful comments on the draft version of this book. Special thanks are extended to people who kindly assisted us in publishing this book. For example, Mr. Ronan Nugent worked hard for the copy-editing of this book. Ms. Ulrike Stricker gave us helpful comments on the layout and production. And general comments are given by Mr. Ralf Gerstner, who patiently and kindly contacted us. Some simulation results in this book were checked by my students. It is a pleasure to acknowledge the help of Takashi Yamamoto, Gaku Nakai, Teppei Seguchi, Yohei Shibata, Masayo Udo, Shiori Kaige, and Satoshi Namba.

Sakai, Osaka, March 2003   *Hisao Ishibuchi*

Contents

1. Linguistic Information Granules

In this book, we handle classification and modeling as linguistic rule extraction from numerical data. When rule extraction problems involve continuous attributes such as height, weight, and length, those attributes are usually discretized into several intervals in the field of machine learning [30]. In some situations, human knowledge exactly corresponds to interval discretization of continuous attributes. For example, the domain of age is divided into two intervals by the threshold age 20 in the following knowledge: "People under 20 are not allowed to smoke". Many laws are related to interval discretization of age. Various fare systems are also based on interval discretization of age (e.g., the bus fare for children between the ages of 6 and 12 is half of that for adults). Other familiar examples of interval discretization are weight divisions in boxing, wrestling, and judo. In these sports, weight is divided into some intervals (e.g., heavyweight, cruiserweight, light heavyweight, super middleweight, middleweight, etc.). Matchmaking is usually done within the same weight division. While we can show many examples of interval discretization, all of them come from artificially specified systems. In our everyday conversations, we usually do not use interval discretization. Instead of interval discretization, we use fuzzy discretization with no sharp boundaries. For example, let us consider the situation where a girl tells us that her father is tall. In this situation, we do not know the exact height of her father. We do not know the exact range (i.e., interval) of the height of her father, either. We just know that her father is tall. While the statement that her father is tall is vague, it gives us significant information about the height of her father. In this example, we do not have any exact interval corresponding to the linguistic term *tall* but have a vague range. Almost all linguistic terms in everyday conversations are related to vague ranges (not exact intervals). We can give many examples of linguistic terms with vague ranges. For example, the following statements include linguistic terms with vague ranges: she can run *fast*, his house is *large*, and my blood pressure is *high*. In these statements, *fast*, *large*, and *high* are not related to any exact intervals with clear boundaries.

We construct if–then rules using linguistic terms to handle classification and modeling problems. Linguistic rules for classification problems have linguistic conditions in the antecedent part and a class label in the consequent part. When our classification problem involves two continuous attributes of length and width, an example of linguistic rules is "If the length is *large* and the width is *large* then Class 1". On the other hand, linguistic rules for modeling problems have linguistic conditions in the antecedent part and linguistic terms in the consequent part. When our modeling problem involves two input variables and a single output variable, an example of linguistic rules is "If the first input is *small* and the second input is *large* then the output is *medium*". Throughout this book, we show how these linguistic rules can be generated from numerical data. We also examine the classification and modeling performance of linguistic rules. We expect that the performance of linguistic models (i.e., linguistic rule-based systems) is inferior to complicated nonlinear mathematical models. For improving the performance of linguistic models, we examine some tricks such as assigning a certainty factor to each rule and replacing a consequent linguistic term with a real number. Through computer simulations on simple numerical examples and real-world data sets, it is shown that the performance of linguistic models is significantly improved by such tricks.

The main advantage of using linguistic terms with vague ranges is the intuitive interpretability of linguistic rules. We can easily understand linguistic rules because they are based on linguistic terms as in our everyday conversations. While complicated nonlinear mathematical models such as neural networks are usually handled as black-box models, linguistic rule-based systems are transparent models. In this book, emphasis is placed on interpretability as well as accuracy when we tackle classification and modeling problems. That is, we try to design linguistic models with high interpretability as well as high accuracy. In addition to the performance of linguistic rules, we discuss their interpretability in this book. The design of linguistic models is viewed as finding a good tradeoff between interpretability and accuracy. Some users may prefer somewhat complicated linguistic models with high accuracy while other users may prefer very simple ones with high interpretability. Thus the design of linguistic models is also treated in the framework of multi-objective optimization. Multi-objective genetic algorithms are used to find a number of alternative rule-based systems with different accuracy and interpretability.

1.1 Mathematical Handling of Linguistic Terms

A mathematical framework for handling linguistic terms is fuzzy logic proposed by Zadeh in 1965 [190]. The concept of linguistic terms was introduced by Zadeh [191]. Recently fuzzy logic has been recognized as a useful mathematical tool for handling continuous attributes in rule-based systems [147]. Fuzzy rule-based systems have been successfully applied to various application fields such as control, modeling, and classification [117, 118, 119, 156].

A fuzzy set is a generalized concept of a standard non-fuzzy set. First let us consider a standard non-fuzzy set. For example, let A be a set of positive integers less than or equal to 5. The standard non-fuzzy set A is written as

$$A = \{1, 2, 3, 4, 5\}. \tag{1.1}$$

All positive integers less than or equal to 5 are included in A and any other integers are excluded from A. In this case, the membership of each integer in A is clear. That is, we know whether each integer is included in A or excluded from A. Now let us consider a set of small positive integers. We denote this set by B. We may be sure that the smallest positive integer "1" is included in B. We may also be sure that large integers such as "100" are not included in B. Let us assume that a small positive integer x (e.g., 1) is included in B. In this case, we may think that the next integer $x + 1$ is also included in B because the difference between x and $x + 1$ is only 1. In the same manner, we may also think that $x + 2$ is included in B because $x + 1$ is in B and the difference between $x + 1$ and $x + 2$ is only 1. This leads to the counter-intuitive result that all positive integers are included in the set B of small positive integers. If we try to define the set B using interval discretization, we have to specify a threshold integer θ such that θ is included in B while $\theta + 1$ is not included in B. The use of such a threshold value is counter-intuitive because the difference between θ and $\theta + 1$ is only 1. For example, it is not natural to think that "6" is not a small positive integer when we think that "5" is a small positive integer.

The difficulty in handling the set B of small positive integers within the framework of the standard set theory stems from the fact that the linguistic term *small* cannot be specified by interval discretization. In fuzzy logic (more specifically, fuzzy set theory), the set B of small positive integers is handled as a fuzzy set. It is assumed that each integer has a different grade of membership in the fuzzy set B. We may think that "1" and "2" have the maximum grade of membership (i.e., grade 1.0) in the fuzzy set B while "3" has a slightly smaller grade of membership (e.g., 0.9) than "1" and "2". Table 1.1 shows the membership grade of each integer in the fuzzy set B. We intuitively specify those grades of membership in Table 1.1. Readers may assign a different grade to each integer depending on their subjective understanding of the linguistic term *small*. The fuzzy set B specified by the membership grades in Table 1.1 is written as follows:

$$B = \left\{ \frac{1.0}{1}, \frac{1.0}{2}, \frac{0.9}{3}, \frac{0.8}{4}, \frac{0.5}{5}, \frac{0.2}{6}, \frac{0.1}{7} \right\}. \tag{1.2}$$

As shown in (1.2), fuzzy sets are denoted in the form of {membership grade/element}. Elements with no membership grade (i.e., grade 0.0) are omitted. In (1.2), integers larger than 7 have no membership grade in the fuzzy set B. As shown in Table 1.1, the maximum and minimum membership grades are 1.0 and 0.0 in fuzzy logic, respectively.

Table 1.1. Examples of membership grades in the fuzzy set B of small positive integers

Integer	1	2	3	4	5	6	7	8	9	10
Membership	1.0	1.0	0.9	0.8	0.5	0.2	0.1	0.0	0.0	0.0

When we have a fuzzy concept on a continuous attribute, we cannot write all elements with positive membership grades in the same manner as (1.2). For handling such a situation, fuzzy logic uses a membership function for defining a fuzzy concept. In Fig. 1.1, we show an example of a membership function that defines the fuzzy concept *tall*. We intuitively define this membership function on the continuous domain of height (i.e., the horizontal axis of Fig. 1.1). Readers may have different membership functions for the fuzzy concept *tall*. In fuzzy logic, membership functions are usually denoted by $\mu(\cdot)$. Let us denote the height by x as in Fig. 1.1. Then the membership function of the fuzzy concept *tall* in Fig. 1.1 is mathematically written as

$$\mu_{tall}(x) = \begin{cases} 0, & \text{for } x \leq 170, \\ (x-170)/10, & \text{for } 170 < x < 180, \\ 1, & \text{for } 180 \leq x. \end{cases} \tag{1.3}$$

The subscript *tall* of the membership function $\mu_{tall}(\cdot)$ denotes the label of the fuzzy set. This membership function specifies a membership grade of every particular value of height to the fuzzy concept *tall*. For example, the membership grade of the height 176 cm can be calculated from (1.3) as 0.6. As shown in Fig. 1.1, a membership function on a continuous attribute can be viewed as a mapping from its domain interval to the unit interval $[0, 1]$. Usually the domain on which a membership function is defined is referred to as the universe of discourse in fuzzy logic.

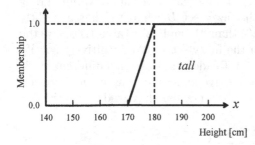

Fig. 1.1. An example of a membership function

1.2 Linguistic Discretization of Continuous Attributes

We use some linguistic terms for describing a continuous attribute. For example, we may use the three linguistic terms of *light*, *middle*, and *heavy* for describing weight. This means that the domain interval of weight is discretized into the three linguistic terms *light, middle,* and *heavy.* Figure 1.2 shows membership functions of these three linguistic terms, which are intuitively specified based on our subjective understanding of these linguistic terms. When the linguistic discretization into the three linguistic terms in Fig. 1.2 is given, we only use those three linguistic terms in our fuzzy models for describing weight. That is, numerical information with respect to weight is granulized into those three linguistic terms.

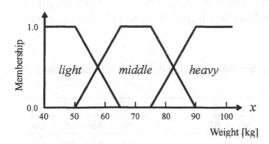

Fig. 1.2. Linguistic discretization of weight into three linguistic terms

The membership function of each linguistic term mathematically specifies its meaning. As we have already mentioned, the membership function is determined according to our subjective understanding of each linguistic term. Readers may assign a different membership function to each linguistic term in Fig. 1.2. Of course, the meaning of each linguistic term depends on the situation. For example, the meaning of the linguistic term *heavy* with respect to high school students is different from its meaning in the context of heavy professional wrestlers. Moreover, readers may have a different number of linguistic terms. The number of linguistic terms depends on the situation. It also depends on the culture. For example, there exist many linguistic terms for describing rain in Japanese. Some languages spoken in dry regions with little rain may have far fewer linguistic terms for describing rain than Japanese.

While people do not always have the same understanding of each linguistic term, we can usually communicate with each other using linguistic terms without mentioning their exact definitions. This is because our everyday conversations usually do not require any exact definition of each linguistic term. Everyone has a vague understanding of each linguistic term. This corresponds to linguistic discretization with fuzzy boundaries in Fig. 1.2. While people may depict different membership functions for the same linguistic term, they may have large overlaps. Thanks to such overlaps in our understanding of each linguistic term, we can communicate with each other using linguistic terms.

To illustrate linguistic rule extraction from numerical data based on linguistic discretization, let us consider the situation where we ask eleven examinees whether they feel comfortable in a small car or not. Suppose that we have the responses in Table 1.2 from the eleven examinees on the comfortableness of the small car. Numerical data in Table 1.2 are depicted in Fig. 1.3 together with the linguistic discretization of weight into the three linguistic terms. From Fig. 1.3, we can extract the following linguistic rules:

> If the weight is *heavy* then they do not feel comfortable in a small car.
> If the weight is *middle* then they do not feel comfortable in a small car.
> If the weight is *light* then they feels comfortable in a small car.

We explain formal mathematical procedures for linguistic rule extraction in the next chapter for classification problems. Here we show these linguistic rules just to illustrate the relation between linguistic discretization and rule extraction.

Table 1.2. Responses from eleven examinees (artificial data for illustration purposes)

Examinee (p)	1	2	3	4	5	6	7	8	9	10	11
Weight (x_p)	45	50	55	60	65	70	75	80	85	90	95
Comfortableness	yes	yes	yes	no	yes	no	no	no	no	no	no

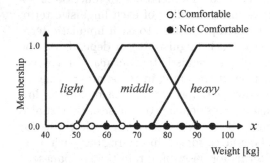

Fig. 1.3. Responses from eleven examinees in Table 1.2

Of course, different linguistic rules have been obtained from different linguistic discretization. In this book, we assume that linguistic discretization of the domain interval of each attribute is given. That is, we assume that a set of linguistic terms is given for describing each attribute. This assumption corresponds to the fact that we usually use a fixed number of linguistic terms to describe each attribute in our everyday conversations. In many machine learning techniques for handling continuous attributes such as decision trees [143], the domain interval of each continuous attribute is discretized into several intervals according to some performance criterion using numerical data. That is, threshold values are specified or adjusted using numerical data. On the contrary, we use a given set of linguistic terms for each attribute. In some cases, linguistic discretization of each attribute may be obtained from human users or domain experts. There are, however, other cases where no linguistic discretization is available for each attribute. In these cases, we have to specify a set of linguistic terms for each attribute. We use homogeneous discretization of the domain interval because such discretization is more easily understood by human users than inhomogeneous discretization. Figure 1.4 shows some examples of homogeneous discretization of the domain interval $[0, 1]$ into several linguistic terms with triangular membership functions. On the other hand, Fig. 1.5 shows an example of inhomogeneous discretization. From the comparison between Fig. 1.4 and Fig. 1.5, we can see that homogeneous discretization is much more interpretable than inhomogeneous discretization. The interpretability of linguistic discretization (or fuzzy discretization in general) has been discussed in many studies. For example, see Oliveira [134], Pedrycz & Oliveira [140], and Suzuki & Furuhashi [161]. While we do not discuss the determination of membership functions from numerical data, we examine the effect of the granularity (i.e., resolution of linguistic discretization: the number of linguistic terms K in Fig. 1.4) on the performance of linguistic models through computer simulations. We also compare linguistic models based on linguistic discretization with non-fuzzy rule-based systems based on interval discretization. These computer simulations will clearly demonstrate some characteristic features of linguistic models. Furthermore we demonstrate the effect of using a certainty factor (i.e., rule weight) for each linguistic rule on the performance of linguistic models.

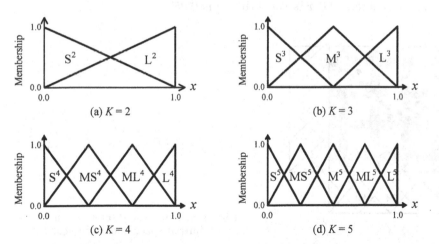

Fig. 1.4. Examples of homogeneous linguistic discretization of the domain interval $[0, 1]$. The meaning of each label is as follows: S: *small*, MS: *medium small*, M: *medium*, ML: *medium large*, and L: *large*. The superscript on each label denotes the granularity of the corresponding linguistic discretization (i.e., the number of linguistic terms: K)

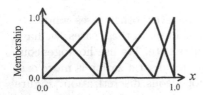

Fig. 1.5. Example of inhomogeneous discretization

In the case of modeling problems, we assume that linguistic discretization is given for each of the input and output variables. Figure 1.6 illustrates a single-input and single-output modeling problem where five linguistic terms (i.e., S: *small*, MS: *medium small*, M: *medium*, ML: *medium large*, and L: *large*) are given to describe both the input variable x and the output variable y. From this figure, we can generate the following five linguistic rules by choosing a consequent linguistic term for each antecedent condition:

> If x is *small* then y is *large*.
> If x is *medium small* then y is *medium*.
> If x is *medium* then y is *medium*.
> If x is *medium large* then y is *medium large*.
> If x is *large* then y is *medium*.

We explain formal mathematical procedures for linguistic rule extraction in a later chapter for modeling problems. We also use a different form of linguistic rules where the consequent part is defined by real numbers instead of linguistic terms (e.g., "If x is *small* then y is 0.95").

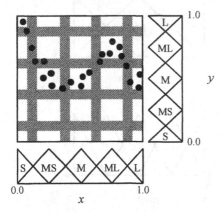

Fig. 1.6. Linguistic discretization of the input–output space and numerical data

As shown in Fig. 1.6, linguistic rules for modeling problems correspond to cells (i.e., patches) in grid spaces defined by linguistic discretization of input and output variables. Linguistic rule extraction can be viewed as the choice of such cells. The point is that each attribute is discretized into several linguistic terms for generating linguistic rules. This corresponds to our knowledge and memory in everyday situations. For example, when we talk about our friends, we usually do not mention the exact values of their height, weight, salary, age, etc. Instead, we describe them using linguistic terms (e.g., she is *tall*). In many cases, we do not know the exact values of those attributes for our friends. We may, however, have linguistic knowledge about these attributes. This contrasts with information processing in computer systems where exact values are stored and processed. In this book, we intend to handle classification and modeling problems using linguistic terms in a similar manner to our everyday information processing. Since we use only a small number of pre-specified linguistic terms, the performance of linguistic rules seems to be inferior to that of complicated nonlinear mathematical models. On the other hand, linguistic rules have high interpretability. We do not try to design mathematical models with high accuracy but design linguistic models with high interpretability. We do not adjust (i.e., modify) the membership function of each linguistic term. This is because the adjustment of the membership function leads to the modification of the meaning of each linguistic term. We try to improve the performance of linguistic models by finding good linguistic rules. This involves not only the specification of the consequent part but also input selection and rule selection. Through the use of computer simulations in this book, the classification and modeling performance of linguistic models are examined. Simulation results show that linguistic models have high performance while we may expect low performance of linguistic models from the fact that we use a small number of pre-specified linguistic terms without modifying their membership functions.

This book can be viewed as an attempt to summarize a part of recent studies in a rapidly emerging field of computer science called "computing with words". We concentrate our attention on classification and modeling using linguistic rules. For more general discussions on the field of computing with words, see the edited books by Wang [177] and Zadeh & Kacprzyk [192]. Shanahan [152] discussed Cartesian granule models from the viewpoints of fuzzy set theory, fuzzy logic, probability theory, machine learning, and data mining. The edited books by Casillas et al. [18, 19] include various topics related to the accuracy, complexity, and interpretability of fuzzy rule-based models. These books may be good choices for advanced readers after reading this book.

2. Pattern Classification with Linguistic Rules

In this chapter, we describe a heuristic approach to linguistic rule extraction from numerical data for pattern classification problems. We also explain a single winner-based fuzzy reasoning method for classifying new patterns by generated linguistic rules. Learning of linguistic rules is discussed in the next chapter. Handling of high-dimensional classification problems is discussed in later chapters where input selection, rule selection, and genetics-based machine learning techniques are described.

2.1 Problem Description

Let us assume that we have m labeled patterns $\boldsymbol{x}_p = (x_{p1}, \ldots, x_{pn})$, $p = 1, 2, \ldots, m$, from M classes for an n-dimensional pattern classification problem where x_{pi} is the attribute value of the i-th attribute in the p-th pattern $\boldsymbol{x}_p$. Each attribute is in general continuous (i.e., each attribute value x_{pi} is a real number). Each attribute, however, can be discrete (i.e., binary, ternary, etc.). We also assume that a set of linguistic terms is given for describing each attribute. Our task is to generate linguistic rules (i.e., to construct a linguistic rule-based system) from the given numerical data using the given linguistic terms. Figure 1.3 in the previous chapter is an example of our linguistic rule extraction problem where eleven patterns from two classes and three linguistic terms for each attribute are given in a single-dimensional continuous pattern space.

For simplicity of explanation, we assume that each attribute value is normalized into a real number in the unit interval $[0, 1]$. This means that the n-dimensional pattern space of our pattern classification problem is normalized into the n-dimensional unit hypercube $[0, 1]^n$. In computer simulations in this book, this normalization is performed as a preprocessing procedure. An example of our pattern classification problem is shown in Fig. 2.1 where 30 patterns from two classes and three linguistic terms for each attribute are given in the two-dimensional pattern space $[0, 1]^2$.

Linguistic rules for our n-dimensional pattern classification problem are written in the following form:

$$\text{Rule } R_q\text{: If } x_1 \text{ is } A_{q1} \text{ and } \ldots \text{ and } x_n \text{ is } A_{qn} \text{ then Class } C_q, \qquad (2.1)$$

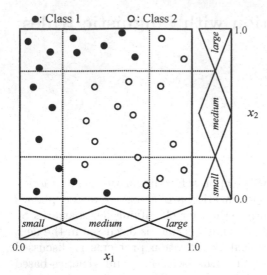

●: Class 1   ○: Class 2

Fig. 2.1. A simple example of our linguistic rule extraction problem where 30 patterns are given from two classes (15 patterns from each class). The normalized domain interval $[0, 1]$ of each attribute is discretized into three linguistic terms

where R_q is the label of the q-th linguistic rule, $x = (x_1, \ldots, x_n)$ is an n-dimensional pattern vector, A_{qi} is a linguistic term given for the i-th attribute, and C_q is a consequent class. When K linguistic terms are given for each of the n attributes, we have K^n linguistic rules of the form (2.1). In Fig. 2.1, we have nine linguistic rules (e.g., "If x_1 is *small* and x_2 is *small* then Class 1").

We also use linguistic rules of the following form with a rule weight:

Rule R_q: If x_1 is A_{q1} and ... and x_n is A_{qn}

then Class C_q with CF_q,   (2.2)

where CF_q is a rule weight (i.e., certainty factor) of the q-th linguistic rule R_q. The effect of using rule weights on the performance of linguistic rule-based classification systems was discussed in Ishibuchi & Nakashima [67]. The rule weight CF_q, which is a real number in the unit interval $[0, 1]$, denotes the strength of the linguistic rule R_q. Linguistic rules with the maximum rule weight 1.0 have the largest effect on the classification of new patterns. On the other hand, linguistic rules with the minimum rule weight 0.0 have no effect on the classification of new patterns. Heuristic specification methods of rule weights are discussed later in this chapter. Learning algorithms of rule weights are described in the next chapter.

2.2 Linguistic Rule Extraction for Classification Problems

We describe how the consequent class and the rule weight of each linguistic rule can be specified from numerical data. The consequent class of each linguistic rule is uniquely determined from training patterns compatible with its antecedent part. There are, however, several alternative definitions of its rule weight. Roughly speaking, the consequent class of each linguistic rule is the dominant class in the cell corresponding to its antecedent part. For example, the consequent class for the antecedent part "If x_1 is *small* and x_2 is *large*" is determined as Class 1 in Fig. 2.1 because there are many closed circles (i.e., Class 1 patterns) and no open circles (i.e., Class 2 patterns) around the top-left corner of the pattern space $[0, 1]^2$. When all patterns compatible with the antecedent part are from a single class (i.e., the consequent class of the linguistic rule), the rule weight is its maximum value (i.e., 1.0). The larger is the ratio of compatible patterns from the consequent class to all compatible patterns, the higher is the rule weight. In this section, we describe a heuristic specification method of the consequent class. We also describe four alternative heuristic definitions of the rule weight of each linguistic rule.

2.2.1 Specification of the Consequent Class

When we use interval discretization for each attribute, it is easy to count the number of patterns compatible with the antecedent part of each rule. On the other hand, we have to take into account a compatibility grade of each pattern with the antecedent part in the case of linguistic discretization. To calculate the compatibility grade of the pattern $x_p = (x_{p1}, \ldots, x_{pn})$ with the antecedent part of the linguistic rule R_q, first the compatibility grade of each attribute value x_{pi} with the corresponding linguistic term A_{qi} is calculated as $\mu_{A_{qi}}(x_{pi})$ where $\mu_{A_{qi}}(\cdot)$ is the membership function of the linguistic term A_{qi}. Then the compatibility grade of the pattern x_p with the antecedent part of R_q is calculated from the compatibility grade $\mu_{A_{qi}}(x_{pi})$. In many studies on fuzzy rule-based systems, the minimum operator and the product operator have been used to calculate the compatibility grade with the antecedent part. When the minimum operator is used, the compatibility grade is calculated as

$$\mu_{A_q}(x_p) = \min\left\{\mu_{A_{q1}}(x_{p1}), \ldots, \mu_{A_{qn}}(x_{pn})\right\}, \qquad (2.3)$$

where $A_q = (A_{q1}, \ldots, A_{qn})$. For simplicity of notation, A_q is used to denote the antecedent part "If x_1 is A_{q1} and ... and x_n is A_{qn}" of the linguistic rule R_q in this book. On the other hand, the compatibility grade is calculated as follows when the product operator is used:

$$\mu_{A_q}(x_p) = \mu_{A_{q1}}(x_{p1}) \times \ldots \times \mu_{A_{qn}}(x_{pn}). \qquad (2.4)$$

Traditionally the minimum operator has often been used in the literature. Recently the product operator has been frequently used especially in adaptive fuzzy rule-based systems. This is because the derivation of learning algorithms is easier for the product operator than for the minimum operator. We illustrate the difference in the compatibility grade between these two operators in Fig. 2.2 and Fig. 2.3. Let us consider the pattern $x_p = (0.25, 0.25)$

denoted by a closed circle in these figures. The compatibility grade of this pattern with the antecedent part "If x_1 is *medium* and x_2 is *medium*" is calculated using the minimum operator as

$$\mu_{A_q}(x_p) = \min\{\mu_{medium}(0.25), \mu_{medium}(0.25)\}$$
$$= \min\{0.5, 0.5\}$$
$$= 0.5, \tag{2.5}$$

where $A_q = (medium, medium)$. On the other hand, the compatibility grade is calculated using the product operator as

$$\mu_{A_q}(x_p) = \mu_{medium}(0.25) \times \mu_{medium}(0.25)$$
$$= 0.5 \times 0.5$$
$$= 0.25. \tag{2.6}$$

Figure 2.2 and Fig. 2.3 show contour lines of the compatibility grade for the cases of the minimum operator and the product operator, respectively. Contour lines are square in the case of the minimum operator in Fig. 2.2 while they are somewhat circular in the case of the product operator in Fig. 2.3. In almost all computer simulations in this book, we use the product operator. The minimum operator is used only when these two operators are compared with each other.

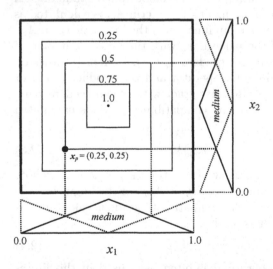

Fig. 2.2. Contour lines of the compatibility grade with the antecedent part "If x_1 is *medium* and x_2 is *medium*" in the case of the minimum operator

Let D be the set of the given training patterns: $D = (x_1, \ldots, x_m)$. The cardinality of D is m (i.e., $|D| = m$). Let $D(A_q)$ be the fuzzy set of compatible training patterns with the antecedent part A_q of the linguistic rule R_q. Then the total compatibility grade with the antecedent part A_q is calculated as

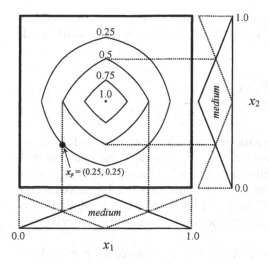

Fig. 2.3. Contour lines of the compatibility grade with the antecedent part "If x_1 is *medium* and x_2 is *medium*" in the case of the product operator

$$|D(\boldsymbol{A}_q)| = \sum_{p=1}^{m} \mu_{\boldsymbol{A}_q}(\boldsymbol{x}_p). \qquad (2.7)$$

$|D(\boldsymbol{A}_q)|$ can be viewed as the cardinality of the fuzzy set $D(\boldsymbol{A}_q)$. In the case of interval discretization (i.e., in the case where A_{qi} is an interval), $|D(\boldsymbol{A}_q)|$ is the number of compatible training patterns with the antecedent part $\boldsymbol{A}_q$.

Using (2.4), we can define the compatibility grade of each training pattern $\boldsymbol{x}_p$ with the linguistic rule R_q (i.e., with both the antecedent part $\boldsymbol{A}_q$ and the consequent class C_q) as

$$\mu_{R_q}(\boldsymbol{x}_p) = \begin{cases} \mu_{\boldsymbol{A}_q}(\boldsymbol{x}_p), & \text{if } p \in \text{Class } C_q, \\ 0, & \text{if } p \notin \text{Class } C_q. \end{cases} \qquad (2.8)$$

Let $D(\boldsymbol{A}_q) \cap D(C_q)$ be the fuzzy set of compatible training patterns with both the antecedent part $\boldsymbol{A}_q$ and the consequent class C_q. Then the total compatibility grade with the linguistic rule R_q (i.e., with both $\boldsymbol{A}_q$ and C_q) is calculated as

$$|D(\boldsymbol{A}_q) \cap D(C_q)| = \sum_{p=1}^{m} \mu_{R_q}(\boldsymbol{x}_p) = \sum_{p \in \text{Class } C_q} \mu_{\boldsymbol{A}_q}(\boldsymbol{x}_p). \qquad (2.9)$$

$|D(\boldsymbol{A}_q) \cap D(C_q)|$ can be viewed as the total compatibility grade of training patterns from Class C_q with the antecedent part $\boldsymbol{A}_q$. In the case of interval discretization, $|D(\boldsymbol{A}_q) \cap D(C_q)|$ is the number of compatible training patterns from Class C_q with the antecedent part $\boldsymbol{A}_q$.

In the field of data mining, two measures are often used to evaluate association rules [4, 5]. They are "confidence" and "support". These concepts can be easily extended to the case of linguistic rules [57, 95]. We use the confidence to describe four heuristic definitions of the rule weight of each linguistic rule.

The linguistic rule R_q in (2.1) can be viewed as a linguistic association rule $\boldsymbol{A_q} \Rightarrow C_q$. The confidence $c(\boldsymbol{A_q} \Rightarrow C_q)$ of the linguistic association rule $\boldsymbol{A_q} \Rightarrow C_q$ is defined as

$$c(\boldsymbol{A_q} \Rightarrow C_q) = \frac{|D(\boldsymbol{A_q}) \cap D(C_q)|}{|D(\boldsymbol{A_q})|} = \frac{\sum\limits_{p \in \text{Class } C_q} \mu_{\boldsymbol{A_q}}(\boldsymbol{x}_p)}{\sum\limits_{p=1}^{m} \mu_{\boldsymbol{A_q}}(\boldsymbol{x}_p)}. \qquad (2.10)$$

The confidence $c(\boldsymbol{A_q} \Rightarrow C_q)$ is the ratio of compatible patterns with both the antecedent part $\boldsymbol{A_q}$ and the consequent class C_q to compatible patterns with the antecedent part $\boldsymbol{A_q}$. The confidence $c(\boldsymbol{A_q} \Rightarrow C_q)$ measures the validity of the linguistic association rule $\boldsymbol{A_q} \Rightarrow C_q$. The confidence can be viewed as the fuzzy conditional probability of Class C_q [171]. Note that the definition of the confidence $c(\boldsymbol{A_q} \Rightarrow C_q)$ in (2.10) can be used for linguistic discretization and interval discretization.

On the other hand, the support $s(\boldsymbol{A_q} \Rightarrow C_q)$ of the association rule $\boldsymbol{A_q} \Rightarrow C_q$ is defined as

$$s(\boldsymbol{A_q} \Rightarrow C_q) = \frac{|D(\boldsymbol{A_q}) \cap D(C_q)|}{|D|} = \frac{\sum\limits_{p \in \text{Class } C_q} \mu_{\boldsymbol{A_q}}(\boldsymbol{x}_p)}{m}. \qquad (2.11)$$

The support $s(\boldsymbol{A_q} \Rightarrow C_q)$ is the ratio of compatible patterns with both the antecedent part $\boldsymbol{A_q}$ and the consequent class C_q to the given m training patterns. The support $s(\boldsymbol{A_q} \Rightarrow C_q)$ measures the coverage of training patterns by the linguistic association rule $\boldsymbol{A_q} \Rightarrow C_q$. As the confidence in (2.10), the definition of the support $s(\boldsymbol{A_q} \Rightarrow C_q)$ in (2.11) can be used for linguistic discretization and interval discretization.

To illustrate these two measures (i.e., confidence and support) of linguistic association rules, let us again consider the two-class pattern classification problem in Fig. 1.3 of the previous chapter. First we show how $c(middle \Rightarrow uncomfortable)$ and $s(middle \Rightarrow uncomfortable)$ are calculated. The fuzzy set $D(middle)$ of examinees compatible with the linguistic term $middle$ in Fig. 1.3 is explicitly written as

$$D(middle) = \left\{ \frac{0.33}{55}, \frac{0.67}{60}, \frac{1.0}{65}, \frac{1.0}{70}, \frac{1.0}{75}, \frac{0.67}{80}, \frac{0.33}{85} \right\}, \qquad (2.12)$$

where the denominator and the numerator show the weight x_p of each examinee and its membership value $\mu_{middle}(x_p)$, respectively. As we have already explained in the previous chapter, each element in (2.12) should not be viewed as a fraction but as a pair consisting of an element and its membership value. The total compatibility grade with the linguistic term $middle$ is calculated from (2.12) as

$$|D(middle)| = 0.33 + 0.67 + 1.0 + 1.0 + 1.0 + 0.67 + 0.33 = 5.0. \qquad (2.13)$$

From Fig. 1.3, the total compatibility grade $|D(middle) \cap D(uncomfortable)|$ is calculated as

$$|D(middle) \cap D(uncomfotable)| = 0.67 + 1.0 + 1.0 + 0.67 + 0.33$$
$$= 3.67. \qquad (2.14)$$

Thus the confidence and the support are calculated as

$$c(middle \Rightarrow uncomfortable) = \frac{3.67}{5.0} = 0.734, \qquad (2.15)$$

$$s(middle \Rightarrow uncomfortable) = \frac{3.67}{11} = 0.334. \qquad (2.16)$$

In the same manner, the confidence and the support of the linguistic association rule "*middle $\Rightarrow$ comfortable*" are calculated as

$$c(middle \Rightarrow comfortable) = \frac{1.33}{5.0} = 0.266, \qquad (2.17)$$

$$s(middle \Rightarrow comfortable) = \frac{1.33}{11} = 0.121. \qquad (2.18)$$

Since $c(middle \Rightarrow uncomfortable)$ is larger than $c(middle \Rightarrow comfortable)$, we choose the linguistic association rule "*middle $\Rightarrow$ uncomfortable*" rather than "*middle $\Rightarrow$ comfortable*". In the same manner, we can choose the consequent class for each of the other antecedent linguistic terms. That is, we can generate linguistic association rules "*light $\Rightarrow$ comfortable*" and "*heavy $\Rightarrow$ uncomfortable*" in addition to "*middle $\Rightarrow$ uncomfortable*".

As shown in the above example, it is natural to choose the consequent class C_q with the maximum confidence for the antecedent part A_q as

$$c(A_q \Rightarrow C_q) = \max\{c(A_q \Rightarrow \text{Class } h)|h = 1, 2, \ldots, M\}. \qquad (2.19)$$

Note that the same consequent class C_q is obtained if we use the support $s(\cdot)$ instead of the confidence $c(\cdot)$ in (2.19). When multiple classes have the same maximum confidence (i.e., when C_q cannot be uniquely specified), we do not generate any linguistic rule with the antecedent part A_q. Using (2.19), we determine the consequent class for each of the nine cells in Fig. 2.1. Generated linguistic rules are summarized in Fig. 2.4. The same consequent class is specified for each linguistic rule independent of the choice between the minimum operator and the product operator in this numerical example. From the comparison between Fig. 2.1 and Fig. 2.4, we can see that the dominant class in each cell is chosen as the consequent class for the corresponding linguistic rule. It should be noted that the dotted lines in these figures are not sharp boundaries but fuzzy boundaries between cells because we use linguistic discretization.

2.2.2 Specification of the Rule Weight

The confidence $c(A_q \Rightarrow C_q)$ can be directly used as the rule weight CF_q of the linguistic rule R_q in (2.2) as in Cordon et al. [26]. That is, the rule weight CF_q of the linguistic rule R_q in (2.2) is specified as

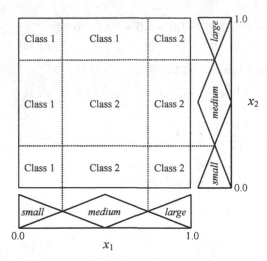

Fig. 2.4. Nine linguistic rules generated from numerical data in Fig. 2.1

$$CF_q^{\mathrm{I}} = c(\boldsymbol{A}_q \Rightarrow C_q). \tag{2.20}$$

The superscript "I" shows that (2.20) is the first alternative definition of the rule weight CF_q.

Ishibuchi et al. [81] used a different heuristic definition of the rule weight CF_q:

$$CF_q^{\mathrm{II}} = c(\boldsymbol{A}_q \Rightarrow C_q) - c_{\mathrm{Average}}, \tag{2.21}$$

where c_{Average} is the average confidence over linguistic rules with the same antecedent part $\boldsymbol{A}_q$ but different consequent classes:

$$c_{\mathrm{Average}} = \frac{1}{M-1} \left(\sum_{\substack{h=1 \\ h \neq C_q}}^{M} c(\boldsymbol{A}_q \Rightarrow \text{Class } h) \right). \tag{2.22}$$

This definition of CF_q can be easily understood if we consider the case of $M = 2$ (i.e., two-class pattern classification problems). In this case, CF_q is calculated as follows when the consequent class is Class 1 (i.e., when $c(\boldsymbol{A}_q \Rightarrow \text{Class } 1) > c(\boldsymbol{A}_q \Rightarrow \text{Class } 2)$):

$$CF_q^{\mathrm{II}} = c(\boldsymbol{A}_q \Rightarrow \text{Class } 1) - c(\boldsymbol{A}_q \Rightarrow \text{Class } 2). \tag{2.23}$$

When the consequent class is Class 2 (i.e., when $c(\boldsymbol{A}_q \Rightarrow \text{Class } 1) < c(\boldsymbol{A}_q \Rightarrow \text{Class } 2)$), CF_q is calculated as

$$CF_q^{\mathrm{II}} = c(\boldsymbol{A}_q \Rightarrow \text{Class } 2) - c(\boldsymbol{A}_q \Rightarrow \text{Class } 1). \tag{2.24}$$

As we can see from (2.23) and (2.24), the rule weight CF_q by the second definition is a real number such that $0 < CF_q^{\mathrm{II}} \leq 1$. On the other hand, the rule weight CF_q by the first definition is always larger than 0.5 in the case of two-class pattern classification problems: $0.5 < CF_q^{\mathrm{I}} \leq 1$ when $M = 2$. The difference between these two definitions is illustrated in Fig. 2.5. In this figure, the value of CF_q calculated by each definition is shown in the corresponding cell. The first and second values in each cell are the values of the rule weight calculated by the first and second definitions for the corresponding linguistic rule, respectively. From this figure, we can see that the rule weight of each linguistic rule is larger in the case of the first definition than the case of the second definition. We can also see that the rule weights of linguistic rules around the class boundary are smaller than those far from the class boundary.

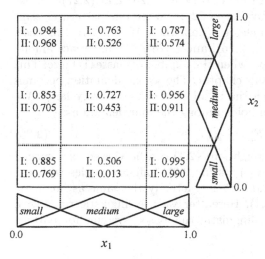

Fig. 2.5. Rule weights of the nine linguistic rules in Fig. 2.4 calculated by the two definitions from numerical data in Fig. 2.1. The product operator was used to calculate the compatibility grade of each pattern

Other definitions of the rule weight CF_q are possible. For example, the following definition is simpler and more intuitively understandable than the second definition in (2.21):

$$CF_q^{\mathrm{III}} = c(\boldsymbol{A}_q \Rightarrow C_q) - c_{\text{Second}}, \qquad (2.25)$$

where c_{Second} is the second largest confidence among M linguistic rules with the antecedent part $\boldsymbol{A}_q$:

$$c_{\text{Second}} = \max\left\{ c(\boldsymbol{A}_q \Rightarrow \text{Class } h)|h = 1, 2, \ldots, M, h \neq C_q \right\}. \qquad (2.26)$$

In the third definition in (2.25), the rule weight is defined as the difference between the largest confidence and the second largest confidence. Note that $\boldsymbol{A}_q \Rightarrow C_q$ always has the maximum confidence among the M linguistic rules with the antecedent part $\boldsymbol{A}_q$ from the specification of the consequent class C_q.

The following definition is also possible:

$$CF_q^{\mathrm{IV}} = c(\boldsymbol{A}_q \Rightarrow C_q) - c_{\text{Sum}}, \qquad (2.27)$$

where c_{Sum} is the sum of the confidence over linguistic rules with the same antecedent part $\boldsymbol{A}_q$ but different consequent classes from C_q:

$$c_{\text{Sum}} = \sum_{\substack{h=1 \\ h \neq C_q}}^{M} c(\boldsymbol{A}_q \Rightarrow \text{Class } h).$$ (2.28)

While CF_q is always positive in the first three definitions, CF_q^{IV} can be negative even when the consequent class C_q is uniquely determined by (2.19). We do not use linguistic rules with negative rule weights (i.e., negative certainty grades) in linguistic models. Thus some linguistic rules may be removed from linguistic models when we use the fourth definition of the rule weight CF_q^{IV}.

Note that the third and fourth definitions in (2.25) and (2.27) are exactly the same as the second definition in (2.21) when our pattern classification problem involves only two classes (i.e., when $M = 2$). In this case, $c_{\text{Average}} = c_{\text{Second}} = c_{\text{Sum}}$ in (2.22), (2.26), and (2.28). The difference among these definitions becomes significant when the number of classes is large. This is illustrated in a later section of this chapter. The second definition becomes similar to the first definition when the number of classes is very large. We can see that the following relation holds among the four definitions:

$$CF_q^{\text{IV}} \leq CF_q^{\text{III}} \leq CF_q^{\text{II}} \leq CF_q^{\text{I}}.$$ (2.29)

Linguistic rules with no rule weights in (2.1) can be viewed as a special case of linguistic rules with rule weights in (2.2). Linguistic rules with the same rule weight (e.g., $CF_q = 1.0, \forall q$) are actually the same as linguistic rules with no rule weights in (2.1). Hereafter we use linguistic rules with rule weights in (2.2) to illustrate linguistic rule-based systems for pattern classification problems.

2.3 Classification of New Patterns by Linguistic Rules

We describe two fuzzy reasoning methods for classifying new patterns using linguistic rules. One is a single winner-based method where a single winner rule is used for classifying each pattern. The other is a voting-based method where the classification of each pattern is performed through a voting procedure by all linguistic rules. Various fuzzy reasoning methods for classification problems were discussed in Cordon et al. [26] and Ishibuchi et al. [68].

2.3.1 Single Winner-Based Method

Let S be a set of linguistic rules of the form (2.2). The rule set S can be viewed as a linguistic rule-based classification system. The single winner rule R_w in the rule set S is determined for a new pattern $\boldsymbol{x}_p = (x_{p1}, \ldots, x_{pn})$ as

$$\mu_{\boldsymbol{A}_w}(\boldsymbol{x}_p) \cdot CF_w = \max \left\{ \mu_{\boldsymbol{A}_q}(\boldsymbol{x}_p) \cdot CF_q | R_q \in S \right\}.$$ (2.30)

That is, the winner rule has the maximum product of the compatibility grade and the rule weight. If multiple linguistic rules have the same maximum product but different consequent classes for the new pattern $\boldsymbol{x}_p$, the classification of x_p is rejected. The classification is also rejected if no linguistic rule is compatible with the new pattern x_p. When we use the single winner-based method, each linguistic rule has its decision region. That is, each linguistic rule is responsible for the classification of new patterns in its decision region. This leads to high transparency of the classification process of new patterns. Since we know which linguistic rule classifies a new pattern, we can explain why that pattern is classified as a particular class by our linguistic rule-based classification system. This is an advantage of the single winner-based method over other fuzzy reasoning methods such as a voting-based method by multiple linguistic rules.

In Fig. 2.6, we show the decision region of each linguistic rule in Fig. 2.4. The boundary between decision regions of linguistic rules with different consequent classes corresponds to the classification (i.e., decision) boundary between two classes, which is depicted by bold lines in Fig. 2.6. As we can see from Fig. 2.6, the classification boundary is not always parallel to each axis of the pattern space. This contrasts with classification results by rule-based systems with interval discretization where the classification boundary is always parallel to each axis. Generally speaking, the larger is the rule weight in linguistic rule-based classification systems, the larger is the decision region. The rule weight of each linguistic rule is specified by the first definition in Fig. 2.6. On the other hand, Fig. 2.7 shows the decision region of each linguistic rule when its rule weight is specified by the second definition. From the comparison between Fig. 2.6 and Fig. 2.7, we can see that different classification boundaries are obtained from the two definitions of the rule weight of each linguistic rule. This suggests the possibility that the performance of linguistic rule-based classification systems can be improved by adjusting the rule weight of each linguistic rule.

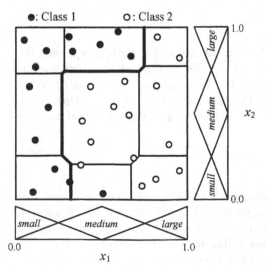

Fig. 2.6. Decision regions of the nine linguistic rules in Fig. 2.4. We used the first definition to specify the rule weight of each linguistic rule. The rule weight of each linguistic rule is shown in the corresponding cell in Fig. 2.5. The bold line shows the classification boundary between two classes

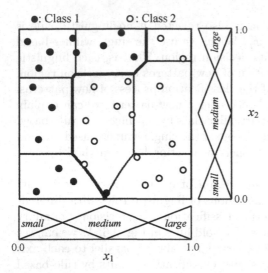

Fig. 2.7. Decision regions of the nine linguistic rules. In this figure, the second definition is used to specify the rule weight of each linguistic rule

As shown in Kuncheva [117], the classification region of each linguistic rule is rectangular when we use linguistic rules with no rule weights (or equivalently linguistic rules with the same rule weight). This situation is illustrated in Fig. 2.8. The same decision region of each linguistic rule as in Fig. 2.8 can be generated from interval discretization of each axis of the pattern space. This is illustrated in Fig. 2.9. This observation suggests that the rule weight of each linguistic rule plays an important role in linguistic rule-based classification systems. Classification results by linguistic rule-based systems with no rule weights are sometimes exactly the same as those based on interval discretization. We compare linguistic discretization with interval discretization in detail in a later chapter.

2.3.2 Voting-Based Method

When we use a voting-based method to classify a new pattern x_p, each linguistic rule votes for its consequent class. The product of the compatibility grade and the rule weight is used as the importance (i.e., strength) of the vote by each linguistic rule. When the new pattern x_p is to be classified by the linguistic rule set S using the voting-based method, the total vote for each class is calculated as follows:

$$V_{\text{Class } h} = \sum_{\substack{R_q \in S \\ C_q = h}} \mu_{A_q}(x_p) \cdot CF_q. \tag{2.31}$$

While a single responsible linguistic rule is identified for the classification of each pattern in the case of the single winner-based method, all compatible linguistic rules are responsible for the classification of each pattern with different grades of responsibility. This makes it difficult to explain why a new pattern is classified as a particular class by the linguistic rule set S.

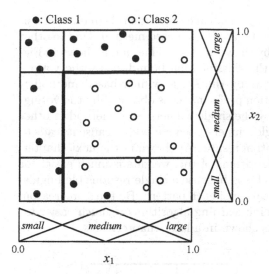

Fig. 2.8. Decision regions of the nine linguistic rules with no rule weights

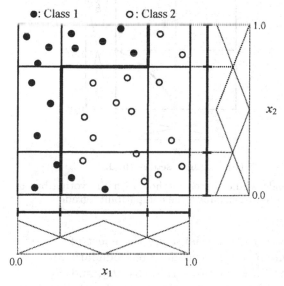

Fig. 2.9. Decision regions of the nine rules generated from interval discretization of each axis of the pattern space. Threshold values in interval discretization are the same as crossing points of neighboring membership functions in linguistic discretization

To illustrate the difference between the single winner-based method and the voting-based method, let us consider the following four linguistic rules, which are also shown in Fig. 2.10 (a).

R_1: If x_1 is *small* and x_2 is *small* then Class 1 with $CF_1 = 1.0$,
R_2: If x_1 is *small* and x_2 is *large* then Class 1 with $CF_2 = 1.0$,
R_3: If x_1 is *large* and x_2 is *small* then Class 2 with $CF_3 = 1.0$,
R_4: If x_1 is *large* and x_2 is *large* then Class 1 with $CF_4 = 1.0$.

Figure 2.10 (a) shows the decision region of each linguistic rule and the classification boundary when we use the single winner-based method. On the other hand, the classification boundary by the voting-based method is shown in Fig. 2.10 (b). As shown in Fig. 2.10, the classification boundary by the voting-based method is smooth while that by the single winner-based method is piece-wise linear. Higher classification performance is obtained by the voting-based method in some cases and by the single winner-based method in other cases. In this book, we use the single winner-based method because it leads to higher interpretability of classification results. As shown in the next chapter, the implementation of learning algorithms of rule weights is much easier for the single winner-based method. This is because a single responsible linguistic rule is identified for the classification of each pattern. By the same reason, the design of genetics-based machine learning algorithms is much easier for the single winner-based method as shown in a later chapter.

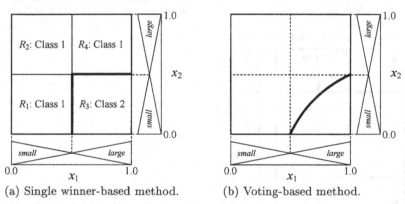

(a) Single winner-based method.   (b) Voting-based method.

Fig. 2.10. Comparison of the single winner-based method with the voting-based method. The product operator is used to calculate the compatibility grade

Using the same four linguistic rules, we illustrate the effect of the rule weight CF_q of each linguistic rule R_q on the classification boundary. First we decrease the rule weights of the three linguistic rules R_1, R_2, and R_4 with Class 1 in the consequent part. We specify the rule weight of each linguistic rule as

$$CF_1 = CF_2 = CF_4 = 0.5, \ CF_3 = 1.0. \tag{2.32}$$

The classification boundary is shown in Fig. 2.11. Since the relative weight of R_3 with Class 2 in the consequent part is large, the region of Class 2 is also large in Fig. 2.11. Another example is shown in Fig. 2.12 where the rule weight of each linguistic rule is specified as

$$CF_1 = 0.7, \ CF_2 = 0.3, \ CF_3 = 0.9, \ CF_4 = 0.2. \tag{2.33}$$

From Fig. 2.11 and Fig. 2.12, we can see that the rule weight of each linguistic rule has a large effect on the classification boundary. Note that we did not modify the membership function of each linguistic term in these figures.

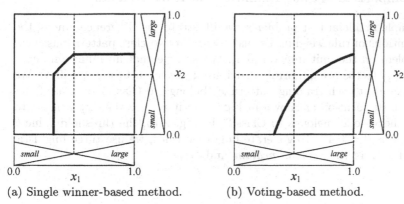

(a) Single winner-based method.   (b) Voting-based method.

Fig. 2.11. Classification boundary when the relative rule weight of R_3 with Class 2 in the consequent part is large

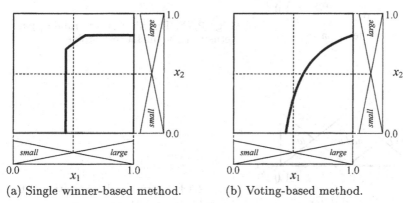

(a) Single winner-based method.   (b) Voting-based method.

Fig. 2.12. Classification boundary when different weights are assigned to the four linguistic rules

2.4 Computer Simulations

We compare the four definitions of rule weights with one another through computer simulations on a class of simple artificial test problems and two well-known real-world data sets: iris data and wine data. We also examine the effect of the granularity of linguistic discretization (i.e., the number of linguistic terms) on the performance of linguistic rule-based systems.

2.4.1 Comparison of Four Definitions of Rule Weights

Using simple artificial test problems, we illustrate the difference among the four definitions of rule weights. Let us consider a two-class pattern classification problem on the unit interval $[0, 1]$. We assume that an infinite number of training patterns are uniformly distributed in the pattern space $[0, 1]$. We also assume that each training pattern x_p belongs to Class 1 or Class 2 depending on its location as shown in Fig. 2.13: if $x_p \leq \theta$ then x_p belongs to Class 1 otherwise x_p belongs to Class 2. In Fig. 2.13, the threshold value θ is specified as $\theta = 0.47$. To generate linguistic rules, we use three linguistic terms in Fig. 2.14 (i.e., *small*, *medium*, and *large*).

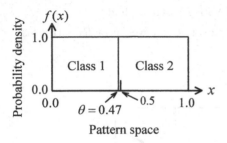

Fig. 2.13. Distribution of training patterns in an artificial test problem

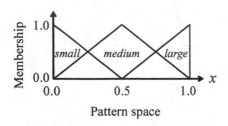

Fig. 2.14. Linguistic discretization with three linguistic terms

Using the uniform distribution of training patterns in Fig. 2.13 and the three linguistic terms in Fig. 2.14, we can generate the following linguistic rules:

   R_1: If x is *small* then Class 1 with CF_1,
   R_2: If x is *medium* then Class 2 with CF_2,
   R_3: If x is *large* then Class 2 with CF_3.

Rule weights of these linguistic rules are calculated from the uniform distribution of training patterns as

$$CF_1^{\mathrm{I}} = 0.996, \ CF_2^{\mathrm{I}} = 0.558, \ CF_3^{\mathrm{I}} = 1.000, \tag{2.34}$$

$$CF_1^{\mathrm{II}} = 0.993, \ CF_2^{\mathrm{II}} = 0.116, \ CF_3^{\mathrm{II}} = 1.000, \tag{2.35}$$

$$CF_1^{\mathrm{III}} = 0.993, \ CF_2^{\mathrm{III}} = 0.116, \ CF_3^{\mathrm{III}} = 1.000, \tag{2.36}$$

$$CF_1^{\mathrm{IV}} = 0.993, \ CF_2^{\mathrm{IV}} = 0.116, \ CF_3^{\mathrm{IV}} = 1.000. \tag{2.37}$$

Since our test problem is a two-class pattern classification problem (i.e., $M = 2$), the second definition is exactly the same as the third and fourth definitions. We can observe a large difference in the rule weight CF_2 of the second linguistic rule R_2 between the first definition and the other definitions. The confidence is calculated for this linguistic rule and the other linguistic rule "$medium \Rightarrow$ Class 1" with the same antecedent linguistic term $medium$ and a different consequent class as

$$c(medium \Rightarrow \text{Class 1}) = 0.442, \tag{2.38}$$

$$c(medium \Rightarrow \text{Class 2}) = 0.558. \tag{2.39}$$

Thus the rule weight CF_2 of the linguistic rule "R_2: $medium \Rightarrow$ Class 2" is very small in the last three definitions. On the other hand, the rule weight CF_2 is not small in the first definition because the confidence $c(medium \Rightarrow$ Class 2) is directly used as the rule weight.

Using the three linguistic rules, we estimate the class boundary between the two classes. The estimated class boundary $\hat{\theta}$ is calculated as follows: $\hat{\theta} = 0.320$ by the first definition and $\hat{\theta} = 0.448$ by the other definitions. The estimated class boundary $\hat{\theta}$ has a large error in the case of the first definition while it is close to the actual threshold 0.47 in the case of the other definitions. The large error in the case of the first definition is due to the large rule weight CF_2^{I} of the second linguistic rule R_2. Since the rule weight CF_2^{I} is not negligible, the second linguistic rule R_2 has a significant effect on the classification of new patterns around the center of the pattern space $[0, 1]$. That is, the second linguistic rule R_2 has a large decision region in which R_2 is selected as the winner rule. As a result, the estimated class boundary $\hat{\theta}$ is pushed to $\hat{\theta} = 0.320$. On the other hand, the rule weight CF_2 is very small when we use the other definitions. Thus the second linguistic rule R_2 has a very small decision region. As a result, the estimated class boundary $\hat{\theta}$ is close to the boundary between the two dominant rules R_1 and R_3 (i.e., $x = 0.5$).

In the same manner, we calculate the estimated class boundary $\hat{\theta}$ between the two classes for our test problem with various specifications of the actual threshold value θ. We examine 51 versions of our test problem with different values of θ: $\theta = 0.25, 0.26, 0.27, \ldots, 0.75$. Simulation results are summarized in Fig. 2.15. This figure shows the relation between the actual threshold θ and the estimated class boundary $\hat{\theta}$. The line in this figure shows the desired ideal relation $\hat{\theta} = \theta$. From the figure, we can see that the difference between

θ and $\hat{\theta}$ is very large in the case of the first definition. On the other hand, the estimated class boundary $\hat{\theta}$ is almost the same as the actual threshold θ when we use the other definitions. This figure suggests that the direct use of the confidence $c(A_q \Rightarrow C_q)$ as the rule weight CF_q (i.e., the first definition CF_q^{I}) may lead to large classification errors.

It should be noted that our simulation results in Fig. 2.15 were obtained using the single winner-based method. Different results can be derived from other fuzzy reasoning methods (see, for example, Berg et al. [171]).

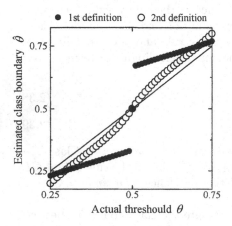

Fig. 2.15. Simulation results by the four definitions of rule weights for the two-class artificial test problem in Fig. 2.13. Results by the last three definitions are the same

Let us extend our test problem in Fig. 2.13 to an M-class pattern classification problem ($M > 2$). For simplicity of discussion, we assume that the unit interval $[0, 1]$ in Fig. 2.13 is a part of a larger entire pattern space. We also assume that training patterns from the other classes (i.e., Class 3, ..., Class M) exist in the other region of the pattern space. From these assumptions, we can discuss the specification of rule weights locally in the unit interval $[0, 1]$. In this situation, the increase in the number of classes has no effect on the rule weight specification except for the second definition. Only the second definition depends on the number of classes (i.e., M) as shown in (2.22). Thus the second definition is not the same as the third and fourth definitions when pattern classification problems involve more than two classes. For example, the rule weights of the three linguistic rules are calculated from the second definition for the case of $M = 5$ and $\theta = 0.47$ as

$$CF_1^{\mathrm{II}} = 0.996, \ CF_2^{\mathrm{II}} = 0.448, \ CF_3^{\mathrm{II}} = 1.000. \tag{2.40}$$

The class boundary between the two classes is calculated as $\hat{\theta} = 0.345$ by the second definition while the actual threshold is $\theta = 0.47$. Note that the class boundary was calculated as $\hat{\theta} = 0.448$ from the second definition when $M = 2$. This result suggests that the increase in the number of classes has a bad effect on the classification performance of linguistic rule-based systems constructed by the second definition of rule weights.

In the same manner as Fig. 2.15, we calculate the estimated class boundary $\hat{\theta}$ using the second definition of rule weights for three specifications of M (i.e., $M = 2, 5, 10$). Simulation results are summarized in Fig. 2.16. From this figure, we can see that the difference between the actual threshold θ and the estimated class boundary $\hat{\theta}$ increases as the value of M increases. This is because the rule weight CF_2^{II} of the second linguistic rule R_2 becomes unnecessarily large when our test problem involves more than two classes as shown in (2.40).

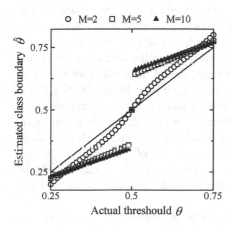

Fig. 2.16. Simulation results by the second definition of rule weights for M-class test problems

2.4.2 Simulation Results on Iris Data

The iris data set is one of the most frequently used data sets in the literature. This data set is a three-class pattern classification problem involving 150 samples (50 samples from each class) with four continuous attributes. The data set is available from the UCI Machine Learning Repository (http://www.ics.uci.edu/~mlearn/MLRepository.html). It is known that linear models work very well on the iris data set. Weiss & Kulikowski [178] examined the classification performance of nine classification methods (e.g., nearest neighbor and neural networks) where the highest classification rate (i.e., 98.0%) on test patterns was obtained by linear models.

Through computer simulations on the iris data set, we compare the four definitions of rule weights. We also examine the effect of the granularity of linguistic discretization on the classification performance of linguistic rule-based systems. Furthermore we compare the product operator with the minimum operator. In our computer simulations, the granularity of linguistic discretization means the number of linguistic terms in Fig. 1.4 of Chap. 1. First all the attribute values were normalized into real numbers in the unit interval $[0, 1]$. This means that the iris data set was handled as a three-class pattern classification problem in the four-dimensional unit hypercube $[0, 1]^4$. This pattern space was discretized into $K \times K \times K \times K$ cells using K linguistic terms on each axis of the pattern space. We examined four different sets of linguistic terms in Fig. 1.4 of Chap. 1 (i.e., $K = 2, 3, 4, 5$). For example, each axis of the pattern space was discretized into two linguistic terms as in Fig. 2.12 when $K = 2$. In this case, the pattern space was discretized into $2 \times 2 \times 2 \times 2$ cells. A linguistic rule was generated for each cell using a heuristic method described in this chapter. When there was no compatible training pattern in a cell, the corresponding linguistic rule was not generated.

First we examined the performance of linguistic rule-based systems on training patterns. All the 150 samples were used as training patterns for generating linguistic rules, and the same 150 samples were used for calculating the performance of generated linguistic rules. Table 2.1 summarizes the number of generated linguistic rules, the number of cells, and the rate of the number of generated linguistic rules to the number of cells when we used the first definition of rule weights and the product operator. From Table 2.1, we can see that many rules could not be generated when linguistic discretization was fine (e.g., $K = 5$). This is because there were no compatible patterns in many small cells constructed from fine linguistic discretization. At the same time, we can also see from Table 2.1 that the number of generated linguistic rules was very large, especially when linguistic discretization was fine. Rule selection is discussed in a later chapter of this book for finding only a small number of important linguistic rules.

The number of generated linguistic rules in the cases of the second and third definitions is always the same as the case of the first definition. Only in the case of the fourth definition may rule weights of some linguistic rules be negative for multi-class pattern classification problems with more than two classes. Linguistic rules with negative rule weights were removed from linguistic rule-based systems in our computer simulations in this book. Table 2.2 shows the number of linguistic rules where we used the fourth definition and the product operator. From the comparison between Table 2.1 and Table 2.2, we can see that some rules were removed when linguistic discretization was coarse (i.e., $K = 2$). This is because large cells constructed from coarse linguistic partitions tend to include training patterns from multiple classes. On the contrary, small cells are not likely to include training patterns from more than two classes. When each linguistic rule does not have compatible patterns from more than two classes, the fourth definition of rule weights is the same as the third definition independent of the total number of classes involved in pattern classification problems.

We examined four granularities of linguistic discretization (i.e., $K = 2, 3, 4, 5$) and the four definitions of rule weights. We also examined the case of no rule weight. Table 2.3 shows the classification rate on training patterns for each combination of the granularity and the rule weight definition where the product operator was used to calculate the compatibility grade. From this table, we can see that higher classification rates were obtained from finer

Table 2.1. Relation between the number of generated linguistic rules and the granularity of linguistic discretization in the case of the first definition of rule weights. The same results are obtained with respect to the number of generated linguistic rules from the second and third definitions of rule weights

Granularity	$K = 2$	$K = 3$	$K = 4$	$K = 5$
# of generated rules	16	62	133	186
# of cells: K^4	16	81	256	625
Rate of generated rules	1.00	0.77	0.52	0.30

Table 2.2. Relation between the number of generated linguistic rules and the granularity of linguistic discretization in the case of the fourth definition of rule weights. Linguistic rules with negative weights are removed from Table 2.1

Granularity	$K = 2$	$K = 3$	$K = 4$	$K = 5$
# of generated rules	12	62	133	186
# of cells: K^4	16	81	256	625
Rate of generated rules	0.75	0.77	0.52	0.30

linguistic discretization. That is, high classification rates on training patterns were realized by dividing the pattern space into many small cells. In Table 2.3, the highest classification rate in each row is highlighted by bold letters. The highest classification rate in Table 2.3 is indicated by *. For comparison, Table 2.4 shows the simulation results when we used the minimum operator.

Table 2.3. Classification rates on training patterns in the iris data set. All the 150 samples in the iris data set were used for generating linguistic rules of length 4. The product operator was used to calculate the compatibility grade

Granularity	Rule weight definition				
	No weight	1st def.	2nd def.	3rd def.	4th def.
$K = 2$	**71.3%**	70.7%	67.3%	68.0%	66.0%
$K = 3$	92.0%	92.7%	**94.0%**	**94.0%**	**94.0%**
$K = 4$	80.0%	90.7%	92.7%	**97.3%**∗	**97.3%**∗
$K = 5$	94.7%	96.0%	96.0%	**96.7%**	**96.7%**

* Best result in this table

We also examined the performance of linguistic rule-based systems on test patterns. We used the leaving-one-out technique [178] where the 150 samples in the iris data set were divided into 149 training patterns and a single test pattern. The design of a linguistic rule-based system using 149 training patterns and the performance evaluation of the designed system using a single test pattern were iterated 150 times so that all the 150 samples were used as test patterns just once. In general, the number of iterations of such a design–evaluation trial in the leaving-one-out technique is the same as the number of given samples.

Table 2.4. Classification rates on training patterns in the iris data set. The minimum operator was used to calculate the compatibility grade

Granularity	Rule weight definition				
	No weight	1st def.	2nd def.	3rd def.	4th def.
$K = 2$	68.7%	80.7%	**91.3%**	75.3%	70.7%
$K = 3$	91.3%	**96.7%**∗	96.0%	94.7%	90.0%
$K = 4$	82.0%	88.7%	92.0%	**95.3%**	**95.3%**
$K = 5$	94.7%	**96.0%**	**96.0%**	**96.0%**	**96.0%**

* Best result in this table

Simulation results on the iris data using the leaving-one-out technique are summarized in Table 2.5 where the product operator was used to calculate the compatibility grade. For comparison, Table 2.6 shows the simulation results when we used the minimum operator.

Table 2.5. Classification rates on test patterns in the iris data set. The leaving-one-out technique was used to examine the generalization ability of linguistic rule-based classification systems. In each trial of the leaving-one-out technique, 149 samples were used as training patterns for generating linguistic rules of length 4. The product operator was used to calculate the compatibility grade

Granularity	Rule weight definition				
	No weight	1st def.	2nd def.	3rd def.	4th def.
$K = 2$	**71.3%**	70.0%	67.3%	68.0%	66.0%
$K = 3$	92.0%	92.0%	**93.3%**	**93.3%**	**93.3%**
$K = 4$	78.7%	88.7%	89.3%	**94.0%**	**94.0%**
$K = 5$	94.7%	**95.3%**∗	**95.3%**∗	**95.3%**∗	**95.3%**∗

* Best result in this table

Table 2.6. Classification rates on test patterns in the iris data set. The minimum operator was used to calculate the compatibility grade

Granularity	Rule weight definition				
	No weight	1st def.	2nd def.	3rd def.	4th def.
$K = 2$	68.7%	79.3%	**88.0%**	72.3%	69.3%
$K = 3$	91.3%	93.3%	**95.3%**	94.0%	90.0%
$K = 4$	80.7%	86.7%	91.3%	**94.7%**	**94.7%**
$K = 5$	94.7%	**96.0%**∗	95.3%	95.3%	95.3%

* Best result in this table

2.4.3 Simulation Results on Wine Data

The wine data set is a 13-dimensional pattern classification problem with 178 samples from three classes. We chose this data set because it involves many continuous attributes. This data set is also available from the UCI Machine Learning Repository, like the iris data set. We first normalized each attribute value into a real number in the unit interval $[0, 1]$. Thus the pattern space of the wine data was normalized into the 13-dimensional unit hypercube $[0, 1]^{13}$. Then we calculated average classification rates on test patterns as well as training patterns. All the given 178 samples were used as training patterns when we examined the classification performance of linguistic rule-based systems on training patterns. On the other hand, we used the leaving-one-out technique when we examined the classification performance on test patterns as in our previous computer simulations on the iris data. In the leaving-one-out technique, the given 178 samples were divided into 177 training patterns and a single test pattern. The product operator was used to calculate the compatibility grade in our computer simulations on the wine data.

As in the previous computer simulations, we examined the four granularities (i.e., $K = 2, 3, 4, 5$) and the five specifications of rule weights (i.e., their four definitions and the case of no rule weights). Since it is difficult to examine K^{13} cells in the 13-dimensional pattern space corresponding to the linguistic discretization of each axis into K linguistic terms, we only generated short linguistic rules with a few antecedent conditions. The number of antecedent conditions is referred to as the rule length in this book. For example, the length of the following linguistic rule is two:

$$\text{Rule } R_q \text{: If } x_i \text{ is } A_{qi} \text{ and } x_j \text{ is } A_{qj} \text{ then Class } C_q \text{ with } CF_q, \qquad (2.41)$$

where x_i and x_j are two attributes chosen from the 13 attributes in the wine data (i.e., $i, j \in \{1, 2, \ldots, 13\}$). The total number of combinations of antecedent linguistic terms for generating linguistic rules of the length L is calculated as $_{13}C_L \times K^L$ where $_{13}C_L$ is the number of combinations of choosing L attributes from the 13 attributes and K^L is the number of combinations of K linguistic terms for the selected K attributes. Table 2.7 summarizes the number of generated linguistic rules when all the 178 samples were used as training patterns. In this table, the first definition of rule weights was used (the same results were obtained from the second and third definitions as we have already explained). It should be noted that the number of short linguistic rules is much smaller than the number of combinations of linguistic terms for generating linguistic rules of length 13 (i.e., K^{13}).

We can construct a linguistic rule-based classification system using all or some of linguistic rules in Table 2.7. As an example, we constructed a linguistic rule-based system using linguistic rules of length 2 for each specification of the granularity of linguistic discretization. Classification rates of such a linguistic rule-based system on training patterns are summarized in Table 2.8 where the five specifications of rule weights and the four granularities of linguistic discretization are examined. In the same manner, we examined the performance of linguistic rules of length 2 on test patterns using the leaving-

Table 2.7. The number of generated linguistic rules of each length from the 178 training patterns in the wine data. The first definition of rule weights was used in this table. The same results were obtained with respect to the number of generated linguistic rules from the second and third definitions

Granularity	Length of linguistic rules (L)				
	Length 0	Length 1	Length 2	Length 3	Length 4
$K = 2$	1	26	312	2288	11440
$K = 3$	1	39	701	7585	54633
$K = 4$	1	52	1201	15766	129624
$K = 5$	1	65	1768	25589	220876

one-out technique. Classification rates on test patterns are summarized in Table 2.9.

Table 2.8. Classification rates on training patterns in the wine data set. All the 178 samples in the wine data set were used to generate linguistic rules of length 2

Granularity	Rule weight definition				
	No weight	1st def.	2nd def.	3rd def.	4th def.
$K = 2$	84.8%	90.4%	**94.9%**	92.7%	92.7%
$K = 3$	70.2%	94.9%	**96.6%**	**96.6%**	94.4%
$K = 4$	71.9%	96.6%	97.2%	**98.3%**	97.8%
$K = 5$	74.7%	94.4%	97.2%	**98.9%∗**	97.8%

∗ Best result in this table

Table 2.9. Classification rates on test patterns in the wine data set. The leaving-one-out technique was used to examine the generalization ability of linguistic rule-based classification systems. In each trial of the leaving-one-out technique, 177 samples were used as training patterns for generating linguistic rules of length 2

Granularity	Rule weight definition				
	No weight	1st def.	2nd def.	3rd def.	4th def.
$K = 2$	80.3%	90.4%	**92.7%**	91.6%	90.4%
$K = 3$	68.0%	93.3%	**95.5%∗**	**95.5%∗**	93.3%
$K = 4$	68.5%	93.3%	**94.9%**	**94.9%**	**94.9%**
$K = 5$	69.7%	89.9%	92.7%	93.3%	**93.8%**

∗ Best result in this table

In Table 2.8 and Table 2.9, we used a large number of linguistic rules. From the viewpoint of interpretability, rule-based systems with only a small number of rules are desirable. While we discuss rule selection in detail in a later chapter, here we show simulation results using a simple heuristic rule selection method for comparing the five specifications of rule weights. In the computer simulations, first we generated linguistic rules of length 3 or less

from training patterns. We used all the 14 linguistic terms in Fig. 1.4 of Chap.
1 for generating linguistic rules. That is, we simultaneously used linguistic
terms with different granularities. In this case, the total number of combinations of antecedent linguistic terms for generating linguistic rules of length L
is calculated as $_{13}C_L \times 14^L$. The generated linguistic rules were divided into
three groups according to their consequent classes. Linguistic rules in each
group were sorted in descending order of a rule selection criterion. We used
the product of the confidence $c(\cdot)$ and the support $s(\cdot)$ as the rule selection
criterion in our computer simulations in this subsection. When multiple linguistic rules had the same value with respect to the rule selection criterion,
they were randomly sorted (i.e., random tiebreak). We constructed a linguistic rule-based system by choosing the first N rules from each group. Using
various values of N (i.e., $N = 1, 2, \ldots, 10$), we examined the classification
performance of linguistic rule-based systems with different sizes. For decreasing the effect of the random tiebreak, we calculated average results over 1000
iterations of our computer simulation to evaluate the performance on training patterns. By the same reason, the leaving-one-out technique was iterated
20 times (i.e., 20×178 trials) to evaluate the performance on test patterns.
Simulation results on training patterns and test patterns are summarized in
Table 2.10 and Table 2.11, respectively. In these tables, the best result in
each row and the best result in each table are indicated by bold type and *,
respectively.

Table 2.10. Classification rates on training patterns in the wine data set. First
linguistic rules of length 3 or less were generated. Then a pre-specified number
of linguistic rules were selected from the generated rules using a rule selection
criterion. The product of the confidence and the support was used as the rule
selection criterion

# of rules	No weight	1st def.	2nd def.	3rd def.	4th def.
3	**89.89%**	**89.89%**	**89.89%**	89.33%	**89.89%**
6	91.01%	91.57%	91.01%	**92.13%**	91.01%
9	93.26%	**93.82%**	92.13%	**93.82%**	**93.82%**
12	93.26%	93.82%	92.70%	**94.94%**∗	**94.94%**∗
15	88.76%	92.70%	92.13%	**94.94%**∗	**94.94%**∗
18	91.01%	91.57%	92.70%	**94.94%**∗	94.38%
21	91.01%	91.57%	92.70%	**94.38%**	93.82%
24	92.13%	92.13%	92.70%	**94.38%**	93.82%
27	90.45%	92.13%	92.70%	**94.38%**	93.82%
30	90.45%	92.13%	92.70%	**94.94%**∗	93.82%

* Best result in this table

2.4.4 Discussions on Simulation Results

From the simulation results in this section, we can see that the best results
were obtained from the third definition of rule weights on the average. This

Table 2.11. Classification rates of small linguistic rule-based systems on test patterns in the wine data set. Linguistic rule-based systems were designed in the same manner as Table 2.9

# of rules	No weight	1st def.	2nd def.	3rd def.	4th def.
3	**89.89%**	**89.89%**	**89.89%**	89.33%	**89.89%**
6	80.34%	83.15%	**85.96%**	84.83%	85.39%
9	88.76%	91.57%	92.13%	**93.26%**	**93.26%**
12	**93.26%**	**93.26%**	92.70%	**93.26%**	**93.26%**
15	88.76%	91.57%	91.57%	**94.38%**∗	93.26%
18	88.20%	89.89%	89.89%	**92.13%**	91.01%
21	89.33%	89.33%	89.33%	**91.57%**	91.01%
24	88.20%	89.33%	89.33%	**91.57%**	91.01%
27	88.20%	89.89%	90.45%	**92.70%**	91.57%
30	90.45%	90.45%	91.01%	**93.26%**	92.13%

* Best result in this table

coincides with the discussions in the previous section using a class of artificial test problems. Hereafter we use the third definition of rule weights in this book. We can also see from the simulation results that the use of rule weights improved the performance of linguistic rule-based systems. In the next chapter, we present two learning schemes of rule weights. The performance of linguistic rule-based systems is further improved by the adjustment of rule weights.

In this section, we also examined the relation between the granularity of linguistic discretization and the performance of linguistic rule-based systems. In general, higher classification rates on training patterns are obtained from finer linguistic discretization. Classification rates on test patterns are not monotonic with respect to the granularity of linguistic discretization (e.g., see Table 2.9). While coarse linguistic discretization cannot approximate desirable classification boundaries very well, fine linguistic discretization is likely to fit training patterns excessively (i.e., overfitting training patterns). Too fine linguistic discretization usually leads to very high classification rates on training patterns but low classification rates on test patterns. In this book, we assume that a set of linguistic terms is given for each attribute by human users or domain experts according to their knowledge and intuition. Our approaches in this book use the given set of linguistic terms for each attribute. Thus the above discussions on the relation between the granularity of linguistic discretization and the performance of linguistic rule-base systems are useful only when linguistic terms are not given (i.e., when we have to specify linguistic discretization for each attribute).

Slightly better results were obtained from the product operator than the minimum operator in our computer simulations on the iris data. Hereafter we use the product operator to calculate the compatibility grade. In recent studies on fuzzy rule-based systems, the product operator has often been used instead of the minimum operator.

In the computer simulations on the wine data, we used a heuristic rule selection method for choosing a tractable number of linguistic rules. In the first computer simulation, we used all linguistic rules of length 2. In the second computer simulation, the product of the confidence and the support was used to select a small number of rules from linguistic rules of length 3 or less. Simulation results in this section can be improved by using more sophisticated techniques for selecting linguistic rules. In a later chapter, we discuss other heuristic rule selection criteria. For various rule selection criteria, see Ishibuchi & Yamamoto [93]. We also describe a genetic algorithm-based approach to linguistic rule selection.

3. Learning of Linguistic Rules

In this chapter, we describe two approaches to the learning of rule weights. One is a reward–punishment learning scheme and the other is an analytical learning scheme. We also mention the adjustment of the membership function of each linguistic term. As in the previous chapter, we use linguistic rules of the following form for our n-dimensional pattern classification problem:

$$\text{Rule } R_q: \text{ If } x_1 \text{ is } A_{q1} \text{ and } \dots \text{ and } x_n \text{ is } A_{qn}$$
$$\text{then Class } C_q \text{ with } CF_q. \quad (3.1)$$

3.1 Reward–Punishment Learning

A simple approach to the learning of rule weights is a reward–punishment learning scheme [132]. The basic idea of this learning scheme is to increase or decrease the rule weight of a winner rule according to the classification result (i.e., correct classification or misclassification) of each training pattern.

3.1.1 Learning Algorithm

Let S be a set of linguistic rules with rule weights in the form (3.1). The rule set S can be viewed as a linguistic rule-based system. In the learning of rule weights, each training pattern x_p is presented to the linguistic rule-based system S. Since we use the single winner-based method, a single winner rule is identified for each training pattern. When a training pattern is correctly classified by the winner rule R_w, its rule weight CF_w is increased as the reward of the correct classification in the following manner:

$$CF_w^{\text{New}} = CF_w^{\text{Old}} + \eta^+ \cdot (1 - CF_w^{\text{Old}}), \quad (3.2)$$

where η^+ is a positive constant for increasing the rule weight ($0 < \eta^+ < 1$). Note that the updated rule weight by (3.2) is always a real number in the unit interval $[0, 1]$ when its initial value is a real number in $[0, 1]$. If the update rule in (3.2) is iteratively applied to the rule weight of a particular linguistic rule (i.e., if the linguistic rule continues to correctly classify training patterns), its rule weight gradually approaches the maximum value of 1.0.

On the other hand, when a training pattern is misclassified by the winner rule R_w, its rule weight CF_w is decreased as the punishment of the misclassification in the following manner:

$$CF_w^{\text{New}} = CF_w^{\text{Old}} - \eta^- \cdot CF_w^{\text{Old}}, \qquad (3.3)$$

where η^- is a positive constant for decreasing the rule weight ($0 < \eta^- < 1$). As in (3.2), the updated rule weight by (3.3) is always a real number in the unit interval $[0, 1]$ when its initial value is a real number in $[0, 1]$. If the update rule in (3.3) is iteratively applied to the rule weight of a particular linguistic rule (i.e., if the linguistic rule continues to misclassify training patterns), its rule weight gradually approaches the minimum value of 0.0.

Only the rule weight of the winner rule is adjusted in the learning for each training pattern depending on its classification result (i.e., correct classification or misclassification). Since the number of correctly classified training patterns is usually much larger than that of misclassified training patterns, a much smaller value is assigned to the learning rate η^+ for increasing rule weights than the learning rate η^- for decreasing rule weights (e.g., $\eta^+ = 0.001$ and $\eta^- = 0.1$). When the classification of a training pattern is rejected, rule weights of no linguistic rules are adjusted. The classification of a training pattern is rejected when no linguistic rules are compatible with the pattern. The rejection also happens when multiple linguistic rules with different consequent classes have the same maximum product of the compatibility grade and the consequent rule weight (i.e., when there exist multiple winner rules with different classes for a training pattern). In the latter case, the pattern is located on the classification boundary generated by the linguistic rule-based system.

The reward–punishment learning scheme can be written as the following algorithm:

[Reward–Punishment Learning Algorithm]

Step 1: Choose a single training pattern.

Step 2: Classify the training pattern by the linguistic rule-based system.

Step 3: If the training pattern is correctly classified, increase the rule weight of the winner rule using (3.2). If the training pattern is misclassified, decrease the rule weight of the winner rule using (3.3). When the classification of the training pattern is rejected, do not change the rule weights of any linguistic rules.

Step 4: If a pre-specified stopping condition is satisfied, terminate this algorithm. Otherwise, return to Step 1.

Learning results of the reward–punishment learning scheme depend on the order of training patterns to be presented to the linguistic rule-based system. Usually all the given training patterns are presented to the linguistic rule-based system in a random order. After all the training patterns are examined, they are presented again in a random order. The presentation of all the training patterns is referred to as a single epoch (or a single sweep). In this book, we use the term "epoch" to describe the number of iterations of the learning algorithm. The upper bound of epochs can be used as a stopping condition of the learning algorithm. Of course, the learning algorithm is usually terminated when all training patterns are correctly classified.

In computer simulations in this book, we handle the two learning rates η^+ and η^- as constant. In real-world applications, the use of variable learning rates may improve the performance of adjusted linguistic rule-based systems. That is, the values of η^+ and η^- can be gradually decreased during the iterative execution of the reward–punishment learning scheme. They can also be adjusted during the learning according to the classification rate of the linguistic rule-based system.

3.1.2 Illustration of the Learning Algorithm Using Artificial Test Problems

For visually illustrating the reward–punishment learning scheme, we applied the learning algorithm to a linguistic rule based system with the following four linguistic rules for a simple two-dimensional pattern classification problem in Fig. 3.1:

R_1: If x_1 is *small* and x_2 is *small* then Class 1 with CF_1,

R_2: If x_1 is *small* and x_2 is *large* then Class 1 with CF_2,

R_3: If x_1 is *large* and x_2 is *small* then Class 1 with CF_3,

R_4: If x_1 is *large* and x_2 is *large* then Class 2 with CF_4.

Together with 20 training patterns, Fig. 3.1 shows the classification boundary when all the four linguistic rules have the same rule weight (their initial rule weights were specified as $CF_q = 0.5$ for $q = 1, 2, 3, 4$). In this figure, three patterns are misclassified by the linguistic rule-based system with the four linguistic rules whose rule weights are the same. For applying the learning algorithm to the linguistic rule-based system, first we randomly specified an order of the given 20 patterns. Then we iteratively presented the given patterns in the specified order to the linguistic rule-based system. The first four patterns are indicated in Fig. 3.1 for illustration purposes. The values of the learning rates η^+ and η^- were specified as $\eta^+ = 0.001$ and $\eta^- = 0.1$ in this computer simulation.

As shown in Fig. 3.1, the first pattern x_1 is correctly classified by the linguistic rule R_1. Thus the rule weight CF_1 of R_1 is increased by (3.2) as

$$CF_1 = 0.5 + 0.001 \cdot (1 - 0.5) = 0.5005. \tag{3.4}$$

The second pattern x_2 is misclassified by the linguistic rule R_3. Thus the rule weight CF_3 of R_3 is decreased by (3.3) as

$$CF_3 = 0.5 - 0.1 \cdot 0.5 = 0.45. \tag{3.5}$$

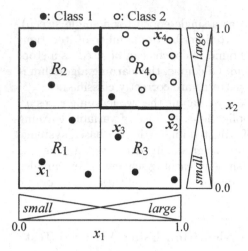

Fig. 3.1. A two-dimensional test problem with 20 training patterns. The decision region of each linguistic rule and the classification boundary correspond to the case with the same rule weight

The third pattern x_3 is correctly classified by the same rule R_3. Thus the rule weight CF_3 is increased by (3.2) as

$$CF_3 = 0.45 + 0.001 \cdot (1 - 0.45) = 0.45055. \tag{3.6}$$

The fourth pattern x_4 is correctly classified by the linguistic rule R_4. Thus the rule weight CF_4 is increased by (3.2) as

$$CF_4 = 0.5 + 0.001 \cdot (1 - 0.5) = 0.5005. \tag{3.7}$$

In this manner, the rule weight of each linguistic rule is updated by presenting all the given training patterns to the linguistic rule-based system. In Fig. 3.2, we show the classification boundaries after a single epoch and seven epochs. As shown in Fig. 3.2, three patterns are misclassified after a single epoch and all the given patterns are correctly classified after seven epochs. Table 3.1 shows the values of the rule weights and the number of misclassified training patterns after each epoch.

Table 3.1. Simulation results by the reward–punishment learning algorithm on the artificial test problem in Fig. 3.1. The second row "Errors" shows the number of misclassified training patterns

Epoch	0	1	2	3	4	5	6	7
Errors	3	3	3	2	1	2	1	0
CF_1	0.5000	0.5015	0.5030	0.5045	0.5065	0.5084	0.5104	0.5124
CF_2	0.5000	0.5015	0.5030	0.5045	0.5065	0.5080	0.5099	0.5119
CF_3	0.5000	0.4066	0.3311	0.2999	0.2713	0.2456	0.2225	0.2240
CF_4	0.5000	0.4541	0.4131	0.3770	0.3826	0.3498	0.3557	0.3621

We also applied the learning algorithm to the following three linguistic rules that were used for our single-dimensional artificial test problem in Fig.

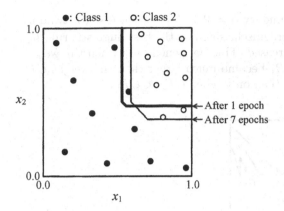

Fig. 3.2. Classification boundaries after a single epoch and seven epochs

2.13 of Chap. 2:

R_1: If x is *small* then Class 1 with CF_1,

R_2: If x is *medium* then Class 2 with CF_2,

R_3: If x is *large* then Class 2 with CF_3.

Note that the membership function of each linguistic term in these linguistic rules (i.e., Fig. 2.14) is different from the above computer simulation (i.e., Fig. 3.1).

We adjusted the rule weights of the three linguistic rules using the reward–punishment learning scheme. The initial rule weights were specified as $CF_1 = CF_2 = CF_3 = 0.5$. Training patterns were randomly generated from the pattern space $[0, 1]$ in Fig. 2.13 according to the uniform distribution in the pattern space $[0, 1]$. The execution of the learning algorithm was iterated until 10000 training patterns were examined. The values of the learning rates η^+ and η^- were specified as $\eta^+ = 0.0005$ and $\eta^- = 0.2$. In Fig. 3.3, we show how the rule weights were updated during the iterative execution of the learning algorithm. On the other hand, Fig. 3.4 shows how the estimated class boundary was adjusted. The estimated class boundary was calculated as $\hat{\theta} = 0.25$ by the linguistic rules with the initial rule weights $CF_1 = CF_2 = CF_3 = 0.5$. Since the actual threshold θ in Fig. 2.13 is $\theta = 0.47$ in our single-dimensional artificial test problem, training patterns in the interval $[\hat{\theta}, \theta]$ were misclassified by the second linguistic rule R_2 in the early stage of the learning. Thus the value of CF_2 was rapidly decreased by the learning algorithm as shown in Fig. 3.3. At the same time, the values of CF_1 and CF_3 were gradually increased because the first and third linguistic rules always correctly classified training patterns in their decision regions. Since compatible training patterns with the third linguistic rule are always Class 2 patterns (i.e., training patterns in the interval $[0.5, 1.0]$ are always from Class 2; see Fig. 2.13), CF_3 continued to be increased during the execution of the leaning algorithm. On the other hand, we can observe some drops in the value of CF_1 in Fig. 3.3. When the estimated class boundary $\hat{\theta}$ became larger than the actual class boundary $\theta = 0.47$ (i.e., when $\theta < \hat{\theta}$), training patterns in the interval $[\theta, \hat{\theta}]$ were misclassified by the first linguistic rule R_1. Thus the value of CF_1 was decreased. This happened only when the weight CF_1 of the first linguistic rule R_1 became much larger than the weight CF_2 of the second linguistic rule R_2 (i.e., only when $CF_2 \ll CF_1$).

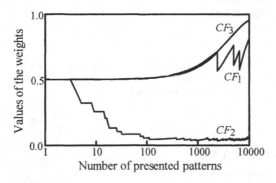

Fig. 3.3. Rule weight update during the iterative execution of the reward–punishment learning scheme

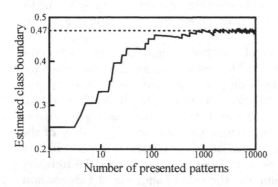

Fig. 3.4. Adjustment of the estimated class boundary during the iterative execution of the reward–punishment learning scheme

Learning results of the reward–punishment learning scheme strongly depend on the values of the learning rates η^+ and η^-. To demonstrate this dependency, we performed the same computer simulation as in Fig. 3.3 and Fig. 3.4 using various specifications of η^+ and η^-. Since learning results also depend on the order of training patterns, we performed our computer simulation 20 times for each combination of η^+ and η^-. In each trial, a different set of randomly generated 10000 training patterns was used in the learning of the rule weights. That is, we used 20 sets of 10000 training patterns in our computer simulations. Table 3.2 summarizes the average value of the estimated class boundary $\hat{\theta}$ after the presentation of 10000 training patterns over 20 trials for each combination of η^+ and η^-. From this table, we can see that the estimated class boundary $\hat{\theta}$ was far from the actual threshold value $\theta = 0.47$ when the specifications of η^+ and η^- were not appropriate.

Table 3.2. Average values of the estimated class boundary $\hat{\theta}$. The actual threshold θ is $\theta = 0.47$. The derivation $|\hat{\theta} - \theta|$ can be viewed as an error measure. Reasonable specifications of η^+ and η^- satisfy the inequality relation $\eta^+ \ll \eta^-$

η^+	η^-			
	0.1	0.01	0.001	0.0001
0.1	0.309	0.259	0.251	0.250
0.01	0.421	0.315	0.259	0.251
0.001	0.463	0.422	0.314	0.257
0.0001	0.470	0.460	0.379	0.270

3.1.3 Computer Simulations on Iris Data

For examining the effect of the rule weight learning on the performance of linguistic rule-based classification systems, we applied the reward–punishment learning scheme to the iris data. As in Sect. 2.4.2, we discretized the normalized pattern space $[0, 1]^4$ into $K \times K \times K \times K$ cells using K linguistic terms on each attribute. We examined four values of K: $K = 2, 3, 4, 5$. Linguistic discretization corresponding to each value of K is shown in Fig. 1.4 of Chap. 1. For specifying initial rule weights, we used the third definition of rule weights. We also examined the case with the same initial rule weight for all linguistic rules (i.e., $CF_q = 0.5$, $^\forall q$). In computer simulations, training patterns were presented in a random order. The values of η^+ and η^- were specified as $\eta^+ = 0.001$ and $\eta^- = 0.1$.

In Table 3.3, we show simulation results on training patterns using the initial weights specified by the third definition. Average classification rates were calculated for each value of K over 20 independent trials with different orders of presentation of the 150 training patterns. The learning of rule weights in each trial was iterated for 100 epochs even when all training patterns were correctly classified before the 100th epoch. On the other hand, Table 3.4 shows simulation results on training patterns in the case of the same initial rule weight for all linguistic rules. These tables show that the learning of rule weights significantly improved classification rates on training patterns, especially when we used coarse linguistic discretization (e.g., $K = 2$). When linguistic discretization was fine (e.g., $K = 5$), classification rates were already high before the learning algorithm was applied to linguistic rule-based systems. Thus the effect of the rule weight learning was not so significant compared with the case of coarse discretization. From the comparison between Table 3.3 and Table 3.4, we can see that similar results were obtained after enough iterations of the learning algorithm independent of the initial specifications of rule weights (except for the case of $K = 2$).

We also examined classification rates on test patterns using the leaving-one-out technique. This technique was iterated ten times using different orders of presentation of 149 training patterns. Simulation results are summarized in Table 3.5 and Table 3.6. As we have already mentioned, the increase

Table 3.3. Classification rates on training patterns in the iris data set. Rule weights were adjusted by the reward–punishment learning scheme from their initial values heuristically specified by the third definition

Granularity	Number of epochs						
	0	1	2	5	10	50	100
$K = 2$	68.0%	78.2%	84.7%	90.2%	91.5%	92.7%	92.0%
$K = 3$	94.0%	95.1%	96.1%	96.4%	96.7%	98.3%	98.2%
$K = 4$	97.3%	97.3%	97.3%	98.0%	98.0%	99.9%	99.5%
$K = 5$	96.7%	96.7%	96.2%	96.0%	97.0%	99.3%	99.7%

Table 3.4. Classification rates on training patterns in the iris data set. Rule weights were adjusted by the reward–punishment learning scheme from their common initial value of 0.5

Granularity	Number of epochs						
	0	1	2	5	10	50	100
$K = 2$	71.3%	86.4%	92.7%	93.7%	95.3%	96.7%	96.7%
$K = 3$	92.0%	95.0%	96.8%	96.5%	97.0%	97.3%	97.8%
$K = 4$	82.7%	88.0%	91.8%	95.5%	96.5%	99.9%	99.9%
$K = 5$	94.7%	95.2%	95.4%	94.7%	95.5%	99.4%	99.4%

in classification rates on training patterns does not always lead to the increase in classification rates on test patterns. In Table 3.5 and Table 3.6, the rule weight learning significantly improved the generalization ability of linguistic rule-based systems on test patterns when linguistic discretization was coarse (e.g., $K = 2$). We can also observe overfitting of linguistic rule-based systems to training patterns. For example, the average classification rate in the case of $K = 5$ in Table 3.6 was first improved during the learning of rule weights. After reaching its peak value (i.e., 95.3% classification rate), the average classification rate was decreased by further learning. From the comparison between Table 3.5 and Table 3.6, we can see that similar results were obtained on test patterns after enough iterations of the learning algorithm independent of the initial specifications of rule weights as in Table 3.3 and Table 3.4 on training patterns (except for the case of $K = 2$).

Table 3.5. Classification rates on test patterns in the iris data set. Rule weights were adjusted by the reward–punishment learning scheme from their initial values heuristically specified by the third definition

Granularity	Number of epochs						
	0	1	2	5	10	50	100
$K = 2$	68.0%	80.2%	83.9%	89.5%	89.0%	89.1%	88.7%
$K = 3$	93.3%	95.6%	96.6%	96.6%	95.3%	94.9%	95.2%
$K = 4$	94.0%	96.0%	96.0%	96.3%	95.8%	96.0%	96.0%
$K = 5$	95.3%	94.7%	94.7%	94.7%	94.0%	95.3%	96.1%

Table 3.6. Classification rates on test patterns in the iris data set. Rule weights were adjusted by the reward–punishment learning scheme from their common initial value of 0.5

Granularity	Number of epochs						
	0	1	2	5	10	50	100
$K = 2$	71.3%	90.8%	93.0%	92.9%	92.5%	93.2%	93.2%
$K = 3$	92.0%	96.5%	96.1%	96.4%	96.3%	95.0%	95.0%
$K = 4$	81.3%	88.3%	88.7%	91.4%	92.3%	96.2%	96.6%
$K = 5$	94.7%	95.3%	95.3%	94.7%	94.7%	94.5%	94.1%

3.1.4 Computer Simulations on Wine Data

The wine data set was also used to examine the effect of the rule weight learning on the classification performance of linguistic rule-based systems. We applied the learning algorithm to linguistic rule-based systems constructed in Table 2.10 and Table 2.11 in the previous chapter. Linguistic rule-based systems in those tables were constructed by choosing a small number of linguistic rules of length 3 or less using the product of the confidence and the support as a rule selection criterion. Candidate rules from which linguistic rules were selected were generated using all the 14 linguistic terms with different granularities in Fig. 1.4 of Chap. 1.

We used the third definition for specifying the initial rule weight of each linguistic rule. Simulation results on training patterns and test patterns are summarized in Table 3.7 and Table 3.8. From these tables, we can see that the classification performance of linguistic rule-based systems on the wine data was improved by the rule weight learning. When the number of linguistic rules was very small (e.g., only three rules), the rule weight learning could not improve classification rates on training patterns as well as test patterns. On the other hand, the effect of the rule weight learning was significant when the number of linguistic rules was not too small. This is because the rule weight learning cannot adjust the classification boundary when there is no overlap between linguistic rules with different consequent classes. The adjustment of the classification boundary can be performed only in the overlapping region of such linguistic rules in the pattern space. When the number of linguistic rules is very small, there seems to be no large overlapping region in which the classification boundary can be adjusted.

3.2 Analytical Learning

The reward–punishment learning scheme gradually adjusts the rule weight of each linguistic rule. Thus many epochs are usually required for the adjustment of rule weights, especially when the learning rates are small. In this section, we explain an analytical learning scheme.

Table 3.7. Classification rates on training patterns in the wine data set. Rule weights were adjusted by the reward–punishment learning scheme from their initial values specified by the third definition

# of rules	Number of epochs						
	0	1	2	5	10	50	100
3	89.3%	89.1%	89.0%	88.8%	89.0%	89.1%	89.1%
6	92.1%	91.5%	91.6%	92.4%	90.3%	91.1%	91.1%
9	93.8%	93.9%	94.3%	95.0%	95.6%	93.8%	93.8%
12	94.9%	94.4%	94.7%	94.3%	94.4%	95.7%	96.0%
15	94.9%	94.7%	95.1%	95.4%	97.0%	95.6%	95.7%
18	94.9%	95.6%	96.4%	98.3%	98.7%	98.7%	98.4%
21	94.4%	95.3%	96.2%	98.3%	98.9%	98.7%	98.4%
24	94.4%	95.3%	96.2%	98.3%	98.9%	98.2%	98.1%
27	94.4%	95.3%	96.2%	98.3%	98.3%	97.9%	98.3%
30	94.9%	95.7%	95.8%	98.2%	98.2%	98.3%	97.8%

Table 3.8. Classification rates on test patterns in the wine data set. Rule weights were adjusted by the reward–punishment learning scheme from their initial values specified by the third definition

# of rules	Number of epochs						
	0	1	2	5	10	50	100
3	89.3%	88.3%	88.5%	88.2%	88.2%	88.4%	88.4%
6	84.8%	86.2%	87.2%	87.6%	86.7%	87.1%	87.3%
9	93.3%	93.7%	92.9%	91.7%	91.9%	92.4%	92.5%
12	93.3%	93.8%	93.5%	93.0%	92.4%	93.7%	93.5%
15	94.4%	93.8%	94.4%	93.5%	92.9%	92.7%	93.6%
18	92.1%	93.2%	93.7%	93.6%	93.8%	95.1%	94.4%
21	91.6%	91.6%	92.5%	94.1%	95.5%	93.3%	95.3%
24	91.6%	92.1%	92.8%	93.7%	94.4%	94.0%	95.0%
27	92.7%	93.2%	92.2%	93.8%	94.8%	93.7%	93.9%
30	93.3%	93.8%	93.5%	94.4%	94.4%	94.1%	93.4%

3.2.1 Learning Algorithm

When a training pattern x_p is classified by our linguistic rule-based system S, the single winner-based method identifies a single winner rule R_w that has the maximum product of the compatibility grade and the rule weight among linguistic rules in S. Let t_p be the actual class (i.e., target class) of x_p. When the consequent class C_w of the winner rule R_w is the same as t_p, x_p is correctly classified. Otherwise, it is misclassified. From the definition of the winner rule R_w, the following relation holds when x_p is correctly classified:

$$\max\{\mu_{A_q}(x_p) \cdot CF_q | C_q = t_p, R_q \in S\} = \mu_{A_w}(x_p) \cdot CF_w. \tag{3.8}$$

On the other hand, the following relation holds when x_p is misclassified:

$$\max\{\mu_{A_q}(x_p) \cdot CF_q | C_q = t_p, R_q \in S\} < \mu_{A_w}(x_p) \cdot CF_w. \tag{3.9}$$

Let R_{q*} be the linguistic rule with the maximum value in the left hand side of (3.9). R_{q*} can be viewed as the most promising linguistic rule for correctly classifying the training pattern x_p. Using R_{q*}, (3.9) is rewritten as

$$\mu_{A_{q*}}(x_p) \cdot CF_{q*} < \mu_{A_w}(x_p) \cdot CF_w. \tag{3.10}$$

In this formulation, the consequent class C_w of the winner rule is different from the actual class of x_p (i.e., $C_w \neq t_p$) because x_p is misclassified. For correctly classifying x_p, it is required to reverse the inequality in (3.10) by adjusting our linguistic rule-based system so that the following inequality holds:

$$\mu_{A_{q*}}(x_p) \cdot CF_{q*} > \mu_{A_w}(x_p) \cdot CF_w. \tag{3.11}$$

When the left hand side of (3.10) is zero (i.c., when x_p is not covered by any linguistic rule with the same consequent class as the actual class of x_p), we do not try to correctly classify x_p. In this case, the misclassification of x_p does not invoke any modification procedure of our linguistic rule-based system. In the following explanations, we assume that x_p is covered by at least one linguistic rule with the same consequent class as the actual class of x_p (i.c., the left hand size of (3.10) is positive).

There are two alternative ways in the adjustment of rule weights for reversing the inequality in (3.10):

(1) To increase the rule weight CF_{q*} of the linguistic rule R_{q*} in the left hand side of (3.10) as

$$CF_{q*}^{\text{New}} = \frac{\mu_{A_w}(x_p)}{\mu_{A_{q*}}(x_p)} \cdot CF_w^{\text{Old}} + \epsilon, \tag{3.12}$$

where ϵ is a very small positive real number. The inequality relation (3.11) holds after this modification. This adjustment is not always possible. When the right hand side of (3.12) is larger than 1, we do not adopt this adjustment.

(2) To decrease the rule weight CF_w of the winner rule R_w in the right hand side of (3.10) as

$$CF_w^{\text{New}} = \frac{\mu_{A_{q*}}(x_p)}{\mu_{A_w}(x_p)} \cdot CF_{q*}^{\text{Old}} - \epsilon. \tag{3.13}$$

When the right hand side of (3.13) is smaller than 0, we specify CF_w^{New} as $CF_w^{\text{New}} = 0$. The inequality relation (3.11) holds after this modification. If R_{q*} becomes the new winner rule after the adjustment of CF_w based on (3.13), x_p is correctly classified. On the other hand, x_p is still misclassified if another linguistic rule becomes the new winner rule. In the latter case, (3.13) is applied to the new winner rule again. This procedure is iterated until R_{q*} becomes the winner rule (i.e., until x_p is correctly classified).

When x_p is misclassified, our linguistic rule-based system is modified by (3.12) or (3.13). We calculate the classification rate of each of the three alternatives (i.e., the current linguistic rule-based system before the modification and two modified ones) on training patterns. Then we replace the current linguistic rule-based system with the best one among the three alternatives. When all the given training patterns are correctly classified, the analytical learning scheme no longer changes the current linguistic rule-based system. Even when some training patterns are misclassified, the current linguistic rule-based system is not modified if no improvement in the classification rate can be achieved. The classification rate on training patterns is monotonically improved during the rule weight learning based on the analytical learning scheme.

The analytical learning scheme can be written as the following algorithm:

[Analytical Learning Algorithm]

Step 1: Choose a single training pattern.

Step 2: Classify the training pattern by the linguistic rule-based system.

Step 3: When the training pattern is misclassified, perform the following procedures. Otherwise, go to Step 4.

   (1) Examine the classification performance on training patterns of the three alternative linguistic rule-based systems: the current one and its two modified versions by (3.12) and (3.13). Note that the modification by (3.13) is iterated until the current training pattern chosen in Step 1 is correctly classified. If no modified versions outperform the current one, go to Step 4.

   (2) Replace the current linguistic rule-based system with the better modified version. If the two modified versions have the same classification rate on training patterns, randomly choose one version.

Step 4: If a pre-specified stopping condition is satisfied, terminate this algorithm. Otherwise, return to Step 1.

Learning results of the analytical learning scheme depend on the order of training patterns to be presented to the linguistic rule-based system as in the case of the reward–punishment learning scheme. When there are no misclassified training patterns, rule weights are no longer adjusted by the analytical learning scheme. On the contrary, the reward–punishment learning scheme continues to change the rule weight of the winner rule because the reward is given to the winner rule when a training pattern is correctly classified.

3.2.2 Illustration of the Learning Algorithm Using Artificial Test Problems

For visually illustrating the analytical learning scheme, let us again consider the two-dimensional pattern classification problem in Fig. 3.1. We adjusted the rule weights of the four linguistic rules in Fig. 3.1 using the analytical learning scheme. As in the case of the reward–punishment learning scheme, we specified the initial rule weights as $CF_q = 0.5$ for all the four linguistic rules. Figure 3.1 shows the classification boundary by the initial linguistic rule-based system. The value of ϵ was specified as $\epsilon = 0.001$ in computer simulations.

Since the first training pattern x_1 in Fig. 3.1 is correctly classified by the initial linguistic rule-based system, no rule weights are modified. As shown in Fig. 3.1, the second pattern x_2 is misclassified by the linguistic rule R_3. Thus R_3 is the winner rule R_w for x_2 in (3.10). Since the actual class of x_2 is Class 2, R_4 is chosen as the most promising linguistic rule R_{q*} in (3.10) for correctly classifying the training pattern x_2. One modified version of the current linguistic rule-based system is constructed by increasing the rule weight of the most promising linguistic rule R_{q*} (i.e., R_4) using (3.12) as

$$
\begin{aligned}
CF_4 &= \frac{\mu_{A_3}(x_2)}{\mu_{A_4}(x_2)} \cdot CF_3 + \epsilon \\
&= \frac{0.944 \times 0.555}{0.944 \times 0.445} \cdot 0.5 + 0.001 \\
&\approx 0.625.
\end{aligned}
\tag{3.14}
$$

The rule weights of the other linguistic rules are not adjusted (i.e., $CF_1 = CF_2 = CF_3 = 0.5$). The classification boundary by this modified linguistic rule-based system is shown in Fig. 3.5. As shown in this figure, the training pattern x_2 is correctly classified. The classification boundary is close to x_2 because ϵ is very small. Note that x_2 is located on the classification boundary when ϵ is zero. Some issues related to the location of the classification boundary are discussed in a later section of this chapter.

Another alternative linguistic rule-based system is constructed by decreasing the rule weight of the winner rule R_w for x_2 (i.e., R_3) using (3.13) as

$$
\begin{aligned}
CF_3 &= \frac{\mu_{A_4}(x_2)}{\mu_{A_3}(x_2)} \cdot CF_4 - \epsilon \\
&= \frac{0.944 \times 0.445}{0.944 \times 0.555} \cdot 0.5 - 0.001 \\
&\approx 0.400.
\end{aligned}
\tag{3.15}
$$

The rule weights of the other linguistic rules are not adjusted (i.e., $CF_1 = CF_2 = CF_4 = 0.5$). The classification boundary by this modified linguistic rule-based system is shown in Fig. 3.6. As shown in this figure, the training pattern x_2 is correctly classified. In Fig. 3.6, two training patterns are misclassified while three training patterns are misclassified in Fig. 3.5. Since three training patterns are misclassified by the current linguistic rule-based system in Fig. 3.1, the second modification in Fig. 3.6 is adopted. That is, the rule weights of the four linguistic rules are updated as

$$
CF_1 = CF_2 = CF_4 = 0.5,
\tag{3.16}
$$

$$CF_3 = 0.400. \tag{3.17}$$

After the learning for the second training pattern x_2, the current situation is Fig. 3.6. The third training pattern x_3 in Fig. 3.6 is correctly classified. Thus no rule weights are modified. The fourth training pattern x_4 is also correctly classified. Thus Fig. 3.6 is still the current situation after the presentation of x_4.

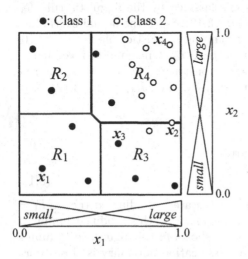

Fig. 3.5. Classification boundary by the modified linguistic rule-based system using (3.12)

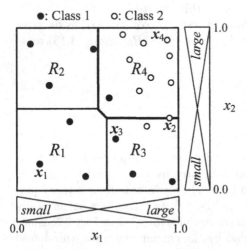

Fig. 3.6. Classification boundary by the modified linguistic rule-based system using (3.13)

In this manner, the rule weight of each linguistic rule is updated by presenting each training pattern to the linguistic rule-based system. In Fig. 3.7, we show the classification boundary after a single epoch. As shown in Fig. 3.7, all the given patterns are correctly classified after a single epoch. Table 3.9 shows the values of the rule weights and the number of misclassified training patterns after each epoch. As shown in this table, the analytical learning scheme needs far fewer epochs than the reward–punishment learning scheme. This is because the amount of adjustment is analytically calculated for updating the rule weight of each linguistic rule in the analytical learning scheme while the weight is incrementally updated without considering the effect of the modification on the classification performance of the linguistic rule-based system in the reward–punishment learning scheme. Of course, much more computation time is required for a single epoch by the analytical learning scheme than the reward–punishment learning scheme.

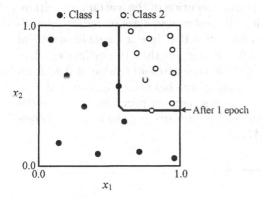

Fig. 3.7. Classification boundary after a single epoch

Table 3.9. Simulation results by the analytical learning scheme on the artificial test problem in Fig. 3.1. The second row "Errors" shows the number of misclassified training patterns

Epoch	0	1
Errors	3	0
CF_1	0.5000	0.5000
CF_2	0.5000	0.6638
CF_3	0.5000	0.3254
CF_4	0.5000	0.5000

We also applied the analytical learning scheme to the single-dimensional artificial test problem in Fig. 2.13. Since Fig. 2.13 is an online-type classification problem where the number of training patterns incrementally increases over time, the application of the analytical learning scheme is not straightforward. In our computer simulation, all the generated training patterns were used to examine the classification performance of the linguistic rule-based system. That is, all the available p patterns $x_1, x_2, \ldots, x_p$ are used for the performance evaluation in the learning for the p-th training pattern x_p. In real-world applications, it is more natural to use a pre-specified number of recent training patterns in the learning. That is, only recent training patterns in a moving window are used in the learning.

We adjusted the rule weights of the three linguistic rules for the single-dimensional artificial test problem using the analytical learning scheme from their initial specifications $CF_1 = CF_2 = CF_3 = 0.5$. Training patterns were randomly generated from the pattern space $[0, 1]$ in Fig. 2.13 according to the uniform distribution as in the computer simulation by the reward–punishment learning scheme in the previous section. The execution of the learning algorithm was iterated until 10000 training patterns were examined. The values of ϵ was specified as $\epsilon = 0.001$. In Fig. 3.8, we show how the rule weights were updated during the iterative execution of the learning algorithm. On the other hand, Fig. 3.9 shows how the estimated class boundary was adjusted. Note that the actual threshold θ is $\theta = 0.47$ in our single-dimensional artificial test problem. From Fig. 3.9, we can see that the estimated class boundary monotonically approaches the actual threshold value of 0.47 from the initial value of 0.25. From the comparison between Fig. 3.9 and Fig. 3.4, we can see that the analytical learning scheme required far fewer epochs than the reward–punishment learning scheme for driving the estimated class boundary to its desired value of 0.47.

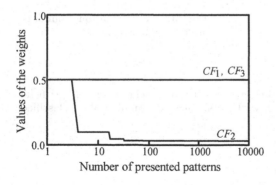

Fig. 3.8. Rule weight update during the iterative execution of the analytical learning scheme

3.2.3 Computer Simulations on Iris Data

In the same manner as the computer simulations on the iris data using the reward–punishment learning scheme in Sect. 3.1.3, we applied the analytical learning scheme to the iris data set. We examined the four granularities of linguistic discretization (i.e., $K = 2, 3, 4, 5$) and the two initial rule weight specifications (i.e., $CF_q = 0.5$, $^\forall q$, and the heuristic specification using the third definition).

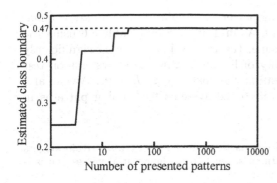

Fig. 3.9. Adjustment of the estimated class boundary during the iterative execution of the analytical learning scheme

Average classification rates on training patterns were calculated over 20 independent trials for each combination of the granularity and the initial rule weight specification. Simulation results on training patterns are summarized in Table 3.10 for the heuristic rule weight specification and Table 3.11 for the initial rule weight 0.5. From these tables, we can see that the analytical learning scheme required only a few epochs to reach to high classification rates on training patterns.

Table 3.10. Classification rates on training patterns in the iris data set. Rule weights were adjusted by the analytical learning scheme from their initial values heuristically specified by the third definition

Granularity	Number of epochs			
	0	1	2	3
$K = 2$	68.0%	94.5%	95.9%	96.2%
$K = 3$	94.0%	97.7%	98.0%	98.0%
$K = 4$	97.3%	98.0%	98.0%	98.0%
$K = 5$	96.7%	98.7%	98.7%	98.7%

Table 3.11. Classification rates on training patterns in the iris data set. Rule weights were adjusted by the analytical learning scheme from their common initial value of 0.5

Granularity	Number of epochs			
	0	1	2	3
$K = 2$	71.3%	95.4%	95.6%	95.7%
$K = 3$	92.0%	98.0%	98.0%	98.0%
$K = 4$	82.7%	95.4%	95.8%	95.8%
$K = 5$	94.7%	97.0%	97.0%	97.0%

We also examined classification rates on test patterns using the leaving-one-out technique. This technique was iterated ten times using different orders of presentation of 149 training patterns. Simulation results are summarized in Table 3.12 and Table 3.13. As in Table 3.5 and Table 3.6 using the reward–punishment learning scheme, the rule weight learning significantly improved the generalization ability of linguistic rule-based systems on test patterns when linguistic discretization was coarse (e.g., $K = 2$). We can also observe overfitting of linguistic rule-based systems to training patterns in some cases.

Table 3.12. Classification rates on test patterns in the iris data set. Rule weights were adjusted by the analytical learning scheme from their initial values heuristically specified by the third definition

Granularity	Number of epochs		
	0	1	2
$K = 2$	68.0%	91.5%	93.6%
$K = 3$	93.3%	95.9%	96.3%
$K = 4$	94.0%	96.0%	96.0%
$K = 5$	95.3%	94.6%	94.6%

Table 3.13. Classification rates on test patterns in the iris data set. Rule weights were adjusted by the analytical learning scheme from their common initial value of 0.5

Granularity	Number of epochs		
	0	1	2
$K = 2$	71.3%	93.6%	93.6%
$K = 3$	92.0%	96.7%	96.7%
$K = 4$	81.3%	89.4%	90.1%
$K = 5$	94.7%	94.0%	94.0%

3.2.4 Computer Simulations on Wine Data

We also performed computer simulations on the wine data using the analytical learning scheme in the same manner as the computer simulations in Sect. 3.1.4 using the reward–punishment learning scheme. Simulation results on training patterns and test patterns are summarized in Table 3.14 and Table 3.15, respectively. As in the case of the iris data, the analytical learning scheme required only a few epochs to reach high classification rates on training patterns. As we have already mentioned in the previous section, the improvement of classification rates on training patterns does not always mean an improvement on test patterns.

Table 3.14. Classification rates on training patterns in the wine data set. Rule weights were adjusted by the analytical learning scheme from their initial values specified by the third definition

# of rules	Number of epochs			
	0	1	2	3
3	89.3%	90.5%	90.5%	90.5%
6	92.1%	94.0%	94.1%	94.1%
9	93.8%	96.5%	96.8%	96.8%
12	94.9%	96.5%	96.6%	96.6%
15	94.9%	96.6%	96.6%	96.6%
18	94.9%	98.2%	98.2%	98.2%
21	94.4%	98.1%	98.1%	98.1%
24	94.4%	98.4%	98.5%	98.5%
27	94.4%	98.3%	98.3%	98.4%
30	94.9%	98.0%	98.2%	98.2%

Table 3.15. Classification rates on test patterns in the wine data set. Rule weights were adjusted by the analytical learning scheme from their initial values specified by the third definition

# of rules	Number of epochs			
	0	1	2	3
3	89.3%	88.9%	88.9%	88.9%
6	84.8%	84.6%	84.6%	84.6%
9	93.3%	93.7%	93.7%	93.7%
12	93.3%	94.0%	94.0%	94.0%
15	94.4%	94.2%	94.2%	94.2%
18	92.1%	93.5%	93.5%	93.5%
21	91.6%	93.5%	93.4%	93.4%
24	91.6%	93.7%	96.7%	93.7%
27	92.7%	92.1%	92.3%	92.3%
30	93.3%	92.8%	93.0%	93.0%

3.3 Related Issues

In this section, we discuss two issues related to the learning of rule weights. One is additional learning when all the training patterns are correctly classified. The other is the learning of the membership function of each linguistic term.

3.3.1 Further Adjustment of Classification Boundaries

As shown in the previous section, the classification boundary obtained by the analytical learning scheme is always close to the training pattern that was used in the final adjustment of rule weights. This is because the value of ϵ in the update rules (3.12) and (3.13) is very small. For examining the effect of the value of ϵ on the location of the classification boundary, we performed computer simulations on the two-dimensional test problem in Fig. 3.1 using various values of ϵ: $\epsilon = 0.001, 0.1, 0.3$. In Fig. 3.7, we have already shown the classification boundary obtained from $\epsilon = 0.001$. Simulation results obtained from $\epsilon = 0.1$ and $\epsilon = 0.3$ are shown in Fig. 3.10 and Fig. 3.11, respectively. In the case of $\epsilon = 0.1$ in Fig. 3.10, the classification boundary is not very close to any training patterns compared with the case of $\epsilon = 0.001$ in Fig. 3.7. On the other hand, all the training patterns could not be correctly classified in the case of $\epsilon = 0.3$ in Fig. 3.11. This is because the value of ϵ (i.e., the amount of adjustment of rule weights) is too large.

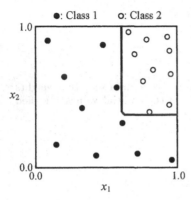

Fig. 3.10. Classification boundary obtained by the analytical learning scheme with $\epsilon = 0.1$

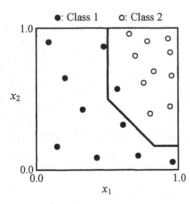

Fig. 3.11. Classification boundary obtained by the analytical learning scheme with $\epsilon = 0.3$

As the above simulation results on the two-dimensional test problem suggest, large values of ϵ make successful execution of the analytical learning scheme very difficult. On the other hand, the classification boundary is very close to training patterns in the case of small values of ϵ.

When we use the reward–punishment learning scheme, we cannot adjust the location of the classification boundary. The rule weight of the winner rule is increased or decreased depending on the classification result (i.e., correct classification or misclassification) of each training pattern. The classification rate of the linguistic rule-based system after the rule weight adjustment is not taken into account in the reward–punishment learning scheme.

Let us consider a very simple single-dimensional pattern classification problem in Fig. 3.12 where ten patterns from two classes are given together with three linguistic terms. Training patterns from Class 1 and Class 2 are depicted by closed circles and open circles in Fig. 3.12, respectively. As in the case of the single-dimensional artificial test problem in the previous computer simulations, we use the following three linguistic rules:

R_1: If x is *small* then Class 1 with CF_1,
R_2: If x is *medium* then Class 2 with CF_2,
R_3: If x is *large* then Class 2 with CF_3.

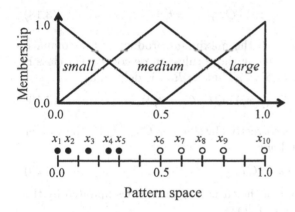

Pattern space

Fig. 3.12. A simple single-dimensional test problem

In Fig. 3.13, we show simulation results (i.e., classification boundaries) by the reward–punishment learning scheme with $\eta^+ = 0.001$ and $\eta^- = 0.1$, and the analytical learning scheme with $\epsilon = 0.001$. The learning of the rule weights based on each scheme was iterated from their initial values $CF_1 = CF_2 = CF_3 = 0.5$ until all the training patterns were correctly classified. The ten training patterns $x_1, x_2, \ldots, x_{10}$ were presented in this order in the learning. As we can see from Fig. 3.13, the classification boundaries in both cases are very close to the fifth training pattern $x_5 = 0.3$. This training pattern was used in the final rule weight adjustment in the analytical learning scheme.

Intuitively we think that the actual class boundary in the simple single-dimensional pattern classification problem in Fig. 3.12 may be around $x = 0.4$ because the largest attribute value from Class 1 is $x = 0.3$ and the smallest attribute value from Class 2 is $x = 0.5$. To drive the classification boundary of the linguistic rule-based system to such an intuitive location, an idea of additional learning was proposed in [132]. The additional learning scheme was utilized when all the training patterns were correctly classified using

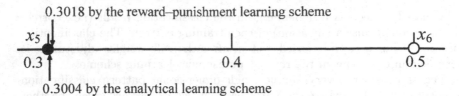

Fig. 3.13. Simulation results by the reward–punishment learning scheme and the analytical learning scheme

the reward–punishment learning scheme. In the following, we explain this additional learning scheme.

Let us assume that a training pattern x_p is correctly classified as Class t_p by the linguistic rule-based system S. That is, we assume that x_p is correctly classified by the winner rule R_w satisfying the following relation:

$$\mu_{A_w}(x_p) \cdot CF_w = \max_{R_q \in S}\{\mu_{A_q}(x_p) \cdot CF_q | C_q = t_p\}. \tag{3.18}$$

Let R_{w*} be the linguistic rule with the maximum product of the compatibility grade and the rule weight among those rules whose consequent class is different from the actual class t_p of x_p. That is, R_{w*} is defined as

$$\mu_{A_{w*}}(x_p) \cdot CF_{w*} = \max_{R_q \in S}\{\mu_{A_q}(x_p) \cdot CF_q | C_q \neq t_p\}. \tag{3.19}$$

Since the training pattern x_p is correctly classified as Class t_p by the winner rule R_w, the following relation holds:

$$\mu_{A_{w*}}(x_p) \cdot CF_{w*} < \mu_{A_w}(x_p) \cdot CF_w. \tag{3.20}$$

In Fig. 3.13, the rule weights of the three linguistic rules updated by the analytical learning scheme were as follows:

$$CF_1 = 0.5000, \; CF_2 = 0.3323, \; CF_3 = 0.5000. \tag{3.21}$$

In Fig. 3.14, we depict the value of $\mu_{A_q}(x) \cdot CF_q$ for each linguistic rule where A_q is *small*, *medium*, or *large*. The first linguistic rule R_1 with *small* in the antecedent part is the winner rule R_w for the fifth training pattern x_5 and the second linguistic rule R_2 with *medium* is R_{w*}.

Let us define σ_p as

$$\sigma_p = \mu_{A_w}(x_p) \cdot CF_w - \mu_{A_{w*}}(x_p) \cdot CF_{w*}. \tag{3.22}$$

As we can see from Fig. 3.14, the smaller is the value of σ_p, the closer is the training pattern x_p to the classification boundary. The basic idea of the additional learning scheme is to drive the classification boundary to the center of two training patterns from different classes by making the value of σ_p large. In each epoch of the additional learning scheme, first a training pattern x_{p*} with the minimum value of σ_p is selected as

$$\sigma_{p*} = \min\{\sigma_p | p = 1, 2, \ldots, m\}. \tag{3.23}$$

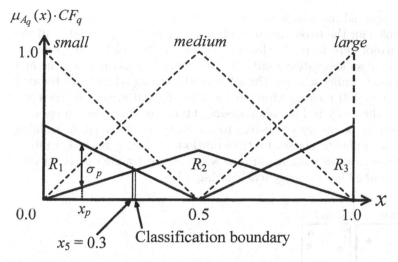

Fig. 3.14. Shape of the product of the compatibility grade and the rule weight for each linguistic rule. The membership function of each linguistic term is shown by dashed lines

Then R_w in (3.18) and R_{w*} in (3.19) are found for the training pattern x_{p*}. To increase the value σ_{p*}, CF_w is increased and CF_{w*} is decreased as

$$CF_w^{\text{New}} = CF_w^{\text{Old}} + \eta \cdot (1 - CF_w^{\text{Old}}), \tag{3.24}$$

$$CF_{w*}^{\text{New}} = CF_{w*}^{\text{Old}} - \eta \cdot CF_{w*}^{\text{Old}}, \tag{3.25}$$

where η is a positive real number (e.g., $\eta = 0.05$). While we treat η as a constant parameter in the following computer simulations, it is possible to treat η as a variable control parameter. That is, η can be decreased during the iterative execution of the additional learning scheme.

We applied the additional learning scheme with $\eta = 0.05$ to the three linguistic rules for the simple single-dimensional test problem in Fig. 3.12 after all the training patters were correctly classified by the analytical learning scheme. Table 3.16 shows how the classification boundary was adjusted by the analytical learning scheme (the first epoch) and the additional learning scheme (the other epochs). From this table, we can see that the classification boundary gradually approached the intuitively acceptable boundary of 0.4.

Table 3.16. The location of the classification boundary after each epoch of the analytical learning scheme and the additional learning scheme

Epoch	0	1	2	3	4	5	10
Boundary	0.250	0.3004	0.3122	0.3233	0.3336	0.3433	0.3829

We also applied the additional learning scheme with $\eta = 0.01$ to the four linguistic rules for the two-dimensional test problem in Fig. 3.1 after all the training patters were correctly classified by the analytical learning scheme. Figure 3.15 shows simulation results by the analytical learning scheme and the additional learning scheme. The additional learning scheme was iterated 100 times (i.e., 100 epochs) after all the training patterns were correctly classified by the analytical learning scheme. From Fig. 3.15, we can see that the classification boundary was driven to the center of two adjacent training patterns from different classes by the additional learning scheme, while it was very close to some training patterns when all the training patterns were correctly classified by the analytical learning scheme.

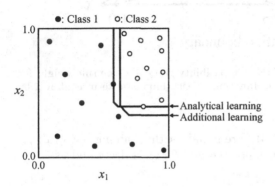

Fig. 3.15. Simulation results by the analytical learning scheme and the additional learning scheme

As we illustrated through the computer simulations on the simple test problems, the additional learning scheme tries to improve the generalization ability of linguistic rule-based systems after all the training patterns are correctly classified. High classification rates on test patterns were reported in Nozaki et al. [132] using a hybrid algorithm of the reward–punishment learning scheme and the additional learning scheme. For example, a 98.0% classification rate on test patterns was obtained for the iris data set using the leaving-one-out technique.

3.3.2 Adjustment of Membership Functions

In this book, we use a set of given linguistic terms for each attribute without modifying their membership functions for constructing linguistic rule-based systems. This means that we use simple grid-type fuzzy partitions of the pattern space for generating linguistic rule-based systems. An example of a simple grid-type fuzzy partition is shown in Fig. 3.16 where the two-dimensional pattern space is discretized into 5×3 cells. In each cell, a single linguistic rule is to be generated from training patterns.

In some studies on fuzzy rule-based classification systems, fuzzy partitions are adjusted (e.g., see [128]). That is, the membership function of each

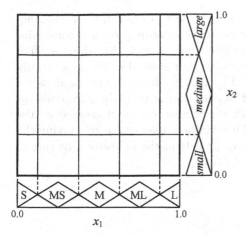

Fig. 3.16. An example of a simple grid-type fuzzy partition

linguistic term is adjusted. An example of an adjustable grid-type fuzzy partition is shown in Fig. 3.17. As we have already discussed in Chap. 1, linguistic interpretation of adjusted membership functions is not always easy. In this book, we use given linguistic terms without adjusting their membership functions for constructing linguistic rule-based systems with high interpretability. In the following, we briefly discuss the adjustment of membership functions.

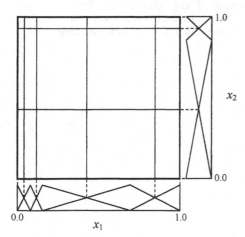

Fig. 3.17. An example of an adjustable grid-type fuzzy partition

The basic idea of the reward–punishment learning scheme can be applied to the learning of membership functions. When a training pattern x_p is correctly classified by the winner rule, the compatibility grade of the training pattern x_p with the winner rule is increased as the reward for the correct classification. This can be implemented by moving the center of the antecedent part of the winner rule toward the training pattern x_p in the n-dimensional pattern space as shown in Fig. 3.18. Usually the neighboring membership functions of the adjusted ones are also modified according to some constraint conditions. For example, the sum of adjacent membership functions is often maintained as 1 for covering the entire pattern space by the membership functions after their adjustment (see Fig. 3.17). On the other hand, when a training pattern x_p is misclassified by the winner rule, the compatibility grade of the training pattern x_p with the winner rule is decreased as the punishment of the misclassification. This can be implemented by moving the center of the antecedent part of the winner rule in the opposite direction of the training pattern x_p as shown in Fig. 3.19.

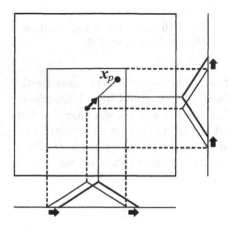

Fig. 3.18. Adjustment of the antecedent part of the winner rule for increasing the compatibility grade with the training pattern denoted by a closed circle

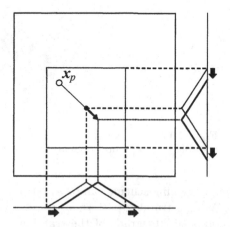

Fig. 3.19. Adjustment of the antecedent part of the winner rule for decreasing the compatibility grade with the training pattern denoted by an open circle

The basic idea of the analytical learning scheme can also be applied to the adjustment of the compatibility grade of each linguistic rule. That is,

instead of adjusting rule weights, it is possible to adjust compatibility grades
for correctly classifying a misclassified training pattern. By the same idea as
the update rule for increasing the rule weight of the most promising linguistic
rule R_{q*} in (3.12), the update rule for increasing the compatibility grade of
R_{q*} can be written as

$$\mu_{A_{q*}}^{\text{New}}(x_p) = \frac{CF_w}{CF_{q*}} \cdot \mu_{A_w}^{\text{Old}}(x_p) + \epsilon. \tag{3.26}$$

This can be implemented by moving the center of the antecedent part of R_{q*}
toward the training pattern x_p as shown in Fig. 3.18. On the other hand, the
update rule for decreasing the compatibility grade of the winner rule R_w can
be written as follows from the same idea as (3.13):

$$\mu_{A_w}^{\text{New}}(x_p) = \frac{CF_{q*}}{CF_w} \cdot \mu_{A_{q*}}^{\text{Old}}(x_p) - \epsilon. \tag{3.27}$$

This can be implemented by moving the center of the antecedent part of R_w
in the opposite direction of the training pattern x_p as shown in Fig. 3.19.

The main drawback of grid-type fuzzy partitions is that the number of
linguistic rules (or fuzzy rules) increases exponentially with the dimensionality of the pattern space. This is often called the "curse of dimensionality".
One popular approach for handling high-dimensional problems is to use scattered fuzzy partitions. Examples of scattered fuzzy partitions are shown in
Fig. 3.20 and Fig. 3.21. The main characteristic feature of scattered fuzzy
partitions is that each fuzzy rule does not use linguistic discretization of each
attribute. Instead, each fuzzy rule has its own multi-dimensional antecedent
fuzzy set. In Fig. 3.20, multi-dimensional antecedent fuzzy sets are decomposable into single-dimensional antecedent fuzzy sets while those in Fig. 3.21
are not decomposable. Scattered fuzzy partitions were used in many studies
on fuzzy rule-based pattern classification [1]. When we use scattered fuzzy
partitions, the number of fuzzy rules is independent of the dimensionality of
the pattern space. Since there is no interaction between antecedent fuzzy sets
of different fuzzy rules, the adjustment of the antecedent part of each fuzzy
rule has high flexibility. Thus we can expect high classification performance
of fuzzy rule-based systems with scattered partitions. The interpretability of
such fuzzy rule-based systems, however, is usually low. It is not easy to understand the meaning of the antecedent part of each fuzzy rule in Fig. 3.20
and Fig. 3.21.

Another approach to the handling of high-dimensional pattern classification problems is the use of tree-type fuzzy partitions. Figure 3.22 shows
an example of a tree-type fuzzy partition. This fuzzy partition corresponds
to the tree structure in Fig. 3.23. Fuzzy rule-based systems with tree-type
fuzzy partitions are often called "fuzzy decision trees". Fuzzy decision trees
can be viewed as an extension of non-fuzzy standard decision trees [143]. See
Janikow [100] for the design of fuzzy decision trees.

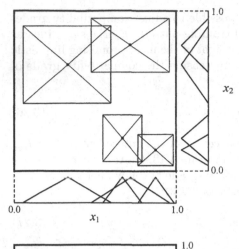

Fig. 3.20. An example of a scattered fuzzy partition with decomposable multi-dimensional antecedent fuzzy sets. Each multi-dimensional antecedent fuzzy set has a pyramidal shape

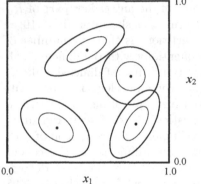

Fig. 3.21. An example of a scattered fuzzy partition with non-decomposable multi-dimensional antecedent fuzzy sets. Each multi-dimensional antecedent fuzzy set has an ellipsoidal shape

Multi-layer structures are also used in fuzzy modeling for high-dimensional problems. An example of a multi-layer structure is shown in Fig. 3.24. A hierarchical fuzzy rule-based system consists of multiple subsystems that are hierarchically combined. Each subsystem is usually a low-dimensional fuzzy rule-based system with grid-type fuzzy partitions. Since each subsystem has only a few input variables, the exponential increase in the number of fuzzy rules can be avoided by the use of multi-layer structures. From the viewpoint of interpretability, multi-layer structures have an inherent drawback in that the interpretation of intermediate variables is very difficult. Intermediate variables are the subsystem's input (or output) variables that are not the input (or output) variables of the entire rule-based system. The design of multi-layer structures of fuzzy rule-based systems was discussed in Ishigami et al. [96] and Shimojima et al. [153].

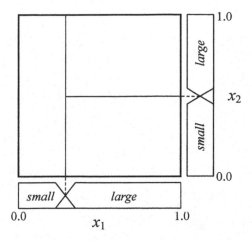

Fig. 3.22. An example of a tree-type fuzzy partition

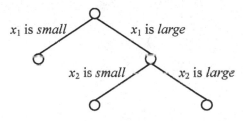

Fig. 3.23. Tree structure corresponding to Fig. 3.22

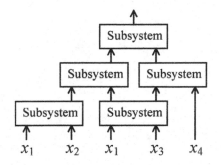

Fig. 3.24. An example of the multi-layer structure of fuzzy rule-based systems

4. Input Selection and Rule Selection

In this chapter, we explain how linguistic rule-based systems with simple grid-type fuzzy partitions can be extended to the case of high-dimensional pattern classification problems. First we mention input selection. Then we describe a genetic algorithm-based approach to rule selection.

4.1 Curse of Dimensionality

As we have already mentioned in the previous section, the main difficulty in applying grid-type fuzzy partitions to high-dimensional pattern classification problems stems from the curse of dimensionality: the exponential increase in the number of linguistic rules with the number of attributes. Let K_i be the number of linguistic terms given for the i-th attribute ($i = 1, 2, \ldots, n$). Then the total number of cells in a grid-type fuzzy partition of the n-dimensional pattern space is $K_1 \times K_2 \times \ldots \times K_n$. For example, there are more than 1 billion cells when five linguistic terms are given for each of the 13 attributes of the wine data set. Thus it is unrealistic to use grid-type fuzzy partitions for high-dimensional pattern classification problems.

From the viewpoint of interpretability of linguistic rule-based systems, the use of grid-type fuzzy partitions can be recommended only for two-dimensional pattern classification problems. In this case, linguistic rule-based systems are concisely written in a two-dimensional tabular form as in Fig. 2.4 of Chap. 2. On the other hand, three-dimensional linguistic rule tables cannot be written in a human understandable manner. For example, let us consider a three-dimensional pattern classification problem with five linguistic terms for each attribute. In this case, the pattern space was discretized into 125 cells by a grid-type fuzzy partition. While computer systems can easily handle 125 linguistic rules with no difficulty, it is not an easy task for human users to intuitively understand a linguistic rule-based system with 125 linguistic rules.

4.2 Input Selection

A straightforward approach to the design of interpretable linguistic rule-based systems is input selection. Input selection has been discussed for many years in the fields of pattern classification and machine learning. For general discussions on input selection, see Blum & Langley [12], Kohavi & John [115], and Liu & Motoda [122, 123]. It was shown in Holte [56] that very good results were obtained for some data sets from the selection of only a single attribute. The relation between the number of attributes and the classification performance of linguistic rule-based systems was examined in Ishibuchi & Yamamoto [91] using sequential feedforward input selection. In this section, we examine the classification performance of linguistic rule-based systems generated from simple grid-type fuzzy partitions with only a few attributes. It is shown through computer simulations that more than two attributes are necessary for designing linguistic rule-based systems with high classification performance for the wine data set. This observation motivates us to use a rule selection method for the wine data set in the next section.

4.2.1 Examination of Subsets of Attributes

The total number of subsets of n attributes is 2^n including the two extreme cases: the whole set with all attributes and an empty set with no attributes. It is possible to find the best subset of attributes by examining all the 2^n subsets only when the following conditions are satisfied:

(a) The design of a classification system using each subset is not time-consuming.
(b) The evaluation of a classification system is not time-consuming.
(c) The number of attributes is small.

Let us consider the wine data set with 13 attributes. The total number of subsets is calculated as $2^{13} = 8192$. If the examination of each subset needs 1 second on the average, the examination of 8192 subsets needs about 2 hours. Thus the examination of all subsets is realistic. Such an enumeration method, however, is impractical when the design of classification systems is time-consuming (e.g., the learning of multi-layer feedforward neural networks with a large number of training patterns). The enumeration of all subsets is also impractical when the number of attributes is large.

While the examination of all subsets is difficult in the case of linguistic rule-based systems for high-dimensional pattern classification problems, small subsets with a few attributes can be efficiently examined. This is because the size of linguistic rule-based systems with a few attributes is very small compared with those with many attributes. Note that the number of linguistic rules increases exponentially with the number of attributes. The number of subsets including k attributes out of the given n attributes is $_nC_k$. For example, the number of subsets with two attributes is calculated for the wine data set with 13 attributes as $_{13}C_2 = 78$. This is much smaller than the total number of subsets 8192. In the next subsection, we examine all subsets of the four attributes in the iris data set. In the case of wine data set with 13 attributes, we examine only small subsets with a few attributes.

4.2.2 Simulation Results

For the iris data set, we examined all subsets of the four attributes. The number of examined subsets is $2^4 - 1 = 15$ excluding an empty set. Simulation results on training patterns and test patterns are summarized in Table 4.1 and Table 4.2, respectively. In computer simulations, each linguistic rule-based system was generated using the third definition of rule weights and a simple grid-type fuzzy partition with the three linguistic terms *small*, *medium*, and *large* as in Fig. 2.1 of Chap. 2. The leaving-one-out technique was used to examine the performance of each subset of the four attributes on test patterns. From Table 4.1 and Table 4.2, we can see that the subset with the single attribute x_4 has better classification ability (i.e., 96.0% on training patterns and test patterns) than all the four attributes in the iris data set (i.e., 94.0% on training patterns and 93.3% on test patterns). We can also see that the classification ability of some subsets is very poor when inappropriate attributes are selected (see the row labeled "Worst classification rate").

Table 4.1. Simulation results on training patterns in the iris data set. All subsets of the four attributes are examined for input selection

Number of attributes: k	1	2	3	4
Number of cells: 3^k	3	9	27	81
Average number of rules	3.0	8.7	23.8	62.0
Best classification rate	96.0%	96.7%	96.7%	94.0%
Average classification rate	77.3%	88.9%	94.2%	94.0%
Worst classification rate	55.3%	66.7%	92.7%	94.0%
Best combination	$\{x_4\}$	$\{x_1, x_4\}$	$\{x_1, x_2, x_4\}$	$\{x_1, x_2, x_3, x_4\}$

Table 4.2. Simulation results on test patterns in the iris data set. All subsets of the four attributes are examined for input selection

Number of attributes: k	1	2	3	4
Number of cells: 3^k	3	9	27	81
Average number of rules	3.0	8.7	23.7	62.0
Best classification rate	96.0%	95.3%	96.0%	93.3%
Average classification rate	76.5%	88.0%	93.2%	93.3%
Worst classification rate	52.0%	64.7%	90.0%	93.3%
Best combination	$\{x_4\}$	$\{x_2, x_4\}$	$\{x_1, x_2, x_4\}$	$\{x_1, x_2, x_3, x_4\}$

For visually illustrating the effect of input selection, we show the normalized 150 patterns in the iris data set using the two-dimensional attribute space with x_1 and x_4 in Fig. 4.1. That is, this figure shows the projection of the normalized 150 patterns onto the x_1–x_4 space. The classification boundary in this figure was depicted by the linguistic rule-based system generated from all the 150 patterns using the two attributes x_1 and x_4. For comparison, we also show the projection onto the x_1–x_2 space in Fig. 4.2. The worst classification rates on training patterns and test patterns were obtained by the two attributes x_1 and x_2 for the case of $k = 2$ in Table 4.1 and Table 4.2 (i.e., 66.7% and 64.7%), respectively. The classification boundary in Fig. 4.2 was depicted by the linguistic rule-based system with the two attributes x_1 and x_2. The comparison between Fig. 4.1 and Fig. 4.2 clearly shows the importance of choosing good attributes for designing linguistic rule-based systems with high classification ability.

●: Class 1   o: Class 2   ▲ : Class 3

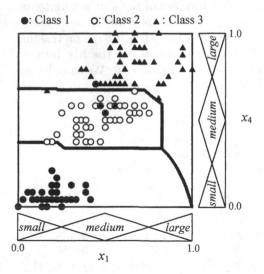

Fig. 4.1. Projection of the normalized 150 patterns in the iris data set onto the x_1–x_4 space and the classification boundary by the linguistic rule-based system with these two attributes in the antecedent part

In Fig. 4.1, only eight linguistic rules were generated. These linguistic rules are shown in Fig. 4.3. We can easily understand the linguistic rule-based system in Fig. 4.3 because the number of linguistic rules is small and each linguistic rule has only two attributes in its antecedent part. As shown in Fig. 4.3, we can generate linguistic rule-based systems with high interpretability by choosing two attributes.

We also examined linguistic rule-based systems with only a few attributes for the wine data set. For each attribute, we used the three linguistic terms *small*, *medium*, and *large* as in the above computer simulations on the iris data set. Since the wine data set has 13 attributes, the number of linguistic rule-based systems with k attributes is $_{13}C_k$. The number of combinations of antecedent linguistic terms in each linguistic rule-based system with k

●: Class 1   ○: Class 2   ▲: Class 3

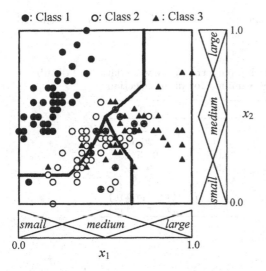

Fig. 4.2. Projection of the normalized 150 patterns in the iris data set onto the x_1–x_2 space and the classification boundary by the linguistic rule-based system with these two attributes in the antecedent part

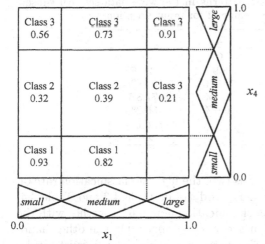

Fig. 4.3. Eight linguistic rules generated from the 150 training patterns in the iris data set using the three linguistic terms *small*, *medium*, and *large* for x_1 and x_4. The other two attributes are removed. In each cell, the corresponding consequent class and rule weight are shown

attributes is 3^k (i.e., 3^k is the number of cells in each of the $_{13}C_k$ grid-type fuzzy partitions). When k is small, it is easy to generate linguistic rules for designing a linguistic rule-based system by examining all the 3^k combinations. The number of linguistic rule-based systems (i.e., $_{13}C_k$) is also small when k is small. On the contrary, 3^k is huge when k is large. This means that it takes a long computation time to examine $_{13}C_k$ linguistic rule-based systems when the number of selected attributes is large. At the same time, linguistic rule-based systems are not interpretable when the number of selected attributes is large. Thus we only examined linguistic rule-based systems with three or less attributes. Simulation results on training patterns and test patterns are summarized in Table 4.3 and Table 4.4, respectively. The leaving-one-out technique was used to calculate the performance of each subset of the 13 attributes on test patterns.

Table 4.3. Simulation results on training patterns in the wine data set. All subsets including three or less attributes are examined for input selection

Number of attributes: k	1	2	3
Number of cells: 3^k	3	9	27
Average number of rules	3.0	8.9	26.5
Best classification rate	68.0%	91.0%	95.5%
Average classification rate	55.4%	70.3%	79.9%
Worst classification rate	43.3%	54.5%	61.8%
Best combination	$\{x_{13}\}$	$\{x_{12}, x_{13}\}$	$\{x_7, x_{10}, x_{13}\}$ $\{x_7, x_{11}, x_{13}\}$

Table 4.4. Simulation results on test patterns in the wine data set. All subsets including three or less attributes are examined for input selection

Number of attributes: k	1	2	3
Number of cells: 3^k	3	9	27
Average number of rules	3	8.9	26.5
Best classification rate	67.4%	90.5%	94.9%
Average classification rate	52.3%	68.1%	77.8%
Worst classification rate	27.0%	50.6%	56.2%
Best combination	$\{x_1\}$	$\{x_{12}, x_{13}\}$	$\{x_7, x_{10}, x_{13}\}$ $\{x_7, x_{11}, x_{13}\}$

When the number of attributes was two, the highest classification rate on training patterns was obtained from x_{12} and x_{13} in Table 4.3 and Table 4.4. Figure 4.4 shows the corresponding classification boundary together with the normalized 178 training patterns in the x_{12}–x_{13} space. On the other hand, Fig. 4.5 shows the corresponding linguistic rule table. The linguistic rule-based system in Fig. 4.5 can be easily understood because it consists of nine linguistic rules with only two antecedent conditions. The classification ability of this linguistic rule-based system, however, is not high (i.e., classification rates are 91.0% on training patterns and 90.5% on test patterns). From Table 4.3 and Table 4.4, we can see that any linguistic rule-based systems with two attributes do not have high classification ability (compare the third column of each table for two attributes with the fourth column for three attributes). This suggests that a linguistic rule-based system with both high comprehensibility and high classification ability cannot be obtained for the wine data set by input selection. In the next section, we show how such a linguistic rule-based system can be obtained by rule selection.

●: Class 1   ○: Class 2   ▲: Class 3

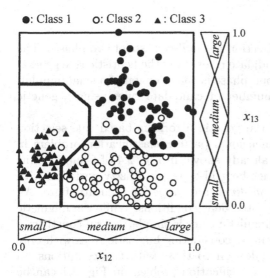

Fig. 4.4. Projection of the normalized 178 patterns in the wine data set onto the x_{12}–x_{13} space and the classification boundary by the linguistic rule-based system with these two attributes in the antecedent part

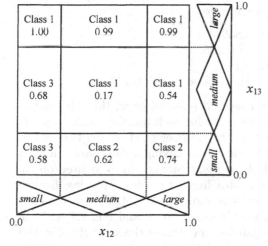

Fig. 4.5. Nine linguistic rules generated from the 178 training patterns in the wine data set using the three linguistic terms on x_{12} and x_{13}. The other eleven attributes are removed

4.3 Genetic Algorithm-Based Rule Selection

The use of genetic algorithms [48, 55] for selecting a small number of linguistic rules from a large number of candidate rules was proposed in Ishibuchi et al. [83, 84]. This idea was extended to the case of two-objective rule selection in [65] for explicitly examining the tradeoff between the number of linguistic rules and the classification ability of linguistic rule-based systems. Genetic algorithm-based rule selection was further extended to the case of three-objective rule selection in [71, 94] by considering the length of each linguistic rule together with the above-mentioned two objectives. In this section, we explain rule selection in the framework of single-objective optimization. Multi-objective rule selection is explained in a later chapter.

4.3.1 Basic Idea

A genetic algorithm-based rule selection method consists of two phases. The first phase is the generation of candidate rules using the heuristic rule generation method in Chap. 2. The second phase is the selection of a small number of linguistic rules from a large number of candidate rules using a genetic algorithm.

We explain the basic idea of the genetic algorithm-based rule selection method using the simple two-dimensional pattern classification problem in Fig. 2.1 of Chap. 2. As we have already shown in Fig. 2.4 of Chap. 2, nine linguistic rules are generated using the grid-type 3×3 fuzzy partition with the three linguistic terms *small*, *medium*, and *large* for each attribute. All the nine linguistic rules have two antecedent conditions. While the linguistic rule-based system with the nine linguistic rules is simple, we can construct a simpler linguistic rule-based system by considering linguistic rules with only a single antecedent condition in addition to those with two conditions. In fact, the two-dimensional pattern classification problem in Fig. 2.1 can be handled by the following four linguistic rules:

If x_1 is *large* then Class 2 with 0.839,
If x_2 is *medium* then Class 2 with 0.255,
If x_2 is *large* then Class 1 with 0.428,
If x_1 is *small* and x_2 is *medium* then Class 1 with 0.705.

The rule weight of each linguistic rule is calculated using the third definition (the same rule weight is also obtained for each linguistic rule from the second and fourth definitions because the number of classes is two in Fig. 2.1). The first linguistic rules can be viewed as having a *don't care* condition on the second attribute x_2. Similarly, a *don't care* condition is used on the first attribute x_1 in the second and third linguistic rules. The classification boundary by these four linguistic rules is shown in Fig. 4.6. From the comparison between Fig. 4.6 with the four linguistic rules and Fig. 2.7 with the nine linguistic rules in Chap. 2, we can see that almost the same classification boundaries were obtained by the two linguistic rule-based systems in Fig. 2.7 and Fig. 4.6. This observation suggests that we may be able to construct simpler linguistic rule-based systems using short linguistic rules (e.g., the first three linguistic rules in the above four rules) than simple grid-type fuzzy partitions without significant deterioration in their classification performance.

In the genetic algorithm-based rule selection method, we use as candidate rules short linguistic rules with some *don't care* conditions as well as standard linguistic rules with no *don't care* conditions. In the case of the two-dimensional pattern classification problem in Fig. 4.6, we examine 16 cells in the four fuzzy partitions in Fig. 4.7 for generating candidate rules. The bottom-right figure is the standard simple grid-type fuzzy partition. In the bottom-left figure, the antecedent condition on the second attribute x_2 is *don't care*. On the other hand, the antecedent condition on the first attribute

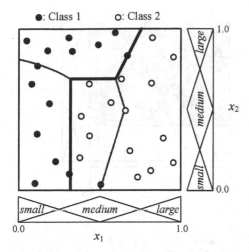

●: Class 1   ○: Class 2

Fig. 4.6. Decision regions of the four linguistic rules and the classification boundary

x_1 is *don't care* in the top-right figure. The single linguistic rule in the top-left figure has two *don't care* conditions (i.e., has no antecedent condition). The shaded regions in Fig. 4.7 correspond to the above-mentioned four linguistic rules in Fig. 4.6.

For high-dimensional pattern classification problems, we only generate short linguistic rules using many *don't care* conditions. We have already employed this trick in the computer simulations on the wine data set in Chaps. 2 and 3. Only short linguistic rules are used as candidate rules in the genetic algorithm-based rule selection method for designing linguistic rule-based systems with high interpretability and high classification ability.

The inclusion or exclusion of each candidate rule is represented by a single binary variable. As a result, any subset of candidate rules is represented by a binary string. The length of the binary string is the same as the number of candidate rules. Genetic algorithms are used to handle such a binary string. The fitness value of each subset is calculated from its classification performance and its cardinality (i.e., the number of linguistic rules). In the following subsections, we explain the genetic algorithm-based rule selection method in detail.

4.3.2 Generation of Candidate Rules

Let K_i be the number of linguistic terms given for the i-th attribute of an n-dimensional pattern classification problem. In addition to the K_i linguistic terms, "*don't care*" is also used for each attribute as an additional antecedent linguistic term (i.e., an additional antecedent fuzzy set) for generating candidate rules. The membership value of *don't care* is always unity in the domain interval of each attribute as shown in Fig. 4.7. The total number of combinations of antecedent fuzzy sets is $(K_1 + 1) \times (K_2 + 1) \times \ldots \times (K_n + 1)$. In Fig.

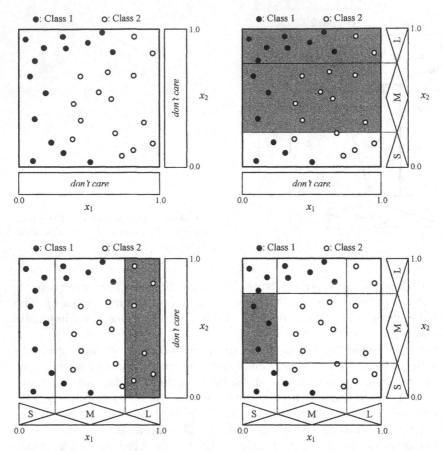

Fig. 4.7. Four fuzzy partitions of the two-dimensional pattern space $[0, 1] \times [0, 1]$. All the 16 cells in the four fuzzy partitions are used for generating candidate rules. Shaded regions correspond to the four linguistic rules in Fig. 4.6

4.7 with the three linguistic terms for each of the two attributes, the total number of combinations of antecedent fuzzy sets is $(3 + 1) \times (3 + 1) = 16$. Each combination of antecedent fuzzy sets corresponds to a single cell in the four fuzzy partitions of the pattern space in Fig. 4.7.

For low-dimensional pattern classification problems, we can examine all combinations of antecedent fuzzy sets for generating candidate rules. The consequent class for each combination is determined by the heuristic rule generation method in Chap. 2. The rule weight of each candidate rule is determined by the third definition in Chap. 2. All the generated rules are used as candidate rules in the genetic algorithm-based rule selection method. For example, 16 combinations of antecedent fuzzy sets are examined for generating candidate rules for the two-dimensional pattern classification problem in Fig. 4.7. Table 4.5 shows the generated candidate rules. All the 15 linguistic rules in Table 4.5 are used as candidate rules. It should be noted that the linguistic rule with the antecedent part "If x_1 is *don't care* and x_2 is *don't care*" is not generated as a candidate rule in Table 4.5. For this linguistic rule with no antecedent condition (i.e., with two *don't care* conditions), all the training patterns are fully compatible. In Fig. 4.7, the number of Class 1 patterns is the same as that of Class 2 patterns. Thus the consequent class of this linguistic rule cannot be uniquely specified by the heuristic rule generation method in Chap. 2. As a result, this linguistic rule is not generated in Table 4.5.

Table 4.5. Candidate rules for the two-dimensional pattern classification problem in Fig. 4.7

Rule	x_1	x_2	Consequent	Weight
R_1	small	don't care	Class 1	0.808
R_2	medium	don't care	Class 2	0.049
R_3	large	don't care	Class 2	0.839
R_4	don't care	small	Class 2	0.074
R_5	don't care	medium	Class 2	0.255
R_6	don't care	large	Class 1	0.428
R_7	small	small	Class 1	0.769
R_8	small	medium	Class 1	0.705
R_9	small	large	Class 1	0.968
R_{10}	medium	small	Class 2	0.013
R_{11}	medium	medium	Class 2	0.453
R_{12}	medium	large	Class 1	0.526
R_{13}	large	small	Class 2	0.990
R_{14}	large	medium	Class 2	0.911
R_{15}	large	large	Class 2	0.574

On the other hand, it is impractical to examine all combinations of antecedent fuzzy sets for generating candidate rules in the case of high-dimensional pattern classification problems. Thus we only generate short linguistic rules with many *don't care* conditions as candidate rules. The shortest linguistic rule for an n-dimensional pattern classification problem has the following form:

$$\text{If (no condition) then Class } C_q \text{ with } CF_q. \tag{4.1}$$

This linguistic rule is the same as the following linguistic rule with n *don't care* conditions:

$$\text{If } x_1 \text{ is } don't\ care \text{ and } \dots \text{ and } x_n \text{ is } don't\ care$$
$$\text{then Class } C_q \text{ with } CF_q. \tag{4.2}$$

All training patterns are fully compatible with the antecedent part of this linguistic rule because there is no antecedent condition. This linguistic rule corresponds to the top-left figure in Fig. 4.7. In the case of Fig. 4.7, we cannot generate the linguistic rule with no antecedent condition because the number of Class 1 patterns is the same as that of Class 2 patterns (see Table 4.5).

The second shortest linguistic rule with a single antecedent condition has the following form:

$$\text{If } x_i \text{ is } A_{qi} \text{ then Class } C_q \text{ with } CF_q. \tag{4.3}$$

The number of linguistic rules of this form is $K_1 + K_2 + \ldots + K_n$. The compatibility grade of each training pattern with the antecedent part of the linguistic rule in (4.3) is the same as that with the linguistic term A_{qi} because there is only a single antecedent condition. The first six candidate rules in Table 4.5, which correspond to the top-right figure and the bottom-left figure in Fig. 4.7, are linguistic rules of this form.

Linguistic rules with two antecedent conditions have the following form:

$$\text{If } x_i \text{ is } A_{qi} \text{ and } x_j \text{ is } A_{qj} \text{ then Class } C_q \text{ with } CF_q. \tag{4.4}$$

The number of linguistic rules of this form is $\sum_{i<j} K_i K_j$. When $K_i = K$ for all i, this is calculated as $_nC_2 \cdot K^2$. In the same manner, we can generate linguistic rules with three antecedent conditions. Generated linguistic rules with three or less antecedent conditions are used as candidate rules in this chapter. When the number of attributes is large (i.e., when n is large), linguistic rules with three antecedent conditions are not examined for generating candidate rules. In this case, linguistic rules with two or less antecedent conditions are used as candidate rules.

4.3.3 Genetic Algorithms for Rule Selection

Let N be the number of candidate rules. Any subset S of the N candidate rules can be represented by a binary string of length N as

$$S = s_1 s_2 \ldots s_N. \tag{4.5}$$

In (4.5), $s_q = 1$ means that the q-th candidate rule R_q is included in the subset S while $s_q = 0$ means that R_q is not included in S. For example, any subset S of the 15 candidate rules in Table 4.5 is represented by a binary string of length 15 (i.e., $S = s_1 s_2 \ldots s_{15}$). The number of linguistic rules in S (i.e., the cardinality of S) is denoted by $|S|$. The cardinality $|S|$ is the same as the number of 1's in the binary string S. For example, the subset including the four linguistic rules in the shaded regions of Fig. 4.7 is represented as

$$S = 001011010000000. \tag{4.6}$$

This binary string shows the following subset of the 15 candidate rules in Table 4.5:

$$S = \{R_3, R_5, R_6, R_8\}. \tag{4.7}$$

Each binary string S can be viewed as a linguistic rule-based system. For assigning a fitness value to the string S, training patterns are classified by linguistic rules in S. Let $NCP(S)$ be the number of correctly classified training patterns by S. The fitness value of S is defined as

$$fitness(S) = NCP(S) - w_{|S|} \cdot |S|, \qquad (4.8)$$

where $|S|$ is the number of linguistic rules in S and $w_{|S|}$ is a positive constant. The second term is added as the penalty with respect to the number of linguistic rules in order to find a small number of linguistic rules with high classification ability. A genetic algorithm is used to search for the optimal subset with the maximum fitness value among the 2^N subsets of the N candidate rules. Of course, the obtained optimal subset depends on the specification of the positive constant $w_{|S|}$. In the field of evolutionary computation, an objective function to be maximized is referred to as a fitness function. In this chapter, $fitness(S)$ in (4.8) is the fitness function in rule selection.

While we consider two different criteria (i.e., classification ability and the number of linguistic rules) in (4.8), they are treated within the framework of single-objective optimization because $w_{|S|}$ is a pre-specified constant. In a later chapter, we explain how rule selection can be treated within in the framework of multi-objective optimization.

Since each feasible solution S (i.e., each subset S) is represented by a binary string with a scalar fitness value, we can directly apply genetic algorithms [48, 55] to the maximization problem of the fitness function in (4.8). First a pre-specified number of initial strings of length N are randomly generated. An initial population consists of the generated strings. It is possible to use some heuristic procedures for generating initial strings. We will use such a heuristic in later chapters. An example of a randomly generated initial population is shown in Table 4.6 where ten binary strings of length 15 are randomly generated for the two-dimensional pattern classification problem in Fig. 4.7. For explanation purposes, the generated strings are sorted in descending order of their fitness values in Table 4.6. The value of $w_{|S|}$ in the fitness function in (4.8) is specified as $w_{|S|} = 0.1$. The number of strings in each population is referred to as the population size, which is denoted as N_{pop} in this book. The population size of the initial population in Table 4.6 is ten (i.e., $N_{\text{pop}} = 10$).

The search for good strings is performed by generating new strings from existing ones in the current population using genetic operations called selection, crossover, and mutation. The point is to use good strings for generating new strings. Selection is a genetic operation that selects a pair of good parent strings from which new strings are generated. Crossover is a genetic operation that combines two parent strings for generating new strings. Mutation is a genetic operation that partially and randomly modifies each string.

Traditionally, roulette wheel selection has been used to select parent strings. In this selection scheme, the selection probability of each string is

Table 4.6. A randomly generated initial population for the two-dimensional pattern classification problem in Fig. 4.7. The value of $w_{|S|}$ is specified as $w_{|S|} = 0.1$ for calculating the fitness value of each string

String	Binary code	$NCP(S)$	$|S|$	$fitness(S)$
S_1	000011010100011	28	6	27.4
S_2	100100011111011	28	9	27.1
S_3	101111110100100	28	9	27.1
S_4	111111101001001	28	10	27.0
S_5	101001111111100	28	10	27.0
S_6	111010001001000	27	6	26.4
S_7	100011000011111	27	8	26.2
S_8	100000001011000	26	4	25.6
S_9	111000111010011	25	9	24.1
S_{10}	010110010110101	22	8	21.2

proportional to its fitness value. That is, a string S_k in the population Ψ has the following selection probability:

$$p(S_k) = \frac{fitness(S_k)}{\sum\limits_{S_j \in \Psi} fitness(S_j)}. \tag{4.9}$$

Roulette wheel selection seems to have two drawbacks. One is the slow convergence in the late stage of evolution. Let us consider a situation where the fitness values of ten strings are $\{96, 94, 93, 93, 92, 90, 90, 88, 87, 85\}$. In this case, the selection probabilities of these strings are almost the same. Thus the selection pressure toward good strings is very low. The other drawback is the premature convergence in the early stage of evolution. Let us consider another situation where the fitness values of ten strings are $\{50, 4, 4, 3, 2, 2, 2, 2, 1, 1\}$. In this case, the first string has a much larger selection probability than the other strings. Thus the selection pressure toward this string is very high. As a result, the first string is frequently selected as parent strings. This leads to the next population consisting of similar strings generated from the first string with the largest fitness value in the previous population.

In the genetic algorithm-based rule selection method in Ishibuchi et al. [83, 84], roulette wheel selection with linear scaling was used as

$$p(S_k) = \frac{fitness(S_k) - f_{\min}(\Psi)}{\sum\limits_{S_j \in \Psi} [fitness(S_j) - f_{\min}(\Psi)]}, \tag{4.10}$$

where $f_{\min}(\Psi)$ is the worst fitness value in the current population Ψ:

$$f_{\min}(\Psi) = \min\{fitness(S_k) | S_k \in \Psi\}. \tag{4.11}$$

Recently binary tournament selection with replacement has often been used in genetic algorithms. In this selection scheme, two strings are randomly selected with replacement. These two strings can be the same (i.e., a single string can be selected twice). The better string with the higher fitness value is selected as a parent string. The selection probability of each string can be analytically calculated for binary tournament selection with replacement. In the case of Table 4.6 with ten strings, the selection probability of the best string S_1 is calculated as

$$p(S_1) = \frac{10 \times 10 - 9 \times 9}{10 \times 10}. \tag{4.12}$$

The denominator is the total number of combinations of selecting two strings from ten strings with replacement. The first term of the numerator is also the total number of combinations of two strings. The second term is the total number of combinations of two strings excluding the best string S_1. In the same manner, the selection probability of the second best string S_2 is calculated as

$$p(S_2) = \frac{9 \times 9 - 8 \times 8}{10 \times 10}. \tag{4.13}$$

While roulette wheel selection depends on the fitness value of each string, tournament selection depends on only the order of the fitness value of each string.

In Table 4.7, we compare the above-mentioned three schemes (i.e., roulette wheel selection, roulette wheel selection with linear scaling, and binary tournament selection with replacement) with one another using the ten strings in Table 4.6. Table 4.7 clearly shows the effect of the linear scaling on the selection probability of each string. This table also shows the difference between roulette wheel selection and binary tournament selection. In this chapter, we use binary tournament selection with replacement in genetic algorithms for rule selection.

Table 4.7. Selection probability of each string in Table 4.6

String	$fitness(S)$	Roulette wheel selection		Binary tournament
		No scaling	Scaling	
S_1	27.4	0.106	0.132	0.190
S_2	27.1	0.105	0.125	0.160
S_3	27.1	0.105	0.125	0.160
S_4	27.0	0.104	0.123	0.120
S_5	27.0	0.104	0.123	0.120
S_6	26.4	0.102	0.110	0.090
S_7	26.2	0.101	0.106	0.070
S_8	25.6	0.099	0.093	0.050
S_9	24.1	0.093	0.062	0.030
S_{10}	21.2	0.082	0.000	0.010

After a pair of parent strings is selected from the current population, a crossover operation is used to generate new strings from the selected parent strings. One-point crossover, two-point crossover, and uniform crossover have frequently been used for binary strings in genetic algorithms. These crossover operations are illustrated in Figs. 4.8 – 4.10 where S_1 and S_2 in Table 4.6 are used as parent strings for illustration purposes.

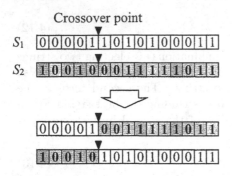

Fig. 4.8. One-point crossover operation

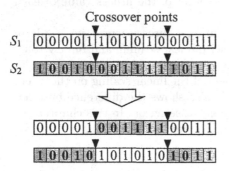

Fig. 4.9. Two-point crossover operation

In the one-point crossover operation in Fig. 4.8, a single crossover point is randomly selected. A different crossover point is selected for a different pair of parent strings. Each parent string is divided into two parts by the single crossover point. Then the right hand side of one parent string is interchanged with the corresponding part of the other parent string.

On the other hand, two crossover points are randomly selected in the two-point crossover operation in Fig. 4.9. Each parent string is divided into three parts by the two crossover points. The substring between the two crossover points of one parent string is interchanged with the corresponding part of the other parent string.

In the uniform crossover operation in Fig. 4.10, locations (i.e., loci) are randomly chosen for crossover. These locations are indicated by * in Fig. 4.10. We randomly assign * to each location with the probability 0.5 for implementing the uniform crossover operation. Values (i.e., genes) in the selected locations of one parent string are exchanged with those of the other parent string. In this chapter, we use the uniform crossover operation because

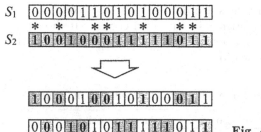

S_1

S_2

Fig. 4.10. Uniform crossover operation

this operation is independent of the order of rules located in each string. On the other hand, the other crossover operations depend on the order of rules (e.g., offspring are likely to inherit adjacent rules from their parents by the one-point and two-point crossover operations).

The uniform crossover operation is applied to each pair of parent strings with a pre-specified crossover probability. This means that the crossover operation is not applied to some pairs of parent strings. In this case, parent strings are not modified by the crossover operation.

A mutation operation is applied to each string after the crossover operation. We use a simple flip-flop mutation operation. This mutation operation is illustrated in Fig. 4.11 where mutated values are indicated by shaded boxes. The mutation operation is applied to each location in each string with a pre-specified mutation operation.

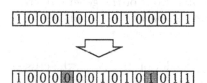

Fig. 4.11. Mutation operation

The best string in the current population is inherited by the next population with no modification. This is referred to as an elitist strategy or elitism. We use this strategy in genetic algorithms for rule selection. In the case of Table 4.7, the best string S_1 is inherited by the next population (see Table 4.8).

As we have explained, the next population is generated from the current one using binary tournament selection with replacement, the uniform crossover, the flip-flop mutation, and the elitist strategy. This is illustrated in Table 4.8 for the current population in Table 4.7. The first column of Table 4.8 shows five pairs of parent strings that are selected by binary tournament selection with replacement. The second column shows new strings after the crossover operation. The crossover operation is not applied to the second pair of parent strings. The best string in Table 4.7 is inserted in the bottom row of the third column as the elite string. The third column shows strings after the mutation operation. Mutated values are underlined in this column. The next population consists of the ten strings in the third column. It should be noted that the elite string is handed down from the current population to the next population with no modification.

Table 4.8. Next population generated from the current population in Table 4.7

	Parent strings	After crossover	After mutation
S_1	000011010100011	100011010100011	100011010100011
S_7	**100011000011111**	000011000011111	000111001011111
S_3	101111110100100	101111110100100	101111100100100
S_1	**000011010100011**	**000011010100011**	001011010100011
S_6	111010001001000	111011101001000	111011101001000
S_4	**111111101001001**	**111110001001001**	101110001001001
S_4	111111101001001	111111101001001	111011101001000
S_4	**111111101001001**	**111111101001001**	111110111001001
S_5	101001111111100	100101111111011	100100111111011
S_2	**100100011111011**	Elite string (S_1)	000011010100011

The above-mentioned genetic operations (i.e., selection, crossover, mutation, and elitist strategy) are iterated to find the optimal rule set with the highest fitness value. Since good strings with high fitness values are selected from the current population for generating the next population, we expect that better strings are obtained through the iterations of the genetic operations. Our genetic algorithm for rule selection can be written as follows:

[Genetic Algorithm for Rule Selection]

Step 0: *Parameter Specification.* Specify the population size N_{pop}, the crossover probability p_c, the mutation probability p_m, and the stopping condition.

Step 1: *Initialization.* Randomly generate N_{pop} binary strings of length N as the initial population.

Step 2: *Genetic Operations.* Calculate the fitness value of each string in the current population. Store the best string as the elite string. Generate ($N_{\text{pop}} - 1$) strings using selection, crossover, and mutation from the current population. The current population is replaced with the newly generated ($N_{\text{pop}} - 1$) strings.

Step 3: *Elitist Strategy.* Add the elite string stored in Step 2 to the current population.

Step 4: *Termination Test.* If the stopping condition is not satisfied, return to Step 2. Otherwise terminate the execution of the algorithm. The best string in the current population is the obtained solution of the rule selection problem.

4.3.4 Computer Simulations

We applied the genetic algorithm-based rule selection method to the two-dimensional test problem in Fig. 4.7 with the 15 candidate rules in Table 4.5. Each subset of the candidate rules was denoted by a binary string of length 15. The value of $w_{|S|}$ in the fitness function (4.8) was specified as $w_{|S|} = 0.1$. This specification means that the first objective (i.e., the number of correctly classified training patterns) is more important than the second objective (i.e., the number of selected linguistic rules). The sensitivity of obtained rule sets to the specification of $w_{|S|}$ is examined later in this subsection through computer simulations with various values of $w_{|S|}$.

In Step 0 of the genetic algorithm for rule selection in the previous subsection, we have to specify some parameter values. In computer simulations on the two-dimensional test problem, we used the following parameter specifications:

Population size: $N_{\text{pop}} = 10$,
Crossover probability: $p_c = 0.8$,
Mutation probability: $p_m = 1/(\text{string length}) = 1/15$,
Stopping condition: 500 iterations (i.e., 500 generation updates).

Since the string length is small (i.e., the search space is small), the population size and the total number of iterations are also small. The above specification of the mutation probability means that each string has a single occurrence of mutation on the average. From the population size and the stopping condition, we can see that 5000 subsets were examined among $2^{15} = 32768$ subsets of the 15 candidate rules. In Step 1, ten strings were randomly generated. We have already shown the generated strings in Table 4.6. The next population was generated by selection, crossover, and mutation in Step 2 and the elitist strategy in Step 3. We have already shown the updated population in Table 4.8. The generation update (i.e., generating the next population from the current one) was iterated 500 times. Then the genetic algorithm was terminated. The following string was obtained as the best string in the final population:

$$S = 001011010000000. \tag{4.14}$$

This string corresponds to the following rule set:

$$S = \{R_3, R_5, R_6, R_8\}. \tag{4.15}$$

We have already used this rule set to explain rule selection in this chapter (see Fig. 4.6 and Fig. 4.7).

We performed the same computer simulation 20 times using different initial populations. The rule set in (4.15) was obtained from 14 trials (out of the 20 trials). To examine the optimality of this rule set, we calculated the fitness values of all the $2^{15} = 32768$ subsets of the 15 candidate rules. From those exhaustive calculations, we confirmed that the rule set in (4.15) is one of the two optimal solutions with the maximum fitness value. The other optimal solution was found from the remaining six trials in the above computer simulations. This means that the genetic algorithm could find the optimal solution by examining 5000 solutions among 32768 possible solutions.

Figure 4.12 shows the average classification rate of the elite string at each generation over the 20 trials. From this figure, we can see that the average classification rate was rapidly improved by the genetic algorithm during the first 100 generations. On the other hand, Fig. 4.13 shows the average cardinality of the elite string at each generation over the 20 trials. From the comparison between Fig. 4.12 and Fig. 4.13, we can see that the decrease in the number of linguistic rules was slower than the increase in the classification rate. This is because the value of $w_{|S|}$ was small (i.e., $w_{|S|} = 0.1$) in the fitness function (4.8).

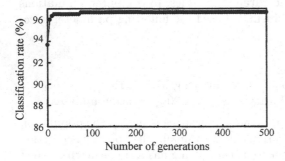

Fig. 4.12. The average classification rate of the elite string at each generation over the 20 trials in the case of $w_{|S|} = 0.1$

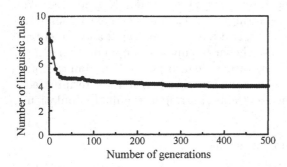

Fig. 4.13. The average cardinality of the elite string at each generation over the 20 trials in the case of $w_{|S|} = 0.1$

We also performed the same computer simulation using a large value for $w_{|S|}$ in the fitness function (4.8). The value of $w_{|S|}$ was specified as $w_{|S|} = 2$. This means that the minimization of the number of linguistic rules is more important than the maximization of the number of correctly classified training patterns. Average simulation results over 20 trials are summarized in Fig. 4.14 and Fig. 4.15. From these figures, we can see that the increase in the number of correctly classified training patterns in Fig. 4.14 was slower than the decrease in the number of linguistic rules in Fig. 4.15. We can also see that the average classification rate deteriorated from Fig. 4.12 to Fig. 4.14 on increasing the value of $w_{|S|}$. At the same time, the average number of linguistic rules was decreased from Fig. 4.13 to Fig. 4.15 by increasing $w_{|S|}$. The following rule set was obtained from all the 20 trials when $w_{|S|}$ was specified as $w_{|S|} = 2$:

$$S = \{R_5, R_8, R_{12}\}. \tag{4.16}$$

This rule set is the optimal solution in the case of $w_{|S|} = 2$. Figure 4.16 shows the decision region of each linguistic rule in the rule set (4.16) together with the classification boundary.

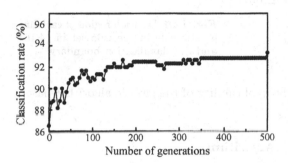

Fig. 4.14. The average classification rate of the elite string at each generation over the 20 trials in the case of $w_{|S|} = 2$

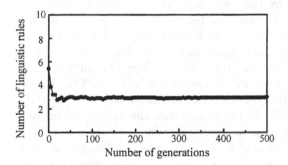

Fig. 4.15. The average cardinality of the elite string at each generation over the 20 trials in the case of $w_{|S|} = 2$

4.4 Some Extensions to Rule Selection

We have already explained the structure of the genetic algorithm-based rule selection method. While the genetic algorithm worked well on the two-dimensional test problem, some extensions are required to improve its efficiency and applicability when it is applied to real-world pattern classification problems with many attributes. In this section, we present some heuristics for

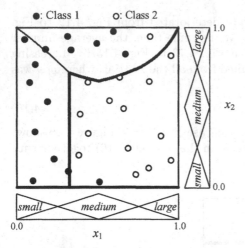

Fig. 4.16. Decision region of each linguistic rule in the rule set in (4.16) and the classification boundary

improving the efficiency and the applicability of the genetic algorithm-based rule selection method.

4.4.1 Heuristics in Genetic Algorithms

One heuristic is the removal of unnecessary linguistic rules from each string S (i.e., each rule set S). Since we use the single winner-based method, the classification of each pattern by the rule set S is performed by finding a single winner rule with the maximum product of the rule weight and the compatibility grade with that pattern as we have already explained in Chap. 2. There may be a case where some linguistic rules in S are not chosen as winner rules for any patterns. We can remove these linguistic rules from S without causing any changes in the classification results by S. That is, the removal of those linguistic rules does not decrease the number of correctly classified training patterns by S. At the same time, the number of linguistic rules is decreased by removing unnecessary linguistic rules. This leads to an improvement in the fitness value of S. Thus we remove all linguistic rules that are not selected as winner rules for any patterns from the rule set S. The removal of those linguistic rules is performed for each string of the current population by changing the corresponding 1's to 0's. This heuristic procedure can be viewed as a kind of local search because each string is modified to improve its fitness value. The removal of unnecessary linguistic rules is performed when the fitness value is calculated (i.e., between the calculation of the number of correctly classified training patterns and the calculation of the number of linguistic rules).

For example, let us consider the following two linguistic rules in Table 4.5 for the two-dimensional test problem in Fig. 4.7:

R_1: If x_1 is *small* and x_2 is *don't care* then Class 1 with 0.808,
R_8: If x_1 is *small* and x_2 is *medium* then Class 1 with 0.705.

When these two linguistic rules are included in the rule set S, R_8 is never chosen as the winner rules of any patterns because both the compatibility grade and the rule weight of R_1 are always larger than R_8. Thus we can remove R_8 from the rule set S without causing any changes in the classification results by S when both R_1 and R_8 are included in S. In this case, the removal of R_8 from S improves the fitness value of S.

Another heuristic is the use of biased mutation probabilities. For efficiently decreasing the number of linguistic rules in each rule set (i.e., the number of 1's in each string), we assign a higher probability to the mutation from 1 to 0 than the mutation from 0 to 1. We briefly explain here the effect of the unbiased mutation on the number of linguistic rules. Let N and p_m be the number of candidate rules (i.e., string length) and the mutation probability, respectively. The number of 1's and 0's in the string S are written as $|S|$ and $N - |S|$, respectively. Thus the expected number of 1's to be mutated to 0 is written for the string S as

$$N_m(1 \to 0) = |S| \cdot p_m. \tag{4.17}$$

On the other hand, the expected number of 0's to be mutated to 1 is written as

$$N_m(0 \to 1) = (N - |S|) \cdot p_m. \tag{4.18}$$

Since initial strings are randomly generated, $|S|$ is almost the same as $N - |S|$. Thus the mutation operation does not change the number of linguistic rules on the average in the initial stage of evolution. Since the goal of rule selection is to find a small number of linguistic rules from a large number of candidate rules, $|S|$ should be much smaller than N in the late stage of evolution. Thus, $|S|$ should be much smaller than $N - |S|$. In this case, $N_m(0 \to 1)$ in (4.18) is much larger than $N_m(1 \to 0)$ in (4.17). This means that the mutation operation increases the number of linguistic rules on the average while the goal of rule selection is to find a small number of linguistic rules. The aim of using biased mutation probabilities is twofold. One is to rapidly decrease the number of linguistic rules in the initial stage of evolution where the number of 1's is almost the same as the number of 0's in each string. The other is to prevent the mutation operation from increasing the number of linguistic rules in the late stage of evolution where the number of 1's is much smaller than the number of 0's.

For simplicity of explanation, let us consider a rule set S with $N = 1010$ and $|S| = 10$. In this case, the number of 1's is 10 and the number of 0's is 1000. When we use an unbiased mutation probability p_m, the expected number of 1's to be mutated to 0 is calculated as

$$N_m(1 \to 0) = |S| \cdot p_m = 10 \cdot p_m. \tag{4.19}$$

On the other hand, the expected number of 0's to be mutated to 1 is calculated as

$$N_m(0 \to 1) = (N - |S|) \cdot p_m = 1000 \cdot p_m. \tag{4.20}$$

Thus we have the following relation:

$$N_m(1 \to 0) = \frac{1}{100} N_m(0 \to 1). \tag{4.21}$$

From this relation, we can see that the mutation operation almost always increases the number of linguistic rules.

We examined the effect of the two heuristics (i.e., the removal of unnecessary linguistic rules and the use of biased mutation probabilities) through computer simulations on the iris data set. First we generated linguistic rules by examining all combinations of the four antecedent fuzzy sets (i.e., *small, medium, large,* and *don't care*) for each of the four attributes (i.e., $4^4 = 256$ combinations). Using all the 150 samples in the iris data set as training patterns, 221 linguistic rules were generated. The other linguistic rules were not generated because their consequent classes could not be uniquely determined by the heuristic rule generation method in Chap. 2. All the generated linguistic rules were used as candidate rules in rule selection.

We used the following four versions of the genetic algorithm-based rule selection method:

GA: Original algorithm in the previous selection with no extension,
R-GA: Modified algorithm with the removal of unnecessary linguistic rules,
B-GA: Modified algorithm with biased mutation probabilities,
RB-GA: Modified algorithm with both heuristics.

These algorithms were applied to the iris data set using the following parameter specifications:

The value of $w_{|S|}$:	$w_{|S|} = 0.1$,
Population size:	$N_{\text{pop}} = 50$,
Crossover probability:	$p_c = 0.8$,
Mutation probability:	$p_m = 1/(\text{string length}) = 1/221$,
Stopping condition:	1000 generation updates.

In the two versions with biased mutation probabilities, the above mutation probability was biased as

$$p_m(0 \to 1) = 1/(\text{string length}) = 1/221,$$
$$p_m(1 \to 0) = 0.1.$$

We applied each algorithm to the iris data set 20 times using different initial populations. Simulation results over 20 trials of each algorithm are summarized in Fig. 4.17 and Fig. 4.18. Figure 4.17 shows the average classification rate by the elite string at each generation. The difference among the four algorithms is not clear in this figure. This is because the two heuristics did not improve the classification performance of each string. On the other hand, Fig. 4.18 shows the average number of linguistic rules in the elite string at each generation. From this figure, we can see that each of the two heuristics had a large effect on the decrease in the number of linguistic rules.

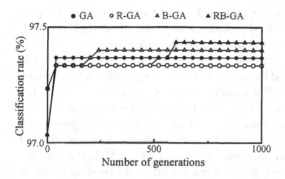

Fig. 4.17. The average classification rate of the elite string at each generation over the 20 trials of each version in computer simulations on the iris data set

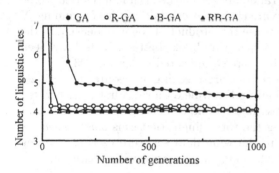

Fig. 4.18. The average cardinality of the elite string at each generation over the 20 trials of each version in computer simulations on the iris data set

Since the number of linguistic rules in each string was rapidly decreased by the two heuristics as shown in Fig. 4.18, computation time was also decreased. The average CPU time of each algorithm over 20 trials is shown in Table 4.9. The average CPU time was measured for each algorithm implemented in the C language on a PC with an Intel Pentium IV 1.5 GHz processor.

Table 4.9. The average CPU time

Algorithm	GA	R-GA	B-GA	RB-GA
CPU time (s)	50.6	27.5	51.1	31.1

4.4.2 Prescreening of Candidate Rules

The efficiency of the genetic algorithm-based rule selection method strongly depends on the number of candidate rules. It is very difficult for genetic algorithms to efficiently find a small number of linguistic rules with high classification ability when the number of candidate rules is huge. The size of the search space in rule selection is 2^N where N is the number of candidate rules. That is, the search space expands exponentially as the number of candidate rules increases. If we can find only good candidate rules by prescreening, the efficiency of genetic algorithms can be significantly improved. In this subsection, we explain such a prescreening procedure.

In the computer simulations on the wine data set in Chap. 2 (i.e., Table 2.10 and Table 2.11), we designed linguistic rule-based systems using a heuristic rule selection method where the product of the confidence $c(\cdot)$ in (2.10) and the support $s(\cdot)$ in (2.11) was used as a rule selection criterion. In this subsection, we use the same heuristic method as a prescreening procedure of candidate rules. As in Chapter 2, generated linguistic rules are divided into M groups according to their consequent classes where M is the number of classes. Linguistic rules in each group were sorted in descending order of the product of the confidence and the support. When multiple linguistic rules have the same product, they are randomly sorted (i.e., random tiebreak). The first N/M rules from each group are chosen as candidate rules for finding N candidate rules in total. While we use the product of the confidence and the support as a rule selection criterion in this book, better results have been reported for some tet problems by more complicated criteria in [93]

We examined the effectiveness of this prescreening procedure of candidate rules through computer simulations on the wine data set. First we generated linguistic rules with three or less antecedent conditions (i.e., with ten or more *don't care* conditions) using the three linguistic terms *small*, *medium*, and *large*. All the 178 samples in the wine data set were used as training patterns. Table 4.10 summarizes the number of generated linguistic rules.

Table 4.10. The number of generated linguistic rules with each number of antecedent conditions. The three linguistic terms *small*, *medium*, and *large* were used to generate linguistic rules

Number of antecedent conditions				Total
0	1	2	3	
1	39	701	7585	8326

Using the prescreening procedure, we found a set of candidate rules. Table 4.11 shows the relation between the number of candidate rules and their classification ability on training patterns. For comparison, Table 4.11 also shows the classification ability of candidate rules obtained by other rule selection criteria (i.e., confidence and support). To decrease the effect of the random tiebreak, the average classification rate was calculated over 100 computer simulations for each case. Note that classification rates in Table 4.11 were measured on training patterns for the candidate rules before rule selection.

From Table 4.11, we can see that the highest classification rates were obtained when candidate rules were prescreened using the product of the confidence and the support.

Table 4.11. Classification rates on training patterns of candidate rules obtained by the prescreening procedure for the wine data set

Number of candidate rules	Rule selection criterion		
	Product	Confidence	Support
3	68.0%	16.2%	43.3%
6	94.4%	28.6%	42.1%
9	92.7%	36.4%	53.9%
30	95.5%	59.1%	78.1%
60	95.5%	64.9%	93.3%
90	95.5%	68.1%	93.8%
300	96.1%	76.1%	95.5%
600	96.1%	79.6%	95.5%
900	96.1%	91.3%	95.5%

We applied the genetic algorithm-based rule selection method to 900 candidate rules obtained by the product criterion. We used the genetic algorithm with the two heuristics (i.e., removal of unnecessary rules and biased mutation probabilities) in the same manner as in the computer simulation on the iris data set in the previous subsection. This computer simulation was performed 20 times using different initial populations. For comparison, we also performed the same computer simulation with no prescreening procedure. That is, all the generated 8326 linguistic rules in Table 4.10 were used as candidate rules. Average simulation results are summarized in Table 4.12. From this table, we can see that almost the same results were obtained from the two cases: with prescreening and without prescreening. We can also see that the prescreening procedure significantly decreased the average CPU time.

Table 4.12. Average results on the wine data set by the genetic algorithm-based rule selection method with/without the prescreening procedure

	Genetic algorithm-based rule selection method	
	With prescreening	Without prescreening
Classification rate	100%	100%
Number of rules	6.9	7.0
CPU times (s)	119.8	546.3

From the comparison between Table 4.11 and Table 4.12, we can see that the genetic algorithm-based rule selection method significantly improved the classification ability of candidate rules. The average classification rate 96.1% of 900 candidate rules in Table 4.11 was improved to 100% by selecting 6.9

linguistic rules on the average in Table 4.12. We can also see from Table 4.11 that small rule sets designed by the prescreening procedure have lower classification rates than the average result of the genetic algorithm-based rule selection method in Table 4.12. This is because the classification accuracy of rule sets is taken into account in the genetic algorithm-based rule selection method while the classification ability of individual linguistic rules is independently evaluated in the prescreening procedure using a heuristic rule evaluation criterion. This observation shows the advantage of the genetic algorithm-based rule selection method over heuristic rule selection. Of course, it should be noted that the prescreening procedure is used to find a tractable number of candidate rules in the genetic algorithm-based rule selection method in this chapter.

4.4.3 Computer Simulations

We further examine the genetic algorithm-based rule selection method through computer simulations on the iris data set and the wine data set. We have used the three linguistic terms *small, medium*, and *large* in the previous computer simulations of this chapter. That is, we have used the same fuzzy partition into the three linguistic terms for all attributes of each data set. In this subsection, we use the four fuzzy partitions with different granularities in Fig. 1.4 of Chap. 1. That is, we use the 14 antecedent fuzzy sets in Fig. 1.4 and *don't care* for each attribute. This is to demonstrate how the genetic algorithm-based rule selection method can be employed in the case where we do not know an appropriate fuzzy partition for each attribute. The total number of combinations of antecedent fuzzy sets is $(14+1)^n$ in an n-dimensional pattern classification problem. Thus far more candidate rules are generated in computer simulations of this subsection than the case with the three linguistic terms in the previous computer simulations.

In the application of the genetic algorithm-based rule selection method to the iris data set, we generated 32840 linguistic rules by examining all the $(14+1)^4$ combinations of antecedent fuzzy sets for generating candidate rules. While it is not impossible to use all the generated 32840 linguistic rules as candidate rules with no prescreening, a long computation time is required to find good rule sets. Thus we chose 900 candidate rules using the prescreening procedure. We applied the genetic algorithm with the two heuristics to the 900 candidate rules in the same manner as in the previous computer simulations on the iris data set. We examined four specifications of $w_{|S|}$: $w_{|S|} = 0.1, 0.5, 1$, and 5. Note that the value of $w_{|S|}$ can be viewed as the penalty with respect to the number of linguistic rules. A large value of $w_{|S|}$ tends to decrease the number of linguistic rules at the expense of the classification ability of rule sets. On the other hand, a small value of $w_{|S|}$ may lead to relatively large rule sets with high classification ability.

For each specification of $w_{|S|}$, the computer simulation was iterated 20 times. Average simulation results are summarized in Table 4.13. This table clearly shows the effect of the value of $w_{|S|}$ on the characteristic features of obtained rule sets. When $w_{|S|}$ is very large (i.e., $w_{|S|} = 5$), only three linguistic rules were selected. That is, only a single linguistic rule was selected for each class. On the other hand, many linguistic rules with high classification ability were selected when $w_{|S|}$ is very small (i.e., $w_{|S|} = 0.1$).

Table 4.13. Simulation results on training patterns of the iris data set using various specifications of the penalty with respect to the number of linguistic rules in the fitness function

Value of $w_{|S|}$	0.1	0.5	1	5
Classification rate	99.3%	98.7%	98.0%	97.7%
Number of rules	5.5	4.7	3.3	3.0

As shown in Table 4.13, rule sets with different sizes can be obtained from multiple runs of the genetic algorithm-based rule selection method using different specifications of $w_{|S|}$. In a later chapter, we discuss the handling of rule selection in the framework of multi objective optimization where a number of rule sets can be obtained from a single run of a multi-objective genetic algorithm.

In Fig. 4.19, we show an example of a rule set with three linguistic rules selected by the genetic algorithm-based rule selection method with $w_{|S|} = 5$ (i.e., a large penalty value with respect to the number of linguistic rules). Each shaded triangle shows an antecedent fuzzy set. Each real number in parentheses is the rule weight of the corresponding linguistic rule. This rule set can correctly classify 146 training patterns (i.e., 97.3% of the 150 samples in the iris data set). We can see from Fig. 4.19 that very simple linguistic rules were selected. Thus this rule set is easily understood by human users. While we did not use input selection in an explicit manner, the selected three linguistic rules do not have antecedent conditions on x_1 and x_2.

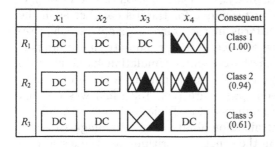

Fig. 4.19. An example of a rule set with three linguistic rules selected by the genetic algorithm-based rule selection method with $w_{|S|} = 5$ for the iris data set

In Fig. 4.20, we show an example of an obtained rule set in the case of a small penalty value with respect to the number of linguistic rules (i.e., $w_{|S|} = 0.1$). This rule set can correctly classify 150 training patterns (i.e.,

100% of the 150 samples). The classification rate of the rule set in Fig. 4.20 is higher than that of the rule set in Fig. 4.19 (i.e., 97.3%). At the same time, the rule set in Fig. 4.20 is more complicated than that in Fig. 4.19. The rule set in Fig. 4.20 includes more linguistic rules, and each linguistic rule has more antecedent conditions. From the comparison between Fig. 4.19 and Fig. 4.20, we can see a tradeoff between the classification ability of each rule set and its complexity. This tradeoff is handled by the value of $w_{|S|}$ in the genetic algorithm-based rule selection method in this chapter. The tradeoff is further discussed in a later chapter in the framework of multi-objective optimization.

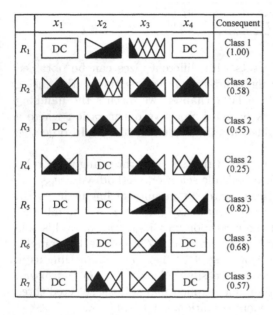

Fig. 4.20. An example of a rule set obtained by the genetic algorithm-based rule selection method with $w_{|S|} = 0.1$ for the iris data set

To examine the generalization ability (i.e., classification rates on test patterns), we used the leaving-one-out technique for the iris data set as in the computer simulations on test patterns in the previous chapters. The prescreening of candidate rules and the selection from candidate rules were performed in the same manner as in the computer simulation for Table 4.13 using 149 training patterns. The remaining single pattern was used as a test pattern. The whole leaving-one-out procedure (i.e., 150 runs) was iterated ten times. Simulation results are summarized in Table 4.14. Since we did not use any trick to improve the generalization ability of selected linguistic rules during the evolution of rule sets in the genetic algorithm-based rule selection method, the classification rates of selected linguistic rules on test patterns are not so high in Table 4.14. The fitness function in (4.8) of this chapter was designed to maximize the classification rate on training patterns and minimize the number of linguistic rules. Thus it may be necessary to change the fitness function if our goal is to find a rule set with high generalization ability. Discussions on the adjustment of classification boundaries in Sect. 3.3 may be useful for modifying the fitness functions.

Table 4.14. Average simulation results on test patterns of the iris data set

Value of $w_{|S|}$	0.1	0.5	1	5
Classification rate	93.5%	93.3%	93.2%	93.8%
Number of rules	5.2	4.6	3.5	3.0

We also applied the leaving-one-out procedure to the wine data set using the 14 antecedent fuzzy sets and *don't care* as in the above computer simulations on the iris data set. The total number of combinations of antecedent fuzzy sets is $(14 + 1)^{13}$, which is much larger than $(14 + 1)^4$ in the case of the iris data set. It is impractical to generate candidate rules by examining all the 15^{13} combinations of antecedent fuzzy sets. Thus we only examined short linguistic rules with three or less antecedent conditions (i.e., with ten or more *don't care* conditions). The number of generated candidate rules of each length is summarized in Table 4.15. We selected 900 candidate rules from the generated 711716 candidate rules using the prescreening procedure. In Table 4.16, we show the relation between the number of candidate rules and their classification performance on training patterns. We used the product of the confidence and the support as the prescreening criterion of candidate rules.

Table 4.15. The number of generated linguistic rules using 14 antecedent fuzzy sets and *don't care* for each attribute of the wine data set

Length of rules	0	1	2	3	Total
Number of rules	1	182	14781	696752	711716

The genetic algorithm with the two heuristics was used to select a small number of linguistic rules from the 900 candidate rules. We used the same parameter specifications as in the previous computer simulations on the iris data set for Table 4.13. Simulation results are summarized in Table 4.17. From this table, we can see that rule sets with high classification rates were obtained by selecting a small number of linguistic rules from the 900 candidate rules. Note that the classification rate of the 900 candidate rules is 96.1% (see Table 4.16). Figure 4.21 and Fig. 4.22 show examples of obtained rule sets in the cases of $w_{|S|} = 5$ and $w_{|S|} = 0.1$, respectively. From these figures and Table 4.17, we can see that rule sets with different sizes were obtained from various specifications of $w_{|S|}$. The rule set in Fig. 4.21 can correctly classify 174 patterns (i.e., 97.8% of the 178 samples of the wine data set). This rule set has high interpretability because the number of rules is very small and each rule has only a few antecedent conditions. While we did not use input

Table 4.16. Classification rates on training patterns of candidate rules obtained by the prescreening procedure for the wine data set

Number of candidate rules	Rule selection criterion		
	Product	Confidence	Support
3	89.3%	11.0%	60.7%
6	92.1%	17.8%	52.2%
9	93.8%	21.3%	61.2%
30	94.9%	28.7%	88.2%
60	94.4%	30.3%	86.5%
90	96.1%	32.0%	88.2%
300	96.1%	32.4%	96.6%
600	96.6%	71.3%	96.1%
900	96.1%	98.2%	96.1%

selection in an explicit manner, only a few attributes are used in the obtained rule set in Fig. 4.21. It should be noted that all the 13 attributes were used for generating candidate rules. On the other hand, the rule set in Fig. 4.22 can correctly classify 178 training patterns (i.e., 100% of the 178 samples). This rule set has higher classification ability and lower interpretability than the rule set in Fig. 4.21.

Table 4.17. Simulation results on training patterns of the wine data set using various specifications of the penalty with respect to the number of linguistic rules in the fitness function

Value of $w_{|S|}$	0.1	0.5	1	5
Classification rate	100%	100%	99.9%	98.7%
Number of rules	5.6	5.1	3.2	3.0

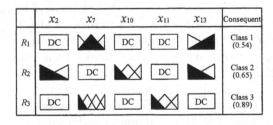

Fig. 4.21. An example of a rule set obtained by the genetic algorithm-based rule selection method with $w_{|S|} = 5$ for the wine data set

We also examined the average classification rate on test patterns of the wine data set using the leaving-one-out technique in the same manner as the previous computer simulations on the iris data set for Table 4.14. The whole leaving-one-out procedure (i.e., 178 runs) was iterated ten times. Simulation results are summarized in Table 4.18. From the comparison between Table 4.17 and Table 4.18, we can see that there are differences of about 5% between

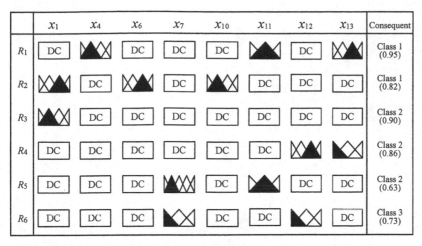

Fig. 4.22. An example of a rule set obtained by the genetic algorithm-based rule selection method with $w_{|S|} = 0.1$ for the wine data set

simulation results on training patterns and test patterns. This observation suggests the overfitting to training patterns of rule sets obtained by the genetic algorithm-based rule selection method. As we have already mentioned with respect to the simulation results on the iris data set where there were also differences of about 5% between training set performance (Table 4.13) and test set performance (Table 4.14), it may be necessary to change the fitness function if our goal is to find a rule set with high generalization ability. It is interesting to note that the increase in the number of linguistic rules did not always lead to an increase in the classification rate on test patterns in Table 4.14 and Table 4.18.

Table 4.18. Average simulation results on test patterns of the wine data set

Value of $w_{|S|}$	0.1	0.5	1	5
Classification rate	94.7%	95.4%	95.7%	94.4%
Number of rules	5.6	5.2	4.3	3.0

Fig. 5.2 ...

5. Genetics-Based Machine Learning

In the previous chapter, genetic algorithms were used as an optimization tool for rule selection. In this chapter, genetic algorithms are used as a machine learning tool for designing linguistic rule-based classification systems. While a rule set was represented as a binary string in the previous chapter, each linguistic rule is coded using its antecedent fuzzy sets in this chapter. Genetic algorithms for machine learning are referred to as genetics-based machine learning (GBML) algorithms. GBML algorithms are usually divided into two categories: Michigan approach and Pittsburgh approach. Each rule is represented by a string and handled as an individual in the Michigan approach. A population of strings corresponds to a rule set. On the other hand, a rule set is represented by a concatenated string and handled as an individual in the Pittsburgh approach. In this chapter, we first explain GBML algorithms in these two approaches for designing linguistic rule-based classification systems. Then we describe the hybridization of these two approaches into a single hybrid GBML algorithm. For further discussions on fuzzy GBML algorithms, see Cordón et al. [24] where various fuzzy GBML algorithms are described.

As in the previous chapter, we use linguistic rules of the following form for our n-dimensional pattern classification problem:

Rule R_q: If x_1 is A_{q1} and ... and x_n is A_{qn}

$$\text{then Class } C_q \text{ with } CF_q. \qquad (5.1)$$

It is assumed that m training patterns $x_p = (x_{p1}, \ldots, x_{pn})$, $p = 1, 2, \ldots, m$, are given from M classes as in the previous chapter.

5.1 Two Approaches in Genetics-Based Machine Learning

Genetics-based machine learning (GBML) algorithms categorized as the Michigan approach are often referred to as classifier systems [14]. It should be noted that classifier systems are totally different from classification systems. Classifier systems are genetic algorithms for generating rules (i.e., designing rule-based systems) while classification systems are computer systems that perform pattern classification. The main characteristic feature of Michigan-style GBML algorithms is the handling of a single rule as an individual (i.e., as a string). Thus a fitness value is assigned to a single rule. A population of individuals corresponds to a single rule set. The performance of a rule set (i.e., population) is not utilized in the evolution of rules. This means that rule sets are not directly optimized. On the other hand, GBML algorithms categorized as Pittsburgh approach [155] handle a rule set as an individual. A rule set is represented by a concatenated string where each substring denotes a single rule. A population of strings corresponds to multiple rule sets. A fitness value is assigned to a rule set. Thus rule sets are directly optimized through the maximization of their fitness values in the evolution of rule sets. The performance of each rule in a rule set is not utilized in the evolution of rule sets in Pittsburgh-style GBML algorithms. Differences between the Michigan and Pittsburgh approaches are summarized in Table 5.1.

Table 5.1. Differences between Michigan approach and Pittsburgh approach

	Michigan approach	Pittsburgh approach
Individual	A single rule	A single rule set
Population	A single rule set	Multiple rule sets
Evaluation of each rule	Yes	No
Evaluation of each rule set	No	Yes
Fitness calculation	For each rule	For each rule set
Selection	Good rules	Good rule sets
Crossover	Between rules	Between rule sets

Since the early 1990s, genetic algorithms have been used for the design of fuzzy rule-based systems mainly in the area of fuzzy control. Fuzzy GBML algorithms have also been proposed for pattern classification problems. Examples of recent fuzzy GBML algorithms for pattern classification problems are Castillo et al. [20], Ishibuchi et al. [71], and Setnes & Roubos [151]. Many fuzzy GBML algorithms have been proposed in the framework of the Pittsburgh approach [17, 54, 138]. This is because Pittsburgh-style GBML algorithms can directly optimize fuzzy rule-based systems (i.e., rule sets). Examples of early studies on fuzzy GBML algorithms categorized as the Pittsburgh approach are Karr [102], Nomura et al. [131], and Thrift [165]. Fuzzy GBML algorithms categorized as the Michigan approach have also been proposed since the early 1990s. Those algorithms are often referred to as fuzzy classifier systems. Examples of early studies on fuzzy classifier systems are Parodi & Bonelli [135] and Valenzuela-Rendon [170]. In Cordón et al. [24], fuzzy GBML algorithms in a different approach called iterative rule learning are described as well as those in the Pittsburgh and Michigan approaches.

5.2 Michigan-Style Algorithm

A Michigan-style fuzzy GBML algorithm (i.e., fuzzy classifier system) was proposed by Ishibuchi et al. [69] for designing linguistic rule-based systems for high-dimensional pattern classification problems. Its search ability to find good rule sets was examined in [66, 70]. In this subsection, we explain their Michigan-style GBML algorithm.

5.2.1 Coding of Linguistic Rules

In the Michigan-style GBML algorithm in [69], each linguistic rule is represented by a string and handled as an individual. A population consists of a pre-specified number of linguistic rules. Because the consequent class and the rule weight of each linguistic rule can be easily specified from the given training patterns by the heuristic rule generation procedure in Chap. 2, they are not used in the coding of each linguistic rule (i.e., they are not included in a string). Each linguistic rule is represented by a string using its antecedent fuzzy sets. For explanation purposes, we assume that all the n attributes of our n-dimensional pattern classification problem have three linguistic terms *small, medium,* and *large.* As in the previous chapter, we also use *don't care* in addition to these three linguistic terms as antecedent fuzzy sets. The total number of combinations of these antecedent fuzzy sets is $(3+1)^n$. Each combination of antecedent fuzzy sets (i.e., each linguistic rule) is represented by a string of length n written in an alphabet with four symbols. Each symbol denotes an antecedent fuzzy set (i.e., one of the three linguistic terms or *don't care*). We use the following four symbols to denote the four antecedent fuzzy sets:

1: *small,*
2: *medium,*
3: *large,*
#: *don't care.*

For example, the following linguistic rule for a five-dimensional pattern classification problem is coded as "#1#23":

Rule R_q: If x_2 is *small* and x_4 is *medium* and x_5 is *large*
then Class C_q with CF_q,

where x_1 and x_3 have *don't care* conditions. It should be noted that the consequent class C_q and the rule weight CF_q are not included in the string "#1#23". They are specified by the heuristic rule generation procedure in Chap. 2.

5.2.2 Genetic Operations

First the Michigan-style GBML algorithm randomly generates a pre-specified number of linguistic rules (say, N_{rule} linguistic rules) as an initial population.

For our n-dimensional pattern classification problem, N_{rule} strings of the length n are generated by randomly choosing each of the four symbols with the probability $1/4$.

Next the fitness value of each linguistic rule in the current population is evaluated. Let S be the set of linguistic rules in the current population. The evaluation of each linguistic rule is performed by classifying all the given training patterns by the rule set S using the single winner-based method described in Chap. 2. In the single winner-based method, only a single winner rule is responsible for the classification of each training pattern. The winner rule receives a unit reward when it correctly classifies a training pattern. After all the given training patterns are classified by the rule set S, the fitness value $fitness(R_q)$ of each linguistic rule R_q in S is calculated as

$$fitness(R_q) = NCP(R_q), \tag{5.2}$$

where $NCP(R_q)$ is the number of correctly classified training patterns by R_q. It should be noted that the following relation holds between the classification performance $NCP(R_q)$ of each linguistic rule R_q and the classification performance $NCP(S)$ of the rule set S used in the fitness function in Chap. 4:

$$NCP(S) = \sum_{R_q \in S} NCP(R_q). \tag{5.3}$$

The Michigan-style fuzzy GBML algorithm is implemented so that only a single copy is selected as a winner rule when multiple copies of the same linguistic rule are included in the rule set S. In genetic algorithms for optimization problems, multiple copies of the same string usually have the same fitness value. This often leads to undesired early convergence of the current population to a single solution. In the Michigan-style fuzzy GBML algorithm in this section, only a single copy can have a positive fitness value and the other copies have zero fitness. This prevents the current population from being dominated by many copies of a single or few linguistic rules.

Then new linguistic rules are generated from linguistic rules in the current population using genetic operations. As parent strings, two linguistic rules are selected from the current population. As in the genetic algorithm for rule selection in the previous chapter, we use binary tournament selection with replacement. That is, two linguistic rules are randomly selected from the current population and the better rule with the higher fitness value is chosen as a parent string. A pair of parent strings is chosen by iterating this procedure twice. While the original fuzzy classifier system in Ishibuchi et al. [69] used the roulette wheel selection, we use binary tournament selection with replacement in this chapter as in the genetic algorithm for rule selection in the previous chapter.

From the selected pair of parent strings, two new strings are generated by a crossover operation. As in the previous chapter, we use the uniform crossover operation, which is illustrated in Fig. 5.1 for a five-dimensional pattern classification problem. Crossover positions indicated by "*" are randomly chosen for each pair of parent strings. The crossover operation is applied to each pair of parent strings with a pre-specified crossover probability. After new strings are generated by the crossover operation, each symbol of the generated strings is randomly replaced with a different symbol by a mutation operation with a pre-specified mutation probability. Usually the same mutation probability is assigned to every position of each string. The mutation operation is illustrated in Fig. 5.2 where mutated values are indicated by an underline. The selection, crossover, and mutation are iterated until a pre-specified number of new strings (say, N_{replace} strings) are generated.

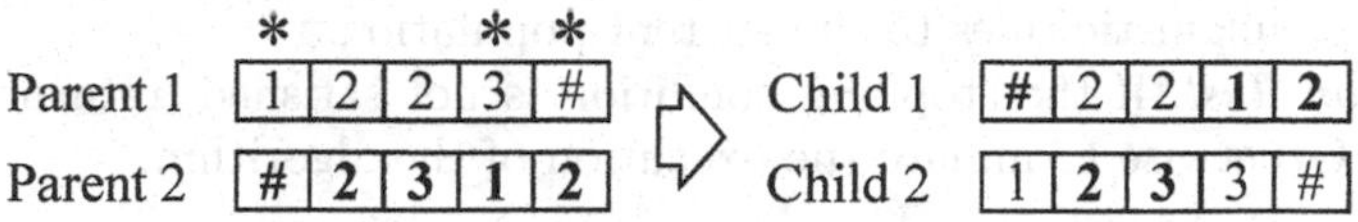

Fig. 5.1. Illustration of the uniform crossover in the Michigan-style fuzzy GBML algorithm

Fig. 5.2. Illustration of the mutation operation in the Michigan-style fuzzy GBML algorithm. This mutation is also used in the Pittsburgh-style fuzzy GBML algorithm

Finally the worst N_{replace} strings with the smallest fitness values in the current population are removed, and the newly generated N_{replace} strings are added to the remaining strings to form a new population. Because the number of removed strings is the same as the number of added strings, every population consists of the same number of strings. That is, every rule set has the same number of linguistic rules. This generation update can be viewed as the elitist strategy where the number of elite strings is $(N_{\text{rule}} - N_{\text{replace}})$.

The above procedures are applied to the new population again. The generation update is iterated until a pre-specified stopping condition is satisfied. In the computer simulations of this chapter, we use the total number of iterations (i.e., the total number of generation updates) as the stopping condition as in the genetic algorithm for rule selection in the previous chapter.

5.2.3 Algorithm

The Michigan-style fuzzy GBML algorithm for designing a linguistic rule-based system can be written as follows:

[Michigan-Style Fuzzy GBML Algorithm]

Step 0: *Parameter Specification.* Specify the number of linguistic rules N_{rule}, the number of replaced rules N_{replace}, the crossover probability p_c, the mutation probability p_m, and the stopping condition.

Step 1: *Initialization.* Randomly generate N_{rule} linguistic rules (i.e., N_{rule} strings of length n) as an initial population.

Step 2: *Genetic Operations.* Calculate the fitness value of each linguistic rule in the current population. Generate N_{replace} linguistic rules using selection, crossover, and mutation from existing linguistic rules in the current population.

Step 3: *Generation Update (Elitist Strategy).* Remove the worst N_{replace} linguistic rules from the current population and add the newly generated N_{replace} linguistic rules to the current population.

Step 4: *Termination Test.* If the stopping condition is not satisfied, return to Step 2. Otherwise terminate the execution of the algorithm.

During the execution of the Michigan-style fuzzy GBML algorithm, we monitor the classification rate of the current population on the given training patterns. The rule set (i.e., population) with the highest classification rate is chosen as the final solution by this algorithm.

In this section, we explain the simplest version of the Michigan-style fuzzy GBML algorithm. Many heuristics can be combined with the above-mentioned algorithm. For example, the search ability of this algorithm can be improved by adding a misclassification penalty term to the fitness function in (5.2), using a tailored initial population, and generating new linguistic rules from misclassified or rejected training patterns [66, 70]. Some heuristics are explained in a later subsection.

5.2.4 Computer Simulations

We applied the Michigan-style fuzzy GBML algorithm to the wine data set using the three linguistic terms and *don't care* for each of the 13 attributes. The total number of combinations of antecedent fuzzy sets is $(3+1)^{13}$. Each combination of antecedent fuzzy sets (i.e., each linguistic rule) is denoted by a string of length 13. It should be noted that we do not have to use any prescreening procedure. The search space in the Michigan-style GBML algorithm consists of all the $(3+1)^{13}$ linguistic rules.

In Step 0 of the algorithm in the previous subsection, we have to specify some parameter values. In our computer simulations, they were specified as follows:

Number of linguistic rules:	$N_{\text{rule}} = 10$,
Number of replaced rules:	$N_{\text{replace}} = 2$,
Crossover probability:	$p_c = 0.8$,
Mutation probability:	$p_m = 1/(\text{string length}) = 1/13$,
Stopping condition:	1000 iterations
	(i.e., 1000 generation updates).

From these parameter specifications, we can see that 1000 rule sets with ten linguistic rules were examined in our computer simulation. It should be noted that the total number of rule sets with ten linguistic rules is $_NC_{10}$ where $N = (3+1)^{13}$. Among such a huge number of rule sets, we only examined 1000 combinations in our computer simulation.

In Step 1, ten linguistic rules were randomly generated. The generated linguistic rules and their fitness values are shown in Table 5.2. The fitness value of each linguistic rule was calculated by classifying all the 178 samples in the wine data set using the ten linguistic rules in the current population. For explanation purposes, the generated linguistic rules are sorted in descending order of their fitness values in Table 5.2. Since the initial linguistic rules were randomly generated, the fitness values of many linguistic rules are zero in Table 5.2. These linguistic rules did not correctly classify any training patterns. The rule set in Table 5.2 can correctly classify 54 training patterns (i.e., 30.3% of the 178 samples in the wine data set). This number is the sum of the fitness values of all the ten linguistic rules in Table 5.2.

Table 5.2. Ten randomly generated initial linguistic rules for the wine data set with 13 attributes. Each linguistic rule is denoted by a string of length 13

Rule	String													$fitness(R_q)$
R_1	2	#	2	#	#	2	1	2	1	2	2	2	1	42.0
R_2	3	2	3	1	2	2	2	1	1	1	3	3	2	6.0
R_3	#	2	1	2	1	2	1	1	#	#	2	1	1	2.0
R_4	1	3	2	#	1	#	2	2	2	#	1	1	1	2.0
R_5	3	1	3	3	2	3	#	3	#	2	1	#	2	1.0
R_6	1	#	1	3	#	2	#	#	2	#	3	#	#	1.0
R_7	1	#	2	3	3	2	3	2	1	#	3	3	3	0.0
R_8	1	1	#	2	2	1	#	3	3	3	2	3	#	0.0
R_9	2	1	1	3	3	1	1	2	#	3	2	2	#	0.0
R_{10}	2	3	3	2	1	1	#	1	3	1	#	3	#	0.0

In Step 2, two new linguistic rules were generated from the ten linguistic rules in the current population using the selection, crossover, and mutation operations. The generation of new linguistic rules is illustrated in Table 5.3. In Step 3, the two worst linguistic rules were removed from the current population in Table 5.2 and the newly generated linguistic rules were added. The new population is shown in Table 5.4 where the newly generated linguistic rules are inserted into the last two rows. The rule set in Table 5.4 can correctly classify 55 training patterns (i.e., 30.9% of the 178 samples).

Table 5.3. Generating new linguistic rules from the linguistic rules in the current population in Table 5.2

Parent strings	R_4	1	3	2	#	1	#	2	2	2	#	1	1	1
	R_6	1	#	1	3	#	2	#	#	2	#	3	#	#
After crossover		**1**	**#**	**1**	**#**	1	#	#	2	2	#	**3**	**1**	**#**
		1	3	2	3	#	2	2	#	2	#	1	#	1
After mutation		**1**	**#**	**1**	**#**	1	#	#	**3**	2	**2**	**3**	**1**	**#**
		1	3	2	3	#	2	2	#	2	#	1	#	1

Table 5.4. Ten linguistic rules after a single iteration of the Michigan-style fuzzy GBML algorithm. Two newly generated rules are inserted into the last two rows as R_{11} and R_{12}

Rule	String	$fitness(R_q)$
R_1	2 # 2 # # 2 1 2 1 2 2 2 1	40.0
R_2	3 2 3 1 2 2 2 1 1 1 3 3 2	6.0
R_3	# 2 1 2 1 2 1 1 # # 2 1 1	2.0
R_4	1 3 2 # 1 # 2 2 2 # 1 1 1	2.0
R_5	3 1 3 3 2 3 # 3 # 2 1 # 2	1.0
R_6	1 # 1 3 # 2 # # 2 # 3 # #	1.0
R_7	1 # 2 3 3 2 3 2 1 # 3 3 3	0.0
R_8	1 1 # 2 2 1 # 3 3 3 2 3 #	0.0
R_{11}	1 # 1 # 1 # # 3 2 2 3 1 #	0.0
R_{12}	1 3 2 3 # 2 2 # 2 # 1 # 1	3.0

In Fig. 5.3, we show how the classification rate of each population (i.e., each rule set) was improved by the evolution of linguistic rules in the Michigan-style fuzzy GBML algorithm. Figure 5.3 simultaneously shows simulation results of three trials from different initial populations. From this figure, we can see that the classification rate was rapidly improved in the early stage of evolution. We can also see that the classification rate did not increase monotonically (i.e., there were ups and downs). This is because the classification performance of each population was not used for the evolution of linguistic rules by the Michigan-style fuzzy GBML algorithm.

We also performed the same computer simulations as in Fig. 5.3 using five linguistic terms (i.e., *small, medium small, medium, medium large,* and *large*) and *don't care* for each of the 13 attributes of the wine data set. The membership function of the antecedent fuzzy set corresponding to each linguistic term is shown in the bottom-right figure of Fig. 1.4 of Chap. 1. Simulation results are shown in Fig. 5.4. From the comparison between Fig. 5.3 and Fig. 5.4, we can see that the classification rate of each population deteriorated sig-

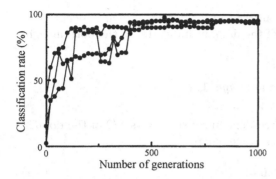

Fig. 5.3. Simulation results of three trials of the Michigan-style fuzzy GBML algorithm on the wine data set using three linguistic terms. The classification rate on training patterns of the current population at each generation is shown for each of the three trials

nificantly by the use of the fine fuzzy partition with the five linguistic terms, especially in the early stage of evolution. This is because the antecedent part of each linguistic rule covers a much smaller portion of the pattern space in Fig. 5.4 than Fig. 5.3. Thus the chance that a randomly generated linguistic rule covers some training patterns is much smaller in Fig. 5.4 than in Fig. 5.3. Actually, the classification rates of initial populations were zero in all trials in Fig. 5.4. This means that no initial linguistic rules correctly classified any training patterns in all trials. Thus all the initial linguistic rules had the same fitness value (i.e., zero fitness). In this case, the genetic search in the Michigan-style fuzzy GBML algorithm was the same as the random search for linguistic rules. When some linguistic rules with positive fitness values were included in the current population, the genetic search tried to find good rules using those linguistic rules as parent strings.

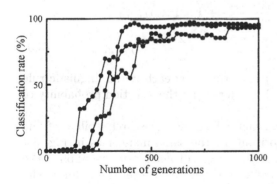

Fig. 5.4. Simulation results of three trials of the Michigan-style fuzzy GBML algorithm on the wine data set using five linguistic terms. The classification rate on training patterns of the current population at each generation is shown for each of the three trials

5.2.5 Extensions to the Michigan-Style Algorithm

As shown in Fig. 5.4, randomly generated initial linguistic rules with fine fuzzy partitions usually do not classify many training patterns in high-dimensional pattern classification problems. This is because each linguistic rule covers a very small portion of the pattern space. When we use the five linguistic terms and *don't care* as antecedent fuzzy sets, each antecedent fuzzy set covers the following portion of the domain interval (see the bottom-right figure of Fig. 1.4 of Chap. 1):

small, large: 1/4,
medium small, medium, medium large: 1/2,
don't care: 1.

Thus a randomly selected antecedent fuzzy set covers 1/2 of the domain interval of each attribute on the average where

$$\left(\frac{1}{4} \times 2 + \frac{1}{2} \times 3 + 1 \times 1\right) \div 6 = \frac{1}{2}. \tag{5.4}$$

As a result, a randomly generated initial linguistic rule for the wine data set with 13 attributes covers $(1/2)^{13} = 1/8192$ of the pattern space. Such a linguistic rule is not likely to cover any of the 178 samples in the wine data set.

A simple trick for expanding the covered area by each initial linguistic rule is to increase the selection probability of *don't care* among the six antecedent fuzzy sets. Let $p_{don't\ care}$ be the selection probability of *don't care* when initial linguistic rules are generated. In this case, the selection probability of each of the other five antecedent fuzzy sets is $(1 - p_{don't\ care})/5$. A randomly selected antecedent fuzzy set with those selection probabilities covers the following portion of the domain interval of each attribute (i.e., (5.4) is modified as follows):

$$\left(\frac{1}{4} \times 2 + \frac{1}{2} \times 3\right) \times \frac{(1 - p_{don't\ care})}{5} + 1 \times 1 \times p_{don't\ care}$$

$$= \frac{2}{5} + \frac{3}{5} \times p_{don't\ care}. \tag{5.5}$$

Thus the portion of the pattern space covered by each initial linguistic rule can be increased from $(1/2)^{13}$ to 1 by increasing the selection probability of *don't care* from 1/6 to 1.

This simple trick has a significant effect on the search ability of the Michigan-style fuzzy GBML algorithm. In the same manner as in Fig. 5.4 except for the selection probability $p_{don't\ care}$ of *don't care*, we applied the Michigan-style fuzzy GBML algorithm to the wine data set three times. The selection probability was specified as $p_{don't\ care} = 3/4$. In this case, the selection probability of each of the other five antecedent fuzzy sets was 1/20. Simulation results are shown in Fig. 5.5. It should be noted that Fig. 5.4 and Fig. 5.5 used the same parameter specifications except for the selection probability $p_{don't\ care}$ of *don't care* for generating initial linguistic rules (i.e., $p_{don't\ care} = 3/4$ in Fig. 5.5 while $p_{don't\ care} = 1/6$ in Fig. 5.4). From the comparison between these two figures, we can see that the classification ability of randomly generated initial linguistic rules was significantly improved.

As a result, the Michigan-style fuzzy GBML algorithm efficiently found good rule sets with high classification rates in the early stage of evolution.

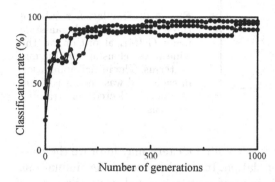

Fig. **5.5.** Simulation results of three trials of the Michigan-style fuzzy GBML algorithm on the wine data set using five linguistic terms. The selection probability of *don't care* for generating initial linguistic rules was increased from 1/6 in Fig. 5.4 to 3/4 in this figure

A more straightforward trick for generating initial linguistic rules with high classification ability is to use training patterns for specifying their antecedent fuzzy sets [00]. To generate an initial population of N_{rule} linguistic rules, first we randomly select N_{rule} training patterns. Next we choose the combination of the most compatible linguistic terms with each training pattern. For example, the combination (*small, medium, large*) is chosen for a three-dimensional training pattern (0.03, 0.52, 0.98). Note that *don't care* is not used in this stage because any attribute values are fully compatible with *don't care* (i.e., because *don't care* is always chosen as the most compatible antecedent fuzzy set for any attribute values). Each linguistic term in the selected combination is replaced with *don't care* using the selection probability $p_{don't\ care}$. The combination of the linguistic terms after this replacement is used as the antecedent part of an initial linguistic rule. This procedure is applied to all the randomly selected N_{rule} training patterns for generating an initial population of N_{rule} linguistic rules.

In the same manner as in Fig. 5.4 and Fig. 5.5 except for the initial populations, we applied the Michigan-style fuzzy GBML algorithm to the wine data set. In each trial, ten training patterns were randomly selected for generating an initial population of ten linguistic rules. The selection probability $p_{don't\ care}$ of *don't care* was specified as $p_{don't\ care} = 1/2$. This means that half of the antecedent fuzzy sets in the initial linguistic rules were replaced with *don't care* on the average. Simulation results are shown in Fig. 5.6. From the comparison of Fig. 5.6 with Fig. 5.4 and Fig. 5.5, we can see that the direct specification of antecedent fuzzy sets from training patterns improved the performance of rule sets in late generations as well as early generations.

The specification of antecedent fuzzy sets from training patterns can be utilized not only for generating an initial population but also for updating the current population. When a training pattern is misclassified or its classification is rejected by the current population, the generation of a new linguistic

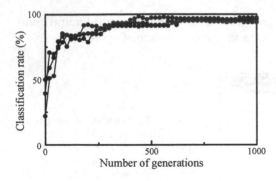

Fig. 5.6. Simulation results of three trials of the Michigan-style fuzzy GBML algorithm on the wine data set using five linguistic terms. The initial population in each trial was generated from randomly selected ten training patterns

rule from the misclassified or rejected training pattern may improve the classification ability of the current population. In the above computer simulations on the wine data set, two linguistic rules were generated using the genetic operations for updating the current population. We modify this generation update procedure as follows. We generate a single linguistic rule using the genetic operations and another linguistic rule from a misclassified or rejected training pattern. When all the training patterns are correctly classified, two linguistic rules are generated using the genetic operations. In the same manner as in Fig. 5.6, we applied the Michigan-style fuzzy GBML algorithm with the modified generation update scheme to the wine data set. Simulation results are shown in Fig. 5.7. From the comparison between Fig. 5.6 and Fig. 5.7, we can see that the modification of the generation update scheme improved the search ability of the Michigan-style fuzzy GBML algorithm to find good linguistic rules in two of the three trials.

One may think that the genetic operations may be unnecessary in the modified generation update scheme. Figure 5.8 shows simulation results where no linguistic rules were generated using the genetic operations. Two linguistic rules were generated for the generation update from misclassified or rejected training patterns. When all the training patterns were correctly classified, the execution of the algorithm was to be terminated in Fig. 5.8. The comparison between Fig. 5.7 and Fig. 5.8 shows the necessity of the genetic operations. While the generation of linguistic rules from misclassified or rejected training patterns is a good idea as shown in Fig. 5.7, the genetic operations are also necessary for designing linguistic rule-based systems with high classification ability. This means that the combination of the most compatible antecedent fuzzy sets with a misclassified or rejected training pattern is not always a good choice for generating a new linguistic rule, though it works very well in many cases.

Another extension to the Michigan-style fuzzy GBML algorithm is the introduction of a penalty term with respect to the number of misclassified training patterns to the fitness function in (5.2) as follows:

$$fitness(R_q) = NCP(R_q) - w_{NMP} \cdot NMP(R_q), \tag{5.6}$$

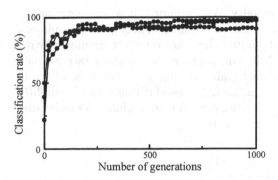

Fig. 5.7. Simulation results of three trials of the Michigan-style fuzzy GBML algorithm on the wine data set using five linguistic terms. The initial population in each trial was generated from ten randomly selected training patterns. For the generation update, a single linguistic rule was generated from a misclassified or rejected training pattern, and another linguistic rule was generated by the genetic operations

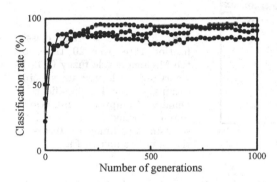

Fig. 5.8. Simulation results of three trials of the Michigan-style fuzzy GBML algorithm on the wine data set using five linguistic terms. The initial population in each trial was generated from randomly selected ten training patterns. For the generation update, two linguistic rules were generated from misclassified or rejected training patterns, and no linguistic rule was generated by the genetic operations

where $NMP(R_q)$ is the number of misclassified training patterns and w_{NMP} is a positive constant. The fitness function in (5.2) can be viewed as a special case of (5.6) with $w_{NMP} = 0$. In (5.6), $NCP(R_q)$ and $NMP(R_q)$ are calculated by classifying all the training patterns by the current population S including the linguistic rule R_q. To understand the effect of the second term of (5.6) on the evolution of linguistic rules, let us consider a linguistic rule that correctly classifies ten patterns and misclassifies three patterns. If the misclassification penalty is zero (i.e., if $w_{NMP} = 0$), the fitness value of this linguistic rule is 10. Thus this linguistic rule is not likely to be removed from the current population. As a result, the three misclassified patterns will also be misclassified in the next population. On the other hand, the fitness value of this linguistic rule is negative (i.e., -5) when $w_{NMP} = 5$. In this case, this linguistic rule will be removed from the current population. As a result, the three misclassified patterns may be correctly classified by other linguistic rules or their classification may be rejected in the next population. From this discussion, we can see that the introduction of the misclassification penalty to the fitness function may improve the search ability of the Michigan-style fuzzy GBML algorithm to find rule sets with high classification ability.

In the same manner as the computer simulation for Fig. 5.7, we performed computer simulations using the Michigan-style fuzzy GBML algorithm with the misclassification penalty. We examined three specifications of w_{NMP}: $w_{NMP} = 0, 3, 10$. For each value of w_{NMP}, the computer simulation was iterated 20 times. It should be noted that the computer simulation with $w_{NMP} = 0$ is the same as Fig. 5.7. The average classification rate at each generation over the 20 trials for each value of w_{NMP} is shown in Fig. 5.9. From this figure, we can see that the average classification rate was slightly improved by increasing the value of w_{NMP} from 0 to 3 while it deteriorated on further increasing the value from 3 to 10.

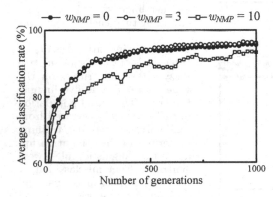

Fig. 5.9. The average classification rate over 20 trials of the Michigan-style fuzzy GBML algorithm with various specifications of the misclassification penalty. Computer simulations were performed on the wine data set using five linguistic terms in the same manner as Fig. 5.7

The effect of the misclassification penalty on the evolution of linguistic rules is more significant when we use coarse fuzzy partitions. In this case, each linguistic rule covers a larger portion of the pattern space than the case of fine fuzzy partitions. As a result, more patterns are correctly and wrongly classified by each linguistic rule. Figure 5.10 shows the simulation results when we used the three linguistic terms for each attribute instead of the five linguistic terms. Computer simulations were performed in the same manner as in Fig. 5.9 except for the fuzzy partition of each attribute. We can observe in Fig.5.10 a large deterioration in the average classification rate when the misclassification penalty w_{NMP} was large (i.e., $w_{NMP} = 10$).

5.3 Pittsburgh-Style Algorithm

It is possible to use the Pittsburgh approach to design linguistic rule-based classification systems with high classification ability and high interpretability. In this section, we explain a Pittsburgh-style fuzzy GBML algorithm. Its characteristic features are explained in comparison with the Michigan-style fuzzy GBML algorithm in the previous section. While the above-mentioned extensions to the Michigan-style algorithm can also be utilized in our Pittsburgh-style algorithm, we describe its simplest version with no extensions in this section to maintain the simplicity of explanation.

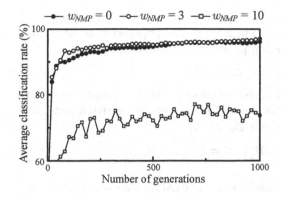

Fig. 5.10. The average classification rate over 20 trials of the Michigan-style fuzzy GBML algorithm with various specifications of the misclassification penalty. Computer simulations were performed on the wine data set using three linguistic terms

5.3.1 Coding of Rule Sets

As in the Michigan-style fuzzy GBML algorithm in the previous section, let N_{rule} be the number of linguistic rules in a rule set S. In our Pittsburgh-style fuzzy GBML algorithm in this section, the rule set S is represented by a concatenated string where each substring of length n denotes a single linguistic rule for our n-dimensional pattern classification problem. The coding of each linguistic rule using its antecedent fuzzy sets is the same as the coding in the Michigan-style algorithm. The length of the string S including N_{rule} linguistic rules is $n \cdot N_{\text{rule}}$. For simplicity of explanation, we assume that all the n attributes of our n-dimensional pattern classification problem have the three linguistic terms *small*, *medium*, and *large*. We also use *don't care* as an additional antecedent fuzzy set. These antecedent fuzzy sets are denoted in the same manner as in the Michigan-style algorithm (i.e., 1: *small*, 2: *medium*, 3: *large*, and #: *don't care*). For example, a rule set of the following four linguistic rules for a five-dimensional pattern classification problem is represented by a string "#1#2# 22### ####1 3###3" of length 20:

Rule R_1: If x_2 is *small* and x_4 is *medium* then Class C_1 with CF_1,
Rule R_2: If x_1 is *medium* and x_2 is *medium* then Class C_2 with CF_2,
Rule R_3: If x_5 is *small* then Class C_3 with CF_3,
Rule R_4: If x_1 is *large* and x_5 is *large* then Class C_4 with CF_4.

As in the Michigan-style algorithm, the consequent class C_q and the rule weight CF_q of each linguistic rule are not included in the string. They are specified by the heuristic rule generation procedure in Chap. 2.

5.3.2 Genetic Operations

In our Pittsburgh-style fuzzy GBML algorithm, first a pre-specified number of rule sets (say, N_{pop} rule sets) with N_{rule} linguistic rules are generated by randomly specifying their antecedent fuzzy sets. An initial population is composed of the generated N_{pop} rule sets where N_{pop} is the population size.

Next each rule set is evaluated by classifying the given training patterns. The fitness value of each rule set S_i in the current population is calculated as follows after all the given training patterns are classified by S_i:

$$fitness(S_i) = NCP(S_i), \quad i = 1, 2, \dots, N_{\text{pop}}, \tag{5.7}$$

where $NCP(S_i)$ is the number of correctly classified training patterns by the rule set S_i. This fitness function of the rule set S_i can be rewritten using the fitness function of each linguistic rule R_q in S_i:

$$fitness(S_i) = \sum_{R_q \in S_i} fitness(R_q), \quad i = 1, 2, \dots, N_{\text{pop}}. \tag{5.8}$$

Next new rule sets are generated from the existing rule sets in the current population by genetic operations. As parent strings, two rule sets are selected from the current population using binary tournament selection with replacement. From the two selected strings, two new strings are generated by the uniform crossover operation with a pre-specified crossover probability. The uniform crossover operation in the Pittsburgh-style algorithm exchanges substrings between the two parent strings. This crossover operation is illustrated in Fig. 5.11 for rule sets with four linguistic rules for a five-dimensional pattern classification problem. Then each symbol of the new strings generated by the crossover operation is randomly replaced with a different symbol using a pre-specified mutation probability as in the Michigan-style algorithm. The selection, crossover, and mutation are iterated until $(N_{\text{pop}} - 1)$ rule sets are generated. Finally the best rule set in the current population is added to the newly generated rule sets as an elite rule set to form a new population including N_{pop} rule sets.

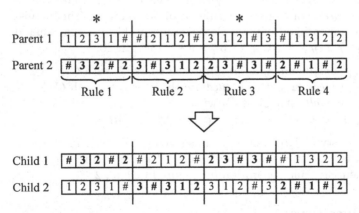

Fig. 5.11. Illustration of the uniform crossover operation in the Pittsburgh approach

The generation update is iterated until a pre-specified stopping condition is satisfied. As in the Michigan-style algorithm in the previous section and the genetic algorithm for rule selection in Chap. 4, we use the total number of iterations as the stopping condition.

5.3.3 Algorithm

Our Pittsburgh-style fuzzy GBML algorithm can be written as follows:

[Pittsburgh-Style Fuzzy GBML Algorithm]

Step 0: *Parameter Specification.* Specify the population size N_{pop}, the number of linguistic rules N_{rule}, the crossover probability p_c, the mutation probability p_m, and the stopping condition.

Step 1: *Initialization.* Randomly generate N_{pop} rule sets with N_{rule} linguistic rules (i.e., N_{pop} strings of length $n \cdot N_{\text{rule}}$) as an initial population.

Step 2: *Genetic Operations.* Calculate the fitness value of each rule set in the current population. Generate $(N_{\text{pop}} - 1)$ rule sets using selection, crossover, and mutation from existing rule sets in the current population.

Step 3: *Generation Update (Elitist Strategy).* Add the best rule set in the current population to the newly generated $(N_{\text{pop}} - 1)$ rule sets to form the next population of the population size N_{pop}.

Step 4: *Termination Test.* If the stopping condition is not satisfied, return to Step 2. Otherwise terminate the execution of the algorithm. The final solution is the best rule set in the final population because the best rule set in the current population is always handed down to the next population by the elitist strategy.

5.3.4 Computer Simulations

To compare the two fuzzy GBML algorithms with each other, we performed computer simulations on the wine data set using the Pittsburgh-style fuzzy GBML algorithm in the same manner as the computer simulations in Sect. 5.2.4 using the Michigan-style fuzzy GBML algorithm with no extensions. Parameter specifications in these two algorithms are summarized in Table 5.5. As the parameter values in Table 5.5 show, our task is to design a classification system with ten linguistic rules. From Table 5.5, we can see that only 1000 rule sets were examined in a single trial of the Michigan-style algorithm while 50000 rule sets were examined in the Pittsburgh-style algorithm.

The average classification rate and the average CPU time of each algorithm over five trials are summarized in Table 5.6 for the case of the three linguistic terms and Table 5.7 for the case of the five linguistic terms. Each algorithm was implemented in the C language and executed on a personal computer with a 1.5 GHz Pentium IV processor. From these tables, we can see that slightly better rule sets were obtained by the Pittsburgh-style algorithm than the Michigan-style algorithm in the case of the three linguistic

Table 5.5. Parameter values in each algorithm

	Michigan	Pittsburgh
Number of linguistic rules	10	10
Number of rule sets	1	50
Crossover probability	0.8	0.8
Mutation probability	1/13	1/13
Number of replaced rules	2	N.A.
Stopping condition (generations)	1000	1000

terms. On the other hand, the performance of the Michigan-style algorithm is clearly better than the Pittsburth-style algorithm in the case of the five linguistic terms. This is because the difference in the search ability between different algorithms is likely to become clear when the search space is large. In both tables, CPU time for the Michigan-style algorithm is much less than the Pittsburgh-style algorithm.

Table 5.6. Average classification rate and average CPU time of each algorithm in the case of the three linguistic terms

	Michigan	Pittsburgh
Classification rate	97.1%	97.3%
CPU time (s)	1.6	303.5

Table 5.7. Average classification rate and average CPU time of each algorithm in the case of the five linguistic terms

	Michigan	Pittsburgh
Classification rate	96.0%	75.4%
CPU time (s)	1.5	236.6

One may think that the rule exchange-type uniform crossover operation in Fig. 5.11 had a bad effect on the search ability of the Pittsburgh-style algorithm. We also performed the same computer simulations using the standard (i.e., gene exchange-type) uniform crossover operation shown in Fig. 5.12. Simulation results are summarized in Table 5.8. From the comparison of Table 5.8 with Table 5.6 and Table 5.7, we can see that the average classification rate by the Pittsburgh-style algorithm for the case of the five linguistic terms was much lower than that by the Michigan-style algorithm independent of the choice of crossover operation. In the following computer simulations, we use the rule exchange-type uniform crossover operation in Fig. 5.11 in the Pittsburgh-style algorithm.

Table 5.8. Average classification rates by the two versions of the Pittsburgh-style algorithm with different crossover operations

Number of linguistic terms	Crossover operation	
	Rule exchange	Gene exchange
Three	97.3%	94.5%
Five	75.4%	62.2%

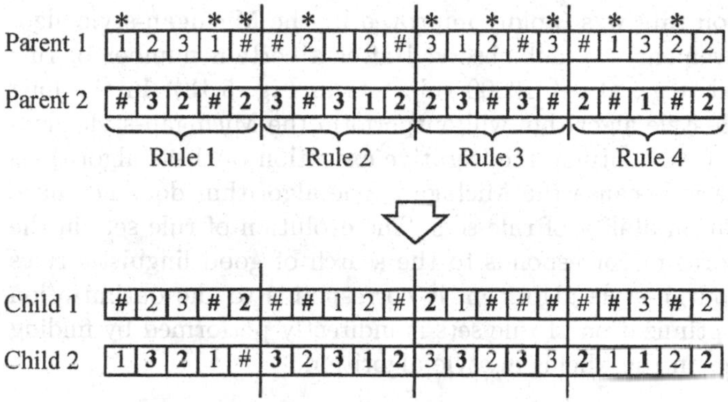

```
           *     * *|    *       |*     *     *|   *     *
Parent 1  [1|2|3|1|#|#|2|1|2|#|3|1|2|#|3|#|1|3|2|2]

Parent 2  [#|3|2|#|2|3|#|3|1|2|2|3|#|3|#|2|#|1|#|2]

          _____/_____/_____/_____/
             Rule 1        Rule 2       Rule 3       Rule 4
```

```
Child 1   [#|2|3|#|2|#|#|1|2|#|2|1|#|#|#|#|#|3|#|2]
Child 2   [1|3|2|1|#|3|2|3|1|2|3|3|2|3|3|2|1|1|2|2]
```

Fig. 5.12. Standard uniform crossover where genes at randomly selected positions are exchanged between two parents

5.4 Hybridization of the Two Approaches

In this section, first we explain the advantages of each of the two fuzzy GBML algorithms through computer simulations. Then we combine the two algorithms into a single hybrid algorithm. Finally we extend the hybrid algorithm to simultaneously perform the maximization of the classification accuracy and the minimization of the number of linguistic rules as in the genetic algorithm for rule selection in Chap. 4.

5.4.1 Advantages of Each Algorithm

To further compare the Pittsburgh-style algorithm with the Michigan-style algorithm, we examined the performance of these two algorithms through computer simulations on the wine data set using various stopping conditions. The simplest version of each algorithm with no extensions was used in the computer simulations of this subsection as in the previous computer simulations in Sect. 5.3.4 for comparing the two algorithms. Simulation results are summarized in Fig. 5.13 for the case of the five linguistic terms and Fig. 5.14 for the case of the three linguistic terms. It should be noted that the horizontal axis of these figures is the number of examined rule sets, which is the same as the number of generations in the case of the Michigan-style algorithm. Each figure shows the average classification rate over five trials of each algorithm.

The average classification rate at each generation was calculated using the best rule set obtained until that generation in each trial. The best rule set is not always the current population in the Michigan-style algorithm while it is always the elite rule set in the current population in the Pittsburgh-style algorithm. From these figures, we can see that the Michigan-style algorithm has a much higher search ability to efficiently find good linguistic rules in the early stage of evolution than the Pittsburgh-style algorithm. That is, the average classification rate was rapidly improved by the Michigan-style algorithm. This improvement was not observed after a certain number of rule sets were examined (e.g., about 10000 rule sets in Fig. 5.13). In the long run, the Pittsburgh-style algorithm will outperform the Michigan-style algorithm in Fig. 5.13 if we continue the iterative execution of these algorithms much further. This is because the Michigan-style algorithm does not have the direct optimization ability of rule sets. The evolution of rule sets in the Michigan-style algorithm corresponds to the search of good linguistic rules while in the Pittsburgh-style algorithm it corresponds to the optimization of rule sets. This optimization of rule sets is indirectly performed by finding good linguistic rules in the Michigan-style algorithm.

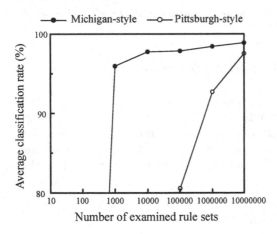

Fig. 5.13. Average simulation results on the wine data set with the five linguistic terms over five trials of each algorithm with various stopping conditions

In order to examine why the Michigan-style algorithm has a high search ability to efficiently find good linguistic rules, we performed computer simulations using partially modified variants of the algorithm. We examined the following three variants of the Michigan-style algorithm.

Entire replacement. In this variant, all linguistic rules in the current population are entirely replaced with newly generated linguistic rules. The entire replacement variant is implemented from our original Michigan-style algorithm by setting the number of replaced rules (i.e., $N_{replace}$) equal to the number of linguistic rules in the current population. In computer simulations, we specified $N_{replace}$ as $N_{replace} = 10$ (see Table 5.5).

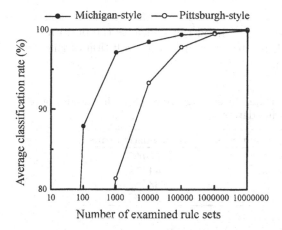

Fig. 5.14. Average simulation results on the wine data set with the three linguistic terms over five trials of each algorithm with various stopping conditions

Random removal. In this variant, randomly selected rules are removed from the current population and replaced with newly generated ones in the generation update procedure. While the worst N_{replace} rules are removed from the current population in our original Michigan-style algorithm, the selection of linguistic rules to be removed in the random removal variant is randomly performed regardless of the fitness value of each rule. In computer simulations, we specified the number of replaced rules as $N_{\text{replace}} = 2$ as in our original algorithm (see Table 5.5).

Random selection. In this variant, parent strings are randomly selected from the current population regardless of their fitness values. That is, the selection probability of each linguistic rule is defined in the random selection variant as $P(R_q) = 1/N_{\text{rule}}$ where N_{rule} is the number of linguistic rules in the current population.

We applied these three variants to the wine data set. Average simulation results over five trials of each variant are summarized in Table 5.9. In this table, the performance of the random selection variant was the worst among the four algorithms. From this poor performance of the random selection variant, we can see that the rule generation from good linguistic rules is an important characteristic feature of the Michigan-style algorithm. On the other hand, the difference in the performance between the original algorithm and the other two variants (i.e., entire replacement and random removal) suggests that the inheritance of good linguistic rules from the current population to the next population is also an important characteristic feature of the Michigan-style algorithm. It should be noted that the Pittsburgh-style algorithm has none of these two characteristic features (i.e., the rule generation from good rules and the inheritance of good rules). In the Pittsburgh-style algorithm, the best rule set is handed down from the current population to the next population as an elite rule set. If good linguistic rules are included in a poor rule set, they are not likely to survive the generation update because poor rule sets do not have high selection probabilities. In the Pittsburgh-style algorithm, new rule sets are generated from good rule sets. This does not mean that new rules are generated from good rules because the performance of each linguistic rule is not taken into account in the evolution of rule sets in the Pittsburgh-style algorithm.

Table 5.9. Average classification rate over five trials of each variant of the Michigan-style algorithm on the wine data set

	Three linguistic terms	Five linguistic terms
Original algorithm	97.1%	96.0%
Entire replacement	89.9%	44.7%
Random removal	89.7%	33.7%
Random selection	60.7%	6.5%

From the simulation results in this subsection, we can see that the Michigan-style algorithm has a high search ability to efficiently find good linguistic rules in the early stage of evolution. The performance of the Michigan-style algorithm deteriorated when we removed the following two characteristic features:

(1) To generate new rules from good rules in the current population.
(2) To pass down good rules from the current population to the next population.

The Pittsburgh-style algorithm has none of these two characteristic features. The search ability of the Pittsburgh-style algorithm to find good linguistic rules in the large search space is inferior to that of the Michigan-style algorithm. The advantage of the Pittsburgh-style algorithm is

(3) To directly optimize rule sets.

The Michigan-style algorithm cannot directly optimize rule sets because the evolution of rule sets is driven only by the performance of each linguistic rule.

5.4.2 Hybrid Algorithm

The aim of the hybridization of the two algorithms is to implement a single hybrid algorithm that has all the above three advantages. Our hybrid algorithm can directly optimize rule sets because its basic framework is the same as the Pittsburgh-style algorithm. The Michigan-style algorithm is used as a mutation operation for partially modifying each string (i.e., each rule set). Our hybrid algorithm can be written as follows:

[Hybrid Fuzzy GBML Algorithm]

Step 0: *Parameter Specification.* Specify the population size N_{pop}, the number of linguistic rules N_{rule}, the number of replaced rules $N_{replace}$, the crossover probability p_{c_P} in the Pittsburgh part, the crossover probability p_{c_M} in the Michigan part, the mutation probability p_{m_P} in the Pittsburgh part, the mutation probability p_{m_M} in the Michigan part, and the stopping condition.

Step 1: *Initialization.* Randomly generate N_{pop} rule sets with N_{rule} linguistic rules (i.e., N_{pop} strings of length $n \cdot N_{\text{rule}}$) as an initial population.

Step 2: *Genetic Operations.* Calculate the fitness value of each rule set in the current population. Generate $(N_{\text{pop}} - 1)$ rule sets using selection, crossover, and mutation from existing rule sets in the current population. The selection and crossover operations are the same as those in the Pittsburgh-style algorithm. The single iteration of the Michigan-style algorithm (i.e., the rule generation and the replacement) is applied as a mutation operation to each of the generated rule sets by the selection and crossover operations in the Pittsburgh part. The mutation probability p_{m_P} is used for the application of the Michigan-style algorithm as a mutation operation. That is, p_{m_P} is the application probability of the Michigan-style algorithm to each rule set.

Step 3: *Generation Update (Elitist Strategy).* Add the best rule set in the current population to the newly generated $(N_{\text{pop}} - 1)$ rule sets to form the next population of the population size N_{pop}.

Step 4: *Termination Test.* If the stopping condition is not satisfied, return to Step 2. Otherwise terminate the execution of the algorithm. The final solution is the best rule set in the final population because the best rule set in the current population is always handed down to the next population by the elitist strategy.

5.4.3 Computer Simulations

We applied our hybrid algorithm to the wine data set in the same manner as in the previous computer simulations using the following parameter values:

Number of linguistic rules: $N_{\text{rule}} = 10$,
Number of rule sets: $N_{\text{pop}} = 50$,
Crossover probabilities: $p_{c_P} = 0.8$ in the Pittsburgh part,
    $p_{c_M} = 0.8$ in the Michigan part,
Mutation probabilities: $p_{m_P} = 0.8$ in the Pittsburgh part,
    $p_{m_M} = 1/13$ in the Michigan part,
Stopping condition: 1000 iterations (i.e., 1000 generations),
Number of replaced linguistic rules in the Michigan part:
    $N_{\text{replace}} = 2$.

It should be noted that the mutation probability of 0.8 in the Pittsburgh part is defined for each string (i.e., for each rule set) while the mutation probability of $1/13$ in the Michigan part is defined for each gene (i.e., for each antecedent fuzzy set).

Average simulation results over five trials of the hybrid algorithm are summarized in Table 5.10 and Table 5.11 where we also cite the corresponding simulation results by the original Michigan-style and Pittsburgh-style algorithms with no modifications. Table 5.10 and Table 5.11 show the average classification rate and the average CPU time of each algorithm, respectively. We can see from Table 5.10 that the hybrid algorithm outperformed the two fuzzy GBML algorithms. This observation suggests that we can successfully implement the advantages of the two algorithms in a single hybrid algorithm. The average CPU time of the hybrid algorithm is of the same order as that of the Pittsburgh-style algorithm. This is because the basic framework of the hybrid algorithm is the Pittsburgh-style algorithm.

Table 5.10. Average classification rate over five trials of each algorithm

	Three linguistic terms	Five linguistic terms
Michigan	97.1%	96.0%
Pittsburgh	97.3%	75.4%
Hybrid algorithm	100.0%	100.0%

Table 5.11. Average CPU time over five trials of each algorithm (seconds)

	Three linguistic terms	Five linguistic terms
Michigan	1.6	1.5
Pittsburgh	304	237
Hybrid algorithm	345	246

5.4.4 Minimization of the Number of Linguistic Rules

We have already examined the three fuzzy GBML algorithms: the Michigan-style algorithm, the Pittsburgh-style algorithm, and their hybrid algorithm. In these algorithms, the number of linguistic rules in each rule set was always constant. That is, the population size in the Michigan-style algorithm and the string length of the other algorithms were fixed. In this subsection, we extend the hybrid algorithm to the case of variable string length to simultaneously perform the minimization of the number of linguistic rules and the maximization of the classification ability of rule sets.

The extended hybrid algorithm is the same as the hybrid algorithm in the previous section except for its crossover operation and fitness function. The main difference is that the string length (i.e., the number of linguistic rules) is not fixed in the extended hybrid algorithm. The number of linguistic rules is changed when new rule sets are generated from parent rule sets by a crossover operation. We use a one-point crossover operation with different crossover points in Fig. 5.15. To decrease the effect of the order of linguistic rules in each string on the genetic search in the extended hybrid algorithm (i.e., to mix up linguistic rules), linguistic rules on one side of one parent are combined with those on the same side of the other parent to form a new string as shown in Fig. 5.15. Since the crossover point in one parent is not always the same as that in the other parent, the string length of new strings is not always the same as that of their parent strings.

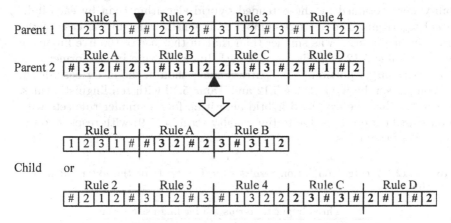

Fig. 5.15. One-point crossover operation with different crossover points. This crossover operation is used in the extended hybrid algorithm to simultaneously perform the minimization of the number of linguistic rules and the maximization of the classification ability of linguistic rules

In the extended hybrid algorithm, we use the following fitness function to evaluate each rule set S:

$$fitness(S) = NCP(S) - w_{|S|} \cdot |S|. \tag{5.9}$$

This fitness function was also used in the genetic algorithm for rule selection in Chap. 4. This means that the task of the extended hybrid algorithm is the same as that of the genetic algorithm-based rule selection method: to find a small number of linguistic rules with a high classification ability.

We applied the extended hybrid algorithm with $w_{|S|} = 1$ to the wine data set. We used the same parameter specifications as in the previous computer simulations with the hybrid algorithm in terms of the number of rule sets (i.e., population size), the crossover probabilities, the mutation probabilities, and the stopping condition. The number of linguistic rules was specified as 10 in initial rule sets, which was changed by the crossover operation during the iterative execution of the extended hybrid algorithm. The number of replaced linguistic rules in the Michigan part was not specified as a constant value. In the Michigan part, 20% of linguistic rules in each rule set were replaced (i.e., $N_{\text{replace}} = \lceil 0.2 \times |S| \rceil$ where $\lceil x \rceil$ denotes the minimum integer that is larger than or equal to x). This is because the number of linguistic rules in each rule set was not constant.

Average simulation results over five trials of the extended hybrid algorithm are shown in Table 5.12. To compare the extended hybrid algorithm with the other three fuzzy GBML algorithms in Table 5.10 and Table 5.11, we did not use any extensions or modifications described in the previous sections. From the comparison of Table 5.12 with Table 5.10 and Table 5.11, we can see that a smaller number of linguistic rules with a high classification ability were obtained by the extended hybrid algorithm than by each individual algorithm. The average number of linguistic rules in the case of the three linguistic terms was smaller than that in the case of the five linguistic terms in Table 5.12. This is because each linguistic rule in the former case can cover a larger portion of the pattern space than in the latter case. From the comparison between Table 5.12 and Table 5.10 with ten linguistic rules, we can see that the extended hybrid algorithm found smaller rule sets with lower classification rates due to the penalty term in (5.9) with respect to the number of fuzzy rules.

Table 5.12. Average simulation results over five trials of the extended hybrid algorithm

	Three linguistic terms	Five linguistic terms
Classification rate	97.5%	97.3%
CPU time (s)	688	688
Number of rules	5.2	7.2

The extended hybrid algorithm uses the same fitness function but a different coding scheme as the genetic algorithm for rule selection in Chap. 4. To compare these two algorithms, we applied the extended hybrid algorithm to the wine data set using the 14 antecedent fuzzy sets in Fig. 1.4 of Chap. 1 and *don't care* as in the computer simulations with the genetic algorithm for rule selection in Chap. 4. While the genetic algorithm-based rule selection method used a prescreening procedure for decreasing the number of candidate rules, the extended hybrid algorithm does not use any trick for decreasing the search space. That is, it tries to maximize the fitness function in the search space with $(14 + 1)^{13}$ combinations of antecedent fuzzy sets for the 13-dimensional wine data set. In computer simulations, we used the following two extensions described for the Michigan-style algorithm:

(1) Specification of antecedent fuzzy sets of initial linguistic rules from training patterns.
(2) Generation of new linguistic rules from misclassified or rejected training patterns.

As in the computer simulations on the wine data set using the genetic algorithm for rule selection in Chap. 4 (i.e., Table 4.17), four values of $w_{|S|}$

were used: $w_{|S|} = 0.1, 0.5, 1, 5$. The average simulation results over five trials of the extended hybrid algorithm are shown in Table 5.13 where the simulation results in Table 4.17 by the genetic algorithm-based rule selection method are also cited. The CPU time for the genetic algorithm-based rule selection method is for both the candidate rule prescreening and the execution of the genetic algorithm. From Table 5.13, we can see that better results were obtained by the genetic algorithm-based rule selection. This may be because the search space of the extended hybrid algorithm is much larger.

Table 5.13. Comparison between the genetic algorithm-based rule selection method and the extended hybrid algorithm of the two fuzzy GBML algorithms

	Value of $w_{|S|}$	0.1	0.5	1	5
	Classification rate	100%	99.6%	97.3%	90.8%
GBML algorithm	Number of rules	18.8	10.2	7.0	3.2
	CPU time (s)	2032	750	498	261
	Classification rate	100%	100%	99.9%	98.7%
Rule selection	Number of rules	5.6	5.1	3.2	3.0
	CPU time (s)	103	180	193	102

We can use the extended hybrid algorithm and the genetic algorithm-based rule selection method for the same task: to find a small number of linguistic rules with a high classification ability. As shown in Table 5.13, somewhat better results were obtained from rule selection. The question is which method should be used for a particular pattern classification problem. There is no general answer to this question. The main difference between these two approaches is that the prescreening procedure of candidate rules is used for decreasing the search space in the genetic algorithm-based rule selection method while the entire search space is handled in the extended hybrid algorithm. Thus the performance of the genetic algorithm-based rule selection method strongly depends on the prescreening procedure. If good linguistic rules are not included in candidate rules, the genetic algorithm for rule selection cannot find good rule sets. On the other hand, the extended hybrid algorithm does not use any prescreening procedure. Thus the search space is not heuristically reduced. While good rule sets were obtained by the extended hybrid algorithm in Table 5.13 for the wine data set, there may be many cases where the extended hybrid algorithm cannot find good rule sets because the search space is too large. In those cases, the genetic algorithm-based rule selection may find good rule sets if the prescreening procedure works well.

6. Multi-Objective Design of Linguistic Models

The extended hybrid fuzzy GBML algorithm in the previous chapter was designed to find a small number of linguistic rules with a high classification ability. The genetic algorithm-based rule selection method in Chap. 4 also tackled the same task. These two algorithms used the same fitness function to simultaneously perform the maximization of classification ability and the minimization of the number of linguistic rules. The minimization of the number of linguistic rules is used to design linguistic rule-based systems with high interpretability. There is a tradeoff between the accuracy and the interpretability of linguistic rule-based systems [18, 19]. istic rule-based systems with both high accuracy and high interpretability. This tradeoff is illustrated in Fig. 6.1. The error on training patterns is monotonically decreased by increasing the complexity of linguistic rule-based systems. On the other hand, the error on test patterns is first decreased and then increased after reaching the minimum error at S^*. Thus the rule set S^* is optimal with respect to the accuracy of linguistic rule-based systems. The accuracy of linguistic rule-based systems deteriorates on decreasing the complexity (i.e., improving the interpretability) from S^*. In some cases, human users may prefer simpler rule-based systems with higher interpretability than S^* even if the classification accuracy deteriorates. That is, the rule set S^* with the highest generalization ability is not always preferred when the interpretability of linguistic rule-based systems is taken into account in addition to the classification accuracy. Recently, several approaches have been proposed for designing fuzzy rule-based systems with high interpretability as well as high accuracy [18, 19, 101, 145, 150, 151]. In this chapter, we discuss the design of linguistic rule-based systems for pattern classification problems in the framework of multi-objective optimization to handle the tradeoff between accuracy and interpretability. Our task in this chapter is not to find a single optimal rule set (e.g., S^* in Fig. 6.1) but to find multiple non-dominated rule sets with respect to the two criteria of accuracy and interpretability.

6.1 Formulation of Three-Objective Problem

While only the number of linguistic rules was considerd in the genetic algorithm-based rule selection method in Chap. 4 and the extended hybrid

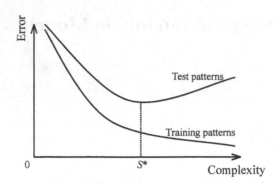

Fig. 6.1. Relation between the error and the complexity of linguistic rule-based systems

fuzzy GBML algorithm in Chap. 5, there are a number of issues that are related to the interpretability of linguistic rule-based systems. For example:

(1) Comprehensibility of fuzzy partitions (e.g., interpretability of each antecedent fuzzy set, separation of neighboring antecedent fuzzy sets, the number of antecedent fuzzy sets for each attribute).
(2) Simplicity of linguistic rule-based systems (e.g., the number of attributes, the number of linguistic rules).
(3) Simplicity of linguistic rules (e.g., type of linguistic rules, the number of antecedent conditions in each linguistic rule).
(4) Simplicity of a classification method (e.g., selection of a single winner rule, voting by multiple rules).

As in the previous chapters, we use the single winner-based method in classification systems with linguistic rules of the following form:

Rule R_q: If x_1 is A_{q1} and ... and x_n is A_{qn}

$$\text{then Class } C_q \text{ with } CF_q. \quad (6.1)$$

It is assumed that linguistic terms are given for each attribute. Thus we do not discuss the first issue: comprehensibility of fuzzy partitions. We do not discuss the last issue, either (i.e., we always use the single winner-based method in this chapter). We measure the simplicity of linguistic rule-based systems by the number of linguistic rules as in Chaps. 4 and 5. That is, the number of linguistic rules is taken into account with respect to the second issue: simplicity of linguistic rule-based systems. Moreover, the number of antecedent conditions of each linguistic rule (i.e., rule length) is taken into account with respect to the third issue: simplicity of linguistic rules.

Ishibuchi et al. [71] formulated the design of linguistic rule-based classification systems as the following three-objective optimization problem:

$$\text{Maximize } f_1(S), \text{ minimize } f_2(S), \text{ and minimize } f_3(S), \quad (6.2)$$

where $f_1(S)$ is the number of correctly classified training patterns by a rule set S (i.e., $NCP(S)$), $f_2(S)$ is the number of linguistic rules in S (i.e., $|S|$), and $f_3(S)$ is the total rule length of linguistic rules in S. Usually there is no optimal rule set with respect to all the above three objectives due to the existence of the above-mentioned tradeoff between accuracy and interpretability. Thus our task is to find multiple rule sets that are not dominated by any other rule sets. A rule set S_B is said to dominate another rule set S_A (i.e., S_B is better than S_A: $S_A \prec S_B$) if all the following inequalities hold:

$$f_1(S_A) \le f_1(S_B), \quad f_2(S_A) \ge f_2(S_B), \quad f_3(S_A) \ge f_3(S_B), \tag{6.3}$$

and at least one of the following inequalities holds:

$$f_1(S_A) < f_1(S_B), \quad f_2(S_A) > f_2(S_B), \quad f_3(S_A) > f_3(S_B). \tag{6.4}$$

The first condition (i.e., all the three inequalities in (6.3)) means that no objective of S_B is worse than S_A (i.e., S_B is not worse than S_A). The second condition (i.e., one of the three inequalities in (6.4)) means that at least one objective of S_B is better than S_A. When a rule set S is not dominated by any other rule sets, S is said to be a Pareto-optimal solution of the three-objective optimization problem in (6.2).

It should be noted that the third objective $f_0(S)$ is not the average rule length but the total rule length. Let us consider another three-objective optimization problem with $f_1(S)$, $f_2(S)$, and $f_{3*}(S)$ where $f_{3*}(S)$ is the average rule length of linguistic rules in S. This three-objective optimization problem is the same as the original formulation in (6.2) except for the third objective. Let us consider a rule set S where the average rule length is larger than 1: $f_{3*}(S) > 1$ (e.g., the rule set with the three linguistic rules in Fig. 4.21 of Chap. 4). We add another linguistic rule of length 1 to this rule set to construct an enlarged rule set S^+. Since $f_{3*}(S) > 1$ and the length of the added linguistic rule is 1, the following relation always holds with respect to the average rule length between S and S^+:

$$f_{3*}(S^+) < f_{3*}(S), \tag{6.5}$$

while the following relation holds with respect to the total rule length:

$$f_3(S^+) > f_3(S). \tag{6.6}$$

This means that the average rule length $f_{3*}(S)$ is improved by adding another linguistic rule of length 1 to the rule set S while the complexity of the rule set S is increased. Even if the added linguistic rule does not improve the classification accuracy of the rule set S (i.e., $f_1(S) \ge f_1(S^+)$), S^+ is not dominated by S when we use the average rule length $f_{3*}(S)$ as the third objective instead of the total rule length $f_3(S)$. This discussion shows that the average rule length is not an appropriate criterion for measuring the simplicity of linguistic rules in the context of multi-objective optimization. Thus we use the total rule length as the third objective $f_3(S)$ in (6.2).

6.2 Multi-Objective Genetic Algorithms

To find non-dominated rule sets of the three-objective optimization problem in (6.2), we use a three-objective genetic algorithm. In this section, we explain its basic framework, which can be used to extend both the genetic algorithm-based rule selection method and the extended hybrid fuzzy GBML algorithm. Recently many evolutionary multi-objective optimization (EMO) algorithms have been proposed [21, 28, 193, 194]. Those EMO algorithms can be applied to the three-objective optimization problem in (6.2). In this section, we explain a slightly modified version of a multi-objective genetic algorithm (MOGA) in [71] because it is easily implemented by simply modifying standard single-objective genetic algorithms. This MOGA has two characteristic features. One is to use a scalar fitness function with random weights to evaluate each solution (i.e., each rule set). Random weights are updated whenever a pair of parent solutions is selected for crossover. That is, the selection of each pair of parent solutions is governed by different weights. A genetic search mechanism in various directions in the three-dimensional objective space is realized by this random weighting scheme. The other characteristic feature is to store all non-dominated solutions as a secondary population separately from the current population. The secondary population is updated at every generation. A small number of non-dominated solutions are randomly chosen from the secondary population and their copies are added to the current population as elite solutions. The convergence speed of the current population to Pareto-optimal solutions is improved by this elitist strategy. Other parts of our MOGA in this chapter are the same as standard single-objective genetic algorithms. The search ability of our three-objective genetic algorithm, which is based on a simple EMO algorithm [127], is not always comparable to that of state-of-the-art EMO algorithms such as NSGA-II [29] and SPEA [194]. In Ishibuchi & Yamamoto [88, 91, 94], the NSGA-II algorithm was used to efficiently find non-dominated rule sets of the three-objective optimization problem in (6.2).

6.2.1 Fitness Function

The fitness value of each string S (i.e., each rule set S) in the current population is defined by the three objectives as

$$fitness(S) = w_1 \cdot f_1(S) - w_2 \cdot f_2(S) - w_3 \cdot f_3(S), \tag{6.7}$$

where w_1, w_2, and w_3 are weights satisfying the following conditions:

$$w_1, w_2, w_3 \geq 0, \tag{6.8}$$

$$w_1 + w_2 + w_3 = 1. \tag{6.9}$$

As we have already mentioned, one characteristic feature of our MOGA in this chapter is to randomly specify the weights whenever a pair of parent strings is selected from the current population. We use binary tournament selection with replacement for the selection of parent strings. Thus we calculate the fitness function in (6.7) for only four rule sets in the current population using the randomly specified weights when a pair of parent strings is selected. When another pair of parent strings is selected, the three weights are randomly updated. That is, the selection of each pair of parent strings is governed by a different weight vector. A pre-specified number of pairs are selected from the current population. New strings are generated from each pair of parent strings using crossover and mutation as in standard single-objective genetic algorithms.

6.2.2 Elitist Strategy

A secondary population stores non-dominated rule sets among examined ones during the execution of our MOGA. The secondary population is updated at every generation so that it includes all non-dominated rule sets and it does not include any dominated ones. Each rule set in the current population is examined to see if it is dominated by any rule sets in the secondary population. If a rule set is not dominated, its copy is added to the secondary population. All solutions in the secondary population dominated by the added copy are removed. In this manner, the secondary population is updated at every generation.

Each non-dominated rule set in the secondary population can be viewed as a kind of elite solution because it is not dominated by any examined rule sets. A pre-specified number (say N_{elite}) of non-dominated rule sets are randomly selected from the secondary population and their copies are added to the current population as elite solutions. This is a simple elitist strategy in EMO algorithms. It is shown in [193, 194] that the use of elitism is essential for designing EMO algorithms with high search ability. Most of the recently proposed EMO algorithms use some form of elitism (see [21, 28]).

6.2.3 Basic Framework of Multi-Objective Genetic Algorithms

The basic framework of our MOGA, which is used in the genetic algorithm-based rule selection method and the extended hybrid fuzzy GBML algorithm, can be written as follows:

[Multi-Objective Genetic Algorithm]

Step 0: *Parameter Specification.* Specify the population size N_{pop}, the number of elite solutions N_{elite}, the parameter values for genetic operations, and the stopping condition.

Step 1: *Initialization.* Randomly generate N_{pop} rule sets as an initial population. Find non-dominated rule sets in the initial population by calculating the three objectives of each rule set. Construct a secondary population using copies of those non-dominated rule sets.

Step 2: *Genetic Operations.* Generate $(N_{\text{pop}} - N_{\text{elite}})$ rule sets using genetic operations (i.e., selection, crossover, and mutation) from the current population. The selection of parent rule sets is performed by iterating the following procedures:

 (a) Randomly specify the three weights as
$$w_i = random_i / (random_1 + random_2 + random_3),$$
$$i = 1, 2, 3, (6.10)$$
 where $random_i$ is a non-negative random real number.

 (b) Select a pair of parent rule sets using binary tournament selection with replacement. The fitness value of each rule set is calculated by the fitness function in (6.7) using the current weight values specified in (6.10).

Step 3: *Evaluation.* Calculate the three objectives of each of the newly generated $(N_{\text{pop}} - N_{\text{elite}})$ rule sets.

Step 4: *Secondary Population Update.* Update the secondary population by examining whether each of the newly generated $(N_{\text{pop}} - N_{\text{elite}})$ rule sets is dominated by any rule sets in the secondary population.

Step 5: *Generation Update (Elitist Strategy).* Randomly select N_{elite} non-dominated rule sets from the secondary population and add their copies to the newly generated $(N_{\text{pop}} - N_{\text{elite}})$ rule sets to form the next population of the population size N_{pop}.

Step 6: *Termination Test.* If the stopping condition is not satisfied, return to Step 2. Otherwise terminate the execution of the algorithm. All the non-dominated rule sets among the examined ones during the execution of the algorithm are stored in the secondary population.

6.3 Multi-Objective Rule Selection

6.3.1 Algorithm

The genetic algorithm for rule selection in Chap. 4 can be directly extended to the case of three-objective rule selection using the framework of our MOGA (and other EMO algorithms) described in Sect. 6.2. The binary coding of each rule set and the genetic operations for generating new rule sets in Chap. 4 can be used in the three-objective genetic algorithm for rule selection with no modifications. As we have already explained in Chap. 4, unnecessary linguistic rules are removed from each rule set. The second and third objectives are calculated for each rule set after unnecessary linguistic rules are removed.

6.3.2 Computer Simulations

We applied the three-objective genetic algorithm for rule selection to the wine data set. We used the 14 antecedent fuzzy sets in Fig. 1.4 of Chap. 1 and *don't care* for generating linguistic rules. As in the computer simulations in Sect. 4.4, we generated linguistic rules of length 3 or less (i.e., linguistic rules with three or less antecedent conditions). The number of generated linguistic rules was 711716. We selected 900 candidate rules from the 711716 linguistic rules using the candidate rule prescreening procedure as in Sect. 4.4

The three-objective genetic algorithm for rule selection was used to find non-dominated rule sets from the 900 candidate rules. Parameter values were specified as follows.

Population size:	$N_{\mathrm{pop}} = 50$,
Number of elite solutions:	$N_{\mathrm{elite}} = 5$,
Crossover probability:	$p_c = 0.8$,
Mutation probability:	$p_m(0 \to 1) = 1/900$,
	$p_m(1 \to 0) = 0.1$,
Stopping condition:	1000 population updates.

We used the same parameter specifications as in the computer simulations in Sect. 4.4 using the genetic algorithm-based rule selection method. It should be noted that we do not have to specify the weight values in the fitness function in (6.7). This is because we use the three objective genetic algorithm with variable weights. If we pre-specify the weight values, single-objective genetic algorithms can be utilized to maximize the fitness function in (6.7) with the constant weights.

Table 6.1 shows non-dominated rule sets obtained by a single run of the three-objective genetic algorithm for rule selection. It should be noted that only 50000 rule sets were examined by the three-objective genetic algorithm for finding the rule sets in Table 6.1. To clearly demonstrate the tradeoff between the accuracy and the interpretability of linguistic rule-based systems, each rule set in Table 6.1 is depicted in the two-dimensional space with the total rule length and the error rate in Fig. 6.2. Some rule sets are not shown because they are out of the range of this figure. The figure clearly shows the tradeoff between the total rule length (i.e., complexity of linguistic rule-based systems) and the error rate (i.e., classification performance). The improvement in the error rate leads to an increase in the total rule length.

Since genetic algorithms are based on a stochastic search mechanism, the obtained rule sets are not always true Pareto-optimal solutions. Thus better solutions may be obtained from multiple runs of the three-objective genetic algorithm for rule selection. Better rule sets may also be obtained by increasing the population size and/or the number of iterations. The increase in the number of candidate rules also increases the chance of finding better rule sets, though it also increases the difficulty of finding good rule sets due to the exponential increase in the size of the search space for rule selection. Table 6.2 shows the simulation results of a single run of the three-objective genetic algorithm for rule selection with a population size of 500 and 10000 iterations. This means that the computation load in Table 6.2 is 100 times as large as in Table 6.1 with a population size of 50 and 1000 iterations. From

Table 6.1. Non-dominated rule sets obtained by a single run of the three-objective genetic algorithm for rule selection with population size of 50 and 1000 iterations

Rule set	Classification rate	Number of rules	Average length
S_1	100.0%	4	2.50
S_2	98.9%	4	2.25
S_3	98.3%	4	2.00
S_4	97.8%	4	1.75
S_5	97.2%	3	2.33
S_6	96.1%	3	2.00
S_7	95.5%	3	1.67
S_8	93.8%	3	1.33
S_9	88.8%	3	1.00
S_{10}	71.9%	2	2.50
S_{11}	70.2%	2	2.00
S_{12}	69.1%	2	1.50
S_{13}	68.0%	2	1.00
S_{14}	39.9%	1	2.00
S_{15}	39.3%	1	1.00

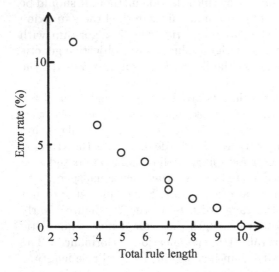

Fig. 6.2. Obtained rule sets in the two-dimensional space with the total rule length and the error rate

the comparison between Table 6.1 and Table 6.2, we can see that simulation results were slightly improved by increasing the computation load. As mentioned in Chap. 4, the efficiency of genetic algorithm-based rule selection strongly depends on the prescreening of candidate rules.

For further discussions on multi-objective genetic rule selection and other simulation results, see Ishibuchi & Yamamoto [94, 88, 89].

Table 6.2. Non-dominated rule sets obtained by a single run of the three-objective genetic algorithm for rule selection with a population size of 500 and 10000 iterations

Rule set	Classification rate	Number of rules	Average length
S_1	100.0%	3	2.33
S_2	99.4%	3	2.00
S_3	98.3%	3	1.67
S_4	97.2%	4	1.00
S_5	96.1%	3	1.33
S_6	96.1%	4	0.75
S_7	94.9%	3	1.00
S_8	88.2%	3	0.67
S_9	73.0%	2	2.50
S_{10}	72.5%	2	2.00
S_{11}	71.9%	2	1.50
S_{12}	69.7%	2	1.00
S_{13}	67.4%	2	0.50
S_{14}	39.9%	1	0.00

6.4 Multi-Objective Genetics-Based Machine Learning

6.4.1 Algorithm

The extended hybrid fuzzy GBML algorithm in Chap. 5 can also be easily adapted to the case of three-objective optimization using the framework of the MOGA described in Sect. 6.2. The coding of each rule set using antecedent fuzzy sets and the genetic operations for generating new rule sets in Chap. 5 can be used in three-objective fuzzy GBML with no modifications. The number of linguistic rules in each rule set is changed by the one-point crossover operation with different crossover points as in Chap. 5. Our three-objective fuzzy GBML algorithm is a hybrid algorithm of the Michigan approach and the Pittsburgh approach. We use the following two heuristics in the three-objective fuzzy GBML algorithm (see Chap. 5).

(1) Heuristic generation of an initial population.
(2) Rule generation from misclassified or rejected training patterns.

6.4.2 Computer Simulations

We applied the three-objective fuzzy GBML algorithm to the wine data set. As in the previous section, we used the 14 antecedent fuzzy sets in Fig. 1.4 of Chap. 1 and *don't care*. The total number of combinations of antecedent fuzzy sets for generating linguistic rules is $(14 + 1)^{13}$. The three-objective fuzzy GBML algorithm was used to construct non-dominated rule sets from such a huge number of possible linguistic rules.

The three-objective fuzzy GBML algorithm was applied to the wine data set using the following parameter specifications:

Number of linguistic rules in initial rule sets: $N_{\text{rule}} = 10$,
Number of rule sets: $N_{\text{pop}} = 50$,
Crossover probabilities: $p_{c_P} = 0.8$ in the Pittsburgh part,
$\qquad\qquad\qquad\quad p_{c_M} = 0.8$ in the Michigan part,
Mutation probabilities: $p_{m_P} = 0.8$ in the Pittsburgh part,
$\qquad\qquad\qquad\quad p_{m_M} = 1/13$ in the Michigan part,
Number of elite solutions: $N_{\text{elite}} = 5$,
Stopping condition: 1000 iterations,
Number of replaced linguistic rules: 20% of existing rules.

The same parameter specifications were used in the computer simulations in Sect. 5.4 using the extended hybrid fuzzy GBML algorithm. As in the case of the three-objective genetic algorithm for rule selection in the previous section, we do not have to specify the weight values in the fitness function in (6.7).

Table 6.3 shows non-dominated rule sets obtained by a single run of the three-objective fuzzy GBML algorithm. As in Table 6.1, only 50000 rule sets were examined by the three-objective fuzzy GBML algorithm for finding the rule sets in Table 6.3. From the comparison between Table 6.1 and Table 6.3, we can see that larger rule sets were obtained from the three-objective fuzzy GBML algorithm. That is, many rule sets in Table 6.3 are inferior to those in Table 6.1 with respect to the comprehensibility of rule sets. This is because the search space in Table 6.1 (i.e., 2^{900}) is much smaller than that in Table 6.3 (i.e., 2^N where $N = 15^{13}$). We also applied the three-objective fuzzy GBML algorithm to the wine data set using a greater computation load than in Table 6.3. That is, the population size and the stopping condition were specified as 500 rule sets and 10000 iterations, respectively. Simulation results are summarized in Table 6.4. From the comparison between Table 6.4 and Table 6.3, we can see that better rule sets were obtained in Table 6.4. Simulation results in Table 6.4, however, are still inferior to those in Table 6.1 by rule selection. This suggests that a greater computation load may be required for finding good rule sets in the huge search space.

Table 6.3. Non-dominated rule sets obtained by a single run of the three-objective fuzzy GBML algorithm with a population size of 50 and 1000 iterations

Rule set	Classification rate	Number of rules	Average length
S_1	100.0%	11	2.00
S_2	99.4%	9	2.22
S_3	98.9%	9	2.00
S_4	98.3%	9	1.78
S_5	97.8%	7	1.86
S_6	97.2%	6	1.67
S_7	96.6%	5	1.80
S_8	96.1%	4	1.75
S_9	96.1%	5	1.20
S_{10}	94.9%	4	1.25
S_{11}	93.3%	4	1.00
S_{12}	91.6%	3	1.00
S_{13}	68.0%	3	0.67
S_{14}	65.7%	2	2.00
S_{15}	65.2%	2	1.00
S_{16}	60.1%	2	0.50
S_{17}	39.9%	1	0.00

Table 6.4. Non-dominated rule sets obtained by a single run of the three-objective fuzzy GBML algorithm with a population size of 500 and 10000 iterations

Rule set	Classification rate	Number of rules	Average length
S_1	100.0%	6	2.67
S_2	100%	7	1.71
S_3	99.4%	5	2.20
S_4	99.4%	6	1.67
S_5	98.9%	5	1.40
S_6	98.3%	4	1.75
S_7	98.3%	5	1.00
S_8	97.8%	4	1.25
S_9	97.2%	4	1.00
S_{10}	96.1%	4	0.75
S_{11}	93.8%	3	1.67
S_{12}	93.3%	3	1.33
S_{13}	92.7%	3	1.00
S_{14}	88.2%	3	0.67
S_{15}	70.2%	2	1.50
S_{16}	69.7%	2	1.00
S_{17}	67.4%	2	0.50
S_{18}	39.9%	1	0.00

7. Comparison of Linguistic Discretization with Interval Discretization

We have already explained several approaches to the design of linguistic rule-based systems for pattern classification problems. In this chapter, we compare linguistic discretization with interval discretization to clearly illustrate characteristic features of linguistic rule-based classification systems. For such a comparison, we specify linguistic discretization in a different manner from the previous chapters. While we assumed in the previous chapters that linguistic discretization is given for each attribute by human users or domain experts, in this chapter we construct linguistic discretization from interval discretization. Figures 7.1 and 7.2 are examples of linguistic discretization generated from interval discretization. Interval discretization in Fig. 7.1 is homogeneous (i.e., five intervals have the same width) while it is inhomogeneous in Fig. 7.2.

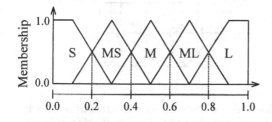

Fig. 7.1. Homogeneous interval discretization into five intervals with the same width and the corresponding linguistic discretization

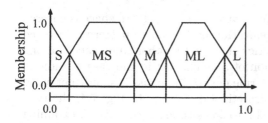

Fig. 7.2. Inhomogeneous interval discretization into five intervals with different widths and the corresponding linguistic discretization

7.1 Effects of Linguistic Discretization

7.1.1 Effect in the Rule Generation Phase

The main characteristic feature of linguistic discretization is the overlap between adjacent antecedent fuzzy sets (i.e., adjacent linguistic terms). This means that many linguistic rules overlap with each other in the pattern space. On the other hand, there is no overlap of rules in the case of interval discretization. This difference is illustrated in Fig. 7.3. In Fig. 7.3 (a), an input pattern denoted by the closed circle in the pattern space is covered by four linguistic rules corresponding to the four shaded cells. In general, an input pattern in the n-dimensional pattern space is covered by 2^n linguistic rules. On the other hand, an input pattern is covered by only a single rule in the case of interval discretization as shown in Fig. 7.3 (b).

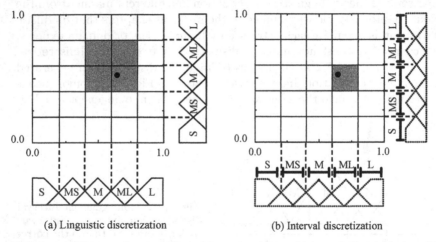

(a) Linguistic discretization   (b) Interval discretization

Fig. 7.3. Difference between fuzzy discretization and interval discretization. Each axis is homogeneously divided into five linguistic terms (S: *small*, MS: *medium small*, M: *medium*, ML: *medium large*, and L: *large*) and five intervals

As shown in Fig. 7.3 (a), an input pattern in the pattern space is covered by multiple linguistic rules. This means that each training pattern is involved in the generation of multiple linguistic rules. On the other hand, each training pattern is involved in the generation of a single rule in the case of interval discretization. This difference in the rule generation phase is significant when training patterns are sparse and discretization is fine. In Fig. 7.4, the two-dimensional pattern space is divided into 25 cells. From the given 14 training patterns (i.e., seven closed circles and seven open circles), 22 linguistic rules in the shaded region in Fig. 7.4 (a) can be generated. On the other hand, only nine rules can be generated in the case of interval discretization in Fig. 7.4 (b).

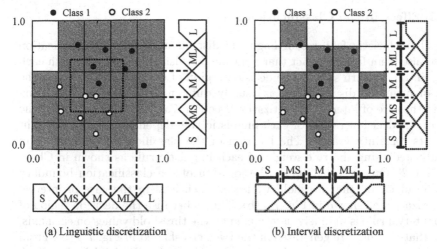

(a) Linguistic discretization   (b) Interval discretization

Fig. 7.4. Training patterns and generated rules

It should be noted that each training pattern has a different influence (i.e., different importance) in the rule generation phase according to its compatibility grade to each linguistic rule. Let us consider the following linguistic rule at the center of the pattern space in Fig. 7.4 (a):

$$\text{If } x_1 \text{ is } medium \text{ and } x_2 \text{ is } medium \text{ then Class 1 with } CF = 0.17. \quad (7.1)$$

The consequent class and the rule weight of this linguistic rule were determined from four training patterns in the large dotted square at the center of the pattern space in Fig. 7.4 (a). In the rule generation phase of this linguistic rule, one training pattern from Class 1 near the center of the pattern space has a larger compatibility grade than two training patterns from Class 2 near the sides of the small cell at the center of the pattern space. The compatibility grades of the four compatible patterns are 0.90 (Class 1 pattern near the center of the pattern space), 0.52 (Class 2 pattern), 0.30 (Class 2 pattern), and 0.26 (Class 1 pattern). The sum of the compatibility grades over the two training patterns from Class 2 is smaller than that of the two Class 1 patterns. As a result, the consequent of the linguistic rule in (7.1) is Class 1.

The corresponding rule was generated in Fig. 7.4 (b) in the case of interval discretization as

$$\text{If } x_1 \text{ is } medium \text{ and } x_2 \text{ is } medium \text{ then Class 2 with } CF = 0.33. \quad (7.2)$$

This rule was generated from three compatible training patterns that are located in the small cell at the center of the pattern space in Fig. 7.4 (b). Note that the linguistic rule in (7.1) and the interval rule in (7.2) have different consequent classes.

7.1.2 Effect in the Classification Phase

The characteristic features of linguistic discretization in the classification phase also stem from the fact that multiple linguistic rules overlap with each other in the pattern space. The decision region of each linguistic rule in the case of linguistic discretization is usually different from the corresponding cell in the case of interval discretization (see Fig. 7.5 (a)). This is because the size of the decision region of each linguistic rule depends on its rule weight (i.e., its certainty grade). The location of the classification boundary can be adjusted using the rule weight of each linguistic rule as shown in Chap. 3 [67, 132]. On the other hand, the location of the classification boundary is determined by the threshold values on each axis in the case of interval discretization as shown in Fig. 7.5 (b). This is because the decision region of each interval rule is uniquely determined by the threshold values on each axis. Note that no rules are generated in the two cells shaded in Fig. 7.5 (b). From these discussions, we expect that good results can be obtained by linguistic rules even when the linguistic discretization of each axis is not appropriately specified. On the other hand, each axis should be appropriately discretized into intervals for generating interval rules with high classification ability.

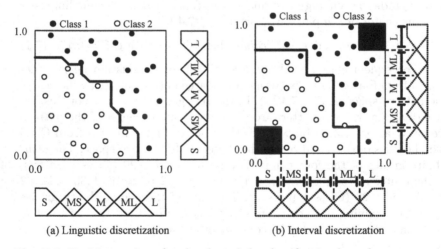

(a) Linguistic discretization   (b) Interval discretization

Fig. 7.5. Decision region of each rule and the classification boundary

Linguistic rules have larger decision regions than the corresponding interval rules when rules are sparse. If there are no adjacent linguistic rules around the linguistic rule in (7.1) with the antecedent part (*medium*, *medium*), its decision region is the dotted square in Fig. 7.4 (a). On the other hand, the decision region of the corresponding interval rule is always the corresponding cell at the center of Fig. 7.4 (b). That is, the size of the decision region is independent of the existence of adjacent interval rules in the case of interval discretization. The size of the decision region of each linguistic rule, however, depends on the existence of adjacent linguistic rules. Thus a small number of sparsely located linguistic rules can classify far more patterns than the corresponding interval rules. In the case of interval discretization, the classification of many patterns will be rejected if the number of interval rules is very small. From these discussions, we expect that a small number of linguistic rules have higher classification ability than the same number of interval rules.

7.1.3 Summary of Effects of Linguistic Discretization

In this section, we have illustrated some effects of linguistic discretization in the rule generation phase and the pattern classification phase. The main positive effects of linguistic discretization on the classification performance of linguistic rule-based systems are summarized as follows:

(1) Multiple linguistic rules can be generated from a single training pattern while only a single rule can be generated in the case of interval discretization. This may lead to better results by linguistic discretization than interval discretization when the number of training patters is very small (i.e., when training patterns are sparse).

(2) The location of the classification boundary can be adjusted using the rule weight of each linguistic rule while it is determined by the specification of threshold values in the case of interval discretization. This may lead to better results by linguistic discretization than interval discretization when the discretization of each axis is not tuned appropriately.

(3) Each linguistic rule can classify a larger region than the corresponding interval rule. This may lead to better results by linguistic discretization than interval discretization when the number of rules is very small (i.e., when rules are sparse).

7.2 Specification of Linguistic Discretization from Interval Discretization

7.2.1 Specification of Fully Fuzzified Linguistic Discretization

The membership function of each fuzzy set in Fig. 7.1 and Fig. 7.2 was generated from the corresponding interval based on the following constraint conditions:

(a) Membership functions are linear (i.e., triangular or trapezoidal).
(b) The sum of neighboring membership functions is 1.
(c) Crossing points of neighboring membership functions coincide with threshold values for interval discretization (see Fig. 7.1 and Fig. 7.2).

(d) The membership value of each intermediate fuzzy set (e.g., MS: *medium small*, M: *medium*, and ML: *medium large* in Fig. 7.1) is 1 at the midpoint of the corresponding interval. The membership value of the smallest fuzzy set (e.g., S: *small* in Fig. 7.1) is 1 at the smallest input value 0 in the domain interval $[0, 1]$. The membership value of the largest fuzzy set (e.g., L: *large* in Fig. 7.1) is 1 at the largest input value 1 in the domain interval $[0, 1]$.

It should be noted that linguistic discretization is not uniquely specified by these constraint conditions from interval discretization. For example, Fig. 7.6 satisfies these constraint conditions as well as Fig. 7.1. While Fig. 7.1 shows fully fuzzified linguistic discretization, Fig. 7.6 shows partially fuzzified linguistic discretization.

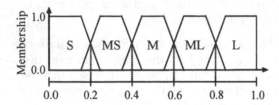

Fig. 7.6. Partially fuzzified linguistic discretization

To represent the grade of fuzzification, let us introduce the fuzzification grade F. When $F = 1$, linguistic discretization is fully fuzzified under the above constraint conditions as shown in Fig. 7.1 and Fig. 7.2. On the other hand, $F = 0$ corresponds to interval discretization with no fuzzification (i.e., no overlap between adjacent fuzzy sets). From fully fuzzified linguistic discretization with $F = 1$ and interval discretization with $F = 0$, we can generate partially fuzzified linguistic discretization with arbitrary grades of fuzzification.

Before explaining the specification of partially fuzzified linguistic discretization, we first show how fully fuzzified linguistic discretization (e.g., Fig. 7.1 and Fig. 7.2) can be obtained from interval discretization based on the above-mentioned four constraint conditions. Let us assume that the unit interval $[0, 1]$ is discretized into K intervals $I_1, I_2, \ldots, I_K$ as shown in Fig. 7.7. We denote each interval I_j by its lower limit L_j and upper limit U_j as $I_j = [L_j, U_j]$, $j = 1, 2, \ldots, K$. For these intervals, the following relations hold (see Fig. 7.7):

$$L_1 = 0, \ U_K = 1, \tag{7.3}$$

$$U_j = L_{j+1} \text{ for } j = 1, 2, \ldots, K - 1. \tag{7.4}$$

Our task is to derive the fully fuzzified linguistic discretization with K fuzzy sets from the interval discretization with those K intervals. Let $A_1, A_2, \ldots, A_K$ be the K fuzzy sets corresponding to the K intervals $I_1, I_2, \ldots, I_K$.

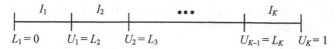

Fig. 7.7. Interval discretization of the unit interval $[0,1]$ into K intervals

As shown in Fig. 7.1 and Fig. 7.2, each fuzzy set A_j is in general trapezoidal from the first constraint condition (a). A triangular fuzzy set can be viewed as a special case of a trapezoidal fuzzy set. We denote the trapezoidal fuzzy set A_j by its four parameters as $A_j = (a_j, b_j, c_j, d_j)$. This notation is illustrated in Fig. 7.8. It should be noted that the fuzzy set A_j is triangular when $b_j = c_j$.

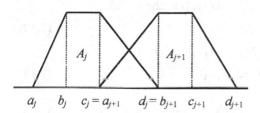

Fig. 7.8. Adjacent trapezoidal fuzzy sets

From the second constraint condition (b), we have the following relations (see Fig. 7.8):

$$a_{j+1} = c_j \text{ and } b_{j+1} = d_j \text{ for } j = 1, 2, \ldots, K - 1. \tag{7.5}$$

In this case, we can see from Fig. 7.8 that the following relation holds:

$$\mu_{A_j}(x) + \mu_{A_{j+1}}(x) = 1 \text{ for } c_j \leq x \leq d_j, \ j = 1, 2, \ldots, K - 1. \tag{7.6}$$

From the fourth constraint condition (d), the left hand side slope of the first fuzzy set A_1 (e.g., S in Fig. 7.1) is specified as

$$a_1 = b_1 = 0. \tag{7.7}$$

The right hand side slope of the last fuzzy set A_K (e.g., L in Fig. 7.1) is specified as

$$c_K = d_K = 1. \tag{7.8}$$

From (7.5), (7.7), and (7.8), we can see that the fuzzy discretization with $A_1, A_2, \ldots, A_K$ is uniquely specified by determining the values of c_j and d_j for $j = 1, 2, \ldots, K - 1$. In the following, we show how these parameters can be determined from the interval discretization with $I_1, I_2, \ldots, I_K$.

The third constraint condition (c) requires the following relation:

$$U_j = \frac{c_j + d_j}{2} \text{ for } j = 1, 2, \ldots, K - 1. \tag{7.9}$$

To handle the fourth constraint condition (d), let us define M_j where the membership value of A_j should be 1 as follows:

$$M_j = \begin{cases} 0, & \text{if } j = 1, \\ (L_j + U_j)/2, & \text{if } 1 < j < K, \\ 1, & \text{if } j = K. \end{cases} \tag{7.10}$$

The fourth constraint condition (d) requires the following relation:

$$M_j \le c_j \le d_j \le M_{j+1} \text{ for } j = 1, 2, \ldots, K - 1. \tag{7.11}$$

The specification of the fully fuzzified linguistic partition means the minimization of c_j and the maximization of d_j under the constraint conditions in (7.9) and (7.11). This optimization problem can be easily solved as follows:

Case 1 (Fig. 7.9 (a)): When $U_j \le (M_j + M_{j+1})/2$, then

$$c_j = M_j \text{ and } d_j = U_j + (U_j - M_j). \tag{7.12}$$

Case 2 (Fig. 7.9 (b)): When $U_j > (M_j + M_{j+1})/2$, then

$$c_j = U_j - (M_{j+1} - U_j) \text{ and } d_j = M_{j+1}. \tag{7.13}$$

Using (7.12) and (7.13), we can specify c_j and d_j for $j = 1, 2, \ldots, K - 1$. Then a_j and b_j are specified from (7.5) for $j = 2, 3, \ldots, K$. The other parameters have already been specified by (7.7) and (7.8). In this manner, we can specify the fully fuzzified linguistic discretization of the domain interval $[0, 1]$ with the K fuzzy sets from the interval discretization with the K intervals.

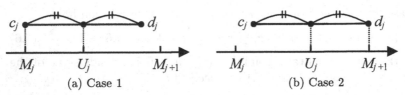

(a) Case 1   (b) Case 2

Fig. 7.9. Illustration of the specification of c_j and d_j

7.2.2 Specification of Partially Fuzzified Linguistic Discretization

Now we show how we can specify the partially fuzzified linguistic discretization with the fuzzification grade F. Let us denote the partially fuzzified trapezoidal fuzzy set A_j with the fuzzification grade F as $A_j^F = (a_j^F, b_j^F, c_j^F, d_j^F)$ where $0 \le F \le 1$. Note that we have already obtained the fully fuzzified trapezoidal fuzzy set $A_j^1 = (a_j^1, b_j^1, c_j^1, d_j^1)$ with the maximum fuzzification grade (i.e., $F = 1$) in the previous subsection. On the other hand, the trapezoidal fuzzy set $A_j^0 = (a_j^0, b_j^0, c_j^0, d_j^0)$ with no fuzzification is the same as the interval I_j:

$$a_j^0 = b_j^0 = L_j, \tag{7.14}$$

$$c_j^0 = d_j^0 = U_j. \tag{7.15}$$

Using the interpolation between A_j^0 and A_j^1, we specify $A_j^F = (a_j^F, b_j^F, c_j^F, d_j^F)$ as follows:

$$a_j^F = a_j^0 + (a_j^1 - a_j^0)F, \tag{7.16}$$

$$b_j^F = b_j^0 + (b_j^1 - b_j^0)F, \tag{7.17}$$

$$c_j^F = c_j^0 + (c_j^1 - c_j^0)F, \tag{7.18}$$

$$d_j^F = d_j^0 + (d_j^1 - d_j^0)F. \tag{7.19}$$

From these formulations, we can generate partially fuzzy linguistic discretization with arbitrary fuzzification grades when the interval discretization is given. Figure 7.6 was drawn using these formulations for $F = 0.5$.

7.3 Comparison Using Homogeneous Discretization

Through computer simulations on the iris data set and the wine data set, we compare linguistic discretization with interval discretization when the domain interval of each attribute is homogeneously divided into multiple intervals with the same width.

7.3.1 Simulation Results on Iris Data

In this subsection, we present simulation results on the iris data set. As in the previous chapters, the iris data set was treated as a three-class pattern classification problem in the four-dimensional unit hypercube $[0, 1]^4$.

First we examined the classification performance of linguistic rule-based systems in the case of sparse training patterns. We randomly selected only five samples from each class as training patterns. Thus the total number of training patterns was 15. These training patterns were used to design a linguistic rule-based system. The other 135 samples were used as test patterns to evaluate the generalization ability of the designed linguistic rule-based system. In our computer simulations in this subsection, the domain interval $[0, 1]$ of each attribute was uniformly divided into K intervals with the same width. The linguistic discretization with K fuzzy sets of the fuzzification grade F was generated from the interval discretization with the K intervals. To generate linguistic rules, K^4 combinations of K antecedent fuzzy sets for each of the four attributes were examined using the heuristic rule generation procedure in Chap. 2. There were many combinations for which linguistic rules could not be generated. This is because training patterns were sparse.

We examined four parameter specifications of K: $K = 2, 3, 4, 5$. For each specification of K, we examined eleven parameter specifications of the fuzzification grade F: $F = 0, 0.1, 0.2, \ldots, 1$. For each combination of K and F, we calculated the average classification rate on test patterns over 500 trials with different choices of 15 training patterns (i.e., different partitions of the 150 samples into 15 training patterns and 135 test patterns). Simulation results are summarized in Fig. 7.10.

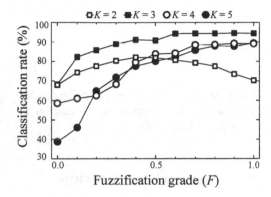

Fig. 7.10. Average classification rates on test patterns. Only 15 samples in the iris data set were used as training patterns

From Fig. 7.10, we can see that the fuzzification of interval discretization improved the generalization ability of linguistic rule-based systems. The main reason for the poor generalization ability of interval discretization (i.e., poor results in Fig. 7.10 in the case of no fuzzification: $F = 0$) is that only a small number of rules were generated from sparse training patterns. As a result, the classification of many test patterns was rejected. The average number of generated linguistic rules is summarized in Table 7.1. From this table, we can see that much far rules were generated in the case of linguistic discretization than interval discretization. We also calculated the average rejection rate for each combination of K and F. Simulation results are summarized in Fig. 7.11. From this figure, we can see that the classification of many test patterns was rejected in the case of a large K (i.e., fine partition) and a small F (i.e., small fuzzification grade). The combination of a large K and a small F means a small decision region of each linguistic rule. Such a small decision region has two negative effects on the classification performance in the case of sparse training patterns. One is that the number of generated rules is small. The other is that each rule can classify only a small number of test patterns. As a result, many test patterns cannot be classified in the case of fine partitions and small fuzzification grades.

Next we examined the classification performance of linguistic rule-based systems in the case of sparse rules. We used the 10-fold cross-validation (10CV) technique to estimate the generalization ability of linguistic rule-based systems. In the 10CV technique, the 150 samples in the iris data set

Table 7.1. Number of generated rules

Partition	Interval discretization ($F = 0$)			
Granularity	2	3	4	5
# of rules	6.5	9.0	14.4	11.8

Partition	Linguistic discretization ($F = 1$)			
Granularity	2	3	4	5
# of rules	16.0	40.3	65.5	87.2

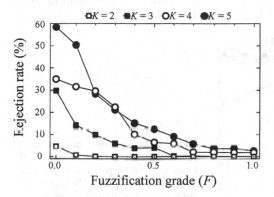

Fig. 7.11. Average rejection rates on test patterns. Only 15 samples in the iris data set were used as training patterns

were randomly divided into ten subsets with five samples from each class (i.e., 15 samples in each subset). Nine subsets were used as training patterns and the remaining subset was used as test patterns. This was iterated ten times so that all subsets were used once as test patterns. The whole 10CV procedure was iterated 50 times using different partitions of the 150 samples into ten subsets for each combination of granularity K and fuzzification grade F. In each trial in the 10CV procedure, K^4 combinations of K antecedent fuzzy sets for each of the four attributes were examined to generate linguistic rules. From the generated linguistic rules, N linguistic rules were selected using the rule prescreening procedure in Chap. 4. Simulation results are summarized in Fig. 7.12 for the case of $N = 3$ (i.e., only a single rule for each class) and Fig. 7.13 for the case of $N = 30$ (i.e., ten rules for each class). These figures show the average classification rate on test patterns for each specification for the granularity K, the fuzzification grade F, and the number of linguistic rules N. From Fig. 7.12, we can see that the effect of fuzzification on the classification performance of linguistic rule-based systems was significant when the number of linguistic rules was very small. On the other hand, this effect was not so significant when the number of linguistic rules was large as shown in Fig. 7.13.

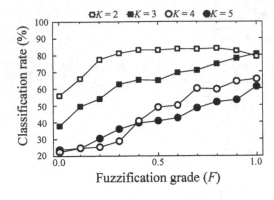

Fig. 7.12. Average classification rates on test patterns obtained from the 10CV procedure for the iris data set using three linguistic rules (i.e., a single linguistic rule for each class)

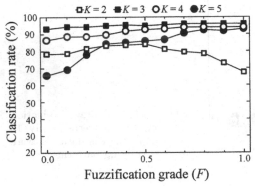

Fig. 7.13. Average classification rates on test patterns obtained from the 10CV procedure for the iris data set using 30 linguistic rules (i.e., ten linguistic rules for each class)

7.3.2 Simulation Results on Wine Data

In this subsection, we present simulation results on the wine data set. As in the previous chapters, the wine data set was treated as a three-class pattern classification problem in the 13-dimensional unit hypercube $[0, 1]^{13}$. In our computer simulations in this subsection, we only generated linguistic rules of length of 2 or less.

Using linguistic rules of this length, we performed almost the same computer simulations on the wine data set as in the previous subsection on the iris data set. First we examined the classification performance of linguistic rule-based systems in the case of sparse training patterns. About 10% of the given samples were randomly selected as training patterns from the wine data set: six samples from Class 1 with 59 samples, seven samples from Class 2 with 71 samples, and five samples from Class 3 with 48 samples. Thus the total number of training patterns was 18. These training patterns were used to design a linguistic rule-based system. The other 160 samples were used as test patterns to evaluate the generalization ability of the designed linguistic rule-based system. For each specification of the granularity K and the fuzzification grade F, we calculated the average classification rate on test patterns over 500 trials with different choices of the 18 training patterns. Simulation results are summarized in Fig. 7.14. From this figure, we can see that the fuzzification of interval discretization significantly improved the generalization ability of linguistic rule-based systems as in Fig. 7.10 on the iris data set when training patterns were sparse.

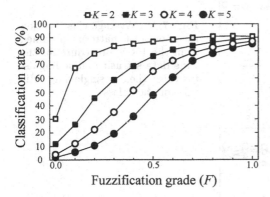

Fig. 7.14. Average classification rates on test patterns. Only 18 samples in the wine data were used as training patterns

Next we examined the classification performance of linguistic rule-based systems in the case of sparse rules. As in the previous subsection, we used the 10CV technique to estimate the generalization ability of linguistic rule-based systems. The whole 10CV procedure was iterated 50 times using different partitions of the wine data set into ten subsets for each specification of the granularity K and the fuzzification grade F. Simulation results are summarized in Fig. 7.15 for the case of $N = 3$ (only a single linguistic rule from each class) and Fig. 7.16 for the case of $N = 30$ (ten linguistic rules from each class). From Fig. 7.15, we can see that the effect of fuzzification on the performance of linguistic rule-based systems was significant when the number of linguistic rules was very small. On the other hand, this effect was not so significant in Fig. 7.16 where the number of fuzzy rules was large. The same observations were obtained from the previous computer simulations on the iris data set (i.e., Fig. 7.12 and Fig. 7.13).

7.4 Comparison Using Inhomogeneous Discretization

In the previous computer simulations, we used homogeneous interval discretization for generating linguistic discretization with arbitrary fuzzification grades. Since the location of classification boundaries totally depends on threshold values in the case of interval discretization, generalization ability can be improved by carefully choosing threshold values for each attribute. In this section, we specify interval discretization using the entropy measure as in Fayyad & Irani [45] and Quinlan [143].

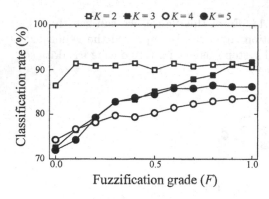

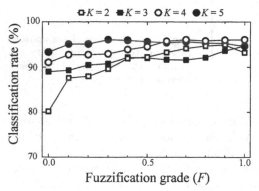

Fig. 7.15. Average classification rates on test patterns obtained from the 10CV procedure for the wine data set using three linguistic rules (i.e., a single linguistic rule for each class)

Fig. 7.16. Average classification rates on test patterns obtained from the 10CV procedure for the wine data set using 30 linguistic rules (i.e., ten linguistic rules for each class)

7.4.1 Entropy-Based Inhomogeneous Interval Discretization

In computer simulations in this section, the domain interval of each attribute was discretized independently of the other attributes. When the domain interval of an attribute was discretized into K intervals $I_1, I_2, \ldots, I_K$ using $(K-1)$ threshold values, the threshold values were selected from $(m-1)$ candidates. Each candidate was the midpoint of a pair of neighboring attribute values in the given m training patterns. All the $_{m-1}C_{K-1}$ combinations were examined to select $(K-1)$ threshold values from $(m-1)$ candidates (for more efficient discretization methods, see [41]). The entropy was calculated for each combination of $(K-1)$ threshold values (i.e., for each discretization). Let D be the set of given training patterns. Using $(K-1)$ threshold values on the attribute to be discretized (i.e., using K intervals $I_1, I_2, \ldots, I_K$ on that attribute), the data set D is divided into K subsets $D_1, D_2, \ldots, D_K$ where D_j is the set of training patterns in the interval I_j. According to the class of each training pattern, each subset D_j is further divided into M subsets $D_{j1}, D_{j2}, \ldots, D_{jM}$ where D_{jh} is the set of training patterns from Class h in the interval I_j. The entropy measure $H(I_1, I_2, \ldots, I_K)$ is defined for the interval discretization $I_1, I_2, \ldots, I_K$ as

$$H(I_1, I_2, \ldots, I_K) = - \sum_{j=1}^{K} \frac{|D_j|}{m} \sum_{h=1}^{M} \frac{|D_{jh}|}{|D_j|} \log_2 \frac{|D_{jh}|}{|D_j|}. \tag{7.20}$$

The combination of $(K - 1)$ threshold values with the minimum entropy was selected for each attribute. We discretized the domain interval of each attribute in this manner as a preprocessing procedure before designing linguistic rule-based systems. From the inhomogeneous interval discretization generated in this manner, we generated the corresponding fully fuzzified linguistic discretization as shown in Fig. 7.2. Then we generated partially fuzzified linguistic discretization with various fuzzification grades F from the inhomogeneous interval discretization and the corresponding fully fuzzified linguistic discretization.

7.4.2 Simulation Results on Iris Data

As in Sect. 7.3.1, we examined the classification performance of linguistic rule-based systems in the case of sparse training patterns (i.e., 15 training patterns from the iris data set). Simulation results are summarized in Fig. 7.17. From this figure, we can see that the classification performance of linguistic rule-based systems on test patterns was improved by increasing the fuzzification grade. This improvement was more significant in the case of fine discretization (e.g., $K = 5$) than coarse discretization (e.g., $K = 2$).

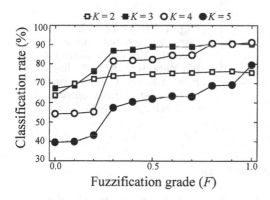

Fig. 7.17. Average classification rates on test patterns in the case of inhomogeneous discretization. Only 15 samples in the iris data set were used as training patterns

We also examined the classification performance of linguistic rule-based systems in the case of sparse rules. As in Sect. 7.3.1, we used the 10CV technique. Simulation results are summarized in Fig. 7.18 for the case of $N = 3$ (i.e., only a single linguistic rule from each class) and Fig. 7.19 for the case of $N = 30$ (i.e., ten linguistic rules from each class). From these figures, we can see that the classification performance of linguistic rule-based systems on test patterns was improved by increasing the fuzzification grade. This improvement was more significant in Fig. 7.18 with only three linguistic rules than Fig. 7.19 with 30 linguistic rules. In the case of $K = 3$ in Fig. 7.19 (i.e., closed squares), we can observe no improvement in the classification rate by the increase of the fuzzification grade.

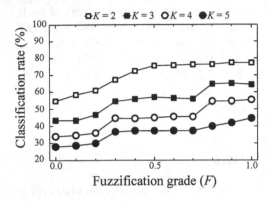

Fig. 7.18. Average classification rates on test patterns obtained from the 10CV procedure for the iris data set using three linguistic rules (i.e., a single linguistic rule for each class). Inhomogeneous discretization was used

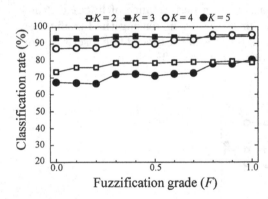

Fig. 7.19. Average classification rates on test patterns obtained from the 10CV procedure for the iris data set using 30 linguistic rules (i.e., ten linguistic rules for each class). Inhomogeneous discretization was used

7.4.3 Simulation Results on Wine Data

In the same manner as in Sect. 7.3.2, we performed computer simulations on the wine data set using inhomogeneous discretization. Linguistic rules of length of 2 or less were used. First we examined the classification performance of linguistic rule-based systems in the case of sparse training patterns (i.e., only 18 training patterns). Simulation results are summarized in Fig. 7.20. From Fig. 7.20, we can see that the classification performance of linguistic rule-based systems was improved by increasing the fuzzification grade when they were generated from sparse training patterns. The same observation was obtained from the previous computer simulations on the iris data set.

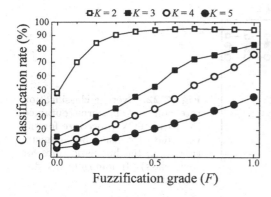

Fig. 7.20. Average classification rates on test patterns using inhomogeneous discretization. Only 18 samples in the wine data set were used as training patterns

Next we examined the classification performance of linguistic rule-based systems in the case of sparse rules using the 10CV technique. Simulation results are summarized in Fig. 7.21 for $N = 3$ (i.e., only a single linguistic rule for each class) and Fig. 7.22 for $N = 30$ (i.e., ten linguistic rules for each class). From Fig. 7.21, we can see that the classification performance of linguistic rule-based systems was improved by increasing the fuzzification grade when the number of linguistic rules was very small. The same observation was obtained from the previous computer simulations on the iris data set. On the other hand, the classification performance was impaired by the fuzzification of interval discretization in Fig. 7.22. Only this figure among simulation results in this chapter shows a clear deterioration in the classification performance by the fuzzification of interval discretization. Thus we conclude that the fuzzification of interval discretization can have a negative effect on the classification performance of rule-based systems when the following conditions are satisfied: the number of training patterns is not too small, the number of rules is not too small, and threshold values for interval discretization are appropriately specified.

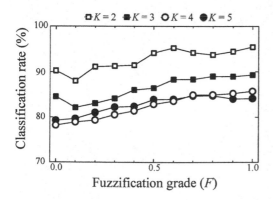

Fig. 7.21. Average classification rates on test patterns obtained from the 10CV procedure for the wine data set using three linguistic rules (i.e., a single linguistic rule for each class). Inhomogeneous discretization was used

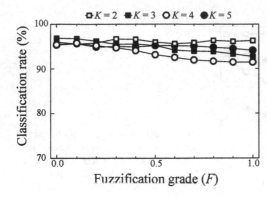

Fig. 7.22. Average classification rates on test patterns obtained from the 10CV procedure for the wine data set using 30 linguistic rules (i.e., ten linguistic rules for each class). Inhomogeneous discretization was used

8. Modeling with Linguistic Rules

We have already explained how linguistic rules can be used for pattern classification problems. In this chapter, we discuss modeling problems using linguistic rules. Our task in this chapter is to extract linguistic rules (i.e., to design a linguistic rule-based system) from numerical data to approximately realize an unknown nonlinear function. First we describe a heuristic approach to linguistic rule extraction from numerical data for modeling problems. Then we explain a fuzzy reasoning method for calculating an output value for an input vector using linguistic rules. In later chapters, we explain rule selection, genetics-based machine learning, and learning of linguistic rules for modeling problems.

8.1 Problem Description

Let us assume that we have m input–output pairs $(\boldsymbol{x}_p, y_p)$, $p = 1, 2, \ldots, m$, as training data where $\boldsymbol{x}_p = (x_{p1}, x_{p2}, \ldots, x_{pn})$ is an n-dimensional input vector and y_p is the corresponding output value. We also assume that linguistic terms are given for describing the input and output variables. This means that a fuzzy partition of the input–output space is given. Our task is to design a linguistic rule-based system to approximately realize an unknown n-input and single-output nonlinear function using the given training data and the given linguistic terms. For simplicity of explanation, we assume that the n-dimensional input space and the single-dimensional output space are normalized into the n-dimensional unit hypercube $[0, 1]^n$ and the unit interval $[0, 1]$, respectively. In Fig. 8.1, we show a simple example of our modeling problem where 20 input–output pairs are given in a two-dimensional input–output space $[0, 1] \times [0, 1]$. Five linguistic terms (i.e., S: *small*, MS: *medium small*, M: *medium*, ML: *medium large*, and L: *large*) are given for both the input and output variables in Fig. 8.1.

The linguistic rules for approximately realizing an n-input and single-output function are written in the following form:

$$\text{Rule } R_q: \text{If } x_1 \text{ is } A_{q1} \text{ and } \ldots \text{ and } x_n \text{ is } A_{qn} \text{ then } y \text{ is } B_q, \tag{8.1}$$

where R_q is the label of the q-th linguistic rule, $\boldsymbol{x} = (x_1, \ldots, x_n)$ is an n-dimensional input vector, A_{qi} is a linguistic term given for the i-th input

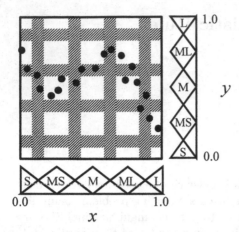

Fig. 8.1. A simple example of our modeling problem where 20 input–output pairs are given. The two-dimensional input–output space is discretized into 25 fuzzy subspaces by five linguistic terms for the input and output variables

variable x_i (i.e., A_{qi} is an antecedent fuzzy set), y is an output variable, and B_q is a linguistic term for the output variable (i.e., B_q is a consequent fuzzy set). When K linguistic terms are given for each of the n input and single output variables (e.g., $K = 5$ in Fig. 8.1), the total number of combinations of antecedent and consequent fuzzy sets is K^{n+1} in (8.1). Our task in this chapter is to generate a linguistic rule-based system, which is a subset of the K^{n+1} combinations of antecedent and consequent fuzzy sets. When we use a grid-type fuzzy partition to generate a linguistic rule table, the number of linguistic rules is K^n because a single linguistic rule is generated for each combination of antecedent fuzzy sets (i.e., for each fuzzy subspace in the n-dimensional input space). In Fig. 8.2, we show an example of a 5×5 fuzzy rule table. This table consists of the following 25 linguistic rules:

$$\text{If } x_1 \text{ is } small \text{ and } x_2 \text{ is } small \text{ then } y \text{ is } small, \qquad (8.2)$$

$$\text{If } x_1 \text{ is } small \text{ and } x_2 \text{ is } medium\ small \text{ then } y \text{ is } medium\ small, \quad (8.3)$$

$$\vdots$$

$$\text{If } x_1 \text{ is } large \text{ and } x_2 \text{ is } large \text{ then } y \text{ is } small. \qquad (8.4)$$

Figure 8.3 shows the corresponding nonlinear function generated by the fuzzy rule table in Fig. 8.2. In this chapter, we explain how linguistic rules (e.g., Fig. 8.2) can be extracted from training data. We also explain how nonlinear functions (e.g., Fig. 8.3) can be depicted from linguistic rule-based systems.

8.2 Linguistic Rule Extraction for Modeling Problems

When the number of input variables is small (e.g., $n = 2$), we can use a linguistic rule-based system in a tabular form as Fig. 8.2. In this case, the

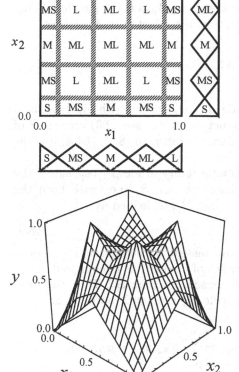

Fig. 8.2. An example of a 5 × 5 fuzzy rule table

Fig. 8.3. The nonlinear function depicted by the fuzzy rule table in Fig. 8.2. The calculation of the output value for each input vector is explained in Sect. 8.2.4

antecedent part of each linguistic rule is specified by the combination of given linguistic terms. The number of linguistic rules is the same as the number of combinations of linguistic terms for the n input variables in the antecedent part. In this section, we explain a heuristic method for determining the consequent part of each linguistic rule. Our heuristic method for modeling problems is similar to the heuristic rule generation method in Chap. 2 for pattern classification problems.

8.2.1 Linguistic Association Rules for Modeling Problems

The linguistic rule R_q in (8.1) can be viewed as a linguistic association rule $A_q \Rightarrow B_q$ where $A_q = (A_{q1}, \ldots, A_{qn})$. While the consequent part is a class label in the pattern classification problems in Chap. 2, B_q is a linguistic term in the modeling problems in this chapter. We extend the two measures (i.e., *confidence* and *support*) in data mining to the case of the linguistic association rule $A_q \Rightarrow B_q$ in the same manner as in Chap. 2 [57, 95].

Let us denote the given training data by D: $D = \{(x_1, y_1), \ldots, (x_m, y_m)\}$. The cardinality of D is m (i.e., $|D| = m$). Let $D(A_q)$ be the fuzzy set of compatible training data with the antecedent part A_q of the linguistic rule R_q. Then the total compatibility grade with the antecedent part A_q is calculated as

$$|D(A_q)| = \sum_{p=1}^{m} \mu_{A_q}(x_p). \tag{8.5}$$

As in Chap. 2, the compatibility grade $\mu_{A_q}(x_p)$ of x_p with A_q is defined by the minimum operator or the product operator (see (2.3) and (2.4) of Chap. 2). In this book, we use the product operator. In (8.5), $|D(A_q)|$ is the cardinality of the fuzzy set $D(A_q)$.

Using the product operator, the compatibility grade $\mu_{R_q}(x_p, y_p)$ of the input–output pair (x_p, y_p) with the linguistic rule R_q (i.e., with both the antecedent part A_q and the consequent part B_q) is defined as

$$\mu_{R_q}(x_p, y_p) = \mu_{A_q}(x_p) \times \mu_{B_q}(y_p). \tag{8.6}$$

It is possible to use the minimum operator instead of the product operator in (8.6). Let $D(A_q) \cup D(B_q)$ be the fuzzy set of compatible training data with both the antecedent part A_q and the consequent part B_q. Then the total compatibility grade with the linguistic rule R_q (i.e., with both A_q and B_q) is calculated as

$$|D(A_q) \cup D(B_q)| = \sum_{p=1}^{m} \mu_{R_q}(x_p, y_p) = \sum_{p=1}^{m} \mu_{A_q}(x_p) \times \mu_{B_q}(y_p). \tag{8.7}$$

As in Chap. 2 for pattern classification problems, the two measures (i.e., *confidence* and *support*) in the field of data mining [4, 5] can be defined for the linguistic association rule $A_q \Rightarrow B_q$ [57, 95]. The confidence $c(A_q \Rightarrow B_q)$ of the linguistic association rule $A_q \Rightarrow B_q$ is defined as

$$c(A_q \Rightarrow B_q) = \frac{|D(A_q) \cup D(B_q)|}{|D(A_q)|} = \frac{\sum\limits_{p=1}^{m} \mu_{A_q}(x_p) \times \mu_{B_q}(y_p)}{\sum\limits_{p=1}^{m} \mu_{A_q}(x_p)}. \tag{8.8}$$

The confidence $c(A_q \Rightarrow B_q)$ is the ratio of compatible training data with both the antecedent part A_q and the consequent part B_q to compatible training data with the antecedent part A_q. The confidence $c(A_q \Rightarrow B_q)$ measures the validity of the linguistic association rule $A_q \Rightarrow B_q$.

On the other hand, the support $s(A_q \Rightarrow B_q)$ of the linguistic association rule $A_q \Rightarrow B_q$ is defined as

$$s(A_q \Rightarrow B_q) = \frac{|D(A_q) \cup D(B_q)|}{|D|} = \frac{\sum\limits_{p=1}^{m} \mu_{A_q}(x_p) \times \mu_{B_q}(y_p)}{m}. \tag{8.9}$$

The support $s(A_q \Rightarrow B_q)$ is the ratio of compatible training data with both the antecedent part A_q and the consequent part B_q to the given training data. The support $s(A_q \Rightarrow B_q)$ measures the coverage of training data by the linguistic association rule $A_q \Rightarrow B_q$.

8.2.2 Specification of the Consequent Part

As in the heuristic rule generation method in Chap. 2 for pattern classification problems, we choose the consequent linguistic term with the maximum confidence for the antecedent part A_q as

$$c(A_q \Rightarrow B_q) = \max\{c(A_q \Rightarrow B_k)|k = 1, 2, \ldots, K\}, \tag{8.10}$$

where B_k, $k = 1, 2, \ldots, K$, are linguistic terms given for the output variable. In Chap. 2, the consequent part of each linguistic rule was specified as the consequent class with the maximum confidence.

We illustrate the heuristic rule generation method in (8.10) using the simple numerical example in Fig. 8.1. The location of each input–output pair in Fig. 8.1 is shown in Table 8.1. Let us consider the specification of the consequent part of the linguistic rule "If x is small then y is B_q". As shown in Fig. 8.1, five linguistic terms are given for the output variable. Thus B_q is one of those five linguistic terms (i.e., S: small, MS: medium small, M: medium, ML: medium large, and L: large). The membership function of each linguistic term is as follows:

$$\mu_S(y) = \max\{0, 1 - 4 \cdot |y|\}, \tag{8.11}$$
$$\mu_{MS}(y) = \max\{0, 1 - 4 \cdot |0.25 - y|\}, \tag{8.12}$$
$$\mu_M(y) = \max\{0, 1 - 4 \cdot |0.5 - y|\}, \tag{8.13}$$
$$\mu_{ML}(y) = \max\{0, 1 - 4 \cdot |0.75 - y|\}, \tag{8.14}$$
$$\mu_L(y) = \max\{0, 1 - 4 \cdot |1 - y|\}. \tag{8.15}$$

The five linguistic terms for the input variable x in Fig. 8.1 have the same membership functions as (8.11)–(8.15).

Table 8.1. Input–output pairs in Fig. 8.1

p	1	2	3	4	5	6	7	8	9	10
x_p	0.01	0.05	0.12	0.14	0.22	0.26	0.29	0.39	0.43	0.53
y_p	0.77	0.63	0.59	0.49	0.44	0.48	0.56	0.53	0.63	0.64
p	11	12	13	14	15	16	17	18	19	20
x_p	0.59	0.64	0.71	0.74	0.79	0.82	0.85	0.89	0.91	0.98
y_p	0.74	0.77	0.73	0.55	0.65	0.54	0.35	0.44	0.28	0.21

To determine the consequent part B_q of the linguistic rule "If x is small then y is B_q" using (8.10), the confidence for each of the five consequent linguistic terms is calculated as

$$c(small \Rightarrow small) = 0.000, \tag{8.16}$$

$$c(small \Rightarrow medium\ small) = 0.016, \tag{8.17}$$

$$c(small \Rightarrow medium) = 0.433, \tag{8.18}$$

$$c(small \Rightarrow medium\ large) = 0.523, \tag{8.19}$$

$$c(small \Rightarrow large) = 0.027. \tag{8.20}$$

Since *medium large* has the maximum confidence among the five consequent linguistic terms, the consequent part is specified as *medium large* for the antecedent linguistic term *small*. In the same manner, we can generate the following five linguistic rules for the simple numerical example in Fig. 8.1:

If x is *small* then y is *medium large*, (8.21)

If x is *medium small* then y is *medium*, (8.22)

If x is *medium* then y is *medium large*, (8.23)

If x is *medium large* then y is *medium large*, (8.24)

If x is *large* then y is *medium small*. (8.25)

If we try to intuitively generate linguistic rules from the given training data in Fig. 8.1, we are likely to generate the same five linguistic rules. That is, our heuristic rule generation method determines the consequent part of each linguistic rule in an intuitively acceptable manner.

To further illustrate our heuristic rule generation method, we applied it to 441 input–output pairs obtained from a nonlinear function in Fig. 8.4. The 441 input–output pairs correspond to the 441 grid points of the uniformly divided 21×21 grid of the two-dimensional input space $[0, 1] \times [0, 1]$. Our task is to approximately represent the nonlinear function in Fig. 8.4 using linguistic rules. When five linguistic terms are given for each of the two input variables as in Fig. 8.2, 25 linguistic rules are to be generated from the 441 input–output pairs. The generated linguistic rules using five linguistic terms for the output variable are shown in Fig. 8.5. From the comparison between Fig. 8.4 and Fig. 8.5, we can see that intuitively acceptable linguistic rules were generated by the heuristic rule generation method.

8.2.3 Other Approaches to Linguistic Rule Generations

Since Mamdani's pioneering work [124], fuzzy rule-based systems have been mainly applied to control problems [118, 119, 156]. In early studies, fuzzy rules were obtained from human experts in the form of linguistic knowledge. Many studies have been proposed for automatically generating fuzzy rules from numerical data. Takagi & Sugeno [162] proposed the well-known Takagi–Sugeno model where a linear function instead of a linguistic term was used in the consequent part as follows:

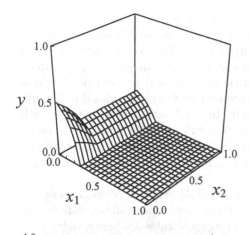

Fig. 8.4. Nonlinear function from which 441 input–output pairs are obtained for generating a linguistic rule-based system

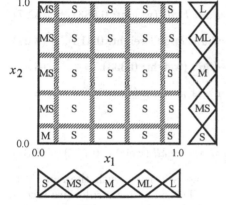

Fig. 8.5. Linguistic rule-based system generated to approximately realize the nonlinear function in Fig. 8.4

R_q: If x_1 is A_{q1} and ... and x_n is A_{qn}

$$\text{then } y_q(x) = a_{q0} + a_{q1}x_1 + \ldots + a_{qn}x_n, \qquad (8.26)$$

where a_{qi} is an adjustable parameter (real number). They proposed a fuzzy modeling method for determining the membership function of each antecedent fuzzy set and the consequent linear function of each fuzzy rule.

For determining fuzzy rules of the form in (8.1), clustering techniques have been used in many fuzzy modeling methods [150, 151, 159]. In clustering-based methods, antecedent and consequent fuzzy sets are usually generated by the projection of each cluster (i.e., multi-dimensional fuzzy set) onto input and output variables. That is, usually clustering-based methods (as well as the Takagi–Sugeno model) do not assume that linguistic terms are given for input and output variables.

Wang & Mendel [176] proposed a rule generation method that used given linguistic terms. In their method, it is assumed that the input–output space has already been divided into fuzzy subspaces by given linguistic terms as in Fig. 8.1. First the linguistic rule with the highest compatibility grade for each input–output pair is identified. That is, m linguistic rules are generated from the given m input–output pairs. Of course, the same linguistic rule may be generated from multiple input–output pairs. The compatibility grade of each linguistic rule with the corresponding input–output pair (i.e., the input–output pair that generates the linguistic rule) is used as the rule weight of the linguistic rule. When there exist inconsistent linguistic rules (i.e., linguistic rules with the same antecedent part but different consequent linguistic terms), the linguistic rule with the largest rule weight is chosen to resolve the inconsistency. Rule weights are used only for resolving the inconsistency in the rule generation method of Wang & Mendel (i.e., rule weights are not used in fuzzy reasoning).

We illustrate the rule generation method of Wang & Mendel using the simple numerical example in Fig. 8.1. From each input–output pair in Fig. 8.1 (i.e., in Table 8.1), the following 20 linguistic rules are generated:

1st pair: If x is *small* then y is *medium large* (weight: 0.883),   (8.27)

2nd pair: If x is *small* then y is *medium large* (weight: 0.416),   (8.28)

3rd pair: If x is *small* then y is *medium* (weight: 0.333),   (8.29)

4th pair: If x is *medium small* then y is *medium* (weight: 0.538), (8.30)

$$\vdots$$

20th pair: If x is *large* then y is *medium small* (weight: 0.773).   (8.31)

From the first three input–output pairs, linguistic rules with the same antecedent part "If x is *small* " are generated. These linguistic rules are inconsistent. Thus the linguistic rule with the largest weight (i.e., (8.27) generated from the first input–output pair) is chosen. In this manner, we have five linguistic rules for the simple numerical example in Fig. 8.1 using the rule generation method of Wang & Mendel. The generated five linguistic rules are the same as those by our heuristic rule generation method in the previous subsection.

The difference between our heuristic method and the rule generation method of Wang & Mendel can be clearly illustrated using Fig. 8.6. In this figure, a single input–output pair $(0.49, 0.24)$ is added to the 20 input–output pairs in Fig. 8.1. Our heuristic method generates the same five linguistic rules for Fig. 8.6 as those for Fig. 8.1. On the other hand, the rule generation method of Wang & Mendel generates the linguistic rule "If x is *medium* then y is *medium small*" for Fig. 8.6 while it generates "If x is *medium* then y is *medium large*" for Fig. 8.1. This is because the consequent linguistic term of each linguistic rule is determined by a single input–output pair with the highest compatibility grade in the rule generation method of Wang & Mendel. On the other hand, it is determined by all the compatible input–output pairs with the antecedent part in our heuristic method.

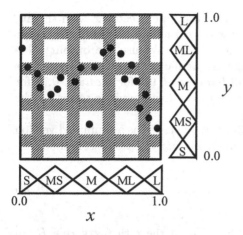

Fig. 8.6. A slightly modified example. A single input–output pair $(0.49, 0.24)$ is added to the 20 input–output pairs in Fig. 8.1

8.2.4 Estimation of Output Values by Linguistic Rules

Fuzzy reasoning for modeling problems in this chapter is to infer an output value for an input vector using linguistic rules. Many fuzzy reasoning methods have been proposed in the literature. They can be classified into two categories: FATI (first aggregate then infer) and FITA (first infer then aggregate). In fuzzy reasoning methods in the FATI category, first an aggregated fuzzy set on the output variable is constructed by combining the consequent part of each linguistic rule. Then a final inferred output value is calculated from the aggregated fuzzy set constructed in the first phase. On the other hand, first a real number is calculated for the consequent part of each linguistic rule in fuzzy reasoning methods in the FITA category. Then a final inferred output value is calculated from the real number for each linguistic rule obtained in the first phase. Fuzzy reasoning methods in the FATI category such as the center-of-gravity method were mainly used in early studies on fuzzy rule-based systems. Recently fuzzy reasoning methods in the FITA category have been frequently used. In this chapter, we use a simple fuzzy reasoning method in the FITA category. See Emami et al. [44] and Cordon et al. [25] for details of these two categories of fuzzy reasoning methods.

8.2.5 Standard Fuzzy Reasoning

Let S be a set of linguistic rules of the form (8.1). The rule set S can be viewed as a linguistic rule-based system. The estimated output value $\hat{y}(x)$ is calculated from the linguistic rule-based system S for an input vector $x = (x_1, x_2, \ldots, x_n)$ as

$$\hat{y}(x) = \frac{\sum_{R_q \in S} \mu_{A_q}(x) \cdot b_q}{\sum_{R_q \in S} \mu_{A_q}(x)}, \tag{8.32}$$

where $\mu_{A_q}(x)$ is the compatibility grade of the input vector x with the antecedent part A_q, and b_q is a representative real number for the consequent linguistic term B_q of the q-th linguistic rule R_q. We use the output value with the maximum membership of the triangular membership function as b_q for B_q (e.g., 0 for *small*, 0.25 for *medium small*, 0.5 for *medium*, 0.75 for *medium large*, and 1 for *large* in the case of the five linguistic terms on the unit interval $[0, 1]$).

The fuzzy reasoning method in (8.32) can be viewed as a simplified version of the Takagi–Sugeno model with the following fuzzy reasoning method:

$$\hat{y}(x) = \frac{\sum\limits_{R_q \in S} \mu_{A_q}(x) \cdot y_q(x)}{\sum\limits_{R_q \in S} \mu_{A_q}(x)}, \tag{8.33}$$

where $y_q(x)$ is the consequent linear function of the q-th fuzzy rule R_q in (8.26).

In Fig. 8.7, we show the estimated output by the five linguistic rules in (8.21)–(8.25) for the simple numerical example in Fig. 8.1. The bold lines in Fig. 8.7 are the input–output relation obtained from the five linguistic rules using the fuzzy reasoning method in (8.32).

For the five linguistic terms for the input variable in Fig. 8.7, the following relation holds for any input value x in the domain interval $[0, 1]$:

$$\mu_S(x) + \mu_{MS}(x) + \mu_M(x) + \mu_{ML}(x) + \mu_L(x) = 1. \tag{8.34}$$

Thus (8.32) can be rewritten for the five linguistic rules in (8.21)–(8.25) as

$$\hat{y}(x) = 0.75 \times \mu_S(x) + 0.5 \times \mu_{MS}(x)$$
$$+ 0.75 \times \mu_M(x) + 0.75 \times \mu_{ML}(x) + 0.25 \times \mu_L(x). \tag{8.35}$$

Using the membership function of each linguistic term, this formulation is further rewritten as

$$\hat{y}(x) = \begin{cases} 0.75 \cdot 4(0.25 - x) + 0.5 \cdot 4x, & \text{if } 0 \leq x < 0.25, \\ 0.5 \cdot 4(0.5 - x) + 0.75 \cdot 4(x - 0.25), & \text{if } 0.25 \leq x < 0.5, \\ 0.75 \cdot 4(0.75 - x) + 0.75 \cdot 4(x - 0.5), & \text{if } 0.5 \leq x < 0.75, \\ 0.75 \cdot 4(1 - x) + 0.25 \cdot 4(x - 0.75), & \text{if } 0.75 \leq x \leq 1. \end{cases} \tag{8.36}$$

The bold lines in Fig. 8.7 correspond to this piece-wise linear function. As shown in Fig. 8.7 and (8.36), we can see that the input–output relation realized from the five linguistic rules is the linear interpolation of the representative real numbers for the consequent linguistic terms of adjacent linguistic rules.

Another example of a fuzzy reasoning result is shown in Fig. 8.8. This figure shows the estimated input–output relation from the 25 linguistic rules in Fig. 8.5. From the comparison between Fig. 8.5 and Fig. 8.8, we can see that the fuzzy reasoning result in Fig. 8.8 is intuitively acceptable.

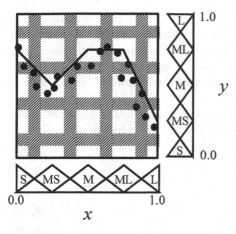

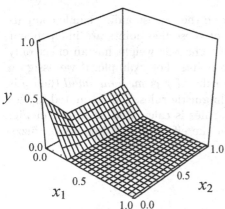

Fig. 8.7. The estimated input–output relation from the five linguistic rules with no rule weights

Fig. 8.8. The input–output relation obtained from the 25 linguistic rules in Fig. 8.5

While the rule weight of each linguistic rule has a large effect on the location of the classification boundary in the application to pattern classification problems in Chap. 2, the rule weight has only a limited effect on the input–output relation realized by the fuzzy reasoning method. Let us consider linguistic rules with rule weights of the following form:

Rule R_q: If x_1 is A_{q1} and ... and x_n is A_{qn}

$$\text{then } y \text{ is } B_q \text{ with } CF_q, \qquad (8.37)$$

where CF_q is the rule weight of the linguistic rule R_q. In this case, the fuzzy reasoning method in (8.32) is modified as

$$\hat{y}(\boldsymbol{x}) = \frac{\displaystyle\sum_{R_q \in S} CF_q \cdot \mu_{A_q}(\boldsymbol{x}) \cdot b_q}{\displaystyle\sum_{R_q \in S} CF_q \cdot \mu_{A_q}(\boldsymbol{x})}. \qquad (8.38)$$

As shown in Fig. 8.7, some input values (vectors) are compatible with only a single linguistic rule. For each of these input values (vectors), the estimated output value is calculated as the representative real number of the consequent linguistic term of the single compatible rule. Thus the rule weight of each linguistic rule has no effect on the calculation of the estimated output values for those input values (vectors).

The bold lines in Fig. 8.7 (i.e., the input–output relation obtained from the five linguistic rules) are determined by the following five points:

$$\hat{y}(x) = 0.75 \quad \text{for } x = 0, \tag{8.39}$$

$$\hat{y}(x) = 0.5 \quad \text{for } x = 0.25, \tag{8.40}$$

$$\hat{y}(x) = 0.75 \quad \text{for } x = 0.5, \tag{8.41}$$

$$\hat{y}(x) = 0.75 \quad \text{for } x = 0.75, \tag{8.42}$$

$$\hat{y}(x) = 0.25 \quad \text{for } x = 1. \tag{8.43}$$

Each of these five points is calculated from the corresponding single compatible linguistic rule. Thus the locations of these five points are independent of the rule weight of each linguistic rule. The rule weight has an effect only on the interpolation between these five points. For example, if we assign a rule weight 0.2 to the second linguistic rule "If x is *medium small* then y is *medium*" and 1.0 to all the other four linguistic rules, the estimated input–output relation from the five linguistic rules is calculated as shown in Fig. 8.9. See [129] for further discussions on the effect of rule weights on fuzzy reasoning results in modeling problems.

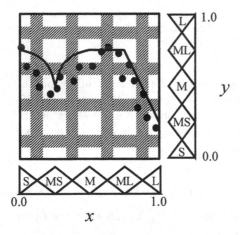

Fig. 8.9. The estimated input–output relation from the five linguistic rules with rule weights. The rule weight of the second linguistic rule is 0.2 and those of the other linguistic rules are 1.0

8.2.6 Limitations and Extensions

As shown in Fig. 8.7 and Fig. 8.8, fuzzy reasoning results (i.e., input–output relations realized by linguistic rules) are piece-wise linear lines (planes, hyperplanes). Since we use given linguistic terms for input and output variables, it is difficult to perform the fine tuning of linguistic rule-based systems. The adjustment of linguistic rule-based systems in a tabular form is performed by replacing the consequent linguistic term of each linguistic rule with another one. Since we use only a small number of linguistic terms for the output variable, the adjustment of linguistic rules by replacing their consequent linguistic terms with other ones is very coarse. In Fig. 8.7, we observe large errors between the given input–output pairs and the estimated input–output relation for *medium large x*. One may think that these errors would be decreased by using a different consequent linguistic term for the fourth linguistic rule. In Fig. 8.10, we show the estimated input–output relation when we use *medium* instead of *medium large* in the consequent part of the fourth linguistic rule. As shown in this figure, the accuracy of the five linguistic rules deteriorates from Fig. 8.7 to Fig. 8.10 on replacing the consequent linguistic term. While the desired input–output relation is somewhere between Fig. 8.7 and Fig. 8.10, we cannot realize such an input–output relation using the given five linguistic terms. This discussion shows that the adjustment of the membership function of each linguistic term is necessary to improve the accuracy of linguistic rule-based systems. Many learning methods based on neural networks and genetic algorithms have been proposed to improve the accuracy of fuzzy rule-based systems [119]. In Chap. 10, we will show how the accuracy of linguistic rule-based systems can be improved by using an adjustable real number in the consequent part of each linguistic rule instead of a linguistic term.

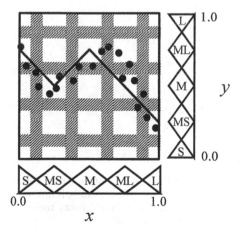

Fig. 8.10. The estimated input–output relation from the five linguistic rules after replacing the consequent linguistic term of the fourth linguistic rule (i.e., *medium large*) with *medium*

Another limitation of linguistic rule-based systems in a tabular form is the scalability to high-dimensional problems with many input variables. As we have already explained for pattern classification problems, the number of linguistic rules in a rule table is K^n when we have K linguistic terms for each of the n input variables. This means that the number of linguistic rules increases exponentially as the number of input variables increases. Thus we cannot use linguistic rule-based systems in a tabular form for high-dimensional problems. As in the case of pattern classification problems, we use short linguistic rules with many *don't care* conditions to handle high-dimensional modeling problems. In Chap. 9, we will explain genetic algorithm-based rule selection and GBML for modeling problems.

8.2.7 Non-Standard Fuzzy Reasoning Based on the Specificity of Each Linguistic Rule

When we simultaneously use general linguistic rules and specific linguistic rules in a single linguistic rule-based system, counter-intuitive fuzzy reasoning results are often obtained [61, 92]. Let us consider the following three linguistic rules for a modeling problem with two input variables x_1 and x_2:

R_1: If x_1 is *small* and x_2 is *small* then y is *medium*, (8.44)

R_2: If x_1 is *small* then y is *medium small*, (8.45)

R_3: y is *small*. (8.46)

The first linguistic rule has two antecedent conditions while the second rule has only a single antecedent condition. The third rule has no antecedent condition (i.e., has two *don't care* conditions). The estimated input–output function is depicted in Fig. 8.11. This figure is obtained from the three linguistic rules using the standard fuzzy reasoning method in (8.32).

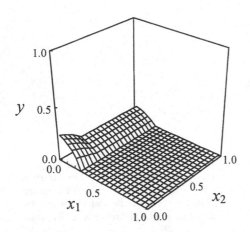

Fig. 8.11. The input–output relation obtained from the three linguistic rules using the standard fuzzy reasoning method in (8.32)

The point is whether the nonlinear function in Fig. 8.11 coincides with our intuition or not (i.e., whether an intuitively constructed nonlinear function from the three linguistic rules is similar to Fig. 8.11 or not). Let us consider the estimated output value for a *small* x_1 and a *small* x_2. For example, all the three linguistic rules are fully compatible with the input vector $x = (0,0)$. Thus the estimated output value for this input vector is calculated as $\hat{y}(x) = 0.25$ as the interpolation of the three linguistic terms *medium*, *medium small*, and *small*. It seems that the estimated output value 0.25 does not coincide with our intuition. When the three linguistic rules in (8.44)–(8.46) are given, usually we intuitively think that the output value would be *medium* for a *small* x_1 and a *small* x_2. This is because we usually use the most specific rule (i.e., (8.44)) when multiple rules are applicable to a current situation. On the other hand, fuzzy reasoning is usually based on the interpolation of compatible rules. As a result, fuzzy reasoning results are often counter-intuitive when general rules (i.e., short rules with many *don't care* conditions) and specific rules (long rules with many antecedent conditions) are simultaneously used in a single linguistic rule-based system.

One might think that the three linguistic rules in (8.44)–(8.46) should not be used in a single rule-based system because they are inconsistent with each other. Several approaches have been proposed for finding inconsistent rules in fuzzy rule-based systems [11, 125, 172, 186]. In those studies, it was implicitly assumed that the inconsistency in fuzzy rule-based systems should be removed or resolved. Recently the importance of outliers and exception rules was recognized in some studies on data mining [113, 114, 160]. This is because interesting rules are likely to be generated from exceptions in many cases. The handling of inconsistent rules has also been studied in the field of default reasoning [9, 49, 141, 144, 147]. Many studies on default reasoning espouse some form of preference for more specific information [9]. When two inconsistent rules are applicable to a current situation, the more specific rule is usually used in the reasoning for this situation. In a data mining algorithm for finding exception rules [160], more specific rules (i.e., exception rules) are implicitly assumed to have priority over general rules. Default reasoning has also been discussed in the framework of possibility theory (for details, see Dubois et al. [31, 32], Dubois & Prade [34, 35, 37], and Yager [182, 183, 184, 185]).

The preference for more specific information is frequently explained in the literature using the following simple example. Let us consider the reasoning about a penguin x using the following three rules:

Rule R_I: Birds fly,   (8.47)

Rule R_II: Penguins are birds,   (8.48)

Rule R_III: Penguins do not fly.   (8.49)

If we use the first two rules R_I and R_II, we conclude that x flies. We usually conclude, however, that x does not fly using the third rule R_III. This is because the third rule R_III is more specific than the first rule R_I.

In order to implement the preference for more specific information, the following non-standard fuzzy reasoning method was proposed in [61, 92] based on the specificity of each linguistic rule:

$$\hat{y}(\boldsymbol{x}) = \frac{\displaystyle\sum_{R_q \in S} w(R_q, \boldsymbol{x}) \cdot \mu_{A_q}(\boldsymbol{x}) \cdot b_q}{\displaystyle\sum_{R_q \in S} w(R_q, \boldsymbol{x}) \cdot \mu_{A_q}(\boldsymbol{x})}. \tag{8.50}$$

This formulation is the same as the standard fuzzy reasoning method in (8.32) when $w(R_q, \boldsymbol{x}) = 1$. In this formulation, $w(R_q, \boldsymbol{x})$ is a rule weight determined by the relative specificity of the linguistic rule R_q. When R_q includes more specific rules, the rule weight $w(R_q, \boldsymbol{x})$ of R_q for $\boldsymbol{x}$ is discounted in the fuzzy reasoning method in (8.50) as follows:

$$w(R_q, \boldsymbol{x}) = \prod_{\substack{R_k \subseteq R_q \\ k \neq q}} (1 - \mu_{A_k}(\boldsymbol{x})). \tag{8.51}$$

On the other hand, $w(R_q, \boldsymbol{x})$ is defined as $w(R_q, \boldsymbol{x}) = 1$ when no rule is included in R_q. This means that the non-standard fuzzy reasoning method in (8.50) is the same the standard fuzzy reasoning method (8.32) when they are used for linguistic rule-based systems in the standard tabular form (e.g., Fig. 8.5). This is because all linguistic rules in the standard tabular form have the same specificity (i.e., no inclusion relations hold among linguistic rules). Different results are obtained from the two fuzzy reasoning methods only when the inclusion relation holds among linguistic rules. Note that the inclusion relation between linguistic rules is defined by their antecedent parts as

$$R_k \subseteq R_q \Leftrightarrow A_{ki} \subseteq A_{qi} \text{ for } i = 1, 2, \ldots, n. \tag{8.52}$$

Let us illustrate the non-standard fuzzy reasoning method using the three linguistic rules in (8.44)–(8.46). Among the three linguistic rules, the inclusion relation $R_1 \subseteq R_2 \subseteq R_3$ holds. Thus $w(R_q, \boldsymbol{x})$ is calculated as

$$w(R_1, \boldsymbol{x}) = 1, \tag{8.53}$$

$$w(R_2, \boldsymbol{x}) = 1 - \mu_{A_1}(\boldsymbol{x})$$
$$= 1 - \mu_S(x_1) \cdot \mu_S(x_2), \tag{8.54}$$

$$w(R_3, \boldsymbol{x}) = (1 - \mu_{A_1}(\boldsymbol{x})) \times (1 - \mu_{A_2}(\boldsymbol{x}))$$
$$= (1 - \mu_S(x_1) \cdot \mu_S(x_2)) \times (1 - \mu_S(x_1)). \tag{8.55}$$

From (8.55), we can see that the rule weight of the most general rule (i.e., R_3: y is *small*) is discounted when the input vector is compatible with the other rules. The weight of R_2 is discounted in (8.54) when the input vector is compatible with the most specific rule R_1. In Fig. 8.12, we show the input–output relation obtained from the three linguistic rules in (8.44)–(8.46) using the non-standard fuzzy reasoning method. We can see from Fig. 8.12 that the non-standard fuzzy reasoning method successfully implements the preference for more specific information through the weighting mechanism using $w(R_q, \boldsymbol{x})$. For example, the estimated output value $\hat{y}(\boldsymbol{x})$ for the input vector $\boldsymbol{x} = (0, 0)$ is 0.5 in Fig. 8.12 with the non-standard fuzzy reasoning method while it was 0.25 in Fig. 8.11 with the standard fuzzy reasoning method. This is because the estimated output value (i.e., $\hat{y}(\boldsymbol{x}) = 0.5$) is calculated only from the most specific linguistic rule R_1 in the case of the non-standard fuzzy reasoning method in Fig. 8.12 while it was calculated as the interpolation of all three linguistic rules compatible with the input vector $\boldsymbol{x} = (0, 0)$ in the case of the standard fuzzy reasoning method in Fig. 8.11.

From the comparison between Fig. 8.12 and Fig. 8.8, we can see that very similar results are obtained from the three linguistic rules in (8.44)–(8.46) and from the 25 linguistic rules in Fig. 8.5. That is, the three linguistic rules with the non-standard fuzzy reasoning method played a very similar role as the 25 linguistic rules in Fig. 8.5 with the standard fuzzy reasoning method. The non-standard fuzzy reasoning method in (8.50) is an attempt to handle linguistic rule-based systems that consist of general and specific linguistic rules. The formulation in (8.50) may need modifications and/or extensions in future studies.

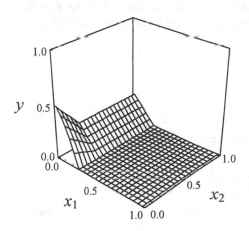

Fig. 8.12. The input–output relation obtained from the three linguistic rules using the non-standard fuzzy reasoning method in (8.50)

8.3 Modeling of Nonlinear Fuzzy Functions

In the previous section, we discussed the estimation of the output value $\hat{y}(\boldsymbol{x})$ from a linguistic rule-based system for an input vector $\boldsymbol{x}$. That is, the linguistic rule-based system was used as an approximator of a nonlinear function. In this section, we briefly discuss the modeling of fuzzy functions using linguistic rule-based systems. This topic will be further discussed in Chap. 14 where fuzzified neural networks are used to approximately realize fuzzy functions.

A function with non-fuzzy input and fuzzy output values is referred to as a fuzzy function in this section. That is, a fuzzy function is a mapping from a non-fuzzy input vector $\boldsymbol{x} = (x_1, x_2, \ldots, x_n)$ to a fuzzy number $\hat{y}(\boldsymbol{x})$.

The fuzzy reasoning method in (8.32) is modified to approximately realize a nonlinear fuzzy function as

$$\tilde{y}(x) = \frac{\sum\limits_{R_q \in S} \mu_{A_q}(x) \cdot B_q}{\sum\limits_{R_q \in S} \mu_{A_q}(x)}. \tag{8.56}$$

In this formulation, the calculation of $\tilde{y}(x)$ is performed using fuzzy arithmetic [106]. We will explain fuzzy arithmetic in detail in Chap. 11 in the context of fuzzification of neural networks. Since the approximation of non-fuzzy functions has been the main research topic in the field of fuzzy rule-based systems, there are not many studies on the approximation of fuzzy functions [78].

Using the five linguistic rules in Fig. 8.7 (i.e., in (8.21)–(8.25)), we illustrate the difference between (8.32) for calculating the estimated real number and (8.56) for calculating the estimated fuzzy number. When the input value $x = 0.125$ is presented to the linguistic rule-based system with the five linguistic rules, the estimated real number $\hat{y}(x)$ is calculated from (8.32) as

$$\begin{aligned}
\hat{y}(x) &= \frac{\mu_S(x) \cdot 0.75 + \mu_{MS}(x) \cdot 0.5}{\mu_S(x) + \mu_{MS}(x)} \\
&= \frac{0.5 \cdot 0.75 + 0.5 \cdot 0.5}{0.5 + 0.5} \\
&= 0.625.
\end{aligned} \tag{8.57}$$

On the other hand, the estimated fuzzy number $\tilde{y}(x)$ is calculated for the input value $x = 0.125$ from (8.56) as

$$\begin{aligned}
\tilde{y}(x) &= \frac{\mu_S(x) \cdot medium\ large + \mu_{MS}(x) \cdot medium}{\mu_S(x) + \mu_{MS}(x)} \\
&= 0.5 \cdot medium\ large + 0.5 \cdot medium.
\end{aligned} \tag{8.58}$$

Intuitively, $\tilde{y}(x)$ is a fuzzy number between *medium large* and *medium*. More specifically, $\tilde{y}(x)$ is the weighted average of *medium large* and *medium*. Using fuzzy arithmetic, the membership function $\tilde{y}(x)$ in (8.58) is calculated as shown in Fig. 8.13.

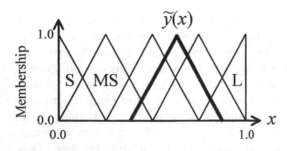

Fig. 8.13. Membership function of $\tilde{y}(x)$ in (8.58)

A fuzzy rule-based system can also be used as an approximator of a fuzzy mapping from a fuzzy input vector to a fuzzy output value. When a fuzzy input vector $\tilde{x} = (\tilde{x}_1, \tilde{x}_2, \ldots, \tilde{x}_n)$ is presented to a fuzzy rule-based system, (8.56) is further extended to calculate the estimated fuzzy output $\tilde{y}(\tilde{x})$ as

$$\tilde{y}(\tilde{x}) = \frac{\sum\limits_{R_q \in S} \mu_{A_q}(\tilde{x}) \cdot B_q}{\sum\limits_{R_q \in S} \mu_{A_q}(\tilde{x})}, \tag{8.59}$$

where $\mu_{A_q}(\tilde{x})$ is the compatibility grade of the fuzzy input vector $\tilde{x}$ with the antecedent part A_q of the linguistic rule R_q. Using fuzzy arithmetic, the estimated fuzzy output $\tilde{y}(\tilde{x})$ is calculated from (8.59) in the same manner as illustrated in (8.58). The problem in (8.59) is the definition of the compatibility grade $\mu_{A_q}(\tilde{x})$ of the fuzzy input vector $\tilde{x}$ with the antecedent part A_q. There may be many alternative definitions. One definition is based on the possibility measure [36] as follows:

$$\mu_{A_q}(\tilde{x}) = \text{Poss}(A_{q1}, \tilde{x}_1) \times \ldots \times \text{Poss}(A_{qn}, \tilde{x}_n), \tag{8.60}$$

where

$$\text{Poss}(A_{qi}, \tilde{x}_i) = \max\{\mu_{A_{qi}}(x) \wedge \mu_{\tilde{\omega}_i}(x) | x \in \Re\}. \tag{8.61}$$

In (8.61), $\wedge$ is the minimum operator (i.e., $a \wedge b = \min\{a, b\}$). Of course, we can use the minimum operator instead of the product operator in (8.60). Other measures may be used in (8.60) instead of the possibility measure. The approximation of fuzzy functions and fuzzy mappings will be further discussed in Chap. 14.

9. Design of Compact Linguistic Models

As in the case of pattern classification problems, genetic algorithm-based rule selection and genetics-based machine learning can be applied to the design of linguistic rule-based systems for modeling problems [85, 90]. These two schemes for pattern classification problems are slightly modified in this chapter to apply them to modeling problems. As in the previous chapter, we use linguistic rules of the following form to approximately realize an n-input and single-output nonlinear function:

$$\text{Rule } R_q\text{: If } x_1 \text{ is } A_{q1} \text{ and } \dots \text{ and } x_n \text{ is } A_{qn} \text{ then } y \text{ is } B_q. \tag{9.1}$$

Our task in this chapter is to design a linguistic rule-based system from the given m input–output pairs (x_p, y_p), $p = 1, 2, \dots, m$, where $x_p = (x_{p1}, x_{p2}, \dots, x_{pn})$ is an n-dimensional input vector and y_p is the corresponding output value. For simplicity of explanation, we assume that the input–output space has already been normalized into the unit hypercube $[0, 1]^{n+1}$. We also assume that K linguistic terms are given for each of the n input and single output variables.

9.1 Single-Objective and Multi-Objective Formulations

9.1.1 Three Objectives in the Design of Linguistic Models

In Chap. 6, we explained the three-objective optimization problem in the design of linguistic rule-based systems for pattern classification problems. The three objectives were the classification accuracy, the number of linguistic rules, and the total rule length of linguistic rules. The first objective should be modified for modeling problems while the other two objectives can be used with no modifications.

Let S be a set of linguistic rules of the form (9.1). In addition to the given K linguistic terms, we use *don't care* as an antecedent fuzzy set (i.e., A_{qi} in (9.1)). This special fuzzy set is not used as a consequent fuzzy set (i.e., B_q in (9.1)) because linguistic rules with *don't care* in the consequent part are meaningless. Thus the total number of possible linguistic rules is $K(K+1)^n$. The rule set S is a subset of these linguistic rules. The rule set S can be viewed as a fuzzy rule-based system for our modeling problem.

We measure the accuracy of the rule set S by the total squared error as

$$f_1(S) = \sum_{p=1}^{m} \{\hat{y}(\boldsymbol{x}_p) - y_p\}^2 / 2, \tag{9.2}$$

where $\hat{y}(\boldsymbol{x}_p)$ is the estimated output value for the input vector $\boldsymbol{x}_p = (x_{p1}, x_{p2}, \ldots, x_{pn})$ by the rule set S. We can use any fuzzy reasoning method for the calculation of $\hat{y}(\boldsymbol{x})$. In this chapter, we use the non-standard fuzzy reasoning method in (8.50) of the previous chapter. Note that the non-standard fuzzy reasoning method is the same as the standard fuzzy reasoning method in (8.32) when no inclusion relation holds among linguistic rules in the rule set S.

Since S is an arbitrary subset of the $K(K+1)^n$ linguistic rules, there are many cases where the entire input space is not covered by the rule set S. This means that the estimated output value $\hat{y}(\boldsymbol{x})$ is not always calculated for an arbitrary input vector $\boldsymbol{x} = (x_1, x_2, \ldots, x_n)$. When there is no compatible linguistic rule in S for the input vector $\boldsymbol{x}_p$, the corresponding estimated output value $\hat{y}(\boldsymbol{x}_p)$ cannot be calculated from S. In this case, the squared error for the input–output pair $(\boldsymbol{x}_p, y_p)$ cannot be calculated in (9.2), either. Thus we use a pre-specified penalty value as the squared error when $\hat{y}(\boldsymbol{x}_p)$ cannot be calculated:

$$(\hat{y}(\boldsymbol{x}_p) - y_p)^2 = \delta^2, \tag{9.3}$$

where δ is a pre-specified positive constant. In our computer simulations in this chapter, we specified the penalty value as $(\hat{y}(\boldsymbol{x}_p) - y_p)^2 = 1$ because the output value y_p is normalized into a real number in the unit interval $[0, 1]$.

As in Chap. 6 for pattern classification problems, the second objective $f_2(S)$ and the third objective $f_3(S)$ are the number of linguistic rules in S (i.e., $|S|$) and the total rule length of linguistic rules in S, respectively.

Using the three objectives, the design of linguistic rule-based systems for modeling problems is formulated as

$$\text{Minimize } f_1(S), \text{ minimize } f_2(S), \text{ and minimize } f_3(S). \tag{9.4}$$

Note that all three objectives are to be minimized. In Chap. 6, the first objective was to be maximized because it was the number of correctly classified training patterns by the rule set S. In this chapter, $f_1(S)$ should be minimized because it is the total squared error.

9.1.2 Handling as a Single-Objective Optimization Problem

When the weight for each objective is available from a human user, the three objectives in (9.4) can be combined into a single scalar objective function as

$$\text{Minimize } f(S) = w_1 \cdot f_1(S) + w_2 \cdot f_2(S) + w_3 \cdot f_3(S), \tag{9.5}$$

where w_1, w_2, and w_3 are non-negative real numbers. The three weights w_1, w_2, and w_3 should be specified according to the user's preference with respect to the three objectives. We assume that the weight values are given by the human user. The minimization problem in (9.5) can be treated in the framework of single-objective optimization. Thus standard optimization techniques are applicable to the design of linguistic rule-based systems. This is an advantage of the single-objective formulation in (9.5) over the multi-objective formulation in (9.4).

The main drawback of the single-objective formulation is related to the specification of the weight values with respect to the three objectives. It is not easy for the human user to appropriately specify the weight values according to their preference with respect to the three objectives. Moreover, the final solution (i.e., the obtained rule set) strongly depends on the specification of the weight values. This dependency is illustrated in Fig. 9.1. For simplicity of explanation, the three-dimensional objective space is represented as a two-dimensional objective space in Fig. 9.1 where the ellipsoidal region shows all subsets (i.e., all rule sets) of the linguistic rules. Figure 9.1 shows the relation between the search direction and the obtained rule set. The search direction is specified by the three weights w_1, w_2, and w_3. When the weight w_1 with respect to the total squared error is much larger than the other two weights w_2 and w_3, a complicated rule set with high accuracy will be obtained (e.g., the rule set S_a will be obtained from the search direction w_a in Fig. 9.1). In this case, the obtained rule set may consist of a large number of long linguistic rules. On the other hand, when the two weights w_2 and w_3 with respect to the complexity of rule sets are much larger than the other weight w_1 for the total squared error, a simple rule set with low accuracy may be obtained (e.g., the rule set S_b will be obtained from the search direction w_b). In this case, the obtained rule set may consist of a small number of short linguistic rules. When the three weights are of the same magnitude, a compromise solution may be obtained (e.g., the rule set S_c will be obtained from the search direction w_c). From these discussions, we can see that the obtained rule set from the single-objective formulation strongly depends on the specification of the three weight values. In real-world applications, the single-objective optimization problem in (9.5) will be solved several times using different weight vectors to find a number of alternative rule sets.

9.1.3 Handling as a Three-Objective Optimization Problem

As in Chap. 6, we can use multi-objective optimization algorithms to find non-dominated rule sets with respect to the three objectives in (9.4). Let us briefly review the concept of non-dominated rule sets for the three-objective optimization problem in (9.4). A rule set S_B is said to dominate another rule set S_A (i.e., S_B is better than S_A) if all the following inequalities hold:

$$f_1(S_A) \geq f_1(S_B), \quad f_2(S_A) \geq f_2(S_B), \quad f_3(S_A) \geq f_3(S_B), \tag{9.6}$$

and at least one of the following inequalities holds:

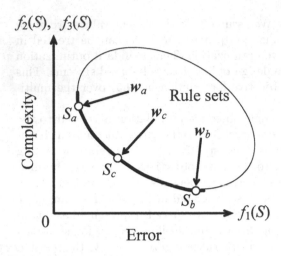

$f_2(S),\; f_3(S)$

Complexity

Rule sets

w_a

S_a

w_c

w_b

S_c

S_b

$f_1(S)$

0

Error

Fig. 9.1. Relation between the search direction and the obtained rule set in the multi-dimensional objective space. The bold curve shows the Pareto front of the multi-objective optimization problem

$$f_1(S_A) > f_1(S_B), \quad f_2(S_A) > f_2(S_B), \quad f_3(S_A) > f_3(S_B). \tag{9.7}$$

The first condition (i.e., all three inequalities in (9.6)) means that no objective of S_B is worse than S_A (i.e., S_B is not worse than S_A). The second condition (i.e., one of the three inequalities in (9.7)) means that at least one objective of S_B is better than S_A. When a rule set S is not dominated by any other rule set, S is said to be a Pareto-optimal solution of the three-objective optimization problem in (9.4). In Fig. 9.1, Pareto-optimal solutions are rule sets on the bold curve. The above conditions in (9.6)–(9.7) are slightly different from Chap. 6. This is because the first objective is to be minimized in this chapter while it was to be maximized in Chap. 6.

When the search space is not large, it may be easy to find all the Pareto-optimal solutions of the three-objective optimization problem in (9.4). On the other hand, when the search space is huge, it is impractical to try to find true Pareto-optimal solutions. In this case, multi-objective optimization algorithms try to find near-optimal solutions. Non-dominated solutions among examined ones are presented to the human user as search results.

In this chapter, we use the multi-objective genetic algorithm (MOGA) in Sect. 6.2 after modifying the definition of the fitness function. For the three-objective optimization problem in (9.4), the fitness value of each rule set S is defined as

$$fitness(S) = -w_1 \cdot f_1(S) - w_2 \cdot f_2(S) - w_3 \cdot f_3(S), \tag{9.8}$$

where w_1, w_2, and w_3 are weights satisfying the following conditions:

$$w_1, w_2, w_3 \geq 0, \tag{9.9}$$

$$w_1 + w_2 + w_3 = 1. \tag{9.10}$$

Since all three objectives are to be minimized, a negative sign is added to each weight in the fitness function in (9.8). The fitness function is supposed to be maximized. The other parts of the MOGA in Sect. 6.2 are used for modeling problems with no modifications.

9.2 Multi-Objective Rule Selection

As we have already explained in Chaps. 4 and 6 for pattern classification problems, genetic algorithm-based rule selection consists of two phases: candidate rule generation and rule selection. In the first phase, a large number of candidate rules are generated. When too many candidate rules are generated, prescreening is used to decrease the number of candidate rules. In the second phase, a small number of linguistic rules are selected from a large number of candidate rules to design a linguistic rule-based system. In the framework of single-objective optimization, a single rule set is obtained. On the other hand, multiple rule sets are obtained as non-dominated solutions of the three-objective optimization problem in (9.4) when we used the MOGA. In this section, we explain a genetic algorithm-based rule selection method that is designed to find multiple non-dominated rule sets of the three-objective optimization problem in (9.4).

9.2.1 Candidate Rule Generation

As we have explained, the total number of combinations of antecedent and consequent fuzzy sets is $K(K+1)^n$ when we use K linguistic terms and *don't care* for each of the n input variables and K linguistic terms for the single output variable. Thus the total number of linguistic rules is also $K(K + 1)^n$. For low-dimensional modeling problems, we can use all the $K(K + 1)^n$ linguistic rules as candidate rules in rule selection.

Let us consider a two-input and single-output nonlinear function in Fig. 9.2. This nonlinear function was depicted using nine linguistic rules in Fig. 9.3. When the three linguistic terms (i.e., S: *small*, M: *medium*, and L: *large*) are given for the two input and single output variables as in Fig. 9.3, the total number of combinations of antecedent and consequent fuzzy sets is $3 \times (3 + 1)^2 = 48$. Thus the total number of possible linguistic rules is also 48. Genetic algorithms can easily handle such a small number of linguistic rules as candidate rules.

9.2.2 Candidate Rule Prescreening

Candidate rule prescreening is a procedure for decreasing the number of candidate rules in a heuristic manner. As we have explained in Chap. 4, candidate rule prescreening significantly improves the efficiency of genetic algorithm-based rule selection. A simple prescreening procedure for modeling problems is to remove linguistic rules with no compatible training data. That is, this

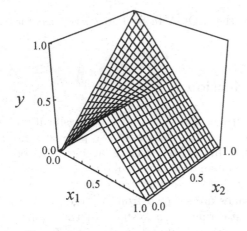

Fig. 9.2. A nonlinear function used as a numerical example. This nonlinear function was depicted from the nine linguistic rules in Fig. 9.3

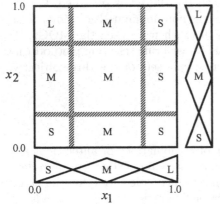

Fig. 9.3. Nine linguistic rules used for depicting the nonlinear function in Fig. 9.2

prescreening procedure removes linguistic rules that satisfy the following relation:

$$\mu_{R_q}(\pmb{x}_p, y_p) = 0, \quad p = 1, 2, \ldots, m. \tag{9.11}$$

The compatibility grade of each input–output pair $(\pmb{x}_p, y_p)$ with the linguistic rule R_q is defined by its antecedent part $\pmb{A}_q$ and the consequent part B_q as

$$\mu_{R_q}(\pmb{x}_p, y_p) = \mu_{A_q}(\pmb{x}_p) \times \mu_{B_q}(y_p). \tag{9.12}$$

Let us assume that 441 input–output pairs are generated as training data from the nonlinear function in Fig. 9.2 using the uniformly divided 21×21 grid of the two-dimensional input space $[0, 1] \times [0, 1]$. While we can generate the 48 candidate rules by considering all the possible combinations of antecedent and consequent fuzzy sets, some rules have no compatible training data. For example, we can see from Fig. 9.2 that the following linguistic rule has no compatible training data:

If x_1 is *large* and x_2 is *large* then y is *large*. (9.13)

Among the possible 48 candidate rules, 8 rules have no compatible training data. Thus the removal of these rules is likely to have no bad effect on the performance of the rule sets finally obtained by genetic algorithm-based rule selection.

For high-dimensional problems, we cannot examine all the $K(K+1)^n$ combinations of antecedent and consequent fuzzy sets for generating candidate rules. This is because the number of these combinations (i.e., $K(K+1)^n$) increases exponentially as the number of input variables (i.e., n) increases. As in Chap. 4, we can use the rule length as a heuristic prescreening criterion for decreasing the number of examined linguistic rules. The total number of possible linguistic rules of length L for an n-input and single-output nonlinear function is $K \cdot {}_nC_L \cdot K^L$ where K is the number of consequent linguistic terms, ${}_nC_L$ is the number of combinations of choosing L out of n input variables, and K^L is the number of combinations of K antecedent linguistic terms for L input variables. The number of short linguistic rules is not large even when the total number of linguistic rules is huge (i.e., $K \cdot {}_nC_L \cdot K^L$ is not large for a small L even when $K(K+1)^n$ is huge).

The fuzzy versions of the two rule evaluation measures (i.e., *confidence* and *support*) described in the previous chapter can be used for candidate rule prescreening. As in Chap. 4 for pattern classification problems, we can find an arbitrary number of candidate rules for modeling problems using a heuristic prescreening criterion. First we generate linguistic rules of length L or less. The confidence and the support are calculated for each of the generated linguistic rules. When L is too large, we are not likely to complete the generation of linguistic rules within the available computation time. On the other hand, when L is too small, we are not likely to generate a large number of good linguistic rules. The value of L should be specified by taking into account various factors such as the available computation time, the number of input variables, the number of given input–output pairs, the number of linguistic terms for input and output variables, etc. As in Chap. 4, the product of the confidence and the support is used as a heuristic prescreening criterion for choosing an arbitrary number of candidate rules from the generated linguistic rules.

9.2.3 Three-Objective Genetic Algorithm for Rule Selection

Let N be the number of candidate rules. As in Chaps. 4 and 6, any subset S of the N candidate rules can be represented by a binary string of length N as

$$S = s_1 s_2 \cdots s_N, \tag{9.14}$$

where $s_q = 1$ and $s_q = 0$ represent the inclusion of the q-th candidate rule R_q in S and the exclusion of R_q from S, respectively.

First a pre-specified number (say N_{pop}) of binary strings of length N are randomly generated as an initial population. The three objectives of each string S (i.e., rule set S) are evaluated. Copies of non-dominated rule sets are stored as a secondary population separately from the current population. In the application of genetic algorithm-based rule selection to pattern classification problems in Chap. 4, unnecessary rules were removed from each rule set S. While only a single winner rule was used to classify each training pattern in the case of pattern classification problems, all compatible rules are used to calculate the estimated output value for each input vector in modeling problems. If a linguistic rule in S has no compatible input vector, that rule has no effect on the calculation of the estimated output for any input vector in the training data. This means that the removal of such a linguistic rule does not change the value of the first objective $f_1(S)$. Thus we can remove all linguistic rules that satisfy the following condition:

$$\mu_{A_q}(x_p) = 0, \quad p = 1, 2, \ldots, m. \tag{9.15}$$

The removal of these linguistic rules improves the second objective $f_2(S)$ and the third objective $f_3(S)$. Usually linguistic rules satisfying (9.15) have already been removed from candidate rules by a prescreening procedure. This is because the prescreening criterion (9.11) always holds if (9.15) holds. Thus we do not use the rule removal procedure based on (9.15) in the genetic algorithm-based rule selection method for modeling problems.

For selecting a pair of parent strings from the current population, the three weights in the fitness function (9.8) are randomly specified as

$$w_i = random_i/(random_1 + random_2 + random_3), \quad i = 1, 2, 3, \tag{9.16}$$

where $random_i$ is a non-negative random real number. Using binary tournament selection with replacement, a pair of parent strings is selected from the current population based on the fitness function (9.8) with the randomly specified weight values in (9.16). When another pair of parent strings is selected from the current population, the three weights are randomly updated by (9.16). That is, the selection of each pair of parent strings is governed by a different weight vector. From each pair of parent strings, we generate new strings by the uniform crossover and the biased mutation as in the case of pattern classification problems in Chap. 4. By iteratively executing the genetic operations (i.e., selection, crossover, and mutation), we generate $(N_{pop} - N_{elite})$ rule sets. The secondary population of non-dominated rule sets is updated using the newly generated rule sets. If a newly generated rule set is not dominated by any other rule sets in the current and secondary populations, its copy is added to the secondary population and all the solutions dominated by the added one are removed from the secondary population. Finally a pre-specified number (say N_{elite}) of non-dominated rule sets are randomly selected from the secondary population and their copies are added to the newly generated $(N_{pop} - N_{elite})$ rule sets to form the next population of N_{pop} rule sets. In this manner, the next population is generated from current and secondary populations using the selection, crossover, mutation, and elitism. The generation update is iterated until a pre-specified stopping condition is satisfied. At each generation, the secondary population is updated to include all the non-dominated rule sets among the examined ones.

9.2.4 Simple Numerical Example

We applied the three-objective genetic algorithm for rule selection to the 441 input–output pairs generated from Fig. 9.2. As in Fig. 9.3, we used the three linguistic terms (i.e., *small, medium,* and *large*) for each of the two input and single output variables. The number of possible combinations of antecedent and consequent fuzzy sets is 48. Since the number of possible combinations is very small, we can use all the 48 linguistic rules as candidate rules. In this case, each rule set is represented by a binary string of length 48. The task of the three-objective genetic algorithm for rule selection is to find non-dominated rule sets from the 48 candidate rules. Our computer simulation was performed using the following parameter specifications:

Population size:	$N_{pop} = 50$,
Number of elite solutions:	$N_{elite} = 5$,
Crossover probability:	$p_c = 0.8$,
Mutation probability:	$p_m(0 \rightarrow 1) = 1/48$,
	$p_m(1 \rightarrow 0) = 0.1$,
Stopping condition:	1000 populations.

After 1000 iterations of the population update using the genetic operations, five rule sets were obtained (i.e., these rule sets were included in the secondary population after the 1000th generation). The obtained rule sets are shown in Table 9.1.

Table 9.1. Non-dominated rule sets for the nonlinear function in Fig. 9.2

Rule set	Total squared error	Number of rules	Average rule length
S_1	441	0	-
S_2	27.6	1	0.0
S_3	7.4	2	0.5
S_4	3.7	3	1.0
S_5	0.0	4	1.25

The simplest rule set S_2 (excluding an empty set S_1) in Table 9.1 includes only a single linguistic rule of length 0. The linguistic rule is

$$R_1: y \text{ is } medium. \tag{9.17}$$

This is a very rough description of the nonlinear function in Fig. 9.2. The second simplest rule set S_3 includes the following linguistic rule in addition to R_1 in (9.17).

R_2: If x_1 is *large* then y is *small*.   (9.18)

In Fig. 9.4, we show the nonlinear function depicted from the rule set $S_3 = \{R_1, R_2\}$ using the non-standard fuzzy reasoning method. From the comparison between Fig. 9.4 and Fig. 9.2, we can see that the rule set S_3 is a rough approximation of the nonlinear function in Fig. 9.2. The accuracy of approximation can be improved by increasing the number of linguistic rules. For example, the rule set S_5 in Table 9.1 includes four linguistic rules, which are shown in Fig. 9.5. The corresponding estimated nonlinear function is shown in Fig. 9.6. From the comparison between Fig. 9.6 and Fig. 9.2, we can see that the rule set S_5 with the four linguistic rules in Fig. 9.5 approximates the nonlinear function in Fig. 9.2 very well (actually the total squared error is zero as shown in Table 9.1). As we can see from Table 9.1, there exists a tradeoff between the accuracy and the complexity of linguistic rule-based systems.

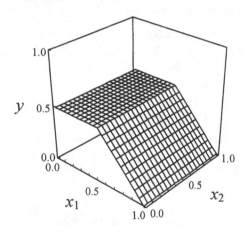

Fig. 9.4. Estimated nonlinear function from the obtained rule set S_3

In the above computer simulation, we used all the 48 linguistic rules as candidate rules for rule selection. As we have already explained, eight linguistic rules have no compatible input–output pairs. Thus these linguistic rules can be removed from candidate rules. We performed the same computer simulation using the remaining 40 linguistic rules as candidate rules. Exactly the same rule sets as Table 9.1 were obtained from this computer simulation.

9.3 Fuzzy Genetics-Based Machine Learning

In the application of linguistic rule-based systems to pattern classification problems, it is easy to implement a Michigan-style genetics-based machine learning (GBML) algorithm as shown in Chap. 5. This is because a single winner rule is responsible for the classification of each training pattern. A

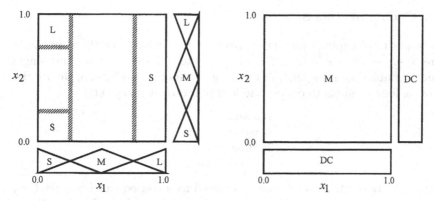

Fig. 9.5. Obtained rule set S_5 with four linguistic rules in Table 9.1 for the nonlinear function in Fig. 9.2

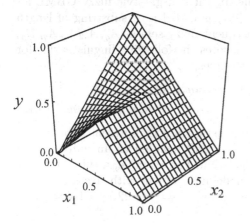

Fig. 9.6. Estimated nonlinear function from the obtained rule set S_5 in Fig. 9.5

reward or penalty will be given to the single winner rule depending on the classification result (i.e., correct classification or misclassification). On the other hand, the definition of a fitness function for each linguistic rule is not easy in modeling problems because multiple linguistic rules are involved in the calculation of the estimated output value for each input vector. Moreover, the evaluation of the estimated output value is not easy, while the evaluation of the classification result is straightforward (i.e., correct classification or misclassification). In this section, we implement a Pittsburgh-style GBML algorithm for the design of linguistic rule-based systems for modeling problems. See [13] for recent developments of Michigan-style fuzzy GBML algorithms (i.e., fuzzy classifier systems).

9.3.1 Coding of Rule Sets

For simplicity of explanation, let us assume that we have the three linguistic terms (i.e., *small*, *medium*, and *large*) for each of the n input and single output variables as in Fig. 9.3. In the same manner as in Chap. 5, we use the following four symbols to denote the four antecedent fuzzy sets:

1: *small*,

2: *medium*,

3: *large*,

#: *don't care*.

It should be noted that *don't care* is not used as a consequent fuzzy set (i.e., it is used only in the antecedent part). The total number of combinations of antecedent and consequent fuzzy sets is $(3 + 1)^n \cdot 3$. Each combination corresponds to a single linguistic rule. In Pittsburgh-style fuzzy GBML algorithms, each linguistic rule R_q in (9.1) is coded as a substring of length $(n + 1)$ using its antecedent and consequent fuzzy sets as $A_{q1} A_{q2} \ldots A_{qn} B_q$. For example, a substring "1##232" denotes the following linguistic rule for a modeling problem with five input variables:

Rule R_1: If x_1 is *small* and x_4 is *medium* and x_5 is *large*

then y is *medium*.   (9.19)

Each rule set S including N_{rule} linguistic rules is represented by a concatenated string of length $(n + 1) \cdot N_{\text{rule}}$ and handled as an individual in our Pittsburgh-style fuzzy GBML algorithm. For example, a rule set of the following four linguistic rules for a modeling problem with five input variables is represented by a concatenated string "1##232 22###1 ####12 3###33" of length 24:

Rule R_1: If x_1 is *small* and x_4 is *medium* and x_5 is *large*

then y is *medium*,   (9.20)

Rule R_2: If x_1 is *medium* and x_2 is *medium* then y is *small*,   (9.21)

Rule R_3: If x_5 is *small* then y is *medium*,   (9.22)

Rule R_4: If x_1 is *large* and x_5 is *large* then y is *large*.   (9.23)

9.3.2 Three-Objective Fuzzy GBML Algorithm

In our three-objective fuzzy GBML algorithm for approximately realizing an n-input and single-output function, each rule set including N_{rule} linguistic rules is represented by a string of length $(n + 1) \cdot N_{\text{rule}}$. First we randomly generate a pre-specified number (say N_{pop}) of strings of length $(n+1) \cdot N_{\text{rule}}$. Then the three objectives of each string S (i.e., rule set S) are evaluated. Copies of non-dominated rule sets are stored as a secondary population separately from the current population.

The selection operation of parent strings is the same as the previous section. That is, the three weights in the fitness function (9.8) are randomly specified for selecting a pair of parent strings as shown in (9.16). We use binary tournament selection with replacement. When another pair of parent strings is selected from the current population, the three weights are randomly updated by (9.16).

From each pair of parent strings, we generate new strings using crossover and mutation. We use the one-point crossover operation with different crossover points as in Chap. 5. This crossover operation is illustrated in Fig. 9.7 (also see Fig. 5.15).

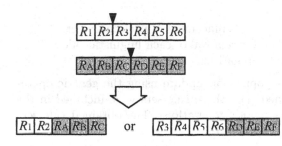

Fig. 9.7. One-point crossover operation with different crossover points

Two mutation operations are applied to each of the generated new strings by the crossover operation. One mutation operation randomly replaces an antecedent or consequent fuzzy set with another one. Note that *don't care* is not used as a consequent fuzzy set, though it is used as an antecedent fuzzy set. This mutation operation is applied to each antecedent or consequent fuzzy set with a pre-specified mutation probability. The other mutation operation is to randomly remove linguistic rules from each rule set. This mutation operation is applied to each linguistic rule with a pre-specified mutation probability. These mutation operations can also be used in the fuzzy GBML algorithms in Chaps. 5 and 6 for classification problems.

By iteratively executing the genetic operations (i.e., selection, crossover, and mutation), we generate $(N_{\mathrm{pop}} - N_{\mathrm{elite}})$ rule sets. The secondary population of non-dominated rule sets is updated using the newly generated rule sets. Finally a pre-specified number (say N_{elite}) of non-dominated rule sets are randomly selected from the secondary population and their copies are added to the newly generated $(N_{\mathrm{pop}} - N_{\mathrm{elite}})$ rule sets to form the next population of N_{pop} rule sets. In this manner, the next population is generated from the current and secondary populations using selection, crossover, mutation, and elitism. The generation update is iterated until a pre-specified stopping condition is satisfied. At each generation, the secondary population is updated to include all the non-dominated rule sets among the examined ones.

9.3.3 Simple Numerical Example

We applied the three-objective fuzzy GBML algorithm to the 441 input–output pairs generated from Fig. 9.2 to design linguistic rule-based systems. As in the previous computer simulation in Sect. 9.2.4, we used the three linguistic terms (i.e., *small*, *medium*, and *large*) for each of the two input and single output variables. Our computer simulation was performed using the following parameter specifications:

Population size: 50,
Number of linguistic rules in each initial rule set: 10,
Number of elite solutions: 5,
Crossover probability: 0.8,
Mutation probability: 0.05 for replacement of each fuzzy set,
                                   0.05 for removal of each linguistic rule,
Stopping condition: 1000 populations.

After 1000 iterations of the population update using the genetic operations, five rule sets were obtained (i.e., these rule sets were included in the secondary population after the 1000th generation). The obtained rule sets are exactly the same as those in Table 9.1.

9.3.4 Some Heuristic Procedures

As we have already mentioned, the total number of possible linguistic rules is $K \cdot (K+1)^n$ when K linguistic terms are given for each of the n input and single output variables. Each substring of length $(n+1)$ corresponds to one of the $K \cdot (K+1)^n$ linguistic rules. Since each rule set S (i.e., each string S) is a subset of the $K \cdot (K+1)^n$ linguistic rules, the size of the search space is 2^N where $N = K \cdot (K+1)^n$. This means that the size of the search space rapidly increases as the number of input variables increases. Thus the three-objective fuzzy GBML algorithm in this section does not always work well on high-dimensional problems while it worked well on the simple numerical example in the previous computer simulation.

We explain two heuristic procedures [85] for improving the search ability of the three-objective fuzzy GBML algorithm to find good rule sets for high-dimensional modeling problems. Both heuristic procedures are applied to rule sets generated by the genetic operations in each generation.

One is a heuristic replacement procedure of the consequent linguistic term of each linguistic rule. Since the genetic operations do not take into account the given input–output pairs, each linguistic rule does not always have an appropriate consequent linguistic term. The heuristic replacement procedure probabilistically replaces the consequent linguistic term of each linguistic rule with a more appropriate one using the information about the given input–output pairs. The replacement probability for each linguistic term from the current one is defined using the confidence as

$$p(B_k) = \frac{c(\mathbf{A}_q \Rightarrow B_k)}{\sum\limits_{k=1}^{K} c(\mathbf{A}_q \Rightarrow B_k)}, \tag{9.24}$$

where K is the number of linguistic terms for the output variable. This procedure is applied to each linguistic rule with a pre-specified probability. In the computer simulations in the next section, the application probability is specified as 0.5.

Let us consider a linguistic rule of the form "If x_1 is *small* and x_2 is *small* then y is B_q" for the simple numerical example in Fig. 9.2 with the 441 input–output pairs. The confidence of each linguistic rule with the antecedent part (*small, small*) is calculated as

$$c((small, small) \Rightarrow small) = 0.49, \tag{9.25}$$

$$c((small, small) \Rightarrow medium) = 0.51, \tag{9.26}$$

$$c((small, small) \Rightarrow large) = 0.00. \tag{9.27}$$

Thus the consequent part of a linguistic rule of the form "If x_1 is *small* and x_2 is *small* then y is B_q" is replaced with *small* or *medium* when the heuristic replacement procedure is applied to the linguistic rule. The replacement probabilities of *small* and *medium* are 0.49 and 0.51, respectively. That is, *small* and *medium* are chosen as the consequent fuzzy set with the probabilities of 0.49 and 0.5, respectively.

The other heuristic procedure is to generate a linguistic rule from an input–output pair with the maximum error. A similar idea was explained for pattern classification problems in Chap. 5. In this procedure, first the squared error for each input–output pair is calculated using each rule set in the current population after the replacement procedure. Next an input–output pair with the maximum error is identified for each rule set. Let $(\boldsymbol{x}_p, y_p)$ be the input–output pair with the maximum error for the rule set S. Then a linguistic rule is generated from this input–output pair. Its antecedent and consequent parts are determined by the most compatible linguistic terms with the input and output values $(\boldsymbol{x}_p, y_p)$. For example, if $\boldsymbol{x}_p = (0.12, 0.48, 0.97)$ and $y_p = 0.57$, then the following linguistic rule is generated:

If x_1 is *small* and x_2 is *medium* and x_3 is *large*

then y is *medium*. (9.28)

Each antecedent linguistic term is replaced with *don't care* using a pre-specified probability. This probability is specified as 0.5 in the computer simulations in the next section. The generated linguistic rule is added to the rule set S. This procedure is applied to each rule set with a pre-specified probability (0.1 in the computer simulations in the next section) after the above-mentioned replacement procedure.

9.4 Comparison of Two Schemes

We compared the following four algorithms with each other through computer simulations on numerical examples:

(1) The genetic algorithm-based rule selection method with no prescreening procedure.
(2) The genetic algorithm-based rule selection method with a heuristic pre-screening procedure.
(3) The fuzzy GBML algorithm with no heuristic procedure.
(4) The fuzzy GBML algorithm with the two heuristic procedures in Sect. 9.3.4.

In the second algorithm, 100 candidate rules were selected using the product of the confidence and the support as a heuristic prescreening criterion. When the total number of candidate rules was not more than 100, all candidate rules were used in rule selection.

Since the evaluation of simulation results by multi-objective optimization methods is not easy, we used these four algorithms as single-objective optimization methods by specifying the three weights as $w_1 = 100$, $w_2 = 1$, and $w_3 = 1$. That is, we used the following fitness function in the four algorithms:

$$fitness(S) = -100f_1(S) - f_2(S) - f_3(S). \tag{9.29}$$

As training data, we generated 441 input–output pairs (x_{p1}, x_{p2}, y_p), $p = 1, 2, \ldots, 441$, from the nonlinear function in Fig. 9.8 using the uniformly divided 21×21 grid of the input space $[0, 1] \times [0, 1]$. That is, $x_{p1} = 0.00, 0.05, \ldots, 1.00$, $x_{p2} = 0.00, 0.05, \ldots, 1.00$, and the value of y_p was calculated from Fig. 9.8. For each of the two input and single output variables, we used five linguistic terms (i.e., *small, medium small, medium, medium large*, and *large*).

We also generated a test problem with three input variables by adding an additional input variable x_3 to the test problem with the two input variables. The value of x_3 in each of the 441 input–output pairs $(x_{p1}, x_{p2}, x_{p3}, y_p)$, $p = 1, 2, \ldots, 441$, was randomly specified as a real number in the unit interval $[0, 1]$. In the same manner, we also generated test problems with four and five input variables.

The length of bit strings in the genetic algorithm-based rule selection (i.e., the first algorithm) becomes extremely long as the number of input variables increases. This is because the number of candidate rules exponentially increases as the number of input variables increases. It is impractical to directly apply the first algorithm to the problems with three and more input variables. Thus, we modify the initialization process of the first algorithm. We pre-specified the probability of $s_i = 1$ for $i = 1, \ldots, N$ in (9.14) as 0.1 in the case of the three and the four input variables and 0.001 in the case of the five input variables. This modification reduces the CPU time of the algorithm since the number of selected rules in the initial population does not become large.

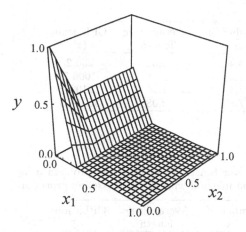

Fig. 9.8. A test problem

We applied each of the four algorithms to each of the four test problems ten times. Average simulation results are summarized in Tables 9.2 – 9.5. In these tables, each algorithm was implemented in the C language and executed on a PC with a Pentium IV 2.80 GHz processor. From the comparison between Table 9.2 and Table 9.3, we can see that the prescreening procedure of candidate rules significantly decreased the CPU time of the genetic algorithm-based rule selection method. As we have already demonstrated in Chapt. 4 for pattern classification problems, candidate rule prescreening is necessary in rule selection for handling high-dimensional problems. However, the performance of the genetic algorithm-based rule selection method with the prescreening procedure is significantly worse than that with no prescreening procedure in some cases. This is because we cannot always successfully select important linguistic rules as candidate rules for the genetic algorithm-based rule selection method by the prescreening procedure. For example, in the case of the four input variables, we did not select the following linguistic rule as a candidate rule:

If x_1 is *small* and x_2 is *small* then y is *large*. (9.30)

The product of the support and the confidence of this linguistic rule is 0.001. This value is the 974th largest in the entire set of the generated linguistic rules. It should be noted that 100 candidate rules were selected in the computer simulations for Table 9.3.

From the comparison between Table 9.4 and Table 9.5, we can see that the search ability of the fuzzy GBML algorithm was improved by the two heuristic procedures. We can also see from Tables 9.2 – 9.5 that better results were obtained by the fuzzy GBML algorithm in Table 9.4 and Table 9.5 than the rule selection method in Table 9.2 and Table 9.3.

Table 9.2. Average simulation results over ten trials for each test problem using the genetic algorithm-based rule selection method with no candidate rule prescreening procedure

Number of input variables	Total squared error	Number of rules	Average rule length	CPU time (s)
2	0.019	3.4	1.03	250.2
3	0.114	4.5	1.18	1006.7
4	0.197	4.1	1.10	12103.1
5	1.074	7.8	2.08	35316.8

Table 9.3. Average simulation results over ten trials for each test problem using the genetic algorithm-based rule selection method with the prescreening procedure

Number of input variables	Total squared error	Number of rules	Average rule length	CPU time (s)
2	0.0	3.0	1.00	163.6
3	0.833	3.0	1.00	155.2
4	0.870	2.0	0.50	146.8
5	8.596	1.0	0.00	102.5

Table 9.4. Average simulation results over ten trials for each test problem using the fuzzy GBML algorithm with no heuristic procedure

Number of input variables	Total squared error	Number of rules	Average rule length	CPU time (s)
2	0.0	3.0	1.00	72.5
3	0.072	3.7	1.11	269.5
4	0.051	3.1	0.97	505.6
5	0.190	3.7	1.16	1243.6

Table 9.5. Average simulation results over ten trials for each test problem using the fuzzy GBML algorithm with the two heuristic procedures

Number of input variables	Total squared error	Number of rules	Average rule length	CPU time (s)
2	0.0	3.0	1.00	597.3
3	0.0	3.0	1.00	4829.2
4	0.0	3.2	1.13	8330.3
5	0.026	3.2	1.13	11010.0

10. Linguistic Rules with Consequent Real Numbers

In this chapter, we use linguistic rules of the following form to approximately realize an n-input and single-output nonlinear function:

$$\text{Rule } R_q: \text{If } x_1 \text{ is } A_{q1} \text{ and } \ldots \text{ and } x_n \text{ is } A_{qn} \text{ then } y \text{ is } b_q, \qquad (10.1)$$

where b_q is an adjustable real number. As in Chaps. 8 and 9, we assume that m input–output pairs (x_p, y_p), $p = 1, 2, \ldots, m$, are given as training data in the normalized input–output space $[0, 1]^{n+1}$. We also assume that K linguistic terms are given for each of the n input variables. The estimated output value $y(x)$ is calculated for the input vector x as

$$\hat{y}(x) = \frac{\sum_{R_q \in S} \mu_{A_q}(x) \cdot b_q}{\sum_{R_q \in S} \mu_{A_q}(x)}, \qquad (10.2)$$

where S is a set of linguistic rules of the form (10.1). This formulation is the same as the standard fuzzy reasoning method in Chap. 8. We can also use the non-standard fuzzy reasoning method in Chap. 8 when S includes linguistic rules with different specificity levels.

10.1 Consequent Real Numbers

Linguistic rules with consequent real numbers in (10.1) can be viewed as a simplified version of the following rule in the Takagi–Sugeno model [162] with a consequent linear function:

$$\text{Rule } R_q : \text{If } x_1 \text{ is } A_{q1} \text{ and } \ldots \text{ and } x_n \text{ is } A_{qn}$$
$$\text{then } y_q(\mathbf{x}) = a_{q0} + a_{q1}x_1 + \ldots + a_{qn}x_n, \qquad (10.3)$$

where a_{qi} is an adjustable real number. In Chaps. 8 and 9, we used the representative real number b_q in fuzzy reasoning for the consequent linguistic term B_q of the linguistic rule R_q of the following form:

$$\text{Rule } R_q: \text{If } x_1 \text{ is } A_{q1} \text{ and } \ldots \text{ and } x_n \text{ is } A_{qn} \text{ then } y \text{ is } B_q. \qquad (10.4)$$

This means that we actually used linguistic rules with consequent real numbers of the form (10.1) in fuzzy reasoning while linguistic rules with consequent linguistic terms of the form (10.2) were used in rule generation in

Chaps. 8 and 9. Wang & Mendel [176] also used real numbers for consequent linguistic terms in fuzzy reasoning while consequent linguistic terms played an important role in their rule generation method. Fuzzy rules with consequent real numbers have often been used in adjustable fuzzy rule-based systems as in Ichihashi & Watanabe [60] and Nomura et al. [130]. This is because fuzzy reasoning and rule adjustment are implemented more easily for consequent real numbers than for consequent linguistic terms.

The accuracy of linguistic rule-based systems can be significantly improved by replacing a fixed consequent linguistic term with an adjustable consequent real number. This is illustrated in Fig. 10.1 where the thick and thin lines are fuzzy reasoning results using fixed consequent linguistic terms and adjustable consequent real numbers, respectively. In Chaps. 8 and 9, the consequent part of each linguistic rule was selected from a set of given linguistic terms. Thus the adjustment of linguistic rule-based systems was very coarse. As a result, good fitting to training data was not always obtained as shown by the thick lines in Fig. 10.1. On the other hand, adjustable consequent real numbers can be tuned to improve the fitting of linguistic rule-based systems to training data as shown by the thin lines in Fig. 10.1. In this chapter, we show how the consequent real number of each linguistic rule of the form (10.1) can be specified and adjusted from training data. We will not discuss the adjustment of antecedent linguistic terms in this book. This is because such adjustment often leads to difficulties in the interpretation of adjusted linguistic rules. Various approaches have been proposed for adjusting antecedent and consequent parts of fuzzy rules using neural learning schemes and genetic algorithms (e.g., [53, 58, 99, 103, 151]).

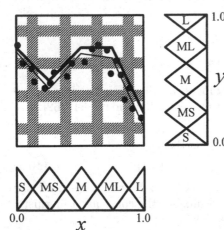

Fig. 10.1. Comparison in fuzzy reasoning results between fixed consequent linguistic terms (thick lines) and adjustable consequent real numbers (thin lines)

10.2 Local Learning of Consequent Real Numbers

The basic idea of local learning is to adjust the consequent part of each linguistic rule using compatible training data independently of other linguistic rules. On the other hand, global learning tries to minimize a global error measure (e.g., total squared error) between the actual output value of each input–output pair and the corresponding estimated output value by a linguistic rule-based system. The difference between local learning and global learning was demonstrated in Ishibuchi et al. [82], Nozaki et al. [133], and Yen & Wang [187]. The main advantage of local learning over global learning is that the learning of each linguistic rule can be performed independently of the learning of other linguistic rules. Another advantage is that local learning usually improves the interpretability of each linguistic rule. Sometimes global learning leads to meaningless results from the viewpoint of interpretability even if a global error measure is very small. In this section, we explain two methods based on the concept of local learning: a heuristic specification method and an incremental learning algorithm of the consequent real number of each linguistic rule.

10.2.1 Heuristic Specification Method

A heuristic method for specifying the consequent real number of each linguistic rule from compatible input–output pairs was proposed in Ishibuchi et al. [82]. In their heuristic method, the consequent real number is specified as the weighted average of output values of compatible input–output pairs as

$$b_q = \frac{\sum\limits_{p=1}^{m} \mu_{A_q}(x_p) \cdot y_p}{\sum\limits_{p=1}^{m} \mu_{A_q}(x_p)} \tag{10.5}$$

where $\mu_{A_q}(x_p)$ is the compatibility grade of the input vector x_p with the antecedent part A_q of the linguistic rule R_q in (10.1). This formulation can be understood more easily by rewriting it as

$$b_q = \sum_{p=1}^{m} w_q(x_p) \cdot y_p, \tag{10.6}$$

where

$$w_q(x_p) = \frac{\mu_{A_q}(x_p)}{\sum\limits_{p=1}^{m} \mu_{A_q}(x_p)}, \tag{10.7}$$

$$\sum_{p=1}^{m} w_q(x_p) = 1. \tag{10.8}$$

In (10.6), $w_q(x_p)$ can be viewed as the weight of the p-th input–output pair (x_p, y_p) in the specification of the consequent real number b_q of the q-th linguistic rule R_q. From (10.6)–(10.8), we can see that the consequent real number b_q is the weighted average of y_p over compatible input–output pairs where the weight of each output value y_p is proportional to the compatibility grade $\mu_{A_q}(x_p)$ of the corresponding input vector x_p with the antecedent part A_q of the linguistic rule R_q. It should be noted that the consequent real number b_q is specified independently of other linguistic rules.

Let us consider the following minimization problem:

$$\text{Minimize} \quad z = \sum_{p=1}^{m} \mu_{A_q}(x_p) \cdot (y_p - b_q)^2 / 2. \tag{10.9}$$

The objective function is a local error measure for the linguistic rule R_q, which is defined independently of other linguistic rules. More specifically, it is the weighted total squared error between the consequent real number b_q and the output value y_p of each input–output pair (x_p, y_p). The weight of each input–output pair (x_p, y_p) is the compatibility grade $\mu_{A_q}(x_p)$ of the input vector x_p with the antecedent part A_q of the linguistic rule R_q. The optimal value of b_q of this minimization problem is obtained from the following equation:

$$\frac{dz}{db_q} = 0. \tag{10.10}$$

This equation is rewritten from (10.9) as

$$\sum_{p=1}^{m} \mu_{A_q}(x_p) \cdot (y_p - b_q) = 0. \tag{10.11}$$

From this equation, we have the heuristic specification method of b_q in (10.5). That is, b_q in (10.5) is the optimal solution of the minimization problem in (10.9) of the weighted total squared error between the consequent real number and the output value of each input–output pair.

We applied the heuristic specification method in (10.5) to the 20 input–output pairs in Fig. 10.1 (i.e., in Table 8.1). The consequent real number of each linguistic rule was specified as follows:

If x is *small* then y is 0.640, $\qquad\qquad\qquad\qquad\qquad$ (10.12)

If x is *medium small* then y is 0.522, $\qquad\qquad\qquad\qquad$ (10.13)

If x is *medium* then y is 0.652, $\qquad\qquad\qquad\qquad\qquad$ (10.14)

If x is *medium large* then y is 0.573, $\qquad\qquad\qquad\qquad$ (10.15)

If x is *large* then y is 0.343. $\qquad\qquad\qquad\qquad\qquad\quad$ (10.16)

The fuzzy reasoning result by these five linguistic rules is shown in Fig. 10.2. The result is not good from the viewpoint of the fitting of the estimated output values to the given input–output pairs. This is because the heuristic specification method (i.e., local learning) does not try to minimize the total

squared error between the estimated output values and the given input–
output pairs.

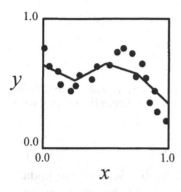

Fig. 10.2. Fuzzy reasoning result using the five linguistic rules obtained by the heuristic specification method of consequent real numbers

As shown in Nozaki et al. [133], the fitting of linguistic rule-based systems to training data can be improved by generalizing the heuristic specification method in (10.5) as

$$b_q = \frac{\sum\limits_{p=1}^{m} [\mu_{A_q}(x_p)]^{\beta} \cdot y_p}{\sum\limits_{p=1}^{m} [\mu_{A_q}(x_p)]^{\beta}}. \tag{10.17}$$

When the value of β is very small (e.g., $\beta = 0.01$), the weights of all compatible input–output pairs are close to 1 (i.e., $[\mu_{A_q}(x_p)]^{\beta} \cong 1$ if $\mu_{A_q}(x_p) > 0$). In this case, the value of b_q in (10.17) is almost the same as the simple average of y_p over compatible input–output pairs. On the other hand, when the value of β is very large (e.g., $\beta = 100$), the weights of almost all input–output pairs become very small. In this case, the value of b_q in (10.17) is mainly calculated from only a few input–output pairs with large compatibility grades. In Fig. 10.3, simulation results for $\beta = 0.1$ and $\beta = 10$ are shown. From this figure, we can see that the fitting of linguistic rule-based systems to training data was improved by using a large value of β. The idea of introducing β to modify the weight of each input–output pair as in (10.17) may be applied to the heuristic rule generation method in Chap. 8.

10.2.2 Incremental Learning Algorithm

The heuristic specification method in (10.5) can be implemented as an incremental learning algorithm for handling a dynamical situation where a target nonlinear function gradually changes over time. Let (x_t, y_t) be the input–output pair obtained at time t ($t = 1, 2, \ldots$). In this case, the consequent real number b_q is updated as

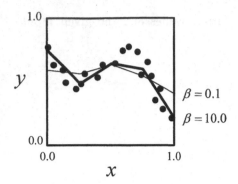

Fig. 10.3. Fuzzy reasoning results by the generalized heuristic specification method

$$b_q^{\text{New}} = (1 - \alpha \cdot \mu_{A_q}(x_t)) \cdot b_q^{\text{Old}} + \alpha \cdot \mu_{A_q}(x_t) \cdot y_t, \qquad (10.18)$$

where b_q^{New} is the value of the consequent real number b_q after the update using the input–output pair (x_t, y_t), b_q^{Old} is the value of b_q before the update, and α is a learning rate. We can rewrite (10.18) as

$$b_{qt} = (1 - \beta_t) \cdot b_{q(t-1)} + \beta_t \cdot y_t, \qquad (10.19)$$

where b_{qt} is the value of b_q after the update using the t-th input–output pair (x_t, y_t) and

$$\beta_t = \alpha \cdot \mu_{A_q}(x_t). \qquad (10.20)$$

From (10.19) and (10.20), we can see that the incremental learning algorithm is a kind of weighted exponential smoothing of compatible input–output pairs.

When the t-th input–output pair (x_t, y_t) is presented to the linguistic rule-based system, all compatible linguistic rules are adjusted by the update rule in (10.18). The amount of modification of the consequent real number of each linguistic rule is proportional to the compatibility grade of the input vector with the antecedent part. When the input vector x_t has a large compatibility grade with the antecedent part A_q of the q-th linguistic rule R_q, the amount of modification of the consequent real number b_q is large. On the other hand, when the input vector x_t is not compatible with A_q of R_q (i.e., when the compatibility grade is zero), the consequent real number b_q is not modified.

The heuristic specification method in (10.5) corresponds to a special case of the incremental learning algorithm. Let us consider the case where the value of α is specified in (10.18) as

$$\alpha = \frac{1}{\displaystyle\sum_{p=1}^{t} \mu_{A_q}(x_p)}. \qquad (10.21)$$

In this case, β_t in (10.20) is

$$\beta_t = \frac{\mu_{A_q}(x_t)}{\displaystyle\sum_{p=1}^{t} \mu_{A_q}(x_p)}. \qquad (10.22)$$

Thus we can solve (10.19) as

$$b_{qt} = \frac{\sum_{p=1}^{t} \mu_{A_q}(\boldsymbol{x}_p) \cdot y_p}{\sum_{p=1}^{t} \mu_{A_q}(\boldsymbol{x}_p)}. \tag{10.23}$$

This equation is the same as the heuristic specification method in (10.5). We can easily see that (10.23) is obtained from (10.19) and (10.22) by iteratively calculating b_{qt} from the case of $t = 1$.

In Fig. 10.4, we show simulation results using the incremental learning algorithm for the five linguistic rules in (10.12)–(10.16). First we specified the initial value of each consequent real number as 0.5. The straight line $y = 0.5$ in Fig. 10.4 corresponds to the initial situation. Then we updated each consequent real number by the incremental learning algorithm using the 20 input–output pairs. The learning rate α was specified as $\alpha = 0.9$. In the execution of the incremental learning algorithm, we presented each of the 20 input–output pairs to the linguistic rule-based system three times (i.e., three epochs). In each epoch, the 20 input–output pairs were presented in a random order. The fuzzy reasoning result after each epoch is shown as a piece-wise linear curve in Fig. 10.4.

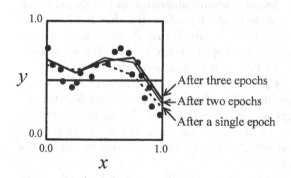

Fig. 10.4. Simulation results by the incremental learning algorithm based on the concept of local learning

10.3 Global Learning

In global learning, the total squared error is usually used as a global error measure to be minimized as

$$\text{Minimize } z = \sum_{p=1}^{m} (\hat{y}(\boldsymbol{x}_p) - y_p)^2 / 2, \tag{10.24}$$

where $\hat{y}(\boldsymbol{x}_p)$ is the estimated output value for the input vector $\boldsymbol{x}_p$ of the input–output pair $(\boldsymbol{x}_p, y_p)$. The objective function in (10.24) is the same as the first objective $f_1(S)$ in the three-objective optimization problem discussed in Chap. 9.

10.3.1 Incremental Learning Algorithm

Ichihashi & Watanabe [60] proposed the following incremental learning algorithm of the consequent real number b_q of each linguistic rule R_q in (10.1):

$$b_q^{\text{New}} = b_q^{\text{Old}} - \alpha \cdot \frac{\delta z_t}{\delta b_q}, \qquad (10.25)$$

where

$$z_t = (\hat{y}(\boldsymbol{x}_t) - y_t)^2 / 2. \qquad (10.26)$$

Using (10.2) for $\hat{y}(\boldsymbol{x}_t)$ in (10.26), we can rewrite (10.25) as

$$b_q^{\text{New}} = b_q^{\text{Old}} - \alpha \cdot \frac{\mu_{\boldsymbol{A}_q}(\boldsymbol{x}_t)}{\sum_{R_q \in S} \mu_{\boldsymbol{A}_q}(\boldsymbol{x}_t)} \cdot (\hat{y}(\boldsymbol{x}_t) - y_t), \qquad (10.27)$$

where S is a rule set (i.e., linguistic rule-based system).

When the t-th input–output pair $(\boldsymbol{x}_t, y_t)$ is presented to the linguistic rule-based system S, all compatible linguistic rules are adjusted by the update rule in (10.27). As in the incremental learning algorithm in (10.18) based on the concept of local learning, the amount of modification in (10.27) for the consequent real number b_q of the q-th linguistic rule R_q is proportional to the compatibility grade $\mu_{\boldsymbol{A}_q}(\boldsymbol{x}_t)$ of the input vector $\boldsymbol{x}_t$ with the antecedent part $\boldsymbol{A}_q$. When the input vector $\boldsymbol{x}_t$ is not compatible with $\boldsymbol{A}_q$ of R_q (i.e., when the compatibility grade is zero), the consequent real number b_q is not modified. This is because linguistic rules that are not compatible with the input vector $\boldsymbol{x}_t$ have no effects on the calculation of the estimated output value $\hat{y}(\boldsymbol{x}_t)$. That is, the consequent real numbers of those linguistic rules have no effects on the squared error z_t in (10.26) to be minimized by the incremental learning algorithm.

The steepest descent learning scheme in (10.25) can also be used for the learning of antecedent linguistic terms. Actually many learning algorithms of fuzzy rule-based systems have been proposed in the framework of steepest descent learning. The incremental learning algorithm in (10.27) is the simplest one among those studies.

In Fig. 10.5, we show simulation results using the incremental learning algorithm in (10.27) for the five linguistic rules in (10.12)–(10.16). As in the computer simulation using local learning in Fig. 10.4 of the previous section, first we specified the initial value of each consequent real number as 0.5. The straight line $y = 0.5$ in Fig. 10.5 corresponds to the initial situation. Then we updated each consequent real number by the incremental learning algorithm in (10.27) using the 20 input–output pairs. The learning rate α was specified as $\alpha = 0.1$. In the execution of the incremental learning algorithm, we presented each of the 20 input–output pairs in a random order to the linguistic rule-based system 100 times (i.e., 100 epochs). The fuzzy reasoning results after a single, ten, and 100 epochs are shown as piece-wise linear curves in Fig. 10.5.

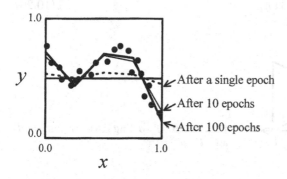

Fig. 10.5. Simulation results by the incremental learning algorithm based on the concept of global learning

The heuristic specification method in the previous section can be used for specifying the initial value of each consequent real number, which is to be further adjusted by the global learning scheme. The heuristic specification of initial values usually improves the learning speed and sometimes improves the generalization ability of adjusted linguistic rule-based systems. The effect of the heuristic specification of initial values on the learning of linguistic rule-based systems was examined in [82, 133].

10.3.2 Comparison Between Two Learning Schemes

Local learning minimizes the difference between the consequent real number and the actual output value of each input–output pair while global learning minimizes the difference between the estimated output value and the actual output value. That is, local learning does not try to minimize the approximation error. This often results in large approximation errors of linguistic rule-based systems obtained by local learning as we have already shown in Fig. 10.2 and Fig. 10.4. On the other hand, global learning always tries to minimize the approximation error. Thus better fitting to training data will always be obtained from global learning than local learning.

As pointed out by Yen & Wang [187], one difficulty of global learning is the interpretability of each linguistic rule. They pointed out this difficulty for the Takagi–Sugeno model with consequent linear functions. More specifically, they demonstrated that the fitting of each consequent linear function to training data is not always good even when the total squared error (i.e., global error measure) is very small. This difficulty of global learning exists not only in the Takagi–Sugeno model but also in linguistic rule-based systems.

For simplicity of explanation, let us assume that we have only two input–output pairs $(0.45, 0.45)$ and $(0.55, 0.55)$ in the two-dimensional input–output space $[0, 1] \times [0, 1]$. We also assume that two linguistic terms *small* and *large* are given to describe the input variable x as shown in Fig. 10.6. In this case, we have the following two linguistic rules:

R_1: If x is *small* then y is b_1,   (10.28)

R_2: If x is *large* then y is b_2.   (10.29)

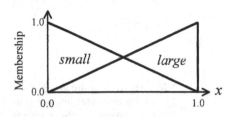

Fig. 10.6. Two linguistic terms *small* and *large*

Since the line $y = x$ has no approximation errors for the two input–output pairs $(0.45, 0.45)$ and $(0.55, 0.55)$, the optimal linguistic rules in global learning are as follows:

R_1: If x is *small* then y is 0,   (10.30)

R_2: If x is *large* then y is 1.   (10.31)

The fuzzy reasoning result by these two linguistic rules corresponds to the line $y = x$ as shown in Fig. 10.7. On the other hand, the following two linguistic rules are obtained from the heuristic specification method based on the concept of local learning in (10.5):

R_1: If x is *small* then y is 0.495,   (10.32)

R_2: If x is *large* then y is 0.505.   (10.33)

The fuzzy reasoning result by these two linguistic rules is shown in Fig. 10.8. The difference between global learning and local learning is clearly shown in Fig. 10.7 and Fig. 10.8.

10.4 Effect of the Use of Consequent Real Numbers

In this section, we discuss the effect of using real numbers instead of linguistic terms in the consequent part of linguistic rules.

10.4.1 Resolution of Adjustment

As we have already explained, we used the same fuzzy reasoning method in (10.2) for linguistic rules with consequent linguistic terms and for those with consequent real numbers. The value of b_q in the fuzzy reasoning method is

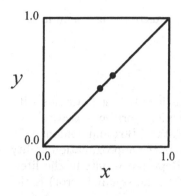

Fig. 10.7. Illustration of global learning. The line shows the fuzzy reasoning result by the two linguistic rules in (10.30) and (10.31)

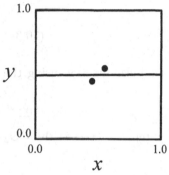

Fig. 10.8. Illustration of local learning. The line shows the fuzzy reasoning result by the two linguistic rules in (10.32) and (10.33)

discrete in the case of consequent linguistic terms while it is continuous in the case of consequent real numbers. When we use the five linguistic terms for the output variable as in Fig. 10.1, the value of b_q is one of the following five real numbers: 0, 0.25, 0.5, 0.75, 1. Thus the fine tuning of the estimated value $\hat{y}(x)$ is impossible. For example, the value of $\hat{y}(x)$ may be increased by replacing the consequent linguistic term *medium* of a linguistic rule with *medium large*. By this replacement, the value of b_q of the adjusted linguistic rule is increased from 0.5 to 0.75. It is impossible to increase the value of b_q to a real number between 0.5 and 0.75 (e.g., 0.6) when we use the five linguistic terms for the output variable as in Fig. 10.1. When we use a coarser fuzzy partition for the output variable, the adjustment of linguistic rules also becomes coarser. For example, when we use the three linguistic terms *small*, *medium*, and *large*, the possible values of b_q are 0, 0.5, and 1. It is impossible to use other values for b_q in the fuzzy reasoning method in (10.2). On the other hand, when we use a finer fuzzy partition for the output variable, the adjustment resolution of linguistic rules also becomes finer. For example, if we use a homogeneous fuzzy partition into eleven linguistic terms for the output variable, the possible values of b_q are $0, 0.1, 0.2, \ldots, 1$. On the other hand, we can use any value for b_q in the case of consequent real numbers.

Thus the use of consequent real numbers corresponds to the use of an infinite number of consequent linguistic terms.

10.4.2 Simulation Results

To examine the approximation ability of linguistic rule-based systems with consequent linguistic terms, we applied the genetic algorithm-based rule selection method in Chap. 9 to the gas furnace data of Box and Jenkins [15]. This data set has been frequently used to evaluate the approximation ability of fuzzy rule-based systems in the literature. Reported results in the literature are shown in Table 10.1 where the MSE (mean squared error) is the following global error measure:

$$\text{MSE} = \frac{1}{m} \sum_{p=1}^{m} (\hat{y}(\boldsymbol{x}_p) - y_p)^2. \tag{10.34}$$

The modeling task is to identify the following nonlinear function using the given training data:

$$y(t) = f(u(t), u(t-1), \ldots, y(t-1), y(t-2), \ldots), \tag{10.35}$$

where $u(t)$ is the gas flow rate at the t-th time step, and $y(t)$ is the CO_2 concentration at the t-th time step.

Table 10.1. Reported results on training data of the gas furnace data of Box and Jenkins in the literature. Methods are sorted in descending order of MSE

Fuzzy models	Number of inputs	Number of rules	MSE
Tong (1980) [166]	2	19	0.469
Xu & Lu (1987) [180]	2	25	0.328
Pedrycz (1984) [136]	2	81	0.320
Yoshinari et al. (1993) [188]	3	6	0.299
Sugeno & Yasukawa (1993) [159]	3	6	0.190
Emami et al. (1998) [42]	3	6	0.158
Lin & Cunnigham (1995) [120]	5	4	0.071
Sugeno & Tanaka (1991) [158]	6	2	0.068
Wang & Langari (1995) [173]	6	2	0.066
Kim et al. (1997) [109]	6	2	0.055
Kim et al. (1998) [111]	6	2	0.048

In our computer simulation, we used only two input variables $u(t-4)$ and $y(t-1)$ which were often selected for the gas furnace data set in the literature. All input and output values in the gas furnace data set were normalized into real numbers in the unit interval $[0, 1]$. For each of the two input and single output variables, we used the five linguistic terms as in Fig. 10.1. The genetic algorithm-based rule selection method with the standard fuzzy reasoning in (10.2) found a rule set with five linguistic rules in Table 10.2. The MSE by this rule set was 0.419. This MSE of 0.419 by the five linguistic rules with the two input variables is good if compared with the reported results in the 1980s in Table 10.1. It is, however, inferior to recently developed methods in Table 10.1. Good results in Table 10.1 were obtained using the Takagi–Sugeno model. Thus each fuzzy rule is not always interpretable. For example, Kim et al. [111] found two fuzzy rules with very good fitting to training data (i.e., the MSE was 0.048). The obtained fuzzy rules in Kim et al. [111] have the following consequent linear functions:

$$y_1(t) = 3.350750 + 0.067303 \cdot u(t) - 0.155765 \cdot u(t-1)$$
$$-0.159554 \cdot u(t-2) + 2.028533 \cdot y(t-1)$$
$$-1.523993 \cdot y(t-2) + 0.433772 \cdot y(t-3), \qquad (10.36)$$

$$y_2(t) = 11.122767 - 0.398395 \cdot u(t) + 1.317115 \cdot u(t-1)$$
$$-1.545791 \cdot u(t-2) + 1.061814 \cdot y(t-1)$$
$$-0.152195 \cdot y(t-2) - 0.119401 \cdot y(t-3). \qquad (10.37)$$

It is not easy to intuitively understand the meaning of fuzzy rules with these consequent linear functions. On the other hand, the interpretation of the five linguistic rules in Table 10.2 is very easy.

Table 10.2. Five linguistic rules selected by the genetic algorithm-based rule selection method. Linguistic rules are sorted according to their consequent linguistic terms. In this table, "-" denotes *don't care*

Rule	Antecedent		Consequent
	$u(t-4)$	$y(t-1)$	$y(t)$
1	-	*small*	*small*
2	*medium large*	-	*medium small*
3	*medium*	*medium*	*medium*
4	-	*medium large*	*medium large*
5	-	*large*	*large*

To improve the fitting ability of our five linguistic rules in Table 10.2, we replaced their consequent linguistic terms with the corresponding real numbers (e.g., 0.25 for *medium small*). Then we adjusted the consequent real numbers using the steepest descent learning in (10.27) with $\alpha = 0.01$. After 100 epochs, the MSE decreased from 0.419 to 0.356. This result shows that the fitting ability of linguistic rules can be improved by using adjustable consequent real numbers instead of fixed consequent linguistic terms.

10.5 Twin-Table Approach

In this section, we show that a linguistic rule table with consequent real numbers can be equivalently represented by two rule tables with consequent linguistic terms. This idea was proposed in Nozaki et al. [133]. The same idea was used in Cordon & Herrera [23].

10.5.1 Basic Idea

As we have already explained, the approximation ability of linguistic rules with consequent linguistic terms is inferior to those with consequent real numbers. This is because the resolution of adjustment is very coarse in the case of consequent linguistic terms. Let us consider the case where we have five consequent linguistic terms in Fig. 10.9. In this case, linguistic rules with consequent linguistic terms are the same as those with only five discrete consequent values: 0, 0.25, 0.5, 0.75, and 1.0. Thus the maximum absolute error by a linguistic rule-based system with the five consequent linguistic terms seems to be about 0.125 (0.125 is half of the difference between the adjacent discrete values).

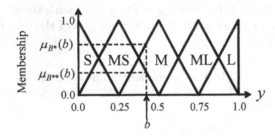

Fig. 10.9. Determination of two consequent linguistic terms from a single consequent real number

The basic idea of the twin-table approach is to use two linguistic rules with consequent linguistic terms to represent a single linguistic rule with a consequent real number. For example, let us consider the following linguistic rule:

$$\text{Rule } R_q \text{: If } x_1 \text{ is } A_{q1} \text{ and } \dots \text{ and } x_n \text{ is } A_{qn} \text{ then } y \text{ is } 0.45. \qquad (10.38)$$

The consequent real number 0.45 is between *medium small* (i.e., 0.25) and *medium* (i.e., 0.5). Thus we use two linguistic rules with *medium small* and *medium* as consequent linguistic terms to represent the linguistic rule in (10.38). Since *medium* has a larger compatibility grade with 0.45 than *medium small*, the linguistic rule with the consequent linguistic term *medium* has a larger rule weight than that with *medium small*. We use the compatibility grade of the consequent real number with each consequent linguistic term as the rule weight of the corresponding linguistic rule. As a result, we have the following two linguistic rules from the single linguistic rule in (10.38):

$$\text{Rule } R_q \text{: If } x_1 \text{ is } A_{q1} \text{ and } \dots \text{ and } x_n \text{ is } A_{qn}$$

$$\text{then } y \text{ is } medium\ small \text{ with } 0.2, \qquad (10.39)$$

Rule R_q: If x_1 is A_{q1} and ... and x_n is A_{qn}

$$\text{then } y \text{ is } medium \text{ with } 0.8. \tag{10.40}$$

10.5.2 Determination of Consequent Linguistic Terms

Let us consider the following linguistic rule with a consequent real number b:

Rule R_q: If x_1 is A_{q1} and ... and x_n is A_{qn} then y is b. (10.41)

When the domain interval of the output variable is partitioned by linguistic terms with triangular membership functions as in Fig. 10.9, the consequent real number b is compatible with two linguistic terms. Let B^* and B^{**} be the linguistic terms with larger and smaller compatibility grades with b, respectively. In Fig. 10.9, B^* and B^{**} are *medium* and *medium small*, respectively. Using the two linguistic terms B^* and B^{**}, we generate the following two linguistic rules:

Rule R_q^*: If x_1 is A_{q1} and ... and x_n is A_{qn}

$$\text{then } y \text{ is } B^* \text{ with } \mu_{B^*}(b), \tag{10.42}$$

Rule R_q^{**}: If x_1 is A_{q1} and ... and x_n is A_{qn}

$$\text{then } y \text{ is } B^{**} \text{ with } \mu_{B^{**}}(b), \tag{10.43}$$

where the compatibility grades $\mu_{B^*}(b)$ and $\mu_{B^{**}}(b)$ are used as the rule weights. In some special cases (e.g., $b = 0.5$ in Fig. 10.9), the consequent real number b is compatible with only a single linguistic term. In this case, B^{**} is not specified. Thus we only generate a single linguistic rule with the consequent linguistic term B^*.

Let b^* and b^{**} be representative real numbers for B^* and B^{**}, respectively (e.g., 0.25 for *medium small*). When B^* and B^{**} have triangular membership functions as in Fig. 10.9, the following relations hold:

$$\mu_{B^*}(b) + \mu_{B^{**}}(b) = 1, \tag{10.44}$$

$$b^* \cdot \mu_{B^*}(b) + b^{**} \cdot \mu_{B^{**}}(b) = b. \tag{10.45}$$

For example, $\mu_{medium}(b) = 0.8$ and $\mu_{medium\ small}(b) = 0.2$ when $b = 0.45$ in Fig. 10.9. Thus we can see that (10.45) holds as follows:

$$0.5 \cdot 0.8 + 0.25 \cdot 0.2 = 0.45. \tag{10.46}$$

From (10.45), we can see that the consequent real number b can be represented by the two linguistic terms B^* and B^{**}.

When a linguistic rule-based system with consequent real numbers is given, we generate two linguistic rules with consequent linguistic terms from each rule with a consequent real number as shown in (10.42) and (10.43). The generated linguistic rule with a larger rule weight (i.e., R_q^* in (10.42)) is included in a main rule table. The other linguistic rule (i.e., R_q^{**} in (10.43)) is included in a secondary rule table. In this manner, we construct two rule tables with consequent linguistic terms from a single rule table with consequent real numbers. It should be noted that all the three rule tables have the same antecedent structure.

Let us assume that a linguistic rule-based system with fuzzy rules of the form in (10.1) is given. Two rule tables with consequent linguistic terms are generated from the given fuzzy rule-based system with consequent real numbers. The main rule table consists of linguistic rules of the following form:

Rule R_q^*: If x_1 is A_{q1} and ... and x_n is A_{qn}

$$\text{then } y \text{ is } B_q^* \text{ with } w_q^*, \qquad (10.47)$$

where B_q^* is the linguistic term with the largest compatibility grade with the consequent real number b_q of the linguistic rule R_q, and the rule weight w_q^* is specified from b_q as

$$w_q^* = \mu_{B_q^*}(b_q). \qquad (10.48)$$

On the other hand, the secondary rule table consists of linguistic rules of the following form:

Rule R_q^{**}: If x_1 is A_{q1} and ... and x_n is A_{qn}

$$\text{then } y \text{ is } B_q^{**} \text{ with } w_q^{**}, \qquad (10.49)$$

where B_q^{**} is the linguistic term with the second largest compatibility grade with b_q, and the rule weight w_q^{**} is specified as

$$w_q^{**} = \mu_{B_q^{**}}(b_q). \qquad (10.50)$$

The fuzzy reasoning method in (10.2) is extended to the case of the two linguistic rule tables as

$$\hat{y}(\mathbf{x}) = \frac{\sum\limits_{R_q \in S} [\mu_{A_q}(\mathbf{x}) \cdot b_q^* \cdot w_q^* + \mu_{A_q}(\mathbf{x}) \cdot b_q^{**} \cdot w_q^{**}]}{\sum\limits_{R_q \in S} [\mu_{A_q}(\mathbf{x}) \cdot w_q^* + \mu_{A_q}(\mathbf{x}) \cdot w_q^{**}]}. \qquad (10.51)$$

From (10.44), (10.45), (10.48), and (10.50), the following relations hold:

$$w_q^* + w_q^{**} = 1, \qquad (10.52)$$

$$b_q^* \cdot w_q^* + b_q^{**} \cdot w_q^{**} = b_q. \qquad (10.53)$$

Thus (10.51) can be rewritten as follows:

$$\hat{y}(\mathbf{x}) = \frac{\sum\limits_{R_q \in S} \mu_{A_q}(\mathbf{x}) \cdot b_q}{\sum\limits_{R_q \in S} \mu_{A_q}(\mathbf{x})}. \qquad (10.54)$$

This is exactly the same as the fuzzy reasoning method in (10.2). This means that a single rule table with consequent real numbers can be equivalently represented by two rule tables with consequent linguistic terms.

10.5.3 Numerical Example

As a numerical example, let us consider the following nonlinear function [159]:

$$y = (1 + x_1^{-2} + x_2^{-1.5})^2, \quad 1 \le x_1 \le 5, \ 1 \le x_2 \le 5. \tag{10.55}$$

This nonlinear function is shown in Fig. 10.10. As training data, we generated 441 input–output pairs (x_{p1}, x_{p2}, y_p), $p = 1, 2, \ldots, 441$, using the uniformly divided 21×21 grid where $x_{p1} = 1.0, 1.2, \ldots, 5.0$, $x_{p2} = 1.0, 1.2, \ldots, 5.0$, and y_p was calculated from (10.55).

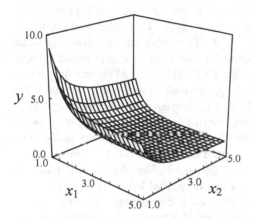

Fig. 10.10. Nonlinear function in (10.55)

First we generated a linguistic rule-based system using the heuristic rule generation method described in Chap. 8. The generated linguistic rule-based system is shown in Fig. 10.11. As shown in this figure, we used five linguistic terms for each of the two input variables. We also used five linguistic terms for the output variable, which are shown in Fig. 10.12. The MSE on the training data in (10.34) was 0.349 by the linguistic rule-based system in Fig. 10.11.

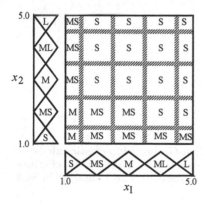

Fig. 10.11. Generated linguistic rule-based system using the heuristic rule generation method in Chap. 8

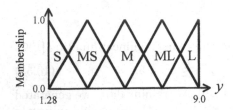

Fig. 10.12. Five linguistic terms used for the output variable

We also generated a linguistic rule-based system with consequent real numbers from the training data using the same antecedent structure as in Fig. 10.11. The consequent real number of each linguistic rule was first specified by the heuristic specification method in Sect. 10.2. The generated linguistic rule-based system is shown in Fig. 10.13. The MSE on the training data was 0.150. This is better than the result by the linguistic rule-based system with consequent linguistic terms in Fig. 10.11 (i.e., the MSE was improved from 0.349 to 0.150). Then each consequent real number was adjusted by the global learning scheme in Sect. 10.3. The incremental learning algorithm was iterated ten times for each input–output pair (i.e., ten epochs) using the learning rate $\alpha = 0.1$. In each epoch, the 441 input–output pairs were presented to the linguistic rule-based system in a random order. The adjusted linguistic rule-based system is shown in Fig. 10.14. The MSE on the training data was improved from 0.150 to 0.104 by the global learning scheme.

From the adjusted linguistic rule table with consequent real numbers in Fig. 10.14, we generated two rule tables using the twin-table approach in this section. The generated rule tables are shown in Fig. 10.15 and Fig. 10.16. We can see that the main rule table in Fig. 10.15 is almost the same as the rule table in Fig. 10.11 generated by the heuristic rule generation method in Chap. 8. The MSE by the main rule table in Fig. 10.15 was 0.278, which is slightly better than the MSE by the heuristic rule table in Fig. 10.11 (i.e., 0.349). On the other hand, the MSE by the secondary rule table in Fig. 10.16 was 1.895, which is much worse than the results by the other rule tables.

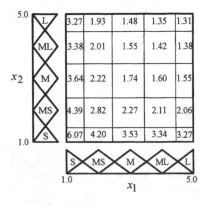

Fig. 10.13. Generated linguistic rule-based system using the heuristic specification method of consequent real numbers in Sect. 10.2

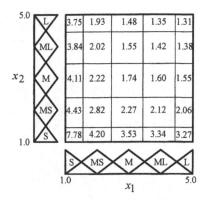

Fig. 10.14. Adjusted linguistic rule-based system using the global learning scheme in Sect. 10.3

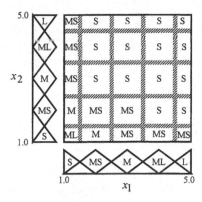

Fig. 10.15. Main rule table

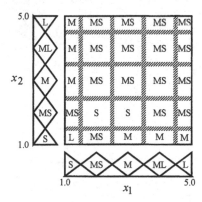

Fig. 10.16. Secondary rule table

11. Handling of Linguistic Rules in Neural Networks

Various hybrid models of fuzzy logic and neural networks have been proposed in the literature. These models are often called fuzzy neural networks. The main line of fuzzy neural networks concerns a class called neuro-fuzzy models. Fuzzy neural networks in this class are basically fuzzy rule-based systems that are adjustable using descent learning algorithms [60, 130]. Neuro-fuzzy models are often represented in neural network structures [10, 58, 99, 128]. They are used as approximators of nonlinear mappings from input vectors to output values. Another class of fuzzy neural networks is neural networks for fuzzy reasoning, which map antecedent linguistic terms to consequent linguistic terms. That is, neural networks are used as approximators of nonlinear mappings from linguistic vectors to linguistic terms. This chapter describes fuzzy neural networks of this class. The learning of neural networks from linguistic rules is discussed in the next chapter.

In this chapter, linguistic rules of the following form are approximately realized by neural networks:

$$\text{Rule } R_q\text{: If } x_1 \text{ is } A_{q1} \text{ and } \dots \text{ and } x_n \text{ is } A_{qn} \text{ then } y \text{ is } B_q, \qquad (11.1)$$

where A_{qi} is an antecedent linguistic term and B_q is a consequent linguistic term. Linguistic rules of the same form were used in Chaps. 8 and 9 for modeling problems. One approach to the handling of linguistic rules is to use preprocessors to transform linguistic terms into real vectors. In this approach, linguistic rules are handled as numerical input–output pairs. There exist two methods in this approach. One method is based on membership values of linguistic terms. The other method is based on upper and lower limits of level sets of linguistic terms. Another approach to the handling of linguistic rules is to use fuzzy arithmetic in neural networks. In this approach, linguistic rules are handled as linguistic input–output pairs while they are handled as numerical input–output pairs in the first approach. The input–output relation of each unit in neural networks is extended to the case of linguistic inputs using fuzzy arithmetic. These two approaches are explained in this chapter.

11.1 Problem Formulation

11.1.1 Approximation of Linguistic Rules

Let us assume that we have N linguistic rules R_q, $q = 1, 2, \ldots, N$. These linguistic rules can be viewed as linguistic input–output pairs (A_q, B_q), $q = 1, 2, \ldots, N$, where $A_q = (A_{q1}, \ldots, A_{qn})$. A simple example of a set of given linguistic rules is as follows:

$$R_1 : \text{If } x \text{ is } small \text{ then } y \text{ is } large, \tag{11.2}$$

$$R_2 : \text{If } x \text{ is } medium \text{ then } y \text{ is } medium, \tag{11.3}$$

$$R_3 : \text{If } x \text{ is } large \text{ then } y \text{ is } small. \tag{11.4}$$

These linguistic rules are viewed as the three linguistic input–output pairs (*small, large*), (*medium, medium*), and (*large, small*). Each linguistic input–output pair (A_q, B_q) is depicted in the input–output space $[0, 1] \times [0, 1]$ in Fig. 11.1 where squares and closed circles correspond to level sets (i.e., α-cuts) of the fuzzy set $A_q \times B_q$ for five levels 0.2, 0.4, 0.6, 0.8, and 1.0. In Fig. 11.1, the membership function of the fuzzy set $A_q \times B_q$ is defined as

$$\mu_{A_q \times B_q}(x, y) = \min\{\mu_{A_q}(x), \ \mu_{B_q}(y)\}. \tag{11.5}$$

The concept of level sets is explained later in this chapter. In Fig. 11.1, each linguistic input–output pair is illustrated as a pyramid-shaped fuzzy set on the two-dimensional input–output space $[0, 1] \times [0, 1]$.

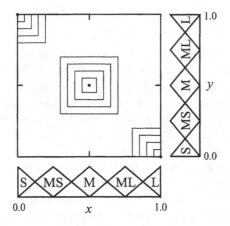

Fig. 11.1. Three linguistic input–output pairs: (*small, large*), (*medium, medium*), and (*large, small*)

Our task in this chapter is to approximately realize the given N linguistic rules of the form in (11.1) using neural networks. This task is rephrased as approximately realizing the given N linguistic input–output pairs (A_q, B_q), $q = 1, 2, \ldots, N$. Thus neural networks are used as approximators of nonlinear mappings from n-dimensional linguistic vectors to linguistic terms.

As in standard learning tasks of neural networks from numerical input–output pairs, there are two issues to be taken into account:

(1) Fitting ability of neural networks. This ability is evaluated by presenting each linguistic input vector A_q in the given linguistic input–output pairs to a trained neural network. The point is whether the actual output from the trained neural network is close to the target linguistic term B_q or not. In the case of the above example with the three linguistic rules in (11.2)–(11.4), the three linguistic input terms *small*, *medium*, and *large* are presented to the trained neural network to check whether the actual outputs are close to the target linguistic terms *large*, *medium*, and *small*, respectively.

(2) Generalization ability of neural networks. This ability is evaluated for new linguistic input vectors that have not been used in the learning of the trained neural network. The point is whether the actual output from the trained neural network is intuitively acceptable or not. For example, *medium small* and *medium large* are presented to the trained neural network in the case of the above example. We may intuitively think from Fig. 11.1 that the corresponding outputs should be *medium large* and *medium small*, respectively. When we have many linguistic input–output pairs, cross-validation techniques (e.g., the leaving-one-out procedure and the 10-fold cross-validation procedure [178]) can be used in the same manner as in the case of numerical input–output pairs.

11.1.2 Multi-Layer Feedforward Neural Networks

We explain some approaches to the handling of linguistic rules by standard feedforward neural networks to which the back-propagation algorithm [146] can be naturally applied. For simplicity of explanation, let us consider a three-layer feedforward neural network, though we can use neural networks with more than three layers in the same manner. We denote the number of input units, hidden units, and output units by n_I, n_H, and n_O, respectively. When an n_I-dimensional input vector $x_q = (x_{q1}, \ldots, x_{qn_I})$ is presented to the neural network, the input–output relation of each unit is written as follows [146]:

$$\text{Input units:} \quad o_{qi} = x_{qi}, \ i = 1, 2, \ldots, n_I. \tag{11.6}$$

$$\text{Hidden units:} \quad o_{qj} = f(net_{qj}), \ j = 1, 2, \ldots, n_H, \tag{11.7}$$

$$net_{qj} = \sum_{i=1}^{n_I} w_{ji} \cdot o_{qi} + \theta_j. \tag{11.8}$$

$$\text{Output units:} \quad o_{qk} = f(net_{qk}), \ k = 1, 2, \ldots, n_O, \tag{11.9}$$

$$net_{qk} = \sum_{j=1}^{n_H} w_{kj} \cdot o_{qj} + \theta_k. \tag{11.10}$$

In this formulation, w_{ji} is the connection weight from the i-th input unit to the j-th hidden unit, θ_j is the bias to the j-th hidden unit, w_{kj} is the connection weight from the j-th hidden unit to the k-th output unit, and θ_k is the bias to the k-th output unit. The weights and biases are adjusted by the learning of the neural network. As in Rumelhart et al. [146], we use the following sigmoidal function as the activation function at the hidden and output units:

$$f(x) = \frac{1}{1 + \exp(-x)}. \tag{11.11}$$

The three-layer feedforward neural network in (11.6)–(11.11) is known as a universal approximator of nonlinear functions [47, 59, 179] when we can use an arbitrary number of hidden units. Linguistic rule-based systems are also universal approximators of nonlinear functions [116, 175] when we can use an arbitrary fine fuzzy partition for each input (and output) variable.

11.2 Handling of Linguistic Rules Using Membership Values

11.2.1 Basic Idea

Standard feedforward neural networks cannot directly handle linguistic input–output pairs. Thus the neural network structure or the data structure should be modified to handle linguistic rules in neural networks. One idea is to represent a linguistic term using its membership values at some discretized points. This idea was proposed by Keller et al. [107, 108]. When the domain interval [0, 1] is discretized into eleven points, a linguistic term is represented by an 11-dimensional numerical vector. For example, *medium* is represented as follows (see Fig. 11.2) using its membership values at the eleven points 0.0, 0.1, 0.2, ..., 1.0:

$$medium = (0.0, 0.0, 0.0, 0.2, 0.6, 1.0, 0.6, 0.2, 0.0, 0.0, 0.0). \tag{11.12}$$

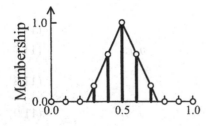

Fig. 11.2. Representation of the linguistic term *medium* using its membership values at the eleven points in the domain interval [0, 1]

11.2.2 Network Architecture

Since each linguistic term is represented by a numerical vector, we can use standard feedforward neural networks. For simplicity of explanation, let us assume that the domain interval of each linguistic term is discretized into the eleven points as shown in Fig. 11.2. In this case, the n-dimensional linguistic input vector $A_q = (A_{q1}, \ldots, A_{qn})$ is represented by an $11n$-dimensional numerical vector. The corresponding linguistic output B_q is represented as an 11-dimensional target vector. Thus we use a standard feedforward neural network with $11n$ input units and 11 output units (i.e., $n_I = 11n$ and $n_O = 11$ in (11.6)–(11.10)).

In Fig. 11.3, we show a three-layer feedforward neural network for the handling of the linguistic input–output pair (*medium*, *medium*) corresponding to the linguistic rule "If x is *medium* then y is *medium*". In this case, the 11-dimensional numerical vector corresponding to *medium* is presented to the neural network. The target vector is the 11-dimensional numerical vector corresponding to *medium*.

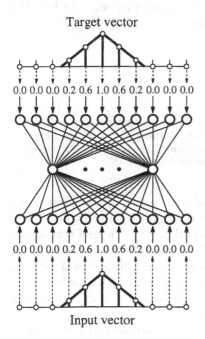

Fig. 11.3. Illustration of the learning of neural networks from the linguistic input–output pair (*medium*, *medium*) using the membership values of each linguistic term

11.2.3 Computer Simulation

We trained a three-layer feedforward neural network with eleven input units, five hidden units, and eleven output units using the three linguistic rules in

(11.2)–(11.4). Each linguistic rule, which is a linguistic input–output pair, was handled as a numerical input–output pair of an 11-dimensional input vector and an 11-dimensional target vector. That is, three numerical input–output pairs were obtained from the three linguistic rules. We used the back-propagation algorithm with the momentum term [146]. This algorithm is explained in the next chapter. The learning rate and the momentum term were specified as 0.25 and 0.9, respectively. The back-propagation algorithm was iterated 1000 times over the three numerical input–output pairs (i.e., 1000 epochs). We calculated the total squared error

$$E = \frac{1}{2} \sum_{p=1}^{3} \sum_{k=1}^{11} (o_{pk} - t_{pk})^2, \tag{11.13}$$

where o_{pk} is the actual output value from the k-th output unit, and t_{pk} is the corresponding target output. After 1000 epochs, the value of the total squared error E in (11.13) was 0.0011. This indicates that good fitting to the three input–output pairs was obtained. For example, Fig. 11.4 shows the actual output vector from the trained neural network for the linguistic input *medium*. We can see that the fitting of the actual output vector in Fig. 11.4 to the linguistic target *medium* is very good.

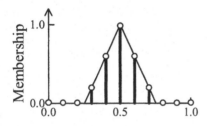

Fig. 11.4. The actual output vector from the trained neural network for the linguistic input *medium*. The corresponding linguistic target is *medium*

To examine the generalization ability of the trained neural network, we presented an 11-dimensional input vector corresponding to the linguistic term *medium small*. The actual output vector from the trained neural network for this input vector is depicted in Fig. 11.5. From intuitive interpolation of the two linguistic rules "If x is *small* then y is *large*" and "If x is *medium* then y is *medium*", we think that the linguistic output should be *medium large* for the linguistic input *medium small*. It is, however, difficult to interpret the actual output vector in Fig. 11.5 as *medium large*.

The main difficulty in the membership value-based method is that actual output vectors from trained neural networks are not always interpreted as linguistic terms. They usually do not represent normal fuzzy sets (i.e., fuzzy sets whose maximum membership value is 1). In many cases, actual output vectors represent membership functions with multiple peaks (i.e., non-convex fuzzy sets). In Fig. 11.5, the membership function constructed by the actual output vector is not normal or convex.

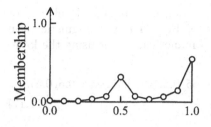

Fig. 11.5. The actual output vector from the trained neural network for the linguistic input *medium small*

11.3 Handling of Linguistic Rules Using Level Sets

11.3.1 Basic Idea

Another trick for transforming a linguistic term into a numerical vector is to use the upper and lower limits of its level sets (i.e., its α-cuts). The h-level set of a linguistic term A (i.e., the α-cut of A for $\alpha = h$) is a closed interval, which is defined as follows (see Fig. 11.6):

$$[A]_h = \{x \mid \mu_A(x) \geq h, \ x \in \Re\} \text{ for } 0 < h \leq 1, \tag{11.14}$$

where $\Re$ is the set of real numbers. In the case of $h = 0$ in (11.14), the h-level set is the same as $\Re$. To avoid such a meaningless result, (11.14) is not applied to the case of $h = 0$. The h-level set of A for $h = 0$ is usually defined as an open interval in the following manner:

$$[A]_h = \{x \mid \mu_X(x) > h, \ x \in \Re\} \text{ for } h = 0. \tag{11.15}$$

We denote the level set using its lower and upper limits as

$$[A]_h = \begin{cases} [[A]_h^L, [A]_h^U] & \text{for } 0 < h \leq 1, \\ ([A]_h^L, [A]_h^U) & \text{for } h = 0, \end{cases} \tag{11.16}$$

where the superscripts L and U represent the lower and upper limits of the level set, respectively.

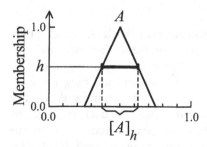

Fig. 11.6. Illustration of the h-level set of a linguistic term A

The idea of decomposing a linguistic term into the upper and lower limits of its level sets was proposed by Uehara & Fujise [168]. Figure 11.7 illustrates the decomposition of the linguistic term *medium* into its six h-level sets for h=0.0, 0.2, 0.4, 0.6, 0.8, 1.0. In the case of Fig. 11.7, the linguistic term *medium* is represented by a 12-dimensional numerical vector using the lower and upper limits of its six level sets as

$$medium = (0.25, 0.75, 0.3, 0.7, 0.35, 0.65, 0.4, 0.6, 0.45, 0.55, 0.5, 0.5).$$

$$(11.17)$$

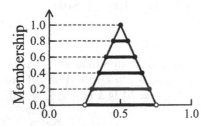

Fig. 11.7. Representation of the linguistic term *medium* using its six h-level sets for h=0.0, 0.2, 0.4, 0.6, 0.8, 1.0

11.3.2 Network Architecture

As in the case of the membership value-based method in the previous section, each linguistic term is represented by a numerical vector in the level set-based method. Thus we can use standard feedforward neural networks. When we use the six level sets of each linguistic term as in Fig. 11.7, the n-dimensional linguistic input vector $\boldsymbol{A}_q = (A_{q1}, \ldots, A_{qn})$ is represented by a $12n$-dimensional numerical vector. The corresponding linguistic output B_q is represented by a 12-dimensional target vector. Thus we use a standard feedforward neural network with $12n$ input units and 12 output units (i.e., $n_I = 12n$ and $n_O = 12$ in (11.6)–(11.10)).

11.3.3 Computer Simulation

We trained a three-layer feedforward neural network with 12 input units, five hidden units, and 12 output units using the three linguistic rules in (11.2)–(11.4). Each linguistic rule was handled as a numerical input–output pair of a 12-dimensional input vector and a 12-dimensional target vector. Thus three numerical input–output pairs were used as training data. The learning of the neural network was performed using the back-propagation algorithm with the momentum term [146] in the same manner as in the previous section. After 1000 epochs, the total squared error was 0.0014. This indicates that good fitting to the three input–output pairs was obtained. For example, Fig. 11.8 shows the actual output vector from the trained neural network for the linguistic input *medium*. We can see from Fig. 11.8 that the fitting of the actual output vector to the linguistic target *medium* is very good.

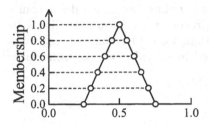

Fig. 11.8. The actual output vector from the trained neural network for the linguistic input *medium*. The corresponding linguistic target is *medium*

To examine the generalization ability of the trained neural network, we presented a 12-dimensional input vector corresponding to the linguistic term *medium small*. The actual output vector from the trained neural network for this input vector is depicted in Fig. 11.9. The intuitively acceptable linguistic output is *medium large* for the linguistic input *medium small*. It is, however, difficult to interpret the actual output vector in Fig. 11.9 as *medium large*.

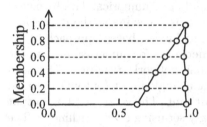

Fig. 11.9. The actual output vector from the trained neural network for the linguistic input *medium small*

The main difficulty in the level set-based approach is that actual output vectors from trained neural networks do not always construct legal fuzzy sets. That is, the following inclusion relation is not always satisfied:

$$[\hat{B}]_h \supseteq [\hat{B}]_k \text{ if } h \leq k, \tag{11.18}$$

where $[\hat{B}]_h$ and $[\hat{B}]_k$ are level sets obtained as output values from trained neural networks. In (11.18), $\hat{B}$ is a fuzzy set constructed from level sets. It should be noted that (11.18) always holds for any fuzzy set. When (11.18) is not satisfied, $\hat{B}$ cannot be viewed as a fuzzy set. In Fig. 11.9, the membership function constructed by the actual output vector from the trained neural network does not satisfy (11.18).

11.4 Handling of Linguistic Rules Using Fuzzy Arithmetic

We have already explained two methods for handling linguistic rules in neural networks. These methods are based on preprocessors that transform linguistic terms into numerical vectors. In this section, we explain another approach where linguistic terms are directly handled in neural networks using fuzzy arithmetic.

11.4.1 Basic Idea

As shown in the previous sections, good fitting to given linguistic rules was obtained by the two methods based on preprocessors. The generalization ability of trained neural networks, however, was not good in those methods. This is because many input and output units were used to handle a single linguistic term. As a result, neural network structures were very complicated in comparison with the complexity of linguistic rules. For example, neural networks with more than ten input and output units were used in the previous computer simulations to handle linguistic rules describing a single-input and single-output nonlinear mapping. In the handling of numerical data by neural networks, the number of input (output) units is the same as the dimensionality of the input (output) space. A fuzzy arithmetic-based approach to the handling of linguistic rules extends neural networks for numerical data to the case of linguistic rules without modifying their network structures. That is, a single input (output) unit is used to handle a single input (output) variable. A linguistic term is presented to each input unit. The corresponding output from each output unit is calculated as a fuzzy set using fuzzy arithmetic. The fuzzy arithmetic-based approach to the handling of linguistic rules by neural networks was proposed in Ishibuchi et al. [63]. The interpolation ability of trained neural networks was examined in [87].

The fuzzy arithmetic-based approach [63, 87] is a special case of fuzzified neural networks. In general, multi-layer feedforward neural networks can be fuzzified by using fuzzy numbers as their inputs, connection weights, and/or targets [16]. Fuzzy numbers (e.g., about 2, approximately 12, etc.) are normal and convex fuzzy sets on the real axis $\Re$ [106]. Linguistic terms such as *small* and *large* can also be viewed as fuzzy numbers. In Hayashi et al. [52], the back-propagation algorithm was directly fuzzified. Learning of fuzzified neural networks was studied by some authors [39, 40, 64].

11.4.2 Fuzzy Arithmetic

Before describing neural networks that can directly handle linguistic rules, we briefly explain fuzzy arithmetic. Fuzzy arithmetic is an extension of standard arithmetic on real numbers to the case of fuzzy numbers. Fuzzy arithmetic is mathematically defined by the extension principle of Zadeh [191] and numerically executed using interval arithmetic [6, 126] on level sets of fuzzy numbers.

In fuzzified neural networks, the following addition and multiplication on fuzzy numbers are used:

$$\mu_{A+B}(z) = \max\{\mu_A(x) \wedge \mu_B(y) \mid x + y = z, \, x \in \Re, \, y \in \Re\}, \quad (11.19)$$

$$\mu_{A \cdot B}(z) = \max\{\mu_A(x) \wedge \mu_B(y) \mid x \cdot y = z, \, x \in \Re, \, y \in \Re\}, \quad (11.20)$$

where upper-case letters (i.e., A and B) are fuzzy numbers, lower-case letters (i.e., x, y, and z) are real numbers, and $\wedge$ is the minimum operator. These two operations on fuzzy numbers are illustrated in Fig. 11.10 and Fig. 11.11, respectively.

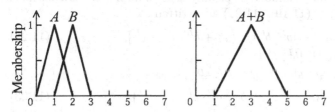

Fig. 11.10. Illustration of the sum $A + B$ of two fuzzy numbers A and B

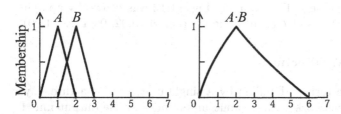

Fig. 11.11. Illustration of the product $A \cdot B$ of two fuzzy numbers A and B

The activation function in (11.11) is extended to the case of a fuzzy input Net as

$$\mu_{f(Net)}(z) = \max\{\mu_{Net}(x) \mid z = f(x), \, x \in \Re\}. \quad (11.21)$$

The nonlinear fuzzy mapping from the fuzzy number Net to the fuzzy number $f(Net)$ is illustrated in Fig. 11.12.

As shown in (11.6)–(11.10), the input–output relation of each unit in standard feedforward neural networks is defined by the addition, multiplication, and activation function. Thus we can define the fuzzy version of the input–output relation using (11.19)–(11.21). Since the exact calculation of fuzzy

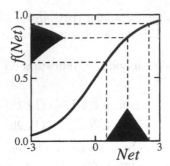

Fig. 11.12. Fuzzy activation function at hidden and output units

arithmetic using the extension principle is not easy, interval arithmetic on multiple level sets of fuzzy numbers is usually used in numerical calculations. The interval versions of (11.19)–(11.21) are written as

$$A + B = [a^L, a^U] + [b^L, b^U] = [a^L + b^L, a^U + b^U], \tag{11.22}$$

$$\begin{aligned} A \cdot B &= [a^L, a^U] \cdot [b^L, b^U] \\ &= [\min\{a^L \cdot b^L, a^L \cdot b^U, a^U \cdot b^L, a^U \cdot b^U\}, \\ &\qquad \max\{a^L \cdot b^L, a^L \cdot b^U, a^U \cdot b^L, a^U \cdot b^U\}], \end{aligned} \tag{11.23}$$

$$f(Net) = f([net^L, net^U]) = [f(net^L), f(net^U)], \tag{11.24}$$

where upper-case letters (i.e., A, B, and Net) are intervals, and superscripts L and U denote the lower and upper limits of intervals, respectively. Fuzzy arithmetic can be numerically executed by applying interval arithmetic to level sets of fuzzy numbers. For example, Fig. 11.12 was drawn by applying (11.24) to the h-level sets of Net for 50 levels (i.e., h=0.02, 0.04, ..., 1.00).

11.4.3 Network Architecture

Since each linguistic term is handled by a single unit, we use a three-layer feedforward neural network with n input units and a single output unit to handle the linguistic rule R_q in (11.1). The number of hidden units, which is denoted by n_H, can be arbitrarily specified. The linguistic rule R_q is handled as the linguistic input–output pair $(\boldsymbol{A}_q, \boldsymbol{B}_q)$. Thus the linguistic vector $\boldsymbol{A}_q = (A_{q1}, \ldots, A_{qn})$ is presented to the neural network. In this case, the input–output relation of each unit is written as follows:

Input units: $O_{qi} = A_{qi}, \ i = 1, 2, \ldots, n.$ \hfill (11.25)

Hidden units: $O_{qj} = f(Net_{qj}), \ j = 1, 2, \ldots, n_H,$ \hfill (11.26)

$$Net_{qj} = \sum_{i=1}^{n} w_{ji} \cdot O_{qi} + \theta_j. \tag{11.27}$$

Output unit: $O_q = f(Net_q),$ \hfill (11.28)

$$Net_q = \sum_{j=1}^{n_H} w_j \cdot O_{qj} + \theta. \tag{11.29}$$

In (11.25)–(11.29), fuzzy numbers are denoted by upper-case letters such as A_{qi}, O_{qi}, and Net_{qj}. While the input vector is fuzzified as $A_q = (A_{q1}, \ldots , A_{qn})$, the connection weights w_{ji}, w_j and the biases θ_j, θ are still real numbers. Fuzzified neural networks with fuzzy connection weights and fuzzy biases will be explained in Chap. 14.

We illustrate the above fuzzification of neural networks using a simple three-layer feedforward neural network in Fig. 11.13 where connection weights and biases are shown as real numbers. Our task in this figure is to calculate the fuzzy output from the output unit when the linguistic vector (*small, medium*) is presented.

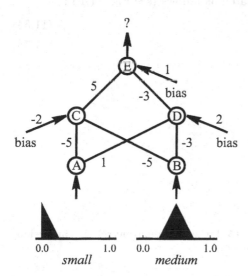

Fig. 11.13. A three-layer feedforward neural network and a linguistic input vector (*small, medium*)

The fuzzy output from each input unit is the same as the linguistic input to that unit as shown in (11.25). Thus the fuzzy outputs from the input units A and B in Fig. 11.13 are *small* and *medium*, respectively. At the hidden unit C, the following fuzzy arithmetic is performed to calculate the fuzzy output O_C:

$$Net_C = -5 \cdot small - 5 \cdot medium - 2, \tag{11.30}$$
$$O_C = f(Net_C). \tag{11.31}$$

The membership functions of O_C and Net_C are shown in Fig. 11.14. The fuzzy output O_D from the hidden unit D is calculated as follows (see Fig. 11.15):

$$Net_D = 1 \cdot small - 3 \cdot medium + 2, \tag{11.32}$$

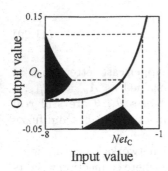

Fig. 11.14. Fuzzy input–output relation at the hidden unit C

$$O_D = f(Net_D). \tag{11.33}$$

Using the fuzzy outputs O_C and O_D from the hidden units, the fuzzy output O_E from the output unit E is calculated as follows (see Fig. 11.16):

$$Net_E = 5 \cdot O_C - 3 \cdot O_D + 1, \tag{11.34}$$

$$O_E = f(Net_E). \tag{11.35}$$

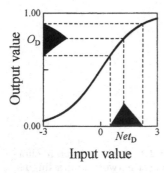

Fig. 11.15. Fuzzy input–output relation at the hidden unit D

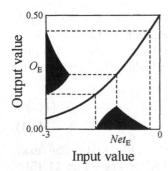

Fig. 11.16. Fuzzy input–output relation at the output unit E

The numerical calculation of fuzzy arithmetic in the neural network in (11.25)–(11.29) is executed using interval arithmetic on level sets of the linguistic input vector $\mathbf{A}_q = (A_{q1}, \ldots, A_{qn})$. Actually, we used interval arithmetic for 50 h-level sets (i.e., $h=0.02, 0.04, \ldots, 1.00$) in Figs. 11.14 – 11.16. The input–output relation in (11.25)–(11.29) for the linguistic input vector $\mathbf{A}_q = (A_{q1}, \ldots, A_{qn})$ is rewritten for the interval input vector $\mathbf{X}_q = (X_{q1}, \ldots, X_{qn})$ as follows (the interval X_{qi} corresponds to the level set of the linguistic term A_{qi}):

Input units: $[o_{qi}^L, o_{qi}^U] = X_{qi} = [x_{qi}^L, x_{qi}^U], i = 1, 2, \ldots, n.$ (11.36)

Hidden units: $[o_{qj}^L, o_{qj}^U] = [f(net_{qj}^L), f(net_{qj}^U)],$

$$j = 1, 2, \ldots, n_H, \quad (11.37)$$

$$net_{qj}^L = \sum_{\substack{i=1 \\ w_{ji} \geq 0}}^{n} w_{ji} \cdot o_{qi}^L + \sum_{\substack{i=1 \\ w_{ji} < 0}}^{n} w_{ji} \cdot o_{qi}^U + \theta_j, \quad (11.38)$$

$$net_{qj}^U = \sum_{\substack{i=1 \\ w_{ji} \geq 0}}^{n} w_{ji} \cdot o_{qi}^U + \sum_{\substack{i=1 \\ w_{ji} < 0}}^{n} w_{ji} \cdot o_{qi}^L + \theta_j. \quad (11.39)$$

Output unit: $[o_q^L, o_q^U] = [f(net_q^L), f(net_q^U)],$ (11.40)

$$net_q^L = \sum_{\substack{j=1 \\ w_j \geq 0}}^{n_H} w_j \cdot o_{qj}^L + \sum_{\substack{j=1 \\ w_j < 0}}^{n_H} w_j \cdot o_{qj}^U + \theta, \quad (11.41)$$

$$net_q^U = \sum_{\substack{j=1 \\ w_j \geq 0}}^{n_H} w_j \cdot o_{qj}^U + \sum_{\substack{j=1 \\ w_j < 0}}^{n_H} w_j \cdot o_{qj}^L + \theta. \quad (11.42)$$

11.4.4 Computer Simulation

As in the previous sections, we used the three linguistic rules in (11.2)–(11.4) as training data. These rules were handled as linguistic input–output pairs (*small, large*), (*medium, medium*), and (*large, small*). A single-input and single-output three-layer feedforward neural network with five hidden units was used to handle such a linguistic input–output pair. That is, the network structure of the neural network is $1 \times 5 \times 1$ while it was $11 \times 5 \times 11$ and $12 \times 5 \times 12$ in the previous sections for handling the same linguistic rules. In the learning of the neural network, we used the h-level sets of each linguistic input–output pair for eleven levels (i.e., $h=0.0, 0.1, 0.2, \ldots, 1.0$). That is, we generated eleven interval input–output pairs from each linguistic input–output pair. In the next chapter, we explain how a learning algorithm of neural networks can be derived for interval input–output pairs. The learning of the neural network was terminated after 1000 epochs. In each epoch, 33 interval input–output pairs were used as training data.

In Fig. 11.17, we show the actual fuzzy output from the trained neural network for the linguistic input *medium*. This figure is depicted using 51 *h*-level sets of the linguistic input *medium* for $h=0.00, 0.02, 0.04, \ldots, 1.00$. We can see that the fuzzy output in Fig. 11.17 is similar to the target output *medium*. While the fitting of the actual fuzzy output in Fig. 11.17 is not bad, it is inferior to the previous results in Fig. 11.4 and Fig. 11.8. This is because the neural network structure is very simple in this section (i.e., $1 \times 5 \times 1$) while it was much more complicated in the previous sections (i.e., $11 \times 5 \times 11$ and $12 \times 5 \times 12$).

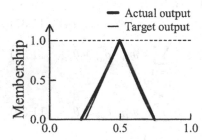

Fig. 11.17. The actual fuzzy output from the trained neural network for the linguistic input *medium*. The corresponding linguistic target is *medium*

To examine the generalization ability of the trained neural network, we presented the linguistic term *medium small*. The corresponding fuzzy output from the trained neural network is shown in Fig. 11.18 using 51 level sets of the linguistic input *medium small*. We can see that the fuzzy output in Fig. 11.18 can be interpreted as *medium large*. From the three linguistic rules (see Fig. 11.1), we intuitively think that the output for the linguistic input *medium small* should be *medium large*. The actual fuzzy output in Fig. 11.18 coincides with this intuition.

From the simulation results in this chapter, we can conclude that the fuzzy arithmetic-based method has lower fitting ability and higher generalization ability than the other methods with preprocessors. Fuzzy outputs from neural networks in the fuzzy arithmetic-based method are always normal and convex fuzzy sets (i.e., fuzzy numbers) when linguistic terms are used as inputs. This feature of fuzzy outputs is easily proven using the characteristic features of fuzzy arithmetic.

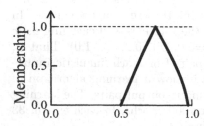

Fig. 11.18. The actual output vector from the trained neural network for the linguistic input *medium small*

12. Learning of Neural Networks from Linguistic Rules

In this chapter, we extend the back-propagation algorithm to the case where linguistic rules instead of numerical data are given as training data. We use the fuzzy arithmetic-based method in Sect. 11.4 to handle linguistic rules. First we explain the learning of standard feedforward neural networks from linguistic rules of the following form for pattern classification problems:

$$\text{Rule } R_q : \text{If } x_1 \text{ is } A_{q1} \text{ and } \ldots \text{ and } x_n \text{ is } A_{qn} \text{ then Class } C_q. \quad (12.1)$$

In this case, target vectors are binary (e.g., $(0, 1, 0)$ for Class 2 in three-class problems) because the consequent part of each linguistic rule is a class label. Then we explain the learning of neural networks from linguistic rules of the following form for modeling problems:

$$\text{Rule } R_q : \text{If } x_1 \text{ is } A_{q1} \text{ and } \ldots \text{ and } x_n \text{ is } A_{qn} \text{ then } y \text{ is } B_q. \quad (12.2)$$

In this case, linguistic terms are used as targets as well as inputs.

12.1 Back-Propagation Algorithm

Before discussing the learning of neural networks from linguistic rules, we explain the back-propagation algorithm [146] for the learning of standard feedforward neural networks from numerical input–output pairs. Let us assume that we have m input–output pairs (x_p, t_p) where $x_p = (x_{p1}, \ldots, x_{pn_I})$ and $t_p = (t_{p1}, \ldots, t_{pn_O})$ are an n_I-dimensional input vector and an n_O-dimensional target vector, respectively. We have already shown the input–output relation of each unit in the three-layer feedforward neural network for the input vector x_p in (11.6)–(11.11) of the previous chapter.

In the back-propagation algorithm, a cost function to be minimized is defined for the input–output pair (x_p, t_p) as the squared error between the actual output vector $o_p = (o_{p1}, \ldots, o_{pn_O})$ from the neural network and the target vector $t_p = (t_{p1}, \ldots, t_{pn_O})$ as:

$$e_p = \frac{1}{2} \sum_{k=1}^{n_O} (t_{pk} - o_{pk})^2. \quad (12.3)$$

The connection weight w_{kj} from the j-th hidden unit to the k-th output unit is updated by the steepest descent scheme as

$$w_{kj}^{\text{New}} = w_{kj}^{\text{Old}} - \eta \cdot \frac{\partial e_p}{\partial w_{kj}}, \tag{12.4}$$

where η is a positive constant (i.e., $0 < \eta$) called the learning rate. The partial derivative in (12.4) is calculated from (12.3) as follows (see [146] for details):

$$\frac{\partial e_p}{\partial w_{kj}} = -(t_{pk} - o_{pk}) \cdot o_{pk} \cdot (1 - o_{pk}) \cdot o_{pj}$$

$$= -\delta_{pk} \cdot o_{pj}, \tag{12.5}$$

where

$$\delta_{pk} = (t_{pk} - o_{pk}) \cdot o_{pk} \cdot (1 - o_{pk}). \tag{12.6}$$

Thus the update rule for w_{kj} is rewritten as

$$w_{kj}^{\text{New}} = w_{kj}^{\text{Old}} + \eta \cdot \delta_{pk} \cdot o_{pj}. \tag{12.7}$$

The update rule for the bias θ_k to the k-th output unit is the same as (12.7) with $o_{pj} = 1$.

In the same manner, the update rule for the connection weight w_{ji} from the i-th input unit to the j-th output unit is written as

$$w_{ji}^{\text{New}} = w_{ji}^{\text{Old}} - \eta \cdot \frac{\partial e_p}{\partial w_{ji}}$$

$$= w_{ji}^{\text{Old}} + \eta \cdot \delta_{pj} \cdot o_{pi}, \tag{12.8}$$

where

$$\frac{\partial e_p}{\partial w_{ji}} = -\delta_{pj} \cdot o_{pi}, \tag{12.9}$$

$$\delta_{pj} = o_{pj} \cdot (1 - o_{pj}) \cdot \sum_{k=1}^{n_O} \delta_{pk} \cdot w_{kj}. \tag{12.10}$$

The update rule for the bias θ_j to the j-th hidden unit is the same as (12.8) with $o_{pi} = 1$.

Usually the momentum term is added to the update rules in (12.7) and (12.8). Let us write the update rules for w_{kj} and w_{ji} as

$$w_{kj}(t + 1) = w_{kj}(t) + \Delta w_{kj}(t), \tag{12.11}$$
$$w_{ji}(t + 1) = w_{ji}(t) + \Delta w_{ji}(t), \tag{12.12}$$

where t indexes the number of updates. Using the momentum term, $\Delta w_{kj}(t)$ and $\Delta w_{ji}(t)$ are specified as

$$\Delta w_{kj}(t) = -\eta \cdot \frac{\partial e_p}{\partial w_{kj}} + \alpha \cdot \Delta w_{kj}(t - 1), \tag{12.13}$$

$$\Delta w_{ji}(t) = -\eta \cdot \frac{\partial e_p}{\partial w_{ji}} + \alpha \cdot \Delta w_{ji}(t - 1), \tag{12.14}$$

where α is a non-negative constant less than 1 (i.e., $0 \leq \alpha < 1$) called the momentum constant. The biases θ_k and θ_j are updated in the same manner as the connection weights w_{kj} and w_{ji}, respectively.

12.2 Learning from Linguistic Rules for Classification Problems

In this section, we discuss the learning of standard multi-layer feedforward neural networks from linguistic rules of the form (12.1) for pattern classification problems. We use a three-layer feedforward neural network with n input units and M output units where M is the number of classes.

12.2.1 Linguistic Training Data

Let us assume that we have m linguistic rules R_q, $q = 1, 2, \ldots, m$, of the form (12.1). As we have already explained in Sect. 11.4, the antecedent part of each linguistic rule is presented to the neural network. That is, the n-dimensional linguistic vector $\boldsymbol{A}_q = (A_{q1}, \ldots, A_{qn})$ is presented. The input–output relation of each unit is defined by fuzzy arithmetic as in Sect. 11.4. The corresponding fuzzy output vector $\boldsymbol{O}_q = (O_{q1}, \ldots, O_{qM})$ is numerically calculated by interval arithmetic on levels sets of $\boldsymbol{A}_q = (A_{q1}, \ldots, A_{qn})$. The target vector $\boldsymbol{t}_q = (t_{q1}, \ldots, t_{qM})$ is defined from the consequent class C_q of the linguistic rule R_q as

$$t_{qk} = \begin{cases} 1, & \text{if } C_q = \text{Class } k, \\ 0, & \text{otherwise}, \end{cases} \qquad k = 1, 2, \ldots, M. \qquad (12.15)$$

In this manner, m input–output pairs $(\boldsymbol{A}_q, \boldsymbol{t}_q)$, $q = 1, 2, \ldots, m$, are generated from the m linguistic rules R_q, $q = 1, 2, \ldots, m$, of the form (12.1) as training data.

12.2.2 Cost Function

The h-level set of the fuzzy output vector $\boldsymbol{O}_q = (O_{q1}, \ldots, O_{qM})$ is calculated by interval arithmetic from the h-level set of the linguistic input vector $\boldsymbol{A}_q = (A_{q1}, \ldots, A_{qn})$ in the numerical calculation of $\boldsymbol{O}_q$. We define a cost function e_{qh} for the h-level set of $\boldsymbol{O}_q$ as

$$e_{qh} = \frac{1}{2} \sum_{k=1}^{M} (t_{qk} - [O_{qk}]_h^L)^2 + \frac{1}{2} \sum_{k=1}^{M} (t_{qk} - [O_{qk}]_h^U)^2, \qquad (12.16)$$

where $[O_{qk}]_h^L$ and $[O_{qk}]_h^U$ are the lower and upper limits of the h-level set $[O_{qk}]_h$ of the fuzzy output O_{qk} from the k-th output unit, respectively. The first and second terms in (12.16) are the squared errors for the lower and upper limits of the h-level set $[O_{qk}]_h$, respectively. In Ishibuchi et al. [63], the following cost function was used:

$$e_{qh} = \frac{1}{2} \sum_{k=1}^{M} \max\{(t_{qk} - o_{qk})^2 \mid o_{qk} \in [O_{qk}]_h\}. \qquad (12.17)$$

Since the derivation of a learning algorithm is easier from (12.16) than from (12.17), we use the cost function in (12.16).

The cost function for the input–output pair (A_q, t_q) is defined as

$$e_q = \sum_h h \cdot e_{qh},$$ (12.18)

where h assumes a pre-specified set of real numbers in the unit interval $[0, 1]$. We use ten values of h in computer simulations in this chapter: $h=0.1, 0.2, \ldots, 1.0$. In (12.18), the cost function e_{qh} for the h-level set is weighted by the value of h. We can also use the following cost function without this weighting scheme:

$$e_q = \sum_h e_{qh}.$$ (12.19)

In the computer simulation of Sect. 11.4, we used this cost function with eleven values of h: $h=0.0, 0.1, 0.2, \ldots, 1.0$.

12.2.3 Extended Back-Propagation Algorithm

The learning of the neural network is performed to minimize the cost function e_{qh} in (12.16). The amount of modification for each connection weight is written as follows:

$$\Delta w_{kj}(t) = -\eta \cdot h \cdot \frac{\partial e_{qh}}{\partial w_{kj}} + \alpha \Delta w_{kj}(t-1),$$ (12.20)

$$\Delta w_{ji}(t) = -\eta \cdot h \cdot \frac{\partial e_{qh}}{\partial w_{ji}} + \alpha \Delta w_{ji}(t-1),$$ (12.21)

where we assume the use of the weighting scheme by the value of h in (12.18). When we use (12.19) instead of (12.18), $\eta \cdot h$ is replaced with η. The biases θ_k and θ_j are updated in the same manner as the connection weights w_{kj} and w_{ji}, respectively.

For simplicity of notation, we denote the h-level set $[A_q]_h$ of the linguistic input vector A_q by the interval input vector $X_q = (X_{q1}, \ldots, X_{qn})$ as in (11.36)–(11.42) of Sect. 11.4. Let $O_q = (O_{q1}, \ldots, O_{qM})$ be the interval output vector calculated by interval arithmetic from X_q. In this case, e_{qh} in (12.16) is rewritten as

$$e_{qh} = \frac{1}{2} \sum_{k=1}^{M} (t_{qk} - o_{qk}^L)^2 + \frac{1}{2} \sum_{k=1}^{M} (t_{qk} - o_{qk}^U)^2,$$ (12.22)

where the interval output O_{qk} from the k-th output unit is calculated as

$$[o_{qk}^L, o_{qk}^U] = [f(net_{qk}^L), f(net_{qk}^U)],$$ (12.23)

$$net_{qk}^L = \sum_{\substack{j=1 \\ w_{kj} \geq 0}}^{n_H} w_{kj} \cdot o_{qj}^L + \sum_{\substack{j=1 \\ w_{kj} < 0}}^{n_H} w_{kj} \cdot o_{qj}^U + \theta_k,$$ (12.24)

$$net_{qk}^U = \sum_{\substack{j=1 \\ w_{kj} \geq 0}}^{n_H} w_{kj} \cdot o_{qj}^U + \sum_{\substack{j=1 \\ w_{kj} < 0}}^{n_H} w_{kj} \cdot o_{qj}^L + \theta_k. \qquad (12.25)$$

From (12.24) and (12.25), we can see that the calculation of O_{qk} depends on the sign of w_{kj}. As a result, the calculation of the partial derivative $\partial e_{qh}/\partial w_{kj}$ also depends on the sign of w_{kj}. When w_{kj} is non-negative (i.e., $w_{kj} \geq 0$), $\partial e_{qh}/\partial w_{kj}$ is calculated from (12.22)–(12.25) as

$$\frac{\partial e_{qh}}{\partial w_{kj}} = -\delta_{qk}^L \cdot o_{qj}^L - \delta_{qk}^U \cdot o_{qj}^U, \qquad (12.26)$$

where

$$\delta_{qk}^L = (t_{qk} - o_{qk}^L) \cdot o_{qk}^L \cdot (1 - o_{qk}^L), \qquad (12.27)$$

$$\delta_{qk}^U = (t_{qk} - o_{qk}^U) \cdot o_{qk}^U \cdot (1 - o_{qk}^U). \qquad (12.28)$$

On the other hand, $\partial e_{qh}/\partial w_{kj}$ is calculated as follows when w_{kj} is negative (i.e., $w_{kj} < 0$):

$$\frac{\partial e_{qh}}{\partial w_{kj}} = -\delta_{qk}^L \cdot o_{qj}^U - \delta_{qk}^U \cdot o_{qj}^L. \qquad (12.29)$$

The calculation of the partial derivative $\partial e_{qh}/\partial w_{ji}$ depends on the sign of w_{ji} because the interval output O_{qj} from the j-th hidden unit is calculated as follows:

$$[o_{qj}^L, o_{qj}^U] = [f(net_{qj}^L), f(net_{qj}^U)], \qquad (12.30)$$

$$net_{qj}^L = \sum_{\substack{i=1 \\ w_{ji} \geq 0}}^{n} w_{ji} \cdot o_{qi}^L + \sum_{\substack{i=1 \\ w_{ji} < 0}}^{n} w_{ji} \cdot o_{qi}^U + \theta_j, \qquad (12.31)$$

$$net_{qj}^U = \sum_{\substack{i=1 \\ w_{ji} \geq 0}}^{n} w_{ji} \cdot o_{qi}^U + \sum_{\substack{i=1 \\ w_{ji} < 0}}^{n} w_{ji} \cdot o_{qi}^L + \theta_j. \qquad (12.32)$$

When w_{ji} is non-negative (i.e., $w_{ji} \geq 0$), $\partial e_{qh}/\partial w_{ji}$ is calculated from (12.22)–(12.25) and (12.30)–(12.32) as

$$\frac{\partial e_{qh}}{\partial w_{ji}} = -\sum_{\substack{k=1 \\ w_{kj} \geq 0}}^{M} (o_{qi}^L \cdot \beta_{qkj}^{LL} + o_{qi}^U \cdot \beta_{qkj}^{UU}) - \sum_{\substack{k=1 \\ w_{kj} < 0}}^{M} (o_{qi}^L \cdot \beta_{qkj}^{UL} + o_{qi}^U \cdot \beta_{qkj}^{LU}),$$

$$(12.33)$$

where

$$\beta_{qkj}^{LL} = \delta_{qk}^{L} \cdot w_{kj} \cdot o_{qj}^{L} \cdot (1 - o_{qj}^{L}), \tag{12.34}$$

$$\beta_{qkj}^{UU} = \delta_{qk}^{U} \cdot w_{kj} \cdot o_{qj}^{U} \cdot (1 - o_{qj}^{U}), \tag{12.35}$$

$$\beta_{qkj}^{UL} = \delta_{qk}^{U} \cdot w_{kj} \cdot o_{qj}^{L} \cdot (1 - o_{qj}^{L}), \tag{12.36}$$

$$\beta_{qkj}^{LU} = \delta_{qk}^{L} \cdot w_{kj} \cdot o_{qj}^{U} \cdot (1 - o_{qj}^{U}). \tag{12.37}$$

On the other hand, $\partial e_{qh}/\partial w_{ji}$ is calculated as follows when w_{ji} is negative (i.e., $w_{ji} < 0$):

$$\frac{\partial e_{qh}}{\partial w_{ji}} = - \sum_{\substack{k=1 \\ w_{kj} \geq 0}}^{M} (o_{qi}^{L} \cdot \beta_{qkj}^{UU} + o_{qi}^{U} \cdot \beta_{qkj}^{LL}) - \sum_{\substack{k=1 \\ w_{kj} < 0}}^{M} (o_{qi}^{L} \cdot \beta_{qkj}^{LU} + o_{qi}^{U} \cdot \beta_{qkj}^{UL}).$$

$$\tag{12.38}$$

When m input–output pairs (A_q, t_q), $q = 1, 2, \ldots, m$, are given as training data, the learning of the neural network is performed using ten levels (i.e., h=0.1, 0.2, ..., 1.0) as follows:

Step 0: Randomly specify initial values of the connection weights and biases. Let $t := 1$.

Step 1: Let $h := 0.1$.

Step 2: Let $q := 1$.

Step 3: Update the connection weights and biases using (12.20) and (12.21).

Step 4: Let $t := t + 1$.

Step 5: Let $q := q + 1$. If $q \leq m$ then go to Step 3.

Step 6: Let $h := h + 0.1$. If $h \leq 1.0$ then go to Step 2, otherwise go to Step 1.

This algorithm is iterated until a pre-specified stopping condition is satisfied.

As an example, let us assume that we have nine linguistic rules in Fig. 12.1 where the consequent class of each linguistic rule is C1, C2, or C3 (i.e., Class 1, Class 2, or Class 3). We trained a three-layer feedforward neural network with two input, five hidden, and three output units using the nine linguistic rules. The learning rate η and the momentum constant α were specified as $\eta = 0.25$ and $\alpha = 0.9$. The above learning algorithm was terminated when it was iterated 1000 times (i.e., 1000 epochs). The trained neural network can be used to classify an arbitrary input vector $x = (x_1, x_2)$ in the pattern space $[0, 1] \times [0, 1]$. The classification is performed by identifying the winner output unit with the maximum output value among the three output units. Figure 12.2 shows the classification boundary obtained from the trained neural network together with the 0.6-level sets of the linguistic input vector $A_{q1} \times A_{q2}$ corresponding to each linguistic rule. From this figure, we can see that an intuitively acceptable result was obtained by the learning of the neural network from the nine linguistic rules.

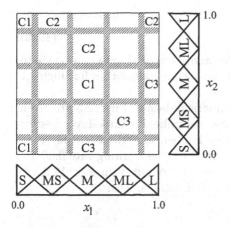

Fig. 12.1. Nine linguistic rules for a pattern classification problem

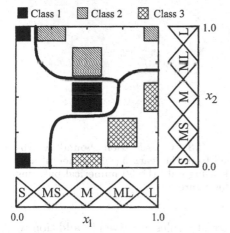

Fig. 12.2. Classification boundary and nine linguistic rules

12.2.4 Learning from Linguistic Rules and Numerical Data

The learning algorithm of neural networks from linguistic rules can be used in the case where both linguistic rules and numerical data are available. Let us assume that a linguistic rule R_q of the form (12.1) is given. As we have already explained, this linguistic rule is handled as a linguistic pattern $A_q = (A_{q1}, \ldots, A_{qn})$. We also assume that a numerical pattern $x_p = (x_{p1}, \ldots, x_{pn})$ from Class C_p is given. These two patterns can be treated in the same framework because both real numbers and linguistic terms are special cases of fuzzy numbers. That is, x_p is handled as a fuzzy pattern $A_p = (A_{p1}, \ldots, A_{pn})$ where each element A_{pi} is viewed as a fuzzy number with the following membership function:

$$
\mu_{A_{pi}}(x) = \begin{cases} 1, & \text{if } x = x_{pi}, \\ 0, & \text{otherwise.} \end{cases} \tag{12.39}
$$

From this membership function, the h-level set of A_{pi} is calculated as

$$[A_{pi}]_h = [x_{pi}, \, x_{pi}] \text{ for } 0 \le h \le 1. \tag{12.40}$$

Using (12.39) and (12.40), linguistic rules and numerical data can be simultaneously used as fuzzy training data in the learning algorithm for linguistic rules.

As an example, let us assume that numerical data in Fig. 12.3 are given. Using 30 numerical patterns in this figure, we trained a three-layer feedforward neural network with two input, five hidden, and three output units by the standard back-propagation algorithm with the learning rate 0.25 and the momentum constant 0.9. The classification boundary in Fig. 12.3 was obtained from the trained neural network after 1000 epochs.

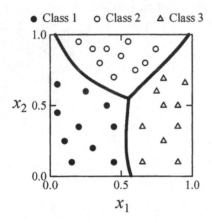

Fig. 12.3. Classification boundary obtained from the learning of the neural network using only the 30 numerical patterns in this figure

We also assume that the following linguistic rules are given in addition to the 30 numerical patterns in Fig. 12.3:

If x_1 is *medium* and x_2 is *medium* then Class 1, $\qquad$ (12.41)

If x_2 is *large* then Class 2. $\qquad$ (12.42)

These two linguistic rules are shown in Fig. 12.4. The first linguistic rule is handled as a linguistic pattern (*medium, medium*). Since the first antecedent condition of the second linguistic rule is *don't care*, this linguistic rule is handled as a linguistic pattern (*don't care, large*). This pattern is the same as ([0, 1], *large*) because the domain interval of the first input variable x_1 is [0, 1]. We used the two linguistic patterns together with the 30 numerical patterns in the learning of the same neural network as in Fig. 12.3. The learning of the neural network was performed using the learning algorithm for linguistic rules. Figure 12.5 shows the classification boundary obtained from the trained neural network after 1000 epochs. From this figure, we can see that the classification boundary follows the two linguistic rules as well as the 30 numerical patterns. The difference between Fig. 12.3 and Fig. 12.5

corresponds to the effect of the two linguistic rules on the learning of the neural network.

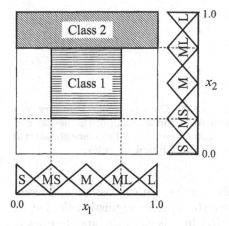

Fig. 12.4. Two linguistic rules

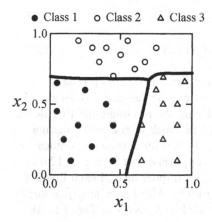

Fig. 12.5. Classification boundary obtained from the learning of the neural network using both the 30 numerical patterns and the two linguistic rules

Further we assume that the following linguistic rule is given in addition to the two linguistic rules in Fig. 12.4 and the 30 numerical patterns in Fig. 12.3:

If x_1 is *large* then Class 3.   (12.43)

This linguistic rule is partially inconsistent with the linguistic rule "If x_2 is *large* then Class 2" in (12.42). In the same manner as in the previous computer simulation in Fig. 12.5, we trained the same neural network using the three linguistic rules and the 30 numerical patterns. The obtained classification boundary after 1000 epochs is shown in Fig. 12.6. From this figure, we can see that the partial inconsistency was resolved by finding a good compromise among the linguistic rules with different consequent classes.

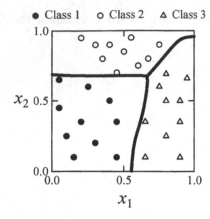

Fig. 12.6. Classification boundary obtained from the learning of the neural network using both the 30 numerical patterns and the three linguistic rules

In our learning algorithm for linguistic rules, we can assign a different grade of importance (i.e., weight or strength) to each linguistic rule. Let ω_q be the importance of the linguistic rule R_q. In this case, the update rules in (12.20) and (12.21) are modified as

$$\Delta w_{kj}(t) = -\omega_q \cdot \eta \cdot h \cdot \frac{\partial e_{qh}}{\partial w_{kj}} + \alpha \cdot \Delta w_{kj}(t-1), \tag{12.44}$$

$$\Delta w_{ji}(t) = -\omega_q \cdot \eta \cdot h \cdot \frac{\partial e_{qh}}{\partial w_{ji}} + \alpha \cdot \Delta w_{ji}(t-1). \tag{12.45}$$

We specified the importance of the last linguistic rule "If x_1 is *large* then Class 3" in (12.43) as 2. The importance of the other linguistic rules and the 30 numerical patterns was specified as 0.5. Using the modified update rules in (12.44)–(12.45), we trained the same neural network in the same manner as in the previous computer simulation in Fig. 12.6. The obtained classification boundary is shown in Fig. 12.7. From the comparison between Fig. 12.6 and Fig. 12.7, we can see that the difference in the importance of each linguistic rule had an effect on the classification boundary. More specifically, a larger area around the top-right corner was classified as Class 3 in Fig. 12.7 than Fig. 12.6.

As shown in the above computer simulations, the learning algorithm of multi-layer feedforward neural networks in this section can be applied to general situations where both linguistic rules and numerical data are available. Moreover, the learning algorithm can handle a different grade of importance attached to each piece of available information. The ability of the learning algorithm to simultaneously handle linguistic rules and numerical data is essential when we cannot construct classification systems with high classification performance by utilizing only one of the two kinds of available information. Better results are usually obtained by simultaneously utilizing linguistic rules and numerical data than utilizing only one of the two kinds of available information [80].

● Class 1   ○ Class 2   △ Class 3

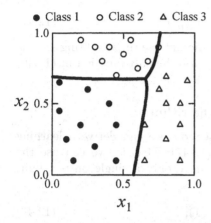

Fig. 12.7. Classification boundary obtained from the learning of the neural network using both the 30 numerical patterns and the three linguistic rules. A much higher grade of importance was assigned to the third linguistic rule "If x_1 is *large* then Class 3" than the other linguistic rules

12.3 Learning from Linguistic Rules for Modeling Problems

In this section, we discuss the learning of standard multi-layer feedforward neural networks from linguistic rules of the form (12.2) for modeling problems. A learning algorithm for this task was derived in Ishibuchi et al. [87]. In this section, we explain their learning algorithm for a three-layer feedforward neural network with n input units and a single output unit.

12.3.1 Linguistic Data

Let us assume that we have m linguistic rules $R_q, q = 1, 2, \ldots, m$, of the form (12.2). From the m linguistic rules, we have m linguistic input–output pairs $(A_q, B_q), q = 1, 2, \ldots, m$, where $A_q = (A_{q1}, \ldots, A_{qn})$. These linguistic input–output pairs are used as training data. When the n-dimensional linguistic vector $A_q = (A_{q1}, \ldots, A_{qn})$ is presented to the neural network, the corresponding fuzzy output O_q is numerically calculated by interval arithmetic on level sets of the linguistic input $A_q = (A_{q1}, \ldots, A_{qn})$ as in the previous section.

12.3.2 Cost Function

The aim of learning is to minimize the difference between the actual fuzzy output O_q and the linguistic target B_q. As in the previous section, a cost function to be minimized is defined using the h-level sets of O_q and B_q as

$$e_q = \sum_h h \cdot e_{qh}, \tag{12.46}$$

where

$$e_{qh} = \frac{1}{2}([B_q]_h^L - [O_q]_h^L)^2 + \frac{1}{2}([B_q]_h^U - [O_q]_h^U)^2. \tag{12.47}$$

In the computer simulation of Chap. 11, we did not use the weighting scheme by the level h in (12.46). In this section, we use the cost function in (12.46) with the weighting scheme.

12.3.3 Extended Back-Propagation Algorithm

In the same manner as in the previous section, we can derive a learning algorithm from the cost function e_{qh} in (12.47). That is, we can use the update rules in (12.20)–(12.21). Since we have only a single output unit, these update rules are rewritten as

$$\Delta w_j(t) = -\eta \cdot h \cdot \frac{\partial e_{qh}}{\partial w_j} + \alpha \cdot \Delta w_j(t-1), \tag{12.48}$$

$$\Delta w_{ji}(t) = -\eta \cdot h \cdot \frac{\partial e_{qh}}{\partial w_{ji}} + \alpha \cdot \Delta w_{ji}(t-1), \tag{12.49}$$

where w_j is the connection weight from the j-th hidden unit to the single output unit.

As in the previous section, let us denote the h-level set $[A_q]_h$ of the linguistic input vector A_q by the interval input vector $X_q = (X_{q1}, \ldots, X_{qn})$ for simplicity of notation. The corresponding interval output $O_q = [o_q^L, o_q^U]$ is calculated by interval arithmetic from X_q as shown in (11.36)–(11.42) of Chap. 11. We also denote the h-level set $[B_q]_h$ of the linguistic target B_q by the interval $T_q = [t_q^L, t_q^U]$. This interval is the target for the interval output O_q. In this case, e_{qh} is rewritten as

$$e_{qh} = \frac{1}{2}(t_q^L - o_q^L)^2 + \frac{1}{2}(t_q^U - o_q^U)^2. \tag{12.50}$$

In the same manner as in the previous section, the partial derivative $\partial e_{qh}/\partial w_j$ is calculated from (12.50) as

$$\frac{\partial e_{qh}}{\partial w_j} = \begin{cases} -\delta_q^L \cdot o_{qj}^L - \delta_q^U \cdot o_{qj}^U & \text{if } w_j \geq 0, \\ -\delta_q^L \cdot o_{qj}^U - \delta_q^U \cdot o_{qj}^L & \text{if } w_j < 0, \end{cases} \tag{12.51}$$

where

$$\delta_q^L = (t_q^L - o_q^L) \cdot o_q^L \cdot (1 - o_q^L), \tag{12.52}$$

$$\delta_q^U = (t_q^U - o_q^U) \cdot o_q^U \cdot (1 - o_q^U). \tag{12.53}$$

The partial derivative $\partial e_{qh}/\partial w_{ji}$ is calculated as follows:

$$\frac{\partial e_{qh}}{\partial w_{ji}} = \begin{cases} -o_{qi}^L \cdot \beta_{qj}^{LL} - o_{qi}^U \cdot \beta_{qj}^{UU} & \text{if } w_j \geq 0 \text{ and } w_{ji} \geq 0, \\ -o_{qi}^L \cdot \beta_{qj}^{UU} - o_{qi}^U \cdot \beta_{qj}^{LL} & \text{if } w_j \geq 0 \text{ and } w_{ji} < 0, \\ -o_{qi}^L \cdot \beta_{qj}^{UL} - o_{qi}^U \cdot \beta_{qj}^{LU} & \text{if } w_j < 0 \text{ and } w_{ji} \geq 0, \\ -o_{qi}^L \cdot \beta_{qj}^{LU} - o_{qi}^U \cdot \beta_{qj}^{UL} & \text{if } w_j < 0 \text{ and } w_{ji} < 0, \end{cases} \tag{12.54}$$

where

$$\beta_{qj}^{LL} = \delta_q^L \cdot w_j \cdot o_{qj}^L \cdot (1 - o_{qj}^L), \tag{12.55}$$

$$\beta_{qj}^{UU} = \delta_q^U \cdot w_j \cdot o_{qj}^U \cdot (1 - o_{qj}^U), \tag{12.56}$$

$$\beta_{qj}^{UL} = \delta_q^U \cdot w_j \cdot o_{qj}^L \cdot (1 - o_{qj}^L), \tag{12.57}$$

$$\beta_{qj}^{LU} = \delta_q^L \cdot w_j \cdot o_{qj}^U \cdot (1 - o_{qj}^U). \tag{12.58}$$

As an example, let us assume that we have five linguistic rules in Fig. 12.8. These linguistic rules are handled as the following linguistic input–output pairs: ((*small*, *small*), *small*), ((*small*, *large*), *medium*), ((*medium*, *medium*), *small*), ((*large*, *small*), *medium*), ((*large*, *large*), *large*). We trained a three-layer feedforward neural network with two input, five hidden, and single output units using the five linguistic input–output pairs. In the learning of the neural network, we used the update rules in (12.48)–(12.49) for ten levels (i.e., $h=0.1, 0.2, \ldots, 1.0$) as in the computer simulations in the previous section for pattern classification problems. Figure 12.9 shows the nonlinear function obtained by the trained neural network after 1000 epochs. From the comparison between Fig. 12.8 and Fig. 12.9, we can see that the fitting of the obtained nonlinear function to the given linguistic rules is very good.

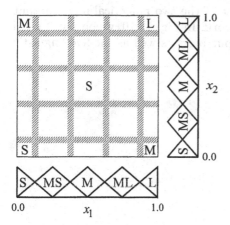

Fig. 12.8. Five linguistic rules for a modeling problem

12.3.4 Learning from Linguistic Rules and Numerical Data

As we have already explained in the previous section, linguistic rules and numerical data can be simultaneously handled in the learning of multi-layer feedforward neural networks because real numbers as well as linguistic terms are special cases of fuzzy numbers. As an example, let us assume that we have two numerical input–output pairs $\{((x_{p1}, x_{p2}), y_p)\} = \{((0.8, 1.0), 0.7),$

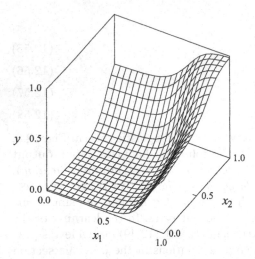

Fig. 12.9. The nonlinear function depicted by the trained neural network. The learning of the neural network was performed using the five linguistic rules in Fig. 12.8

((1.0, 0.8), 0.7)}. We trained the same neural network as in Fig. 12.9 using these two numerical input–output pairs together with the five linguistic rules in Fig. 12.8. Figure 12.10 shows the nonlinear function obtained by the trained neural network after 1000 epochs. The difference between Fig. 12.9 and Fig. 12.10 corresponds to the effect of the two numerical input–output pairs on the learning of the neural network. In Fig. 12.10, we obtained good fitting to the two numerical input–output pairs as well as the five linguistic rules.

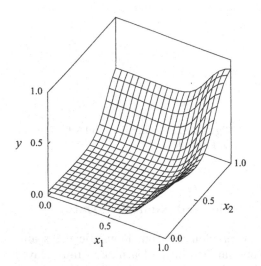

Fig. 12.10. The nonlinear function depicted by the trained neural network. The learning of the neural network was performed by simultaneously utilizing the five linguistic rules in Fig. 12.8 and the two numerical input–output pairs

As in the previous section, the learning algorithm for linguistic rules in this section can handle linguistic rules and numerical data with different grades of importance. As an example, let us assume that we have six linguistic rules in Fig. 12.11 including the following two linguistic rules of length 1:

$$\text{If } x_1 \text{ is } \textit{large} \text{ then } y \text{ is } \textit{small}, \tag{12.59}$$

$$\text{If } x_2 \text{ is } \textit{large} \text{ then } y \text{ is } \textit{large}. \tag{12.60}$$

These two linguistic rules are inconsistent with each other around the top-right corner of the two-dimensional input space $[0, 1] \times [0, 1]$ where both x_1 and x_2 are large. In addition to the six linguistic rules, we also assume that a single input–output pair $((1.0, 1.0), 0.7)$ is given.

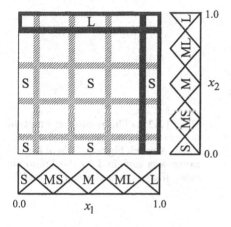

Fig. 12.11. Six linguistic rules for a modeling problem

We trained a neural network in the situation where the linguistic rule "If x_1 is $\textit{large}$ then y is $\textit{small}$" in (12.59) is much more important than the other linguistic rules and the numerical input–output pair. The grade of importance of this linguistic rule was specified as 2. The importance grade 0.1 was assigned to the other linguistic rules and the numerical input–output pair. A neural network with two input, five hidden, and single output units was trained using the six linguistic values and the single input–output pair with different grades of importance in the same manner as in the previous computer simulations. The obtained nonlinear function after 1000 epochs is shown in Fig. 12.12. In this figure, the output value around the top-right corner is $\textit{small}$. This is because the linguistic rule in (12.59) has a higher grade of importance than the other pieces of available information in the learning of the neural network. We also performed the same computer simulation in a different situation where the numerical input–output pair $((1.0, 1.0), 0.7)$ is much more important than the other pieces of available information. The grade of importance of the numerical input–output pair was specified as 2. The importance grade 0.1 was assigned to all the linguistic rules. The obtained nonlinear function after 1000 epochs is shown in Fig. 12.13. In this figure, the output value around the top-right corner is about 0.7. This is because the numerical input–output pair had a higher grade of importance than the linguistic rules in the learning of the neural network. From the simulation results in Fig. 12.12 and 12.13, we can see that the learning algorithm for linguistic rules can take into account the importance of each piece of available information.

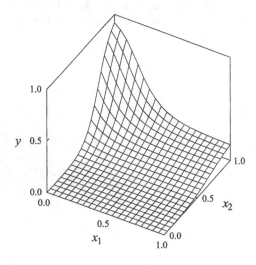

Fig. 12.12. The nonlinear function depicted by the trained neural network. A much higher grade of importance was assigned to the linguistic rule "If x_1 is *large* then y is *small*"

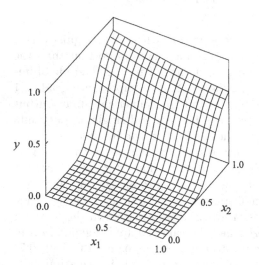

Fig. 12.13. The nonlinear function depicted by the trained neural network. A much higher grade of importance was assigned to the numerical input–output pair ((1.0, 1.0), 0.7)

13. Linguistic Rule Extraction from Neural Networks

We have already explained the learning of standard feedforward neural networks from linguistic rules. In this chapter, we describe a fuzzy arithmetic-based approach to linguistic rule extraction from trained neural networks [72]. The main characteristic feature of this approach is its applicability to arbitrarily trained feedforward neural networks. Usually simplification methods of neural networks such as optimal brain damage [27] and structure learning with forgetting [97] are involved in rule extraction methods. That is, rule extraction methods usually simplify the structure of neural networks. On the contrary, the fuzzy arithmetic-based approach tries to extract linguistic rules without modifying the structure of given neural networks.

Many approaches have been proposed for the extraction of logical rules from neural networks [46, 149, 167]. Andrews et al. [7] and Duch et al. [38] include good surveys in this research field. Since the work of Hayashi [51], fuzzy rule extraction methods from neural networks have also been proposed [98, 104, 105, 169]. Many fuzzy rule extraction methods are based on neuro-fuzzy models, which are fuzzy rule-based systems with neural network structures. In this chapter, we use standard feedforward neural networks for linguistic rule extraction. First we explain how linguistic rules of the following form can be extracted from arbitrarily trained neural networks for n-dimensional modeling problems:

$$\text{Rule } R_q: \text{If } x_1 \text{ is } A_{q1} \text{ and } \ldots \text{ and } x_n \text{ is } A_{qn} \text{ then } y \text{ is } B_q. \qquad (13.1)$$

In the fuzzy arithmetic-based approach, the antecedent part of each linguistic rule is presented to the trained neural network as a linguistic input vector $\boldsymbol{A}_q = (A_{q1}, \ldots, A_{qn})$ to calculate the corresponding fuzzy output value O_q by fuzzy arithmetic. The consequent part B_q is specified based on the fuzzy output value O_q corresponding to the linguistic input vector $\boldsymbol{A}_q$. Next we explain how linguistic rules of the following form can be extracted for M-class pattern classification problems with n attributes:

$$\text{Rule } R_q: \text{If } x_1 \text{ is } A_{q1} \text{ and } \ldots \text{ and } x_n \text{ is } A_{qn}$$
$$\text{then Class } C_q \text{ with } CF_q. \qquad (13.2)$$

The consequent class C_q and the rule weight (i.e., certainty grade) CF_q are specified based on the fuzzy output vector $\boldsymbol{O}_q = (O_{q1}, \ldots, O_{qM})$ calculated for the linguistic input vector $\boldsymbol{A}_q$ by fuzzy arithmetic.

13.1 Neural Networks and Linguistic Rules

In Fig. 13.1, we show relations among numerical data, neural networks, linguistic rules, and human experts. We briefly explain each relation among them (i.e., each arrow in this figure).

Human Experts → Linguistic Rules: In early studies on fuzzy control, fuzzy rules were usually obtained from human experts as linguistic knowledge. The ability to utilize linguistic knowledge is an advantage of fuzzy rule-based systems over other information processing systems.

Human Experts → Neural Networks: The learning of neural networks involves many parameter specifications such as the number of hidden layers, the number of units in each hidden layer, the learning rate, the momentum constant, and the stopping condition. These parameters are specified by human experts (or users).

Numerical Data → Linguistic Rules: Recently many approaches have been proposed for automatically extracting and adjusting linguistic rules from numerical data. The arrow from numerical data to linguistic rules is the main line of recent studies on fuzzy rule-based systems.

Numerical Data → Neural Networks: The main advantage of neural networks over other information processing systems is their high ability to handle numerical data. Almost all learning algorithms of neural networks are for handling numerical data. The arrow from numerical data to linguistic rules has been the main line of studies on neural networks.

Linguistic Rules → Neural Networks: This arrow corresponds to the learning of neural networks from linguistic rules, which has been explained in Chap. 12. Only a few approaches have been proposed in this direction. As shown in Chap. 12, numerical data and linguistic rules can be simultaneously used in the learning of neural networks.

Neural Networks → Linguistic Rules: This arrow corresponds to the linguistic rule extraction from neural networks, which is described in this chapter. As shown in Fig. 13.1, linguistic rules can be obtained from three different kinds of sources: human experts, numerical data, and neural networks. All the obtained linguistic rules can be used in a single linguistic rule-based system. It is also possible to apply a rule selection method to the obtained linguistic rules to design a smaller linguistic rule-based system with a higher performance.

13.2 Linguistic Rule Extraction for Modeling Problems

In this section, we explain the fuzzy arithmetic-based approach to linguistic rule extraction for modeling problems. Linguistic rules of the form in (13.1) are extracted from arbitrarily trained multi-layer feedforward neural networks. We assume that a three-layer feedforward neural network with n input units and a single output unit is given. Our task is to extract linguistic

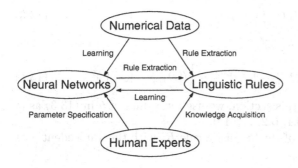

Fig. 13.1. Relations among numerical data, neural networks, linguistic rules, and human experts

rules from the given neural network. As in the other chapters of this book, we assume that a set of linguistic terms is given for each of the n input and single output variables. We also assume that the input space and the output space are the n-dimensional unit hypercube $[0, 1]^n$ and the unit interval $[0, 1]$, respectively.

13.2.1 Basic Idea

The antecedent part of each linguistic rule is constructed by combining given linguistic terms. For simplicity of explanation, let us assume that K linguistic terms are given for each input variable. In this case, there are K^n combinations of antecedent linguistic terms. That is, there are K^n cells in a simple grid-type linguistic rule table. When we use *don't care* for each input variable in addition to the K linguistic terms, the total number of combinations of antecedent linguistic terms is $(K + 1)^n$. Each combination of antecedent linguistic terms corresponds to the antecedent part of a single linguistic rule.

The antecedent part of each linguistic rule is presented to the given neural network as a linguistic input vector $\boldsymbol{A}_q = (A_{q1}, \ldots, A_{qn})$. The corresponding fuzzy output O_q from the neural network is calculated by fuzzy arithmetic as shown in Chap. 11. The consequent part B_q is specified by choosing a single consequent linguistic term from the given ones. This selection is based on the difference between the actual fuzzy output O_q and each candidate linguistic term.

13.2.2 Extraction of Linguistic Rules

Let O_q be the fuzzy output from the neural network when the linguistic vector $\boldsymbol{A}_q = (A_{q1}, \ldots, A_{qn})$ is presented. Our task is to specify the consequent part B_q of the linguistic rule R_q with the antecedent part $\boldsymbol{A}_q$ using the fuzzy output O_q. Let us assume that we have K linguistic terms $D_1, D_2, \ldots, D_K$ to describe the output variable. As in Chap. 12, let us define the difference between D_j and O_q using their h-level sets $[D_j]_h = [[D_j]_h^L, [D_j]_h^U]$ and $[O_q]_h = [[O_q]_h^L, [O_q]_h^U]$ for pre-specified values of h as

$$d(D_j, O_q) = \sum_h h \cdot d([D_j]_h, [O_q]_h), \tag{13.3}$$

where

$$d([D_j]_h, [O_q]_h) = \frac{1}{2}([D_j]_h^L - [O_q]_h^L)^2 + \frac{1}{2}([D_j]_h^U - [O_q]_h^U)^2. \tag{13.4}$$

In computer simulations in this section, we use ten values of h in (13.3) as in the previous chapter: $h = 0.1, 0.2, \ldots, 1.0$.

The consequent part B_q of the linguistic rule R_q with the antecedent part A_q is specified as

$$d(B_q, O_q) = \min\{d(D_j, O_q) \,|\, j = 1, 2, \ldots, K\}. \tag{13.5}$$

That is, the consequent part B_q is the linguistic term with the minimum difference from the actual fuzzy output O_q. For each combination of antecedent linguistic terms (i.e., for each linguistic vector A_q), the corresponding consequent part B_q is specified by (13.5).

13.2.3 Computer Simulations

We illustrate the fuzzy arithmetic-based approach to linguistic rule extraction from trained neural networks for modeling problems using some computer simulations. First we consider the neural network that was trained from the five linguistic rules in Fig. 12.8 in Chap. 12. The nonlinear function realized by the trained neural network was shown in Fig. 12.9. As in Fig. 12.8, we assume that the five linguistic terms are given for each of the two input variables. We also assume that the same five linguistic terms are given for the output variable.

When we do not use *don't care*, the number of combinations of antecedent linguistic terms is 25. Each combination is presented to the trained neural network as a linguistic input vector $A_q = (A_{q1}, A_{q2})$. The corresponding fuzzy output O_q is calculated by fuzzy arithmetic. This calculation is numerically performed for the h-level sets of A_q for $h = 0.1, 0.2, \ldots, 1.0$. The fuzzy output O_q is compared with each of the five linguistic terms using (13.3). The linguistic term with the minimum difference from the fuzzy output O_q is chosen as the consequent part B_q of the linguistic rule R_q with the antecedent part A_q. For example, let us consider the following linguistic rule:

Rule R_q: If x_1 is *medium* and x_2 is *small* then y is B_q. $\qquad$ (13.6)

To determine the consequent part B_q, the antecedent part of the linguistic rule R_q is presented to the trained neural network as the linguistic input vector (*medium, small*). The corresponding fuzzy output O_q is calculated as shown in Fig. 13.2. For illustration purposes, the fuzzy output O_q is depicted using the h-level sets of A_q for 100 values of h (i.e., $h = 0.01, 0.02, \ldots, 1.00$). We do not have to perform interval arithmetic on the h-level sets for such a large number of different values of h for rule extraction purposes. We use only ten levels (i.e., $h = 0.1, 0.2, \ldots, 1.0$) in (13.3) to determine the consequent part B_q. The difference between the fuzzy output O_q and each of the five linguistic terms is calculated as follows:

$$d(small, O_q) = 0.0299, \tag{13.7}$$
$$d(medium\,small, O_q) = 0.5738, \tag{13.8}$$
$$d(medium, O_q) = 1.0544, \tag{13.9}$$
$$d(medium\,large, O_q) = 4.5037, \tag{13.10}$$
$$d(large, O_q) = 6.7851. \tag{13.11}$$

Since *small* has the minimum difference among the five linguistic terms, the consequent part B_q of the linguistic rule R_q in (13.6) with the antecedent part (*medium*, *small*) is specified as *small*. Thus we have the following linguistic rule:

Rule R_q: If x_1 is *medium* and x_2 is *small* then y is *small*.

$$\tag{13.12}$$

From Fig. 12.9 in Chap. 12, we can see that the extracted linguistic rule correctly describes the trained neural network (i.e., the nonlinear function in Fig. 12.9).

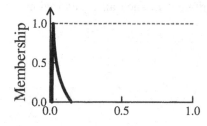

Fig. 13.2. Fuzzy output from the trained neural network for the linguistic input vector (*medium*, *small*)

In the same manner, we determined the consequent linguistic term for each of the 25 combinations of the antecedent linguistic terms. The extracted 25 linguistic rules are summarized in Fig. 13.3. From the comparison between Fig. 12.9 in Chap. 12 and Fig. 13.3, we can see that the extracted 25 linguistic rules describe the trained neural network very well (i.e., they are consistent with the nonlinear function in Fig. 12.9). We can also see from the comparison between Fig. 12.8 in Chap. 12 and Fig. 13.3 that the incomplete linguistic rule-based system in Fig. 12.8 was completed by the linguistic rule extraction method.

Next we applied the linguistic rule extraction method to the trained neural network in Fig. 12.10 of Chap. 12. The trained neural network is similar to that in the above computer simulation because both neural networks were trained using the same five linguistic rules in Fig. 12.8 of Chap. 12. While only the five linguistic rules were used in the learning of the neural network in

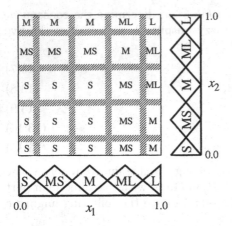

Fig. 13.3. Extracted linguistic rules from the trained neural network in Fig. 12.9

the above computer simulation, the two numerical input–output pairs ((0.8, 1.0), 0.7) and ((1.0, 0.8), 0.7) were also used in the learning of the neural network in this computer simulation. The extracted linguistic rules from the trained neural network in Fig. 12.10 are summarized in Fig. 13.4. From the comparison between Fig. 13.3 and Fig. 13.4, we can see that some linguistic rules are different between these two figures. This means that the output values from the two neural networks are different in such an input region.

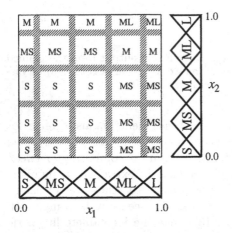

Fig. 13.4. Extracted linguistic rules from the trained neural network in Fig. 12.10

The linguistic rule extraction method can be used to extract linguistic rules with *don't care* conditions. For example, let us consider the extraction of the following linguistic rule from the trained neural network in Fig. 12.9 of Chap. 12:

Rule R_q: If x_1 is *small* then y is B_q,   (13.13) where the antecedent condition on the second input variable x_2 is *don't care*. Since the domain interval of x_2 is the unit interval $[0, 1]$, *don't care* is represented by $[0, 1]$. Thus the linguistic vector (*small*, $[0, 1]$) is presented to the trained neural network in Fig. 12.9 of Chap. 12. Figure 13.5 shows the corresponding fuzzy output O_q calculated by interval arithmetic on the 100 h-level sets of $\mathbf{A}_q$ for $h = 0.01, 0.02, \ldots, 1.00$. The consequent part B_q is specified as *medium small* by calculating the difference between the fuzzy output O_q and each linguistic term. The difference between O_q and *medium small*, however, is not small:

$$d(medium\ small, O_q) = 0.2242. \tag{13.14}$$

This is much larger than the minimum difference 0.0299 in the case of the antecedent part (*medium*, *small*) in (13.7). This is because the fuzzy output in Fig. 13.5 is not similar to any linguistic term.

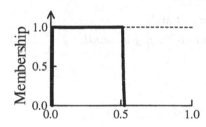

Fig. 13.5. Fuzzy output from the trained neural network for the linguistic input vector (*small, don't care*)

To determine the consequent part B_q of the linguistic rule R_q in (13.13), we also examine a union of multiple adjacent linguistic terms (e.g., *small* or *medium small*) as a candidate consequent part D_j in (13.3). The minimum difference from the fuzzy output O_q is obtained by "*small* or *medium small* or *medium*" among all the possible combinations of multiple adjacent linguistic terms as

$$d(small\ or\ medium\ small\ or\ medium, O_q) = 0.0953. \tag{13.15}$$

Thus we can extract the following linguistic rule from the trained neural network:

Rule R_q: If x_1 is *small* then

y is *small* or *medium small* or *medium*. $\qquad$ (13.16)

In the calculation of the difference from the fuzzy output O_q, a union of multiple linguistic terms is handled as a trapezoidal fuzzy set as shown in Fig. 13.6.

Unions of multiple adjacent linguistic terms can be used not only in the consequent part but also in the antecedent part of each linguistic rule. For example, let us consider the following linguistic rule:

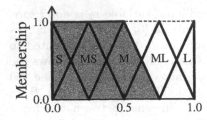

Fig. 13.6. Trapezoidal fuzzy set corresponds to *"small* or *medium small* or *medium"*

Rule R_q: If x_1 is *small* or *medium small* and

x_2 is *small* or *medium small* then y is B_q.   (13.17)

In this case, the linguistic vector (*small* or *medium small, small* or *medium small*) is presented to the trained neural network. The fuzzy output O_q from the trained neural network is calculated as shown in Fig. 13.7. The consequent part B_q is specified from the fuzzy output O_q as

Rule R_q: If x_1 is *small* or *medium small* and

x_2 is *small* or *medium small* then y is *small*.   (13.18)

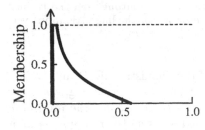

Fig. 13.7. Fuzzy output from the trained neural network for the linguistic input vector (*small* or *medium small, small* or *medium small*)

13.3 Linguistic Rule Extraction for Classification Problems

In this section, we explain the fuzzy arithmetic-based approach to linguistic rule extraction for pattern classification problems. Linguistic rules of the form in (13.2) are extracted from arbitrarily trained multi-layer feedforward neural networks. We assume that a three-layer feedforward neural network with n input units and M output units is given where M is the number of classes. Our task is to extract linguistic rules from the given neural network. As in the previous section, we assume that a set of linguistic terms is given for each of the n input variables. We also assume that the input space is the n-dimensional unit hypercube $[0, 1]^n$.

13.3.1 Basic Idea

As in the case of modeling problems in the previous section, the antecedent part of each linguistic rule is presented to the given neural network as a linguistic input vector $\boldsymbol{A}_q = (A_{q1}, \ldots, A_{qn})$. The corresponding fuzzy output vector $\boldsymbol{O}_q = (O_{q1}, \ldots, O_{qM})$ from the neural network is calculated by fuzzy arithmetic. The consequent class C_q and the rule weight (i.e., certainty grade) CF_q are determined using the fuzzy output vector $\boldsymbol{O}_q$.

When a numerical input vector $\boldsymbol{x}_p = (x_{p1}, \ldots, x_{pn})$ is presented to the trained neural network, the corresponding numerical output vector $\boldsymbol{o}_p = (o_{p1}, \ldots, o_{pM})$ is calculated. Then the input vector $\boldsymbol{x}_p$ is classified by finding the maximum output value in the output vector $\boldsymbol{o}_p$. That is, we usually use the following decision rule based on the single winner output unit:

$$\text{If } {}^\forall k\,(k \neq z), o_{pk} < o_{pz}, \text{ then } \boldsymbol{x}_p \text{ is Class } z. \tag{13.19}$$

The determination of the consequent class C_q is based on the same idea. That is, the consequent class C_q is determined by finding the maximum fuzzy output in the fuzzy output vector $\boldsymbol{O}_q = (O_{q1}, \ldots, O_{qM})$. The rule weight CF_q is calculated from the overlap between the largest fuzzy output and the second largest fuzzy output.

13.3.2 Extraction of Linguistic Rules

By directly extending the decision rule in (13.19) to the case of the linguistic input vector $\boldsymbol{A}_q$, we have the following decision rule:

$$\text{If } {}^\forall k\,(k \neq z), O_{qk} < O_{qz}, \text{ then } \boldsymbol{A}_q \text{ is Class } z. \tag{13.20}$$

To apply this decision rule to the linguistic input vector $\boldsymbol{A}_q$, we have to define the inequality relation $O_{qk} < O_{qz}$ between fuzzy numbers. For this purpose, we use the necessity grade of the inequality between fuzzy numbers that was introduced by Dubois & Prade [33] for ranking fuzzy numbers. The necessity grade of the inequality $O_{qk} < O_{qz}$ is written as follows:

$$\text{Ness}(O_{qk} < O_{qz}) = 1 - \text{Poss}(O_{qk} > O_{qz})$$
$$= 1 - \sup\{\mu_{O_{qk}}(x) \wedge \mu_{O_{qz}}(y) \mid x \geq y, x \in \Re, y \in \Re\}, \tag{13.21}$$

where $\text{Ness}(O_{qk} < O_{qz})$ is the necessity grade of $O_{qk} < O_{qz}$, and $\text{Poss}(O_{qk} > O_{qz})$ is the possibility grade of $O_{qk} > O_{qz}$. This definition of the necessity grade is illustrated in Fig. 13.8. Some examples are shown in Fig. 13.9 to illustrate the definition of the necessity grade.

Using the necessity grade of $O_{qk} < O_{qz}$, let us define the necessity grade that the linguistic input vector $\boldsymbol{A}_q$ belongs to Class z as follows:

$$\text{Ness}(\boldsymbol{A}_q \in \text{Class } z) = \min\{\text{Ness}(O_{qk} < O_{qz}) \mid$$
$$k = 1, 2, \ldots, M, k \neq z\}. \tag{13.22}$$

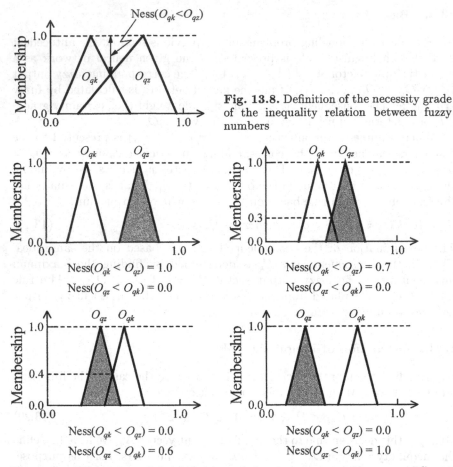

Fig. 13.8. Definition of the necessity grade of the inequality relation between fuzzy numbers

Fig. 13.9. Illustration of the definition of the necessity grade for some different situations

This definition is illustrated in Fig. 13.10 where only Class 3 has a positive necessity grade (the necessity grades of the other classes are zero).

From the relation between possibility and necessity [33, 36], the following relation holds for the necessity grade of the inequality relation between fuzzy numbers:

$$\text{Ness}(O_{qk} < O_{qz}) \cdot \text{Ness}(O_{qz} < O_{qk}) = 0. \tag{13.23}$$

That is, both $O_{qk} < O_{qz}$ and $O_{qz} < O_{qk}$ cannot simultaneously have positive necessity grades (see Fig. 13.9). Now let us assume that Class z has a positive necessity grade for the linguistic input vector $\boldsymbol{A}_q$ (i.e., $\text{Ness}(\boldsymbol{A}_q \in \text{Class } z) > 0$). From the definition in (13.22), we have

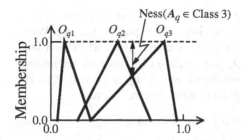

Fig. 13.10. The necessity grade that the linguistic input belongs to Class 3

$$\text{Ness}(\boldsymbol{A}_q \in \text{Class } z) > 0 \Longleftrightarrow \text{Ness}(O_{qk} < O_{qz}) > 0$$
$$\text{for } k = 1, 2, \ldots, M, \, k \neq z. \tag{13.24}$$

From (13.23) and (13.24), we can see that the following relation holds:

$$\text{Ness}(O_{qz} < O_{qk}) = 0 \text{ for } k = 1, 2, \ldots, M, \, k \neq z. \tag{13.25}$$

Thus from (13.22) we have

$$\text{Ness}(\boldsymbol{A}_q \in \text{Class } k) = 0 \text{ for } k = 1, 2, \ldots, M, \, k \neq z. \tag{13.26}$$

This means that only a single class has a positive necessity grade for the linguistic input vector $\boldsymbol{A}_q$. When the necessity grade $\text{Ness}(\boldsymbol{A}_q \in \text{Class } z)$ is positive for Class z, we generate a linguistic rule with $\boldsymbol{A}_q$ in the antecedent part and Class z in the consequent part. We also use the necessity grade $\text{Ness}(\boldsymbol{A}_q \in \text{Class } z)$ as the rule weight CF_q. Thus we generate the following linguistic rule when $\text{Ness}(\boldsymbol{A}_q \in \text{Class } z) > 0$:

If x_1 is A_{q1} and $\ldots$ and x_n is A_{qn}
then Class z with $CF_q = \text{Ness}(\boldsymbol{A}_q \in \text{Class } z)$. (13.27)

There are many cases where no class has a positive necessity grade (see Fig. 13.11). In these cases, we do not generate any linguistic rules with the antecedent part $\boldsymbol{A}_q$ because we cannot specify the consequent class C_q uniquely.

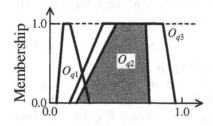

Fig. 13.11. An example of a fuzzy output vector from which the consequent class cannot be uniquely specified

In this subsection, we have already described the fuzzy arithmetic-based approach to linguistic rule extraction for classification problems using the concept of possibility and necessity. This rule extraction method can also be described using the h-level set $[\boldsymbol{A}_q]_h$ of the linguistic input vector $\boldsymbol{A}_q$. When the h-level set $[\boldsymbol{A}_q]_h$ is presented to the trained neural network, the h-level set $[\boldsymbol{O}_q]_h$ of the fuzzy output vector $\boldsymbol{O}_q$ is calculated by interval arithmetic. The decision rule in (13.19) for the real input vector $\boldsymbol{x}_p$ is extended to the case of the h-level set $[\boldsymbol{A}_q]_h$ of the linguistic input vector $\boldsymbol{A}_q$ as

$$\text{If } {}^\forall k\,(k \neq z), [O_{qk}]_h < [O_{qz}]_h, \text{ then } [\boldsymbol{A}_q]_h \text{ is Class } z. \tag{13.28}$$

We define the inequality relation $[O_{qk}]_h < [O_{qz}]_h$ between the h-level sets $[O_{qk}]_h$ and $[O_{qz}]_h$ as

$$[O_{qk}]_h < [O_{qz}]_h \iff [O_{qk}]_h^U < [O_{qz}]_h^L, \tag{13.29}$$

where $[\cdot]_h^L$ and $[\cdot]_h^U$ are the lower and upper limits of the h-level set. This inequality relation is illustrated in Fig. 13.12.

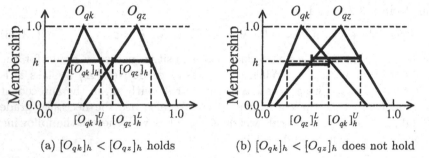

(a) $[O_{qk}]_h < [O_{qz}]_h$ holds   (b) $[O_{qk}]_h < [O_{qz}]_h$ does not hold

Fig. 13.12. Illustration of the inequality relation between the h-level sets $[O_{qk}]_h$ and $[O_{qz}]_h$

When the decision rule (13.28) for the h-level set $[\boldsymbol{A}_q]_h$ of the linguistic input vector $\boldsymbol{A}_q$ holds for Class z, we generate the following interval rule:

$$\text{If } x_1 \text{ is } [A_{q1}]_h \text{ and } \dots \text{ and } x_n \text{ is } [A_{qn}]_h \text{ then Class } z. \tag{13.30}$$

As shown in Fig. 13.13, there is the lower limit h^* of h for which the decision rule (13.28) holds. That is, h^* is defined as

$$h^* = \inf\{h \mid {}^\forall k\,(k \neq z), [O_{qk}]_h < [O_{qz}]_h; 0 \leq h \leq 1\}. \tag{13.31}$$

When the set of h in the righthand side of (13.31) is empty (i.e., there is no h that satisfies the decision rule in (13.28)), we cannot define h^*. In this case, we do not extract the linguistic rule with the antecedent part $\boldsymbol{A}_q$ because the consequent class C_q cannot be uniquely specified (see Fig. 13.11). When the value of h^* can be defined by (13.31), the rule weight CF_q is specified as follows:

$$CF_q = 1 - h^*. \tag{13.32}$$

The consequent class C_q is Class z that satisfies the decision rule (13.28). In this manner, we extract the following linguistic rule from the trained neural network.

$$\text{If } x_1 \text{ is } A_{q1} \text{ and } \ldots \text{ and } x_n \text{ is } A_{qn} \text{ then Class } z \text{ with } CF_q = 1 - h^*.$$

$$(13.33)$$

As we can see from Fig. 13.10 and Fig. 13.13, the rule weight CF_q defined by the necessity grade $\text{Ness}(A_q \in \text{Class } z)$ is the same as $1 - h^*$ calculated from the h-level set of the linguistic input vector A_q.

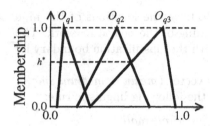

Fig. 13.13. Definition of h^*

13.3.3 Computer Simulations

Using the trained neural network in Fig. 12.2 of Chap. 12, we illustrate the fuzzy arithmetic-based approach to linguistic rule extraction for classification problems. In Chap. 12, the neural network was trained from the nine linguistic rules in Fig. 12.1. We assume that the five linguistic terms are given for each of the two input variables as in Fig. 12.1 and Fig. 12.2. We examine all the 25 combinations of the five linguistic terms as linguistic input vectors. For example, let us consider the following linguistic rule:

$$\text{Rule } R_q \text{: If } x_1 \text{ is } \textit{small} \text{ and } x_2 \text{ is } \textit{medium} \text{ then Class } C_q \text{ with } CF_q.$$

$$(13.34)$$

To determine the consequent class C_q and the rule weight CF_q, the linguistic input vector (*small, medium*) is presented to the trained neural network. The corresponding fuzzy output vector $O_q = (O_{q1}, O_{q2}, O_{q3})$ from the neural network is calculated as shown in Fig. 13.14.

From the fuzzy output vector $O_q = (O_{q1}, O_{q2}, O_{q3})$ in Fig. 13.14, the necessity grade that the linguistic input vector $A_q = (\textit{small, medium})$ belongs to each class is calculated as follows:

$$\text{Ness}(A_q \in \text{Class } 1) = 0.76, \tag{13.35}$$

$$\text{Ness}(A_q \in \text{Class } 2) = 0.00, \tag{13.36}$$

$$\text{Ness}(A_q \in \text{Class } 3) = 0.00. \tag{13.37}$$

Thus we extract the following linguistic rule:

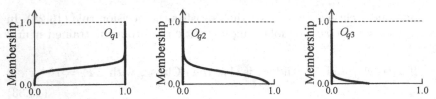

Fig. 13.14. Fuzzy output vector from the trained neural network corresponding to the linguistic input vector (*small, medium*)

$$\text{If } x_1 \text{ is } small \text{ and } x_2 \text{ is } medium \text{ then Class 1 with } 0.76. \tag{13.38}$$

This linguistic rule is intuitively acceptable from the locations of the nine linguistic rules in Fig. 12.1 used in the learning of the neural network. The extracted linguistic rule is also consistent with the classification boundary by the trained neural network in Fig. 12.2.

Let us consider another linguistic input vector (*medium, medium small*). This linguistic input vector corresponds to the following linguistic rule:

$$\text{Rule } R_q : \text{If } x_1 \text{ is } medium \text{ and } x_2 \text{ is } medium\,small$$
$$\text{then Class } C_q \text{ with } CF_q. \tag{13.39}$$

We cannot intuitively specify the consequent class C_q of this linguistic rule from the nine linguistic rules in Fig. 12.1. The linguistic input vector $A_q=(medium, medium\,small)$ is presented to the trained neural network. The corresponding fuzzy output vector $O_q = (O_{q1}, O_{q2}, O_{q3})$ is calculated as shown in Fig. 13.15. We can see that the fuzzy outputs O_{q1} and O_{q3} have a large overlap. This indicates that the linguistic input vector is located near the classification boundary between Class 1 and Class 3. From the fuzzy output vector in Fig. 13.15, the necessity grade that the linguistic input vector $A_q=(medium, medium\,small)$ belongs to each class is calculated as follows:

$$\text{Ness}(A_q \in \text{Class 1}) = 0.00, \tag{13.40}$$
$$\text{Ness}(A_q \in \text{Class 2}) = 0.00, \tag{13.41}$$
$$\text{Ness}(A_q \in \text{Class 3}) = 0.43. \tag{13.42}$$

Thus we extract the following linguistic rule:

$$\text{If } x_1 \text{ is } medium \text{ and } x_2 \text{ is } medium\,small$$
$$\text{then Class 3 with } 0.43. \tag{13.43}$$

The rule weight of the extracted linguistic rule is small. This indicates that the extracted linguistic rule is located near the classification boundary.

In the same manner, we examined all the 25 combinations of the five linguistic terms. The consequent class of each of the extracted linguistic rules is shown in Fig. 13.16. Note that each linguistic rule in Fig. 13.16 has a different rule weight as shown in (13.38) and (13.43). The extracted linguistic rules can be viewed as a linguistic rule-based system. In Fig. 13.17, we show

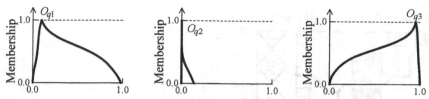

Fig. 13.15. Fuzzy output vector from the trained neural network corresponding to the linguistic input vector (*medium, medium small*)

the classification boundary depicted by the extracted linguistic rules. From the comparison between Fig. 13.17 and Fig. 12.2, we can see that the classification boundary by the extracted linguistic rules is similar to that by the trained neural network.

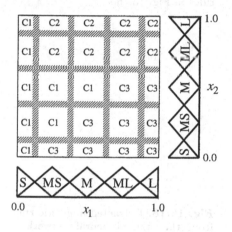

Fig. 13.16. Extracted linguistic rules from the trained neural network in Fig. 12.2

We also extract linguistic rules from the trained neural networks in Fig. 12.3 and Fig. 12.5. In Fig. 12.3, 30 numerical patterns were used as training data. On the other hand, the neural network in Fig. 12.5 was trained from the two linguistic rules in Fig. 12.4 in addition to the same 30 patterns. The classification boundary in Fig. 12.5 is not the same as that in Fig. 12.3 because the two linguistic rules were used only in Fig. 12.5. Extracted linguistic rules from each neural network are shown in Fig. 13.18 and Fig. 13.19. From these figures, we can see that the difference between Fig. 12.3 and Fig. 12.5 leads to the difference between Fig. 13.18 and Fig. 13.19.

13.3.4 Rule Extraction Algorithm

In the previous subsection, we used 100 h-level sets $[A_q]_h$ of the linguistic input vector A_q to calculate the fuzzy output vector O_q (e.g., Fig. 13.14 and

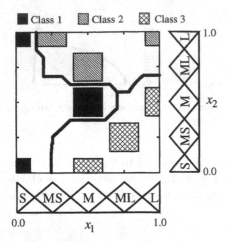

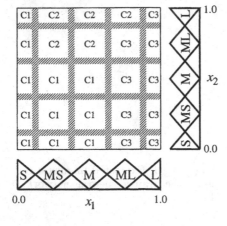

Fig. 13.17. Classification boundary obtained from the extracted linguistic rules in Fig. 13.16

Fig. 13.18. Extracted linguistic rules from the trained neural network in Fig. 12.3

Fig. 13.15). The use of such a large number of level sets was mainly to illustrate the fuzzy arithmetic-based approach to linguistic rule extraction. Each linguistic input vector can be examined more efficiently for determining the consequent class and the rule weight of the corresponding linguistic rule in the following manner:

Step 1: Examine the h-level set of the linguistic input vector A_q for $h = 1$. If the decision rule in (13.28) does not hold, stop the examination of A_q. In this case, we do not generate the corresponding linguistic rule. If (13.28) holds, the consequent class of the linguistic rule is specified as Class z that satisfies (13.28).

Step 2: Examine the h-level set of A_q for $h = 0$. If the decision rule in (13.28) holds, stop the examination of A_q. In this case, the rule weight of

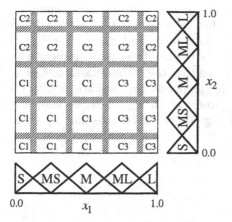

Fig. 13.19. Extracted linguistic rules from the trained neural network in Fig. 12.5

the corresponding linguistic rule is specified as 1. If (13.28) does not hold for $h = 0$, let $h = 0.5$ and $\Delta h = 0.25$.

Step 3: Examine the h-level set of A_q. If the decision rule in (13.28) holds, update the value of h as $h = h - \Delta h$. If (13.28) does not hold, update h as $h = h + \Delta h$.

Step 4: If a pre-specified stopping condition is satisfied, stop the examination of A_q. In this case, we specify the rule weight of the linguistic rule as $1 - h$. Otherwise, update the value of Δh as $\Delta h := \Delta h \times 0.5$ and return to Step 3.

In this algorithm, the value of Δh is exponentially decreased as $\Delta h = 0.25 \times (0.5)^{t-1}$ where t is the number of iterations of the algorithm. For example, the termination after nine iterations is equivalent to the stopping condition $\Delta h \leq 0.001$.

13.3.5 Decreasing the Measurement Cost

The fuzzy arithmetic-based approach to linguistic rule extraction for classification problems can be viewed as a classification method of uncertain patterns by trained neural networks. Such a classification method can be used to decrease the measurement cost for each new pattern to be classified. The decrease in the measurement cost is realized in the following two tricks: to perform a rough measurement of each input variable and to omit the measurement of some input values.

We illustrate each trick using a neural network with the classification boundary in Fig. 13.20, which is actually the same as the trained neural network in Fig. 12.5 used in the previous subsection. When a new pattern $x_p = (x_{p1}, x_{p2})$ is to be classified, x_p is presented to the neural network as an input vector. Then x_p is classified by finding the maximum output value o_{pz} in the output vector $\boldsymbol{o}_p = (o_{p1}, o_{p2}, o_{p3})$ from the neural network, that is, by the decision rule in (13.19). Let us consider the situation where the precise measurement of the exact values of x_1 and x_2 involves a large measurement cost. In this case, one may try to classify $\boldsymbol{x}_p$ without measuring the exact values of x_{p1} and x_{p2}. We assume that the measurement cost of $\boldsymbol{x}_p$ as an interval vector $\boldsymbol{X}_p = (X_{p1}, X_{p2})$ is inexpensive in comparison with the measurement of the exact values of x_{p1} and x_{p2}. In Fig. 13.20, we show two examples of $\boldsymbol{x}_p$ and $\boldsymbol{X}_p$. As shown in Fig. 13.20, we assume that $\boldsymbol{x}_p \in \boldsymbol{X}_p$ (i.e., $x_{p1} \in X_{p1}$ and $x_{p2} \in X_{p2}$).

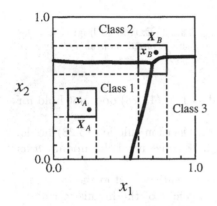

Fig. 13.20. Classification boundary of a trained neural network and new patterns represented by interval input vectors

In Fig. 13.20, we intuitively think that the new input vector $\boldsymbol{x}_A$ can be classified by the trained neural network using its interval estimation $\boldsymbol{X}_A$ without measuring the exact values of x_{A1} and x_{A2}. On the contrary, the classification of the new input vector $\boldsymbol{x}_B$ may require its precise measurement because its interval estimation $\boldsymbol{X}_B$ overlaps with the classification boundary. These intuitive discussions can be mathematically described using the following decision rule for the interval input vector $\boldsymbol{X}_p$:

$$\text{If } {}^{\forall}k\,(k \neq z), O_{pk} < O_{pz}, \text{ then } \boldsymbol{X}_p \text{ is Class } z, \tag{13.44}$$

where the inequality relation between the interval outputs $O_{pk} = [o_{pk}^L, o_{pk}^U]$ and $O_{pz} = [o_{pz}^L, o_{pz}^U]$ is defined as

$$O_{pk} < O_{pz} \iff o_{pk}^U < o_{pz}^L. \tag{13.45}$$

The decision rule in (13.44) for the interval input vector $\boldsymbol{X}_p$ is basically the same as that for the h-level set $[A_q]_h$ of the linguistic input vector $\boldsymbol{A}_q$ illustrated in Fig. 13.12. When the interval input vector $\boldsymbol{X}_p$ can be classified by the decision rule in (13.44), the precise measurement of $\boldsymbol{x}_p$ is not necessary. This is because any input vector $\boldsymbol{x}_p$ in $\boldsymbol{X}_p$ (i.e., ${}^{\forall}\boldsymbol{x}_p \in \boldsymbol{X}_p$) is always classified as Class z when $\boldsymbol{X}_p$ is classified as Class z by the decision rule in (13.44). For any numerical input vector $\boldsymbol{x}_p$ and any interval input vector $\boldsymbol{X}_p$ such that

$x_p \in X_p$, the inclusion relation $o_p \in O_p$ always holds for the corresponding numerical output vector $o_p = (o_{p1}, \ldots, o_{pM})$ and interval output vector $O_p = (O_{p1}, \ldots, O_{pM})$ from the inclusion monotonicity of interval arithmetic [6, 126]. From $o_p \in O_p$, the following relation holds:

$$O_{pk} < O_{pz} \Longrightarrow o_{pk} < o_{pz}. \tag{13.46}$$

This means that x_p is always classified as Class z when X_p is classified as Class z by the decision rule in (13.44).

In Fig. 13.21, we show the interval output vectors O_A and O_B from the trained neural network in Fig. 13.20 corresponding to the interval input vectors X_A and X_B, respectively. From this figure, we can see that X_B is not classifiable by the decision rule in (13.44) while X_A is classifiable. Thus the precise measurement is necessary only for x_B. This result coincides with our intuition obtained from Fig. 13.20.

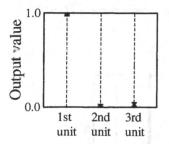 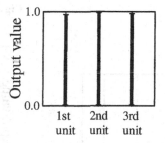

(a) Interval output vector O_A (b) Interval output vector O_B

Fig. 13.21. Interval output vectors corresponding to the interval input vectors X_A and X_B

The decision rule for interval input vectors can also be used to classify incomplete input patterns. In Fig. 13.22, we show an incomplete pattern (?, 0.95) where the first input value has not been measured. Since the pattern space is the unit square $[0, 1] \times [0, 1]$, this incomplete input pattern is represented as an interval input vector $X_p = ([0, 1], [0.95, 0.95])$. When X_p is presented to the trained neural network, the corresponding interval output vector O_p is calculated as shown in Fig. 13.23 (a). Thus X_p is classified as Class 2 by the decision rule in (13.44). It should be noted that an arbitrary numerical input vector x_p in X_p (i.e., $^\forall x_p \in X_p$) is always classified as Class 2 because $o_p \in O_p$ holds. This means that the measurement of the first input vector is not necessary for classifying the incomplete pattern (?, 0.95). On the other hand, no incomplete patterns of the form $(x_{p1}, ?)$ can be classified in Fig. 13.22. For example, Fig. 13.23 (b) shows the interval output vector corresponding to the incomplete pattern (0.5, ?). Only when the second input value is first measured, there is a possibility that the measurement cost can be decreased in the classification phase for new patterns. The determination of the measurement orders was studied in [76] where the decrease in the measurement cost was demonstrated using some real-world pattern classification problems.

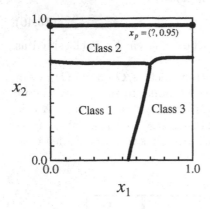

Fig. 13.22. Incomplete pattern (?, 0.95)

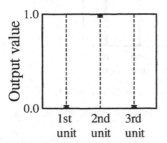
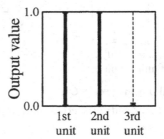

(a) Interval output vector for (?, 0.95)   (b) Interval output vector for (0.5, ?)

Fig. 13.23. Interval output vectors corresponding to incomplete input patterns

13.4 Difficulties and Extensions

We have already explained the fuzzy arithmetic-based approach to linguistic rule extraction for modeling problems and classification problems. One characteristic feature of the fuzzy arithmetic-based approach is its applicability to arbitrarily trained neural networks. It does not require any particular learning algorithm. It does not require numerical training data, either. Thus we can apply the fuzzy arithmetic-based approach to arbitrarily trained multi-layer feedforward neural networks. The high applicability of the fuzzy arithmetic-based approach, however, does not necessarily mean its high performance. In this section, we explain two difficulties: poor scalability to high-dimensional problems and undesirable increase of the excess fuzziness in fuzzy outputs.

13.4.1 Scalability to High-Dimensional Problems

When a trained neural network and linguistic terms are given, the fuzzy arithmetic-based approach examines each combination of linguistic terms. If we have K linguistic terms for each of n input variables, the total number of combinations of linguistic terms is $(K+1)^n$ when *don't care* is used as an additional antecedent fuzzy set. When n is large, it is impossible to examine all the $(K+1)^n$ combinations. Since the available information is only the trained neural network, we cannot evaluate the importance of each combination of antecedent linguistic terms. We cannot find only a small number of significant combinations, either. A simple idea for handling high-dimensional problems is to examine only short linguistic rules with many *don't care* conditions, which was used in Chap. 4. Another idea is to use numerical data to find only a small number of significant combinations of antecedent linguistic terms. We may be able to identify some combinations of antecedent linguistic terms that cover many training patterns. This idea is somewhat different from the original task of linguistic rule extraction from trained neural networks in this chapter. It is rather referred to as linguistic rule extraction from trained neural networks and numerical data.

13.4.2 Increase of Excess Fuzziness in Fuzzy Outputs

An essential difficulty in the fuzzy arithmetic-based approach is the existence of excess fuzziness in fuzzy outputs. In the fuzzy arithmetic-based approach, the fuzzy output vector O_q from the trained neural network is calculated by fuzzy arithmetic for the linguistic input vector A_q. The linguistic rule extraction is totally based on the calculated fuzzy output vector O_q as we have already explained. The problem is that the fuzzy output vector O_q includes a lot of excess fuzziness.

As shown in Chap. 11, the addition, multiplication, and nonlinear mapping by the activation function are defined by the extension principle for fuzzy numbers. This means that the extension principle is locally applied to the input–output relation of each unit as shown in Fig. 13.24. Since the extension principle is locally applied to the input–output relation of each unit, neural networks for linguistic input vectors have the same advantage as standard multi-layer feedforward neural networks: suitability for parallel distributed calculation. At the same time, the local application of the extension principle leads to the existence of excess fuzziness in fuzzy outputs.

Let $G_k(A_q)$ be the fuzzy output O_{qk} from the k-th output unit when the linguistic input vector A_q is presented. The fuzzy output vector O_q from the neural network is written as $O_q = G(A_q) = (G_1(A_q),\ldots,G_M(A_q))$.

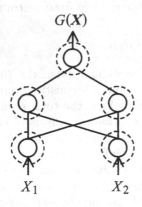

Application area of the extension principle

$G(X)$

X_1 X_2

Fig. 13.24. Local application of the extension principle to each unit

In the same manner, let $g_k(x_p)$ be the output o_{pk} from the k-th output unit when the numerical input vector $x_p = (x_{p1}, \ldots, x_{pn})$ is presented to the same neural network. The output vector o_p from the neural network is written as $o_p = g(x_p) = (g_1(x_p), \ldots, g_M(x_p))$. If we globally apply the extension principle to the mapping $g(x_p) = (g_1(x_p), \ldots, g_M(x_p))$ as shown in Fig. 13.25, the exact fuzzy output $g_k(A_q)$ from the k-th output unit is defined for the linguistic input vector $A_q = (A_{q1}, \ldots, A_{qn})$ as

$$\mu_{g_k(A_q)}(y) = \max\{\mu_{A_{q1}}(x_1) \wedge \ldots \wedge \mu_{A_{qn}}(x_n) \,|\, y = g_k(x), \, x \in \Re^n\}.$$

$$(13.47)$$

This global application of the extension principle defines the exact shape of the fuzzy output when the linguistic input vector A_q is presented to the nonlinear function $g_k(x)$. That is, the global application of the extension principle exactly describes the mapping of the fuzzy input vector A_q by the nonlinear function $g_k(x)$. The calculation of the fuzzy output $g_k(A_q)$ in (13.47), however, is not easy because $g_k(x)$ is highly nonlinear. That is, the calculation in (13.47) involves nonlinear optimization.

The following relation always holds between the fuzzy output $G_k(A_q)$ defined by fuzzy arithmetic (i.e., the local application of the extension principle) and the fuzzy output $g_k(A_q)$ defined by the global application of the extension principle:

$$g_k(A_q) \subseteq G_k(A_q).$$

$$(13.48)$$

The problem is that the equality between $G_k(A_q)$ and $g_k(A_q)$ does not hold in general. That is, $G_k(A_q)$ defined by fuzzy arithmetic is not the same as $g_k(A_q)$ defined by the global application of the extension principle. This is because the definition of $G_k(A_q)$ is based on the local application of the extension principle.

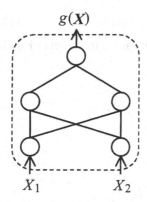

Application area of the extension principle

$g(X)$

X_1 X_2

Fig. 13.25. Global application of the extension principle to the entire neural network

Let us explain the difference between the global and local applications of the extension principle. In the neural network based on fuzzy arithmetic (i e, the local application of the extension principle), the total fuzzy input to the k-th output unit is calculated as

$$Net_k = w_{k1} \cdot O_{q1} + w_{k2} \cdot O_{q2} + \ldots + w_{kn_H} \cdot O_{qn_H} + \theta_k, \qquad (13.49)$$

where $O_{q1}, O_{q2}, \ldots, O_{qn_H}$ are fuzzy outputs from hidden units. In fuzzy arithmetic in (13.49), $O_{q1}, O_{q2}, \ldots, O_{qn_H}$ are handled as independent fuzzy numbers. These fuzzy numbers, however, are not independent because they are written as

$$O_{qj} = \frac{1}{1 + \exp(-\sum_{i=1}^{n} w_{ji} \cdot A_{qi} - \theta_j)}, \; j = 1, 2, \ldots, n_H. \qquad (13.50)$$

That is, all the fuzzy numbers $O_{q1}, O_{q2}, \ldots, O_{qn_H}$ are calculated from the same linguistic input vector $A_q = (A_{q1}, \ldots, A_{qn})$. In fuzzy arithmetic in (13.49), this dependence among the fuzzy numbers $O_{q1}, O_{q2}, \ldots, O_{qn_H}$ is not taken into account. Thus the corresponding fuzzy output $G_k(A_q)$ calculated by fuzzy arithmetic has larger fuzziness than the fuzzy output $g_k(A_q)$ defined by the global application of the extension principle.

For illustration purposes, let us consider a neural network with a fuzzy input vector $A_q = (\tilde{3}, \tilde{2})$ in Fig. 13.26. For simplicity of explanation, we assume that all the input, hidden, and output units of this neural network have the linear activation function: $f(x) = x$. That is, the output from each unit is the same as the total input to that unit. When the fuzzy input vector $A_q = (\tilde{3}, \tilde{2})$ is presented to the neural network, the fuzzy output from each hidden unit is calculated as follows:

Hidden unit C: $O_C = f(1 \cdot \tilde{3} + 1 \cdot \tilde{2} + 0) = \tilde{5}$,   (13.51)
Hidden unit D: $O_D = f(1 \cdot \tilde{3} - 1 \cdot \tilde{2} + 0) = \tilde{1}$.   (13.52)

These two fuzzy numbers $\tilde{5}$ and $\tilde{1}$ are shown in Fig. 13.27. Then the fuzzy output from the output unit is calculated as follows:

$$\text{Output unit: } O_E = G(\tilde{3},\,\tilde{2}) = f(1 \cdot \tilde{5} - 1 \cdot \tilde{1} + 0) = \tilde{4}. \tag{13.53}$$

This fuzzy output $G(\tilde{3},\,\tilde{2})$ calculated by fuzzy arithmetic is shown in Fig. 13.28 (a).

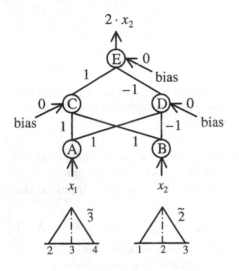

Fig. 13.26. A neural network with the linear activation function

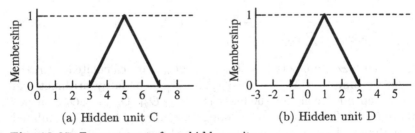

(a) Hidden unit C   (b) Hidden unit D

Fig. 13.27. Fuzzy outputs from hidden units

On the other hand, the exact fuzzy output $g(\boldsymbol{A}_q)$ with no excess fuzziness is defined by globally applying the extension principle to the entire neural network. While the calculation of $g(\boldsymbol{A}_q)$ is very difficult in general, it is easy in Fig. 13.26 because all the input, hidden, and output units of the neural network have the linear activation function $f(x) = x$. The mapping $g(\boldsymbol{x}_p)$ realized by the neural network is calculated as

$$g(\boldsymbol{x}_p) = 1 \cdot (1 \cdot x_{p1} + 1 \cdot x_{p2} + 0) - 1 \cdot (1 \cdot x_{p1} - 1 \cdot x_{p2} + 0) = 2 \cdot x_{p2}. \tag{13.54}$$

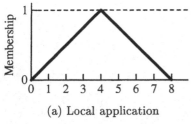
(a) Local application

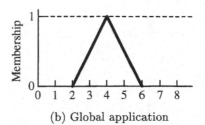
(b) Global application

Fig. 13.28. Comparison of fuzzy outputs from the neural network between the local and global applications of the extension principle

Thus the exact fuzzy output $g(\tilde{3}, \tilde{2})$ with no excess fuzziness is $2 \cdot \tilde{2}$, which is shown in Fig. 13.28 (b). The difference between Fig. 13.28 (a) and Fig. 13.28 (b) is the excess fuzziness involved in the fuzzy output $G(\tilde{3}, \tilde{2})$ in Fig. 13.28 (a).

Excess fuzziness in fuzzy arithmetic corresponds to excess width in interval arithmetic [6, 126]. Calculation of more accurate intervals with less excess width has been studied in the literature. Methods for decreasing excess width such as a subdivision method [126] can be used in the fuzzy arithmetic-based approach to linguistic rule extraction from trained neural networks because fuzzy output vectors are numerically calculated by interval arithmetic on level sets of linguistic input vectors [79].

(a) (b) Digital approximation

14. Modeling of Fuzzy Input–Output Relations

In this chapter, we explain various topics related to the handling of fuzzified systems with fuzzy inputs and/or fuzzy outputs. First we describe some approaches to the modeling of fuzzy number-valued functions. A fuzzy number-valued function with n input variables is written as

$$\tilde{y} = \tilde{f}(x), \tag{14.1}$$

where $\tilde{y}$ is a fuzzy output (i.e., fuzzy number), $\tilde{f}(\cdot)$ is a fuzzy number-valued function, and $x = (x_1, \ldots, x_n)$ is an n-dimensional non-fuzzy input vector. In this chapter, we use "$\sim$" to clearly denote fuzzy numbers (e.g., $\tilde{y}$ in (14.1)). We also use "$\sim$" for fuzzy number-valued functions such as $\tilde{f}(\cdot)$. Real numbers are denoted by lower-case letters without "$\sim$".

Next we describe some approaches to the modeling of fuzzy mappings from fuzzy vectors to fuzzy numbers. A fuzzy mapping with n fuzzy inputs is written as

$$\tilde{y} = \tilde{f}(\tilde{x}), \tag{14.2}$$

where $\tilde{x} = (\tilde{x}_1, \ldots, \tilde{x}_n)$ is an n-dimensional fuzzy vector. Neural networks described in Chap. 11 can be viewed as approximators of $\tilde{f}(\tilde{x})$ in (14.2).

Then we describe fuzzy pattern classification where input vectors and/or classification results are fuzzy. Neural networks used for linguistic rule extraction in Chap. 13 are an example of classification systems for fuzzy input vectors where classification results are not fuzzy. In addition to non-fuzzy classification of fuzzy input vectors, we explain fuzzy classification of non-fuzzy, interval, and fuzzy input vectors where classification results are fuzzy.

14.1 Modeling of Fuzzy Number-Valued Functions

In this section, we explain some approaches to the modeling of fuzzy number-valued functions of the form in (14.1). Fuzzy number-valued functions are realized by linear fuzzy models, fuzzy rule-based systems, fuzzified Takagi–Sugeno models, and fuzzified neural networks.

14.1.1 Linear Fuzzy Regression Models

The main line in fuzzy system research has been fuzzy modeling of nonlinear functions where fuzzy rule-based systems are used as approximators of non-linear mappings from non-fuzzy input vectors to non-fuzzy output values. A large number of fuzzy modeling methods of real number-valued functions have been proposed in the literature. On the other hand, much fewer approaches have been proposed for fuzzy modeling of fuzzy number-valued functions of the form in (14.1).

An early approach to fuzzy modeling of fuzzy number-valued functions is the fuzzy regression analysis of Tanaka et al. [163, 164]. They used the following linear fuzzy model:

$$\tilde{y}(\boldsymbol{x}) = \tilde{a}_0 + \tilde{a}_1 \cdot x_1 + \ldots + \tilde{a}_n \cdot x_n, \tag{14.3}$$

where $\boldsymbol{x} = (x_1, \ldots, x_n)$ is an n-dimensional non-fuzzy input vector, $\tilde{a}_i$ is a fuzzy coefficient (i.e., $\tilde{a}_i$ is a fuzzy number), and $\tilde{y}(\boldsymbol{x})$ is the fuzzy output from the linear fuzzy model corresponding to the input vector $\boldsymbol{x}$. The right hand side of (14.3) is calculated by fuzzy arithmetic [106].

The membership function of the fuzzy output $\tilde{y}(\boldsymbol{x})$ can be easily calculated when each fuzzy coefficient $\tilde{a}_i$ is specified by a parameterized membership function. Since triangular fuzzy coefficients have been traditionally used in fuzzy regression analysis [163, 164], we also assume that each $\tilde{a}_i$ is a triangular fuzzy number. As shown in Fig. 14.1, a triangular fuzzy number $\tilde{a}$ is denoted by its lower limit a^L, center a^C, and upper limit a^U as $\tilde{a} = (a^L, a^C, a^U)$. In the same manner, the fuzzy coefficient $\tilde{a}_i$ is denoted as

$$\tilde{a}_i = (a_i^L, a_i^C, a_i^U), \; i = 0, 1, \ldots, n. \tag{14.4}$$

In this case, the fuzzy output $\tilde{y}(\boldsymbol{x})$ is calculated as a triangular fuzzy number using fuzzy arithmetic:

$$\tilde{y}(\boldsymbol{x}) = (y^L(\boldsymbol{x}), y^C(\boldsymbol{x}), y^U(\boldsymbol{x})), \tag{14.5}$$

where

$$y^L(\boldsymbol{x}) = a_0^L + \sum_{x_i \geq 0} a_i^L \cdot x_i + \sum_{x_i < 0} a_i^U \cdot x_i, \tag{14.6}$$

$$y^C(\boldsymbol{x}) = a_0^C + \sum_{i=1}^{n} a_i^C \cdot x_i, \tag{14.7}$$

$$y^U(\boldsymbol{x}) = a_0^U + \sum_{x_i \geq 0} a_i^U \cdot x_i + \sum_{x_i < 0} a_i^L \cdot x_i. \tag{14.8}$$

A single-input and single-output linear fuzzy model is written as

$$\tilde{y}(x) = \tilde{a}_0 + \tilde{a}_1 x. \tag{14.9}$$

An example of a linear fuzzy model of this form is shown in Fig. 14.2 where

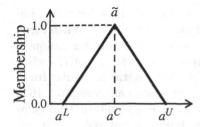

Fig. 14.1. A triangular fuzzy number $\tilde{a} = (a^L, a^C, a^U)$

$$\tilde{a}_0 = (1,\ 1.5,\ 2) \text{ and } \tilde{a}_1 = (1,\ 2,\ 3). \tag{14.10}$$

Three lines in Fig. 14.2 correspond to the lower limit $y^L(x) = 1 + x$, center $y^C(x) = 1.5 + 2x$, and upper limit $y^U(x) = 2 + 3x$. Each triangle corresponds to the membership function of the fuzzy output $\tilde{y}(x)$ for x=1.0, 2.0, 3.0. For example, $\tilde{y}(x)$ is calculated for $x = 3$ as $\tilde{y}(3) = (4,\ 7.5,\ 11)$.

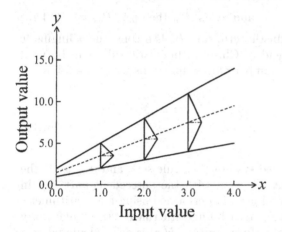

Input value

Fig. 14.2. An example of a linear fuzzy model $\tilde{y}(x) = (1,\ 1.5,\ 2) + (1,\ 2,\ 3)x$

The linear fuzzy model in (14.3) is determined from numerical input–output pairs using linear programming. Let us assume that we have m input–output pairs $(\boldsymbol{x}_p, y_p)$, $p = 1, 2, \ldots, m$, where $\boldsymbol{x}_p = (x_{p1}, \ldots, x_{pn})$. The following linear programming problem is used to determine the linear fuzzy model from the given input–output pairs:

$$\text{Minimize } \sum_{p=1}^{m}(y^U(\boldsymbol{x}_p) - y^L(\boldsymbol{x}_p)), \tag{14.11}$$

$$\text{subject to } y_p \in [\tilde{y}(\boldsymbol{x}_p)]_h,\ p = 1, 2, \ldots, m. \tag{14.12}$$

The objective function is to minimize the total fuzziness of the estimated fuzzy output $\tilde{y}(\boldsymbol{x}_p)$ over the m input–output pairs. The constraint condition means that the h-level set of the linear fuzzy model should include all the given m input–output pairs. This linear programming problem is easily solved when all the fuzzy coefficients $\tilde{a}_i$ are symmetric (i.e., when we have an additional constraint condition $a_i^C = (a_i^L + a_i^U)/2$ for $i=0, 1, \ldots, n$). When fuzzy coefficients are asymmetric triangular fuzzy numbers, they are not uniquely determined from the linear programming problem in (14.11)–(14.12) while their h-level sets are uniquely determined. Thus symmetric triangular fuzzy numbers have been traditionally used in fuzzy regression analysis [163, 164]. Fuzzy regression analysis was extended to the case of asymmetric triangular and trapezoidal fuzzy coefficients [75] where input–output pairs with different importance grades were used as training data. Input-output pairs of non-fuzzy inputs and fuzzy outputs can also be handled by the linear fuzzy model [75, 163].

14.1.2 Fuzzy Rule-Based Systems

In Chap. 8, we used linguistic rules of the following type for modeling problems of n-input and single-output nonlinear functions:

$$\text{Rule } R_q: \text{If } x_1 \text{ is } A_{q1} \text{ and } \ldots \text{ and } x_n \text{ is } A_{qn} \text{ then } y \text{ is } B_q, \qquad (14.13)$$

where A_{qi} is an antecedent linguistic term and B_q is a consequent linguistic term. As we suggested at the end of Chap. 8, linguistic rules can be used for modeling problems of fuzzy number-valued functions using the following fuzzy reasoning method [78]:

$$\tilde{y}(x) = \frac{\sum\limits_{R_q \in S} \mu_{A_q}(x) \cdot B_q}{\sum\limits_{R_q \in S} \mu_{A_q}(x)}, \qquad (14.14)$$

where S is the linguistic rule-based system (i.e., rule set), and $\mu_{A_q}(x)$ is the compatibility grade of the input vector x with the antecedent part A_q. In this formulation, the calculation of $\tilde{y}(x)$ is performed using fuzzy arithmetic [106]. When the consequent part B_q of each linguistic rule is a triangular fuzzy number (b_q^L, b_q^C, b_q^U), the estimated fuzzy output $\tilde{y}(x)$ is also calculated as a triangular fuzzy number $\tilde{y}(x)=(y^L(x), y^C(x), y^U(x))$ in the same manner as (14.5)–(14.8):

$$y^L(x) = \sum_{R_q \in S} \mu_{A_q}^*(x) \cdot b_q^L, \qquad (14.15)$$

$$y^C(x) = \sum_{R_q \in S} \mu_{A_q}^*(x) \cdot b_q^C, \qquad (14.16)$$

$$y^U(x) = \sum_{R_q \in S} \mu_{A_q}^*(x) \cdot b_q^U, \qquad (14.17)$$

where $\mu_{A_q}^*(x)$ is the normalized compatibility grade:

$$\mu_{A_q}^*(x) = \frac{\mu_{A_q}(x)}{\sum\limits_{R_q \in S} \mu_{A_q}(x)}. \qquad (14.18)$$

Since $\mu^*_{A_q}(x)$ is non-negative, the calculation of the estimated triangular fuzzy number $\tilde{y}(x){=}(y^L(x),\, y^C(x),\, y^U(x))$ is simple in (14.15)–(14.17).

The objective function in (14.11) and the constraint condition in (14.12) in fuzzy regression analysis will be utilized to determine the consequent part B_q of each linguistic rule R_q. The consequent part B_q will also be specified in a heuristic manner from compatible input–output pairs with the corresponding antecedent part A_q. Many issues are left for future research, which include the learning of fuzzy rules for modeling problems of nonlinear fuzzy number-valued functions.

14.1.3 Fuzzified Takagi–Sugeno Models

Fuzzy rules in the Takagi–Sugeno model have linear functions in their consequent parts. We extend consequent linear functions to fuzzy number-valued linear functions. That is, we use fuzzy rules of the following type for modeling problems of fuzzy number-valued nonlinear functions:

Rule R_q: If x_1 is A_{q1} and $\ldots$ and x_n is A_{qn}

$$\text{then } \tilde{y}_q(x) = \tilde{b}_{q0} + \tilde{b}_{q1} \cdot x_1 + \ldots + \tilde{b}_{qn} \cdot x_n, \quad (14.19)$$

where $\tilde{b}_{qi}$ is a fuzzy number coefficient. The estimated fuzzy output $\tilde{y}(x)$ for the input vector $x = (x_1, \ldots, x_n)$ is calculated as

$$\tilde{y}(x) = \frac{\sum\limits_{R_q \in S} \mu_{A_q}(x) \cdot \tilde{y}_q(x)}{\sum\limits_{R_q \in S} \mu_{A_q}(x)}$$

$$= \sum\limits_{R_q \in S} \mu^*_{A_q}(x) \cdot \tilde{y}_q(x). \quad (14.20)$$

When each fuzzy number coefficient $\tilde{b}_{qi}$ in (14.19) is a triangular fuzzy number $(b^L_{qi}, b^C_{qi}, b^U_{qi})$, the estimated fuzzy output $\tilde{y}(x)$ is also calculated as a triangular fuzzy number $\tilde{y}(x){=}(y^L(x),\, y^C(x),\, y^U(x))$ where

$$y^L(x) = \sum\limits_{R_q \in S} \mu^*_{A_q}(x) \cdot \left(b^L_0 + \sum\limits_{x_i \geq 0} b^L_i \cdot x_i + \sum\limits_{x_i < 0} b^U_i \cdot x_i \right), \quad (14.21)$$

$$y^C(x) = \sum\limits_{R_q \in S} \mu^*_{A_q}(x) \cdot \left(b^C_0 + \sum\limits_{i=1}^{n} b^C_i \cdot x_i \right), \quad (14.22)$$

$$y^U(x) = \sum\limits_{R_q \in S} \mu^*_{A_q}(x) \cdot \left(b^U_0 + \sum\limits_{x_i \geq 0} b^U_i \cdot x_i + \sum\limits_{x_i < 0} b^L_i \cdot x_i \right). \quad (14.23)$$

As an example, let us consider the following two fuzzy rules:

Rule R_1: If x is A_1 then $\tilde{y}_1(x) = (10, 11, 12) + (0.5, 1, 1.5)x$, (14.24)

Rule R_2: If x is A_2 then $\tilde{y}_2(x) = (2, 4, 6) + (0, 0.25, 0.5)x$. (14.25)

The consequent linear fuzzy models in (14.24) and (14.25) are shown in Fig. 14.3. As in Fig. 14.2, each linear fuzzy model in Fig. 14.3 is represented by three lines: the lower limit, center, and upper limit. When the antecedent fuzzy sets A_1 and A_2 have the membership functions in Fig. 14.4, the fuzzy rule-based system with the above two fuzzy rules represents the nonlinear fuzzy number-valued function $\tilde{y}(x)$ in Fig. 14.5. In this figure, three thick curves show the lower limit, center, and upper limit of $\tilde{y}(x)$ while thin lines show the consequent linear fuzzy models in Fig. 14.3. From Fig. 14.5, we can see that the extended Takagi–Sugeno model in (14.19)-(14.20) is a combination of multiple linear fuzzy models.

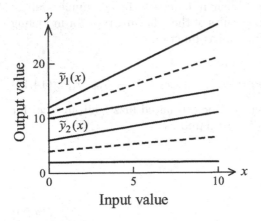

Fig. 14.3. Consequent linear fuzzy models $\tilde{y}_1(x)$ and $\tilde{y}_2(x)$

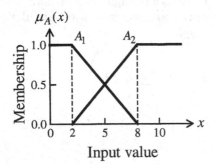

Fig. 14.4. Membership functions of the antecedent fuzzy sets A_1 and A_2

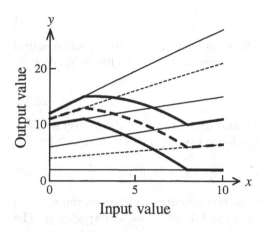

Fig. 14.5. Nonlinear fuzzy number-valued function $\tilde{y}(x)$ realized by the two fuzzy rules

14.1.4 Fuzzified Neural Networks

Modeling problems of nonlinear fuzzy number-valued functions can also be handled by multi-layer feedforward neural networks with fuzzy connection weights [75]. As in Chap. 11, we use a three-layer feedforward neural network with n input units and a single output unit to handle modeling problems of n-input and single-output fuzzy number-valued functions. The input–output relation of each unit of the neural network is fuzzified as follows for the non-fuzzy input vector $x_p = (x_{p1}, \ldots, x_{pn})$:

Input units: $o_{pi} = x_{pi}, i = 1, 2, \ldots, n.$ \hfill (14.26)

Hidden units: $\tilde{o}_{pj} = f(\widetilde{net}_{pj}), j = 1, 2, \ldots, n_H,$ \hfill (14.27)

$$\widetilde{net}_{pj} = \sum_{i=1}^{n} \tilde{w}_{ji} \cdot o_{pi} + \tilde{\theta}_j. \tag{14.28}$$

Output unit: $\tilde{o}_p = f(\widetilde{net}_p),$ \hfill (14.29)

$$\widetilde{net}_p = \sum_{j=1}^{n_H} \tilde{w}_j \cdot \tilde{o}_{pj} + \tilde{\theta}. \tag{14.30}$$

The connection weights $\tilde{w}_{ji}, \tilde{w}_j$ and biases $\tilde{\theta}_j, \tilde{\theta}$ are fuzzy numbers in (14.26)–(14.30). As a result, the activation function $f(\cdot)$ at the hidden and output units is extended to the fuzzy activation function as in Chap. 11. Fuzzy numbers with parameterized membership functions (e.g., triangular and trapezoidal membership functions) are often used as connection weights and biases.

The fuzzified neural network can be trained from numerical input–output pairs $(x_p, y_p), p = 1, 2, \ldots, m$, so that the following relation is approximately satisfied [75]:

$$y_p \in [\tilde{o}_p]_h, \; p = 1, 2, \ldots, m, \tag{14.31}$$

where $[\tilde{o}_p]_h$ is the h-level set of the fuzzy output $\tilde{o}_p$ from the fuzzified neural network when the input vector x_p is presented. The inclusion relation in (14.31) is rewritten as

$$[\tilde{o}_p]_h^L \leq y_p \leq [\tilde{o}_p]_h^U, \tag{14.32}$$

where $[\cdot]_h^L$ and $[\cdot]_h^U$ denote the lower and upper limits of the h-level set. The following cost function is used for the h-level set $[\tilde{o}_p]_h$ of the fuzzy output $\tilde{o}_p$:

$$e_{ph} = \frac{1}{2} \cdot \omega_{ph}^L \cdot (y_p - [\tilde{o}_p]_h^L)^2 + \frac{1}{2} \cdot \omega_{ph}^U \cdot (y_p - [\tilde{o}_p]_h^U)^2, \tag{14.33}$$

where ω_{ph}^L and ω_{ph}^U can be viewed as the penalties related to the squared errors for the lower and upper limits of the h-level set $[\tilde{o}_p]_h$, respectively. The values of ω_{ph}^L and ω_{ph}^U are specified as follows depending on whether the two inequalities in (14.32) are satisfied or not:

$$(\omega_{ph}^L, \omega_{ph}^U) = \begin{cases} (1, \varepsilon), & \text{if } y_p < [\tilde{o}_p]_h^L \leq [\tilde{o}_p]_h^U, \\ (\varepsilon, \varepsilon), & \text{if } [\tilde{o}_p]_h^L \leq y_p \leq [\tilde{o}_p]_h^U, \\ (\varepsilon, 1), & \text{if } [\tilde{o}_p]_h^L \leq [\tilde{o}_p]_h^U < y_p, \end{cases} \tag{14.34}$$

where ε is a small positive constant (i.e., 0.01). The specification of $(\omega_{ph}^L, \omega_{ph}^U)$ in (14.34) means that the penalty is high only when the corresponding inequality is not satisfied in (14.32). A learning algorithm can be derived for the fuzzy connection weights and biases from the cost function (14.33). When the inequality relation in (14.32) is satisfied for an input–output pair, the penalties ω_{ph}^L and ω_{ph}^U are very small. Thus the adjustment of the fuzzy connection weights and biases is also very small. The learning of the fuzzified neural network is significant only when the input–output pair does not satisfy the inequality relation in (14.32). In this manner, the learning of the fuzzified neural network leads to approximate satisfaction of the inequality relation in (14.32).

Using 51 input–output pairs in Fig. 14.6, we trained a fuzzified neural network with a single input unit, five hidden units, and a single output unit. Asymmetric triangular fuzzy numbers were used as connection weights and biases. The learning of the fuzzified neural network was performed using the cost function in (14.33) for $h = 0.2$ and $h = 1$. That is, the cost function for the input–output pair (x_p, y_p) was

$$e_p = \frac{1}{2} \cdot \omega_{p0.2}^L \cdot (y_p - [\tilde{o}_p]_{0.2}^L)^2 + \frac{1}{2} \cdot \omega_{p0.2}^U \cdot (y_p - [\tilde{o}_p]_{0.2}^U)^2$$

$$+ \frac{1}{2} \cdot \omega_{p1}^L \cdot (y_p - [\tilde{o}_p]_1^L)^2 + \frac{1}{2} \cdot \omega_{p1}^U \cdot (y_p - [\tilde{o}_p]_1^U)^2. \tag{14.35}$$

Since we used asymmetric triangular fuzzy numbers for connection weights and biases, the 1-level set of the fuzzy output $\tilde{o}_p$ had no width (i.e., $[\tilde{o}_p]_1^L$

$= [\tilde{o}_p]_1^U$). Thus ω_{ph}^L and ω_{ph}^U were always specified as $\omega_{ph}^L = 1$ and $\omega_{ph}^U = 1$ for $h = 1$. This means that the standard squared error was used for the learning of the fuzzified neural network for the 1-level set of the fuzzy output $\tilde{o}_p$. On the other hand, the learning for the 0.2-level set was performed so that the input–output pair is approximately included in the 0.2-level set of the fuzzy output. For details of the learning algorithm, see Ishibuchi & Nii [75]. Three curves in Fig. 14.6 show the 1-level set and the 0.2-level set of the nonlinear fuzzy number-valued function obtained by the learning of the fuzzified neural network. From this figure, we can see that the 1-level set is similar to simulation results using the standard back-propagation algorithm [146]. We can also see that the 0.2-level set approximately includes all the given input–output pairs.

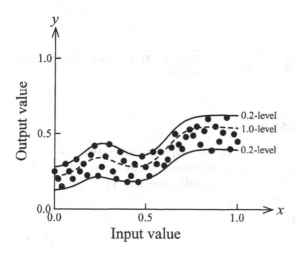

Fig. 14.6. Nonlinear fuzzy number-valued function obtained by the learning of a fuzzified neural network

14.2 Modeling of Fuzzy Mappings

In this section, we explain the approximate realization of fuzzy mappings from fuzzy input vectors to fuzzy output values. Such a fuzzy mapping is obtained by extending the non-fuzzy input vector $x = (x_1, \ldots, x_n)$ in the previous section to the fuzzy input vector $\tilde{x} = (\tilde{x}_1, \ldots, \tilde{x}_n)$.

14.2.1 Linear Fuzzy Regression Models

Sakawa & Yano [148] extended the linear fuzzy model in (14.3) to the case of the fuzzy input vector $\tilde{x} = (\tilde{x}_1, \ldots, \tilde{x}_n)$ as

$$\tilde{y}(\tilde{x}) = \tilde{a}_0 + \tilde{a}_1 \cdot \tilde{x}_1 + \ldots + \tilde{a}_n \cdot \tilde{x}_n. \tag{14.36}$$

This model can be viewed as an approximator of fuzzy mappings from fuzzy input vectors to fuzzy numbers. The fuzzy output $\tilde{y}(\tilde{x})$ in (14.36) is calculated by fuzzy arithmetic. Since the calculation of the fuzzy output $\tilde{y}(\tilde{x})$ involves the product of fuzzy numbers (i.e., $\tilde{a}_i \cdot \tilde{x}_i$), the membership function of $\tilde{y}(\tilde{x})$ cannot be written in a parameterized form even when both $\tilde{x}_i$ and $\tilde{a}_i$ are triangular fuzzy numbers (see Fig. 14.7). To numerically calculate the membership function of $\tilde{y}(\tilde{x})$, interval arithmetic is used on the h-level set of the fuzzy input vector $\tilde{x}$ as in fuzzified neural networks.

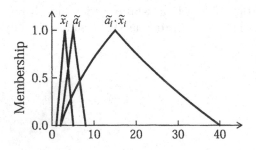

Fig. 14.7. Product of two fuzzy numbers

14.2.2 Fuzzy Rule-Based Systems

Nonlinear fuzzy number-valued functions are approximately realized by linguistic rules in (14.13) using the fuzzy reasoning method in (14.14). The non-fuzzy input vector x in the fuzzy reasoning method in (14.14) can be extended to the fuzzy input vector $\tilde{x}$ as

$$\tilde{y}(\tilde{x}) = \frac{\sum\limits_{R_q \in S} \mu_{A_q}(\tilde{x}) \cdot B_q}{\sum\limits_{R_q \in S} \mu_{A_q}(\tilde{x})}, \tag{14.37}$$

where $\mu_{A_q}(\tilde{x})$ is the compatibility grade of the fuzzy input vector $\tilde{x}$ with the antecedent part A_q of the linguistic rule R_q in (14.13). Since the compatibility grade $\mu_{A_q}(\tilde{x})$ is a non-negative real number, the membership function of the fuzzy output $\tilde{y}(\tilde{x})$ can be represented in a parameterized form as in (14.15)–(14.17) when the consequent linguistic term B_q has a parameterized membership function.

There are many issues to be discussed in future studies. One issue is the definition of the compatibility grade $\mu_{A_q}(\tilde{x})$ of the fuzzy input vector $\tilde{x}$ with the antecedent part A_q of the linguistic rule R_q. Another issue is rule generation for modeling problems of fuzzy mappings.

14.2.3 Fuzzified Takagi–Sugeno Models

The fuzzified Takagi–Sugeno model in (14.19)–(14.20) for modeling problems of nonlinear fuzzy number-valued functions can be further extended to handle fuzzy mappings. Fuzzy rules of the form in (14.19) are further fuzzified as

Rule R_q: If $\tilde{x}_1$ is A_{q1} and $\dots$ and $\tilde{x}_n$ is A_{qn}

$$\text{then } \tilde{y}_q(\tilde{x}) = \tilde{b}_{q0} + \tilde{b}_{q1} \cdot \tilde{x}_1 + \dots + \tilde{b}_{qn} \cdot \tilde{x}_n. \qquad (14.38)$$

As a result, the fuzzy reasoning method in (14.20) is modified as

$$\tilde{y}(\tilde{x}) = \frac{\sum\limits_{R_q \in S} \mu_{A_q}(\tilde{x}) \cdot \tilde{y}_q(\tilde{x})}{\sum\limits_{R_q \in S} \mu_{A_q}(\tilde{x})}. \qquad (14.39)$$

Since the membership function of the fuzzy output from the consequent linear fuzzy model $\tilde{y}_q(\tilde{x})$ cannot be represented in a parameterized form, the calculation of the fuzzy output $\tilde{y}(\tilde{x})$ from the fuzzy rule-based system is numerically performed on level sets of the fuzzy input vector $\tilde{x}$.

14.2.4 Fuzzified Neural Networks

The fuzzified neural network with the non-fuzzy input vector x in the previous section can be extended to the case of the fuzzy input vector $\tilde{x} = (\tilde{x}_1, \dots, \tilde{x}_n)$ as

$$\text{Input units:} \quad \tilde{o}_{qi} = \tilde{x}_{qi}, \; i = 1, 2, \dots, n. \qquad (14.40)$$

$$\text{Hidden units:} \quad \tilde{o}_{qj} = f(\widetilde{net}_{qj}), \; j = 1, 2, \dots, n_H, \qquad (14.41)$$

$$\widetilde{net}_{qj} = \sum_{i=1}^{n} \tilde{w}_{ji} \cdot \tilde{o}_{qi} + \tilde{\theta}_j. \qquad (14.42)$$

$$\text{Output unit:} \quad \tilde{o}_q = f(\widetilde{net}_q), \qquad (14.43)$$

$$\widetilde{net}_q = \sum_{j=1}^{n_H} \tilde{w}_j \cdot \tilde{o}_{qj} + \tilde{\theta}. \qquad (14.44)$$

Fuzzified neural networks of this type are trained using input–output pairs of fuzzy inputs and fuzzy outputs. A learning method similar to the back-propagation algorithm was proposed in [64] for adjusting the fuzzy connection weights and fuzzy biases. The learning was performed by tuning each parameter of the parameterized membership function of each fuzzy connection weight and bias. The learning of fuzzified neural networks was numerically examined in [77] where linguistic rules were used as training data.

14.3 Fuzzy Classification

In this section, we explain fuzzy classification by multi-layer feedforward neural networks. In addition to fuzzy classification of fuzzy patterns, we also explain fuzzy classification of non-fuzzy and interval patterns. For an n-dimensional pattern classification problem with M classes, we use a three-layer feedforward neural network with n input units and M output units.

14.3.1 Fuzzy Classification of Non-Fuzzy Patterns

A non-fuzzy input vector $x_p = (x_{p1}, \ldots, x_{pn})$ is usually classified by finding a single winner output unit with the maximum output value in the corresponding output vector $o_p = (o_{p1}, \ldots, o_{pM})$ from the trained neural network. Each output value o_{pk} can be interpreted as the grade that the input vector x_p belongs to each class. When only a single element of the output vector o_p is approximately equal to 1 and all the other $(M-1)$ elements are approximately equal to 0, we may have high confidence about the classification result of the input vector x_p. On the other hand, the confidence about the classification result is low when no element is close to 1. The confidence is also low when many elements are close to 1.

Two rejection methods examined in Cordella et al. [22] correspond to the above intuitive discussions on the confidence about the classification result of the input vector x_p. One rejection method is to introduce a minimum requirement $\beta_{\max}$ on the maximum output value. That is, the classification of x_p is rejected when the following condition does not hold:

$$o_{pk^*} = \max\{o_{p1}, o_{p2}, \ldots, o_{pk}\} \geq \beta_{\max}. \tag{14.45}$$

The other method is to introduce a minimum requirement $\beta_{\text{difference}}$ on the difference between the largest and second largest output values. That is, the classification of x_p is rejected when the following condition does not hold:

$$o_{pk^*} - o_{pk^{**}} \geq \beta_{\text{difference}}, \tag{14.46}$$

where o_{pk^*} is the largest output value and $o_{pk^{**}}$ is the second largest output value. When we use a rejection method such as (14.45) and (14.46), the pattern space is divided into $(M+1)$ subspaces that correspond to M decision regions and a single rejection region.

These two rejection methods are based on standard feedforward neural networks. Special neural network structures and/or learning algorithms were also proposed for performing pattern classification with a reject option [8, 62, 142]. We explain a simple modification of the back-propagation algorithm by Ishibuchi et al. [62] using the two-class pattern classification problem in Fig. 14.8 where 21 patterns are given in the unit interval [0, 1]. We trained a three-layer feedforward neural network with a single input unit, five hidden units, and a single output unit. The target t_p was specified for the input x_p as

$$t_p = \begin{cases} 1, & \text{if } x_p \text{ is from Class 1,} \\ 0, & \text{if } x_p \text{ is from Class 2.} \end{cases} \tag{14.47}$$

The standard back-propagation algorithm was used for the learning of the neural network using the learning rate 0.25 and the momentum constant 0.9. Figure 14.8 shows the output from the trained neural network after 1000 epochs. From this figure, we can see that the output is not close to 0 or 1 for the input in the overlap region [0.30, 0.65] of patterns from different classes. In this case, rejection methods may work well for identifying the overlap region. Learning results of neural networks strongly depend on parameter specifications such as the number of hidden units and the stopping condition. Figure 14.9 shows a simulation result after 50000 epochs using a three-layer feedforward neural network with 50 hidden units. In this case, rejection methods do not work well for identifying the overlap region of patterns from different classes.

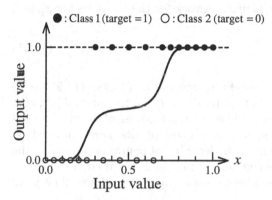

Fig. 14.8. A simulation result after 1000 epochs using a three-layer feedforward neural network with five hidden units

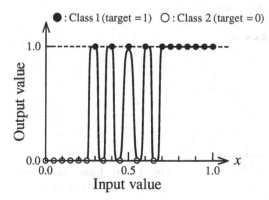

Fig. 14.9. A simulation result after 50000 epochs using a three-layer feedforward neural network with 50 hidden units

Ishibuchi et al. [62] slightly modified the back-propagation algorithm for determining the lower limit o_p^L and the upper limit o_p^U of the output o_p, which are illustrated in Fig. 14.10. When they determine the lower limit o_p^L, they use the following cost function in the learning of a neural network:

$$e_p^L = \frac{1}{2} \cdot \omega_p^L \cdot (t_p - o_p^L)^2, \tag{14.48}$$

where o_p^L is the output from the neural network for the input vector $\boldsymbol{x}_p$, and ω_p^L is specified using a positive small real number ε as

$$\omega_p^L = \begin{cases} \varepsilon, & \text{if } t_p = 1, \\ 1, & \text{if } t_p = 0. \end{cases} \tag{14.49}$$

On the other hand, they use the following cost function in the learning of another neural network when we determine the upper limit o_p^U:

$$e_p^U = \frac{1}{2} \cdot \omega_p^U \cdot (t_p - o_p^U)^2, \tag{14.50}$$

where o_p^U is the output from the neural network for the input vector $\boldsymbol{x}_p$ and

$$\omega_p^U = \begin{cases} 1, & \text{if } t_p = 1, \\ \varepsilon, & \text{if } t_p = 0. \end{cases} \tag{14.51}$$

The basic idea of the above weighting scheme in (14.48)–(14.51) is to approximately include the input–output pair $(\boldsymbol{x}_p, t_p)$ in the interval $[o_p^L, o_p^U]$. We have already explained the same idea for the learning of fuzzified neural networks in Sect. 14.1. It was shown that good results were obtained by gradually decreasing ε from 1 during the learning of neural networks. In the above explanation, two independent neural networks are used to represent the interval $[o_p^L, o_p^U]$. It is also possible to use a single interval neural network [86].

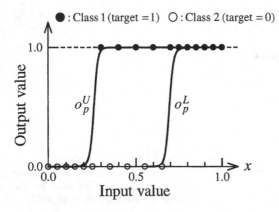

Fig. 14.10. Lower and upper limits of the output o_p

As shown in Fig. 14.10, the output interval $[o_p^L, o_p^U]$ in the overlap region of patterns from different classes is approximately equal to $[0, 1]$. Thus we can use the following decision rules with a rejection option for two-class pattern classification problems:

If $\dfrac{1}{2}(o_p^L + o_p^U) \geq 0.75$ then $\boldsymbol{x}_p$ is Class 1, $\qquad\qquad$ (14.52)

If $\dfrac{1}{2}(o_p^L + o_p^U) \leq 0.25$ then $\boldsymbol{x}_p$ is Class 2, $\qquad\qquad$ (14.53)

If $0.25 < \dfrac{1}{2}(o_p^L + o_p^U) < 0.75$

$\qquad\qquad$ then the classification of $\boldsymbol{x}_p$ is rejected,   (14.54)

where 0.25 and 0.75 are user-definable threshold values (we can use other combinations of threshold values, e.g., 0.1 and 0.9, 0.4 and 0.6, etc.). These decision rules can be easily extended to a more general case with multiple classes.

14.3.2 Fuzzy Classification of Interval Patterns

We have already explained the learning of standard feedforward neural networks using interval input vectors for pattern classification problems in Sect. 12.3. We have also explained the classification of interval input vectors using trained neural networks. Let $\boldsymbol{O}_p = (O_{p1}, \ldots, O_{pM})$ be the interval output vector from a trained neural network for the interval input vector $\boldsymbol{X}_p = (X_{p1}, \ldots, X_{pn})$. When the following relation holds for Class z, the interval input vector $\boldsymbol{X}_p$ is classified as Class z:

If $^\forall k\ (k \neq z), o_{pk}^U < o_{pz}^L$, then $\boldsymbol{X}_p$ is Class z, $\qquad\qquad$ (14.55)

where o_{pk}^U is the upper limit of the interval output O_{pk} from the k-th output unit, and o_{pz}^L is the lower limit of the interval output O_{pz} from the z-th output unit. If there is no class satisfying this relation, the classification of $\boldsymbol{X}_p$ is rejected.

When the classification of $\boldsymbol{X}_p$ is rejected, we can specify a set of possible classes using the following decision rule.

If $^\exists k, o_{pz}^U < o_{pk}^L$, then $\boldsymbol{X}_p$ is not Class z. $\qquad\qquad$ (14.56)

For example, let us consider the interval vector $\boldsymbol{X}_p$ in Fig. 14.11 where the classification boundary is also shown using a trained neural network. The corresponding output vector from the trained neural network is shown in Fig. 14.12. Since no class satisfies the condition in (14.55), the classification of $\boldsymbol{X}_p$ is rejected. The set of possible classes is identified as Class 2 and Class 3 because we know from the decision rule in (14.56) that $\boldsymbol{X}_p$ is not Class 1.

14.3.3 Fuzzy Classification of Fuzzy Patterns

We have already explained the learning of standard feedforward neural networks using linguistic input vectors for pattern classification problems in Sect. 12.2. We have also explained the classification of linguistic input vectors using trained neural networks in Sect. 13.3. Let $\tilde{\boldsymbol{o}}_p = (\tilde{o}_{p1}, \ldots, \tilde{o}_{pM})$ be

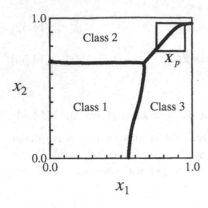

Fig. 14.11. Interval vector and classification boundary

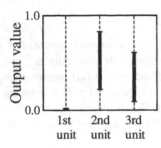

Fig. 14.12. Interval output vector from the trained neural network with three output units

the fuzzy output vector from a trained neural network for the fuzzy input vector $\tilde{x}_p = (\tilde{x}_{p1}, \ldots, \tilde{x}_{pn})$. The classification of the fuzzy input vector $\tilde{x}_p$ is performed using the procedure in Sect. 13.3.4. The classification procedure is based on the following decision rule on the h-level set of the fuzzy input vector $\tilde{x}_p$:

$$\text{If } {}^{\forall}k(k \neq z), [\tilde{o}_{pk}]_h^U < [\tilde{o}_{pz}]_h^L, \text{ then } [\tilde{x}_p]_h \text{ is Class } z, \qquad (14.57)$$

where $[\tilde{o}_{pk}]_h^U$ is the upper limit of the h-level set $[\tilde{o}_{pk}]_h$ of the fuzzy output $\tilde{o}_{pk}$ from the k-th output unit, and $[\tilde{o}_{pz}]_h^L$ is the lower limit of the h-level set $[\tilde{o}_{pz}]_h$ of the fuzzy output $\tilde{o}_{pz}$ from the z-th output unit. The confidence of the classification is specified as $(1 - h^*)$ where h^* is the minimum level for which (14.57) holds. By introducing the minimum requirement for the confidence, we can reject the classification of patterns with low confidence.

14.3.4 Effect of Fuzzification of Input Patterns

It was suggested in [74] that fuzzification of training patterns leads to higher generalization ability of trained neural networks in some cases. Let us assume that we have m training patterns $x_p = (x_{p1}, \ldots, x_{pn})$, $p = 1, 2, \ldots, m$. Each attribute value x_{pi} is fuzzified as a symmetric triangular fuzzy number $\tilde{x}_{pi}$ as shown in Fig. 14.13 where $\lambda_{\text{training}}$ is a small real number that controls the amount of the attached fuzziness. Figure 14.14 demonstrates the effect of fuzzification of training patterns. Non-fuzzy training patterns were used in the learning of a three-layer feedforward neural network by the back-propagation algorithm in Fig. 14.14 (a). On the other hand, fuzzified training patterns with $\lambda_{\text{training}} = 0.1$ were used in Fig. 14.14 (b). The 0-level sets of the fuzzified training patterns are depicted by squares in Fig. 14.14 (b) for four patterns. It should be noted that not only the four patterns but also the other training patterns in Fig. 14.14 (b) were fuzzified in the learning of the neural network. Fuzzification can also be used in the classification phase of new patterns by trained neural networks.

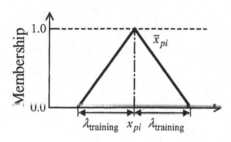

Fig. 14.13. Fuzzification of each input value x_{pi} to a symmetric triangular fuzzy number $\tilde{x}_{pi}$

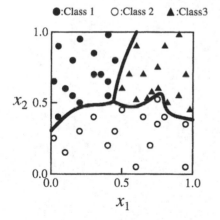

(a) Learning from non-fuzzy patterns

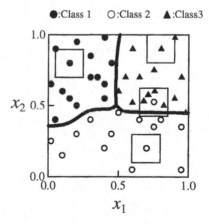

(b) Learning from fuzzified patterns

Fig. 14.14. Comparison between the learning from non-fuzzy training patterns and the learning from fuzzified training patterns

References

1. Abe, S., Lan, M.-S. (1995): A Method for Fuzzy Rules Extraction Directly from Numerical Data and Its Application to Pattern Classification. IEEE Transactions on Fuzzy Systems, $3(1)$, 18–28
2. Abe, S., Lan, M.-S., Thawonmas, R. (1996): Tuning of a Fuzzy Classifier Derived from Data. International J of Approximate Reasoning, $14(1)$, 1–24
3. Abe, S., Thawonmas, R. (1997): A Fuzzy Classifier with Ellipsoidal Regions. IEEE Transactions on Fuzzy Systems, $5(3)$, 358–368
4. Agrawal, R., Mannila, H., Srikant, R., Toivonen, H., Verkamo, A.I. (1996): Fast Discovery of Association Rules. In Fayyad, U.M., Piatetsky-Shapiro, G., Smyth, P., Uthurusamy, R., eds., Advances in Knowledge Discovery & Data Mining, 307–328. AAAI Press, Menlo Park
5. Agrawal, R., Srikant, R. (1994): Fast Algorithms for Mining Association Rules. In Proceedings of 20th International Conferencerence on Very Large Data Bases, 487–499. Expanded version is available as IBM Research Report RJ9839
6. Alefeld, G., Herzberger, J. (1983): Introduction to Interval Computations. Academic Press, New York
7. Andrews, R., Diederich, J., Tickele, A.B. (1995): Survey and Critique of Techniques for Extracting Rules from Trained Artificial Neural Networks. Knowledge-Based Systems, $8(6)$, 373–389
8. Archer, N.P., Wang, S. (1991): Fuzzy Set Representation of Neural Network Classification Boundary. IEEE Transactions on Systems, Man, and Cybernetics, $21(4)$, 735–742
9. Bacchus, F., Grove, A.J., Halpern, J.Y., Koller, D. (1996): From Statistical Knowledge Bases to Degrees of Belief. Artificial Intelligence, $87(1\text{-}2)$, 75–143
10. Berenji, H.R., Khedkar, P. (1992): Learning and Tuning Fuzzy Controllers Through Reinforcements. IEEE Tran on Neural Networks, $3(5)$, 724–740
11. Bien, Z., Yu, W. (1995): Extracting Core Information from Inconsistent Fuzzy Control Rules. Fuzzy Sets and Systems, $71(1)$, 95–111
12. Blum, A.L., Langley, P. (1997): Selection of Relevant Features and Examples in Machine Learning. Artificial Intelligence, $97(1\text{-}2)$, 245–271
13. Bonarini, A. (1999): Comparing Reinforcement Learning Algorithms Applied to Crisp and Fuzzy Learning Classifier Systems. In Proceedings of the Genetic and Evolutionary Computation Conferencerence, 52–67
14. Booker, L.B., Goldberg, D.E., Holland, J.H. (1989): Classifier Systems and Genetic Algorithms. Artificial Intelligence, $40(1\text{-}3)$, 235–282
15. Box, G.E.P., Jenkins, G.M. (1970): Time Series Analysis: Forecasting and Control. Holden-Day, San Francisco
16. Buckley, J.J., Hayashi, Y. (1994): Fuzzy Neural Networks: a Survey. Fuzzy Sets and Systems, $66(1)$, 1–13
17. Carse, B., Fogarty, T.C., Munro, A. (1996): Evolving Fuzzy Rule Based Controllers Using Genetic Algorithms. Fuzzy Sets and Systems, $80(3)$, 273–293

18. Casillas, J., Cordon, O., Herrera, F., Magdalena, L., eds. (2003): Accuracy Improvements in Linguistic Fuzzy Modeling. Physica-Verlag, Heidelberg
19. Casillas, J., Cordon, O., Herrera, F., Magdalena, L., eds. (2003): Interpretabiity Issues in Fuzzy Modeling. Physica-Verlag, Heidelberg
20. Castillo, L., Gonzalez, A., Perez, P. (2001): Including a Simplicity Criterion in the Selection of the Best Rule in a Genetic Fuzzy Learning Algorithm. Fuzzy Sets and Systems, 120(vol 2), 309–321
21. Coello Coello, C.A., van Veldhuizen, D.A., Lamont, G.B. (2002): Evolutionary Algorithms for Solving Multi-Objective Problems. Kluwer Academic Publishers, Boston
22. Cordella, L.P., Stefano, C. De, Tortorella, F., Vento, M. (1995): A Method for Improving Classification Reliability of Multilayer Perceptrons. IEEE Transactions on Neural Networks, 6(5), 1140–1147
23. Cordon, O., Herrera, F. (2000): A Proposal for Improving the Accuracy of Linguistic Modeling. IEEE Transactions on Fuzzy Systems, 8(3), 335–344
24. Cordón, O., Herrera, F., Hoffmann, F., Magdalena, L. (2001): Genetic Fuzzy Systems: Evolutionary Tuning and Learning of Fuzzy Knowledge Bases. World Scientific Publishers, Singapore
25. Cordon, O., Herrera, F., Peregrin, A. (1997): Applicability of the Fuzzy Operations in the Design of Fuzzy Logic Controllers. Fuzzy Sets and Systems, 86, 15–41
26. Cordon, O., Jesus, M.J. Del, Herrera, F. (1999): A Proposal on Reasoning Methods in Fuzzy Rule-based Classification Systems. International Journal of Approximate Reasoning, 20, 21–45
27. Cun, Y. Le, Denker, J.S., Solla, S.A. (1990): Optimal Brain Damage. In Touretzky, D.S., ed., Advances in Neural Information Proceedingsssing Systems 2, 598–605. Morgan Kaufmann, San Mateo
28. Deb, K. (2001): Multi-Objective Optimization Using Evolutionary Algorithms. John Wiley & Sons, Chichester
29. Deb, K., Pratap, A., Agrawal, S., Meyarivan, T. (2002): A Fast and Elitist Multiobjective Genetic Algorithm: NSGA-II. IEEE Transactions on Evolutionary Computation, 6(2), 182–197
30. Dougherty, J., Kohavi, R., Sahami, M. (1995): Supervised and Unsupervised Discretization of Continuous Features. In Proceedings of 12th International Conferencerence on Machine Learning, 194–202
31. Dubois, D., Lang, J., Prade, H. (1994): Automated Reasoning Using Possibilistic Logic: Semantics, Brief Revision, and Variable Certainty Weights. IEEE Transactions on Knowledge and Data Engineering, 6(1), 64–71
32. Dubois, D., Lang, J., Prade, H. (1994): Possibilistic Logic. In Gabbay, D.M., Hogger, C.J., Robinson, J.A., eds., Handbook of Logic in Artificial Intelligence and Logic Programming, Volume 3: Nonmonotonic Reasoning and Uncertain Reasoning, 439–513. Oxford University Press, Oxford
33. Dubois, D., Prade, H. (1983): Ranking Fuzzy Numbers in the Setting of Possibility theory. Information Sciences, 30(3), 183–224
34. Dubois, D., Prade, H. (1987): The Principle of Minimum Specificity as a Basis for Evidential Reasoning. In Bouchon, B., Yager, R.R., eds., Uncertainty in Knowledge Based Systems (Lecture Notes in Computer Science 286), 75–84. Springer-Verlag, Berlin
35. Dubois, D., Prade, H. (1988): Default Reasoning and Possibility Theory. Artificial Intelligence, 35(2), 243–257
36. Dubois, D., Prade, H. (1988): Possibility theory. Plenum Press, New York
37. Dubois, D., Prade, H. (1996): What Are Fuzzy Rules and How To Use Them. Fuzzy Sets and Systems, 84(2), 169–185

38. Duch, W., Adamczak, R., Grabczewski, K. (2001): A New Methodology of Extraction Optimization and Application of Crisp and Fuzzy Logical Rules. IEEE Transactions on Neural Networks, 12(2), 277–306

39. Dunyak, J.P., Wunsch, D. (1999): Fuzzy Number Neural Networks. Fuzzy Sets and Systems, 108(1), 49–58

40. Dunyak, J.P., Wunsch, D. (2000): Fuzzy Regression by Fuzzy Number Neural Networks. Fuzzy Sets and Systems, 112(3), 371–380

41. Elomaa, T., Rousu, J. (1999): General and Efficient Multisplitting of Numerical Attributes. Machine Learning, 36(3), 201–244

42. Emami, M.R., Turksen, I.B., Goldenberg, A.A. (1998): Development of a Systematic Methodology of Fuzzy Logic Modeling. IEEE Transactions on Fuzzy Systems, 6(3), 346–361

43. Emami, M.R., Turksen, I.B., Goldenberg, A.A. (1998): Development of a Systematic Methodology of Fuzzy Logic Modeling. IEEE Transactionsctions on Fuzzy Systems, 6(3), 346–361

44. Emami, M.R., Turksen, I.B., Goldenberg, A.A. (1999): A Unified Parameterized Formulation of Reasoning in Fuzzy Modeling and Control. Fuzzy Sets and Systems, 108, 59–81

45. Fayyad, U.M., Irani, K.B. (1993): Multi-interval Discretization of Continuous-valued Attributes for Classification Learning. In Proceedings of 13th International Joint Conferenceorence on Artificial Intelligence, 1022–1027

46. Fu, L. (1994): Rule Generation from Neural Networks. IEEE Transactions on Systems, Man, and Cybernetics, 24(8), 1114–1124

47. Funahashi, K. (1989): On the Approximate Realization of Continuous Mappings by Neural Networks. Neural Networks, 2, 183–192

48. Goldberg, D.E. (1989): Genetic Algorithms in Search Optimization and Machine Learning. Addison-Wesley, Reading, MA

49. Goldszmidt, M., Pearl, J. (1996): Qualitative Probabilities for Default Reasoning, Belief Revision and Causal Modeling. Artificial Intelligence, 84(1-2), 57–112

50. Halgamuge, S.K., Glesner, M. (1994): Neural Networks in Designing Fuzzy Systems for Real World Applications. Fuzzy Sets and Systems, 65(1), 1–12

51. Hayashi, Y. (1991): A Neural Expert System with Automated Extraction of Fuzzy If-Then Rules and Its Application to Medical Diagnosis. In Lippmann, R.P., Moody, J.E., Touretzky, D.S., eds., Advances in Neural Information Proceedingsssing Systems 3, 578–584. Morgan Kaufmann, San Mateo

52. Hayashi, Y., Buckley, J.J., Czogala, E. (1993): Fuzzy Neural Network with Fuzzy Signals and Weights. International Journal of Intelligent Systems, 8(4), 527–537

53. Herrera, F., Lozano, M., Verdegay, J.L. (1995): Tuning Fuzzy Logic Controllers by Genetic Algorithms. International Journal of Approximate Reasoning, 12(3/4), 299–315

54. Herrera, F., Verdegay, J.L., eds. (1996): Genetic Algorithms and Soft Computing. Physica-Verlag, Heidelberg

55. Holland, J.H. (1975): Adaptation in Natural and Artificial Systems. University of Michigan Press, Ann Arbor

56. Holte, R.C. (1993): Very Simple Classification Rules Perform Well on Most Commonly Used Dataset. Machine Learning, 11, 63–91

57. Hong, T.-P., Kuo, C.-S., Chi, S.-C. (2001): Trade-off Between Computation Time and Number of Rules for Fuzzy Mining from Quantitative Data. International Journal of Uncertainty Fuzziness and Knowledge-Based Systems, 9(5), 587–604

58. Horikawa, S., Furuhashi, T., Uchikawa, Y. (1992): On Fuzzy Modeling Using Fuzzy Neural Networks with the Back-propagation Algorithm. IEEE Transactions on Neural Networks, **3**(5), 801–806

59. Hornik, K. (1989): Multilayer Feedforward Networks Are Universal Approximators. Neural Networks, **2**, 359–366

60. Ichihashi, H., Watanabe, T. (1990): Learning Control by Fuzzy Models Using a Simplified Fuzzy Reasoning. Journal of Japan Society for Fuzzy theory and Systems, **2**(3), 429–437

61. Ishibuchi, H. (1999): A Fuzzy Reasoning Method for Handling Fuzzy Rules with Different Specificity Levels. In Proceedings of 18th International Conferencerence of the North American Fuzzy Information Proceedingsssing Society, 110–114

62. Ishibuchi, H., Fujioka, R., Tanaka, H. (1992): Possibility and Necessity Pattern Classification Using Neural Networks. Fuzzy Sets and Systems, **48**(3), 331–340

63. Ishibuchi, H., Fujioka, R., Tanaka, H. (1993): Neural Networks that Learn from Fuzzy If-Then Rules. IEEE Transactions on Fuzzy Systems, **1**(2), 85–97

64. Ishibuchi, H., Morioka, K., Turksen, I.B. (1995): Learning by Fuzzified Neural Networks. International Journal of Approximate Reasoning, **13**(4), 327–358

65. Ishibuchi, H., Murata, T., Turksen, I.B. (1997): Single-objective and Two-objective Genetic Algorithms for Selecting Linguistic Rules for Pattern Classification Problems. Fuzzy Sets and Systems, **89**(2), 135–149

66. Ishibuchi, H., Nakashima, T. (1999): Improving the Performance of Fuzzy Classifier Systems for Pattern Classification Problems with Continuous Attributes. IEEE Transactions on Industrial Electronics, **46**(6), 157–168

67. Ishibuchi, H., Nakashima, T. (2001): Effect of Rule Weights in Fuzzy Rule-based Classification Systems. IEEE Transactions on Fuzzy Systems, **9**(4), 506–515

68. Ishibuchi, H., Nakashima, T., Morisawa, T. (1999): Voting in Fuzzy Rule-based Systems for Pattern Classification Problems. Fuzzy Sets and Systems, **103**(2), 223–238

69. Ishibuchi, H., Nakashima, T., Murata, T. (1995): A Fuzzy Classifier System that Generates Fuzzy If-Then Rules for Pattern Classification Problems. In Proceedings of 2nd IEEE International Conferencerence on Evolutionary Computation, 759–764

70. Ishibuchi, H., Nakashima, T., Murata, T. (1999): Performance Evaluation of Fuzzy Classifier Systems for Multi-dimensional Pattern Classification Problems. IEEE Transactions on Systems, Man, and Cybernetics, **29**(5), 601–618

71. Ishibuchi, H., Nakashima, T., Murata, T. (2001): Three-objective Genetics-based Machine Learning for Linguistic Rule Extraction. Information Sciences, **136**(1-4), 109–133

72. Ishibuchi, H., Nii, M. (1996): Generating Fuzzy If-Then Rules from Trained Neural Networks: Linguistic Analysis of Neural Networks. In Proceedings of 1996 IEEE International Conferencerence on Neural Networks, 1133–1138

73. Ishibuchi, H., Nii, M. (1998): Fuzzification of Input Vectors for Improving the Generalization Ability of Neural Networks. In Proceedings of 1998 IEEE International Conferencerence on Fuzzy Systems, 1153–1158

74. Ishibuchi, H., Nii, M. (2000): Neural Networks for Soft Decision Making. Fuzzy Sets and Systems, **115**(1), 121–140

75. Ishibuchi, H., Nii, M. (2001): Fuzzy Regression Using Asymmetric Fuzzy Coefficients and Fuzzified Neural Networks. Fuzzy Sets and Systems, **119**(2), 273–290

76. Ishibuchi, H., Nii, M. (2001): Minimizing the Measurement Cost in the Classification of New Samples by Neural-network-based Classifiers. In Pal, N.R., ed.,

Pattern Recognition in Soft Computing Paradigm, 225–248. World Scientific Publishers, Singapore

77. Ishibuchi, H., Nii, M. (2001): Numerical Analysis of the Learning of Fuzzified Neural Networks from Fuzzy If-Then Rules. Fuzzy Sets and Systems, 120(2), 281–307

78. Ishibuchi, H., Nii, M., Oh, C.H. (1999): Approximate Realization of Fuzzy Mappings by Regression Models, Neural Networks and Rule-based Systems. In Proceedings of 1999 IEEE International Conferencerence on Fuzzy Systems, 939–944

79. Ishibuchi, H., Nii, M., Tanaka, K. (1999): Subdivision Methods for Decreasing Excess Fuzziness of Fuzzy Arithmetic in Fuzzified Neural Networks. In Proceedings of 18th International Conference of the North American Fuzzy Information Processing Society, 448–452

80. Ishibuchi, H., Nii, M., Turksen, I.B. (1998): Bidirectional Bridge Between Neural Networks and Linguistic Knowledge: Linguistic Rule Extraction and Learning from Linguistic Rules. In Proceedings of 1998 IEEE International Conferencerence on Fuzzy Systems, 1112–1117

81. Ishibuchi, H., Nozaki, K., Tanaka, H. (1992): Distributed Representation of Fuzzy Rules and Its Application to Pattern Classification. Fuzzy Sets and Systems, 52(1), 21–32

82. Ishibuchi, H., Nozaki, K., Tanaka, H., Hosaka, Y., Matsuda, M (1994): Empirical Study on Learning in Fuzzy Systems by Rice Taste Analysis. Fuzzy Sets and Systems, 64(2), 129–144

83. Ishibuchi, H., Nozaki, K., Yamamoto, N., Tanaka, H. (1994): Construction of Fuzzy Classification Systems with Rectangular Fuzzy Rules Using Genetic Algorithms. Fuzzy Sets and Systems, 65(2/3), 237–253

84. Ishibuchi, H., Nozaki, K., Yamamoto, N., Tanaka, H. (1995): Selecting Fuzzy If-Then Rules for Classification Problems Using Genetic Algorithms. IEEE Transactions on Fuzzy Systems, 3(3), 260–270

85. Ishibuchi, H., Takeuchi, D., Nakashima, T. (2001): GA-based Approaches to Linguistic Modeling of Nonlinear Functions. In Proceedings of 9th IFSA World Congress and 20th NAFIPS International Conferencerence, 1229–1234

86. Ishibuchi, H., Tanaka, H., Okada, H. (1993): An Architecture of Neural Networks with Interval Weights and Its Application to Fuzzy Regression Analysis. Fuzzy Sets and Systems, 57(1), 27–39

87. Ishibuchi, H., Tanaka, H., Okada, H. (1994): Interpolation of Fuzzy If-Then Rules by Neural Networks. International Journal of Approximate Reasoning, 10(1), 3–27

88. Ishibuchi, H., Yamamoto, T. (2003): Effects of Three-Objective Genetic Rule Selection on the Generalization Ability of Fuzzy Rule-Based Systems. In Proceedings of Second International Conferencerence on Evolutionary Multi-Criterion Optimization, 608–622

89. Ishibuchi, H., Yamamoto, T. (2003): Evolutionary Multiobjective Optimization for Generating an Ensemble of Fuzzy Rule-Based Classifiers. In Proceedings of 2003 Genetic and Evolutionary Computation Conferencerence, 1077–1088

90. Ishibuchi, H., Yamamoto, T. (2003): Interpretability Issues in Fuzzy Genetics-Based Machine Learning for Linguistic Modelling. In Lecture Notes in Artificial Intelligence, 2873, 209–228. Springer-Verlag, Berlin

91. Ishibuchi, H., Yamamoto, T. (2003): Tradeoff Between the Number of Fuzzy Rules and Their Classification Performance. In Casillas, J., Cordon, O., Herrera, F., Magdalena, L., eds., Accuracy Improvements in Linguistic Fuzzy Modeling, 72–99. Physica-Verlag, Heidelberg

92. Ishibuchi, H., Yamamoto, T. (2004): An Approach to Fuzzy Default Reasoning for Function Approximation. Soft Computing Journal

93. Ishibuchi, H., Yamamoto, T. (2004): Comparison of Heuristic Criteria for Fuzzy Rule Selection in Classification Problems. Fuzzy Optimization and Decision Making, 3(2), 119–139

94. Ishibuchi, H., Yamamoto, T. (2004): Fuzzy Rule Selection by Multi-Objective Genetic Local Search Algorithms and Rule Evaluation Measures in Data Mining. Fuzzy Sets and Systems, 141(1), 59–88

95. Ishibuchi, H., Yamamoto, T., Nakashima, T. (2001): Fuzzy Data Mining: Effect of Fuzzy Discretization. In Proceedings of 1st IEEE International Conferencerence on Data Mining, 241–248

96. Ishigami, H., Fukuda, T., Shibata, T., Arai, F. (1995): Structure Optimization of Fuzzy Neural Network by Genetic Algorithm. Fuzzy Sets and Systems, 71(3), 257–264

97. Ishikawa, M. (1996): Structural Learning with Forgetting. Neural Networks, 9(3), 509–521

98. Jagielska, I., Matthews, C., Whitfort, T. (1999): An Investigation into the Application of Neural Networks Fuzzy Logic Genetic Algorithms and Rough Sets to Automated Knowledge Acquisition for Classification Problems. Neurocomputing, 24, 37–54

99. Jang, J.-S.R. (1993): ANFIS: Adaptive-network-based Fuzzy Inference System. IEEE Transactions on Systems, Man, and Cybernetics, 23(3), 665–685

100. Janikow, C.Z. (1998): Fuzzy Decision Trees: Issues and Methods. IEEE Transactions on Systems, Man, and Cybernetics, 28(1), 1–14

101. Jin, Y. (2000): Fuzzy Modeling of High-dimensional Systems: Complexity Reduction and Interpretability Improvement. IEEE Transactions on Fuzzy Systems, 8(2), 212–221

102. Karr, C.L. (1991): Design of an Adaptive Fuzzy Logic Controller Using a Genetic Algorithm. In Proceedings of 4th International Conferenceon Genetic Algorithms, 450–457

103. Karr, C.L., Gentry, E.J. (1993): Fuzzy Control of PH Using Genetic Algorithms. IEEE Transactions on Fuzzy Systems, 1(1), 46–53

104. Kasabov, N.K. (2001): On-line Learning Reasoning Rule Extraction and Aggregation in Locally Optimized Evolving Fuzzy Neural Networks. Neurocomputing, 41(1), 25–45

105. Kasabov, N.K., Kim, J., Kozma, R. (1998): A Fuzzy Neural Network for Knowledge Acquisition in Complex Time Series. Control and Cybernetics, 27(4), 593–611

106. Kaufmann, A., Gupta, M.M. (1985): Introduction to Fuzzy Arithmetic. Van Nostrand Reinhold, New York

107. Keller, J.M., Tahani, H. (1992): Backpropagation Neural Networks for Fuzzy Logic. Information Sciences, 62(3), 205–221

108. Keller, J.M., Yager, R.R., Tahani, H. (1992): Neural Network Implementation of Fuzzy Logic. Fuzzy Sets and Systems, 45(1), 1–12

109. Kim, E., Park, M., Ji, S., Park, M. (1997): A New Approach to Fuzzy Modeling. IEEE Transactions on Fuzzy Systems, 5(3), 328–337

110. Kim, E., Park, M., Ji, S., Park, M. (1997): A New Approach to Fuzzy Modeling. IEEE Transactionsctions on Fuzzy Systems, 5(3), 328–337

111. Kim, E., Park, M., Kim, S., Park, M. (1998): A Transactionsormed Input-domain Approach to Fuzzy Modeling. IEEE Transactions on Fuzzy Systems, 6(4), 596–604

112. Kim, E., Park, M., Kim, S., Park, M. (1998): A Transactionsormed Input-Domain Approach to Fuzzy Modeling. IEEE Transactionsctions on Fuzzy Systems, **6**(4), 596–604

113. Knorr, E.M., Ng, R.T. (1999): Finding Intentional Knowledge of Distance-based Outliers. In Proceedings International Conferencerence on Very Large Data Bases, 211–222

114. Knorr, E.M., Ng, R.T., Tucakov, V. (2000): Distance-based Outliers: Algorithms and Applications. International Journal on Very Large Data Bases, **8**(3), 237–253

115. Kohavi, R., John, G.H. (1997): Wrappers for Feature Subset Selection. Artificial Intelligence, **97**(1-2), 273–324

116. Kosko, B. (1994): Fuzzy Systems as Universal Approximators. IEEE Transactions on Computers, **43**(11), 1329–1332

117. Kuncheva, L.I. (2000): Fuzzy Classifier Design. Physica-Verlag, Heidelberg

118. Lee, C.C. (1990): Fuzzy Logic in Control Systems: Fuzzy Logic Controller Part I and Part II. IEEE Transactions on Systems, Man, and Cybernetics, **20**(2), 404–435

119. Leondes, C.T., ed. (1999): Fuzzy theory Systems: Techniques and Applications. Academic Press, San Diego

120. Lin, Y., III, G.A.Cunningham. (1995): A New Approach to Fuzzy-neural System Modelling. IEEE Transactions on Fuzzy Systems, **3**(2), 190–197

121. Lin, Y., III, G.A.Cunningham. (1995): A New Approach to Fuzzy-Neural System Modeling. IEEE Transactionsctions on Fuzzy Systems, **3**(2), 190–198

122. Liu, H., Motoda, H., eds. (1998): Feature Extraction, Construction and Selection: a Data Mining Perspective. Kluwer Academic Publishers, Boston

123. Liu, H., Motoda, H. (1998): Feature Selection for Knowledge Discovery and Data Mining. Kluwer Academic Publishers, Boston

124. Mamdani, E.H., Assilian, S. (1975): An Experiment in Linguistic Synthesis with a Fuzzy Logic Controller. International Journal of Man-Machine Studies, **7**(1), 1–13

125. Mees, W. (1999): Detection of Defects in a Fuzzy Knowledge Base. In Proceedings of 8th IEEE International Conferencerence on Fuzzy Systems, 204–209

126. Moore, R.E. (1979): Methods and Applications of Interval Analysis. SIAM, Philadelphia

127. Murata, T., Ishibuchi, H. (1995): MOGA: Multi-Objective Genetic Algorithms. In Proceedings of 2nd IEEE International Conferencerence on Evolutionary Computation, 289–294

128. Nauck, D., Kruse, R. (1997): A Neuro-fuzzy Method to Learn Fuzzy Classification Rules from Data. Fuzzy Sets and Systems, **89**(3), 277–288

129. Nauck, D., Kruse, R. (1998): How the Learning of Rule Weights Affects the Interpretability of Fuzzy Systems. In Proceedings of 7th IEEE International Conferencerence on Fuzzy Systems, 1235–1240

130. Nomura, H., Hayashi, I., Wakami, N. (1992): A Learning Method of Fuzzy Inference Rules by Descent Method. In Proceedings of 1st IEEE International Conferencerence on Fuzzy Systems, 203–210

131. Nomura, H., Hayashi, I., Wakami, N. (1992): A Self-tuning Method of Fuzzy Reasoning by Genetic Algorithm. In Proceedings of 1992 International Fuzzy Systems and Intelligent Control Conferencerence, 236–245

132. Nozaki, K., Ishibuchi, H., Tanaka, H. (1996): Adaptive Fuzzy Rule-based Classification Systems. IEEE Transactions on Fuzzy Systems, **4**(3), 238–250

133. Nozaki, K., Ishibuchi, H., Tanaka, H. (1997): A Simple but Powerful Heuristic Method for Generating Fuzzy Rules from Numerical Data. Fuzzy Sets and Systems, **86**(3), 251–270

134. Oliveira, V. De (1999): Semantic Constraints for Membership Function Optimization. IEEE Transactions on Systems, Man, and Cybernetics, 29(1), 128–138

135. Parodi, A., Bonelli, P. (1993): A New Approach to Fuzzy Classifier Systems. In Proceedings of 5th International Conferenceon Genetic Algorithm, 223–230

136. Pedrycz, W. (1984): An Identification Algorithm in Fuzzy Relational Systems. Fuzzy Sets and Systems, 13(2), 153–167

137. Pedrycz, W. (1984): An Identification Algorithm in Fuzzy Relational Systems. Fuzzy Sets and Systems, 13(2), 153–167

138. Pedrycz, W., ed. (1997): Fuzzy Evolutionary Computation. Kluwer Academic Publishers, Boston

139. Pedrycz, W., ed. (2001): Granular Computing. Physica-Verlag, Heidelberg

140. Pedrycz, W., Oliveira, V. De (1996): Optimization of Fuzzy Models. IEEE Transactions on Systems, Man, and Cybernetics, 26(4), 627–637

141. Poole, D. (1991): The Effect of Knowledge on Belief: Conditioning Specificity and the Lottery Paradox in Default Reasoning. Artificial Intelligence, 49(1-3), 281–307

142. Purushothaman, G., Karayiannis, N.B. (1997): Quantum Neural Networks (QNN's): Inherently Fuzzy Feedforward Neural Networks. IEEE Transactions on Neural Networks, 8(3), 679–693

143. Quinlan, J.R. (1993): C4.5: Programs for Machine Learning. Morgan Kaufmann Publishers, San Mateo

144. Reiter, R. (1980): A Logic for Default Reasoning. Artificial Intelligence, 13(1/2), 81–132

145. Roubos, H., Setnes, M. (2001): Compact and Transactionsarent Fuzzy Models and Classifiers Through Iterative Complexity Reduction. IEEE Transactions on Fuzzy Systems, 9(4), 516–524

146. Rumelhart, D.E., Hinton, G.E., Williams, R.J. (1986): Learning Internal Representations by Error Propagation. In Rumelhart, D.E., MaClelland, J.L., eds., Parallel Distributed Proceedingsssing, Volume 1, 318–362. MIT Press, Cambridge, MA

147. Russell, S.J., Norvig, P. (1995): Artificial Intelligence: a Modern Approach. Prentice Hall, Upper Saddle River

148. Sakawa, M., Yano, H. (1989): Multiobjective Fuzzy Linear Regression Analysis for Fuzzy Input-Output Data. Journal of Japan Society for Fuzzy theory and Systems, 1(1), 107–116 (in Japanese)

149. Sestito, S., Dillon, T. (1993): Knowledge Acquisition of Conjunctive Rules Using Multilayered Neural Networks. International Journal of Intelligent Systems, 8, 779–805

150. Setnes, M., Babuska, R., Verbruggen, B. (1998): Rule-based Modeling: Precision and Transactionsarency. IEEE Transactions on Systems, Man, and Cybernetics, 28(1), 165–169

151. Setnes, M., Roubos, H. (2000): GA-based Modeling and Classification: Complexity and Performance. IEEE Transactions on Fuzzy Systems, 8(5), 509–522

152. Shanahan, J.G. (2000): Soft Computing for Knowledge Discovery: Introducing Cartesian Granule Features. Kluwer Academic Publishers, Boston

153. Shimojima, K., Fukuda, T., Hasegawa, Y. (1995): Self-tuning Fuzzy Modeling with Adaptive Membership Function Rules and Hierarchical Structure Based on Genetic Algorithm. Fuzzy Sets and Systems, 71(3), 295–309

154. Simpson, P.K. (1992): Fuzzy Min-max Neural Networks - Part I: Classification. IEEE Transactions on Neural Networks, 3(5), 776–786

155. Smith, S.F. (1980): A Learning System Based on Genetic Algorithms. PhD dissertation, University of Pittsburgh, Pittsburgh

156. Sugeno, M. (1985): An Introductory Survey of Fuzzy Control. Information Sciences, **36**(1/2), 59–83
157. Sugeno, M., Tanaka, K. (1991): Successive Identification of a Fuzzy Model and Its Application to Prediction of a Complex System. Fuzzy Sets and Systems, **42**(3), 315–334
158. Sugeno, M., Tanaka, K. (1991): Successive Identification of a Fuzzy Model and Its Applications to Prediction of a Complex System. Fuzzy Sets and Systems, **42**(3), 315–334
159. Sugeno, M., Yasukawa, T. (1993): A Fuzzy-logic-based Approach to Qualitative Modeling. IEEE Transactions on Fuzzy Systems, **1**(1), 7–31
160. Suzuki, E., Kodratoff, Y. (1998): Discovery of Surprising Exception Rules Based on Intensity of Implication. In Zytkow, J.M., Quafafou, M., eds., Principles of Data Mining and Knowledge Discovery (PKDD). Springer-Verlag, Heidelberg
161. Suzuki, T., Furuhashi, T. (2001): Evolutionary Algorithm Based Fuzzy Modeling Using Conciseness Measure. In Proceedings of Joint IFSA and NAFIPS International Conferencerence, 1575–1580
162. Takagi, T., Sugeno, M. (1985): Fuzzy Identification of Systems and Its Applications to Modeling and Control. IEEE Transactions on Systems, Man, and Cybernetics, **15**(1), 116–132
163. Tanaka, H., Hayashi, I., Watada, J. (1989): Possibilistic Linear Regression Analysis for Fuzzy Data. European Journal of Operational Research, **40**(3), 389–396
164. Tanaka, H., Uejima, S., Asai, K. (1982): Linear Regression Analysis with Fuzzy Model. IEEE Transactions on Systems, Man, and Cybernetics, **12**(6), 903–907
165. Thrift, P. (1991): Fuzzy Logic Synthesis with Genetic Algorithms. In Proceedings of 4th International Conferenceon Genetic Algorithms, 509–513
166. Tong, P.M. (1980): The Evaluation of Fuzzy Models Derived from Experimental Data. Fuzzy Sets and Systems, **4**(1), 1–12
167. Towell, G., Shavlik, J.W. (1993): Extracting Refined Rules from Knowledge-based Neural Networks. Machine Learning, **13**, 71–101
168. Uehara, K., Fujise, M. (1990): Learning of Fuzzy-inference Criteria with Artificial Neural Network. In Proceedings of 1st International Conferencerence on Fuzzy Logic and Neural Networks: IIZUKA'90, 193–198
169. Umano, M., Fukunaka, S., Hatono, I., Tamura, H. (1997): Acquisition of Fuzzy Rules Using Fuzzy Neural Networks with Forgetting. In Proceedings of 1997 IEEE International Conferencerence on Neural Networks, 2369–2373
170. Valenzuela-Rendon, M. (1991): The Fuzzy Classifier System: a Classifier System for Continuously Varying Variables. In Proceedings of 4th International Conferenceon Genetic Algorithms, 346–353
171. Berg, J. van den, Kaymak, U., Bergh, W.-M. van den (2002): Fuzzy Classification Using Probability-Based Rule Weighting. In Proceedings International Conferencerence on Fuzzy Systems, 991–996
172. Viaene, S., Wets, G., Vanthienen, J. (2000): A Synthesis of Fuzzy Rule-based System Verification. Fuzzy Sets and Systems, **113**(2), 253–265
173. Wang, L., Langari, R. (1995): Building Sugeno-type Models Using Fuzzy Discretization and Orthogonal Parameter Estimation Techniques. IEEE Transactions on Fuzzy Systems, **3**(4), 454–458
174. Wang, L., Langari, R. (1995): Building Sugeno-type Models using Fuzzy Discretization and Orthogonal Parameter Estimation Techniques. IEEE Transactionsctions on Fuzzy Systems, **3**(4), 454–458

175. Wang, L.-X. (1992): Fuzzy Systems Are Universal Approximators. In Proceedings of 1st IEEE International Conferencerence on Fuzzy Systems, 1163–1170
176. Wang, L.X., Mendel, J.M. (1992): Generating Fuzzy Rules by Learning from Examples. IEEE Transactions on Systems, Man, and Cybernetics, 22(6), 1414–1427
177. Wang, P., ed. (2001): Computing with Words. John Wiley & Sons, New York
178. Weiss, S.M., Kulikowski, C.A. (1991): Computer Systems That Learn. Morgan Kaufmann Publishers, San Mateo
179. White, H. (1990): Connectionist Nonparametric Regression: Multilayer Feedforward Networks Can Learn Arbitrary Mappings. Neural Networks, 3, 535–549
180. Xu, C.W., Lu, Y.Z. (1987): Fuzzy Model Identification and Self-learning for Dynamic Systems. IEEE Transactions on Systems, Man, and Cybernetics, 17(4), 683–689
181. Xu, C.W., Lu, Y.Z. (1987): Fuzzy Model Identification and Self-Learning for Dynamic-Systems. IEEE Transactionsctions on Systems, Man, and Cybernetics, 17(4), 683–689
182. Yager, R.R. (1987): Possibilistic Qualification and Default Rules. In Bouchon, B., Yager, R.R., eds., Uncertainty in Knowledge Based Systems (Lecture Notes in Computer Science 286), 41–57. Springer-Verlag, Berlin
183. Yager, R.R. (1987): Using Approximate Reasoning to Represent Default Knowledge. Artificial Intelligence, 31(1), 99–112
184. Yager, R.R. (1988): A Generalized View of Non-monotonic Knowledge: A Set of Theoretic Perspectives. International Journal of General Systems, 14, 251–265
185. Yager, R.R. (1988): A Mathematical Programming Approach to Inference with the Capability to Implement Default Rules. International Journal of Man-Machine Studies, 29, 685–714
186. Yager, R.R., Larsen, H.L. (1991): On Discovery Potential Inconsistencies in Validating Uncertain Knowledge Bases by Reflecting on the Input. IEEE Transactions on Systems, Man, and Cybernetics, 21(4), 790–801
187. Yen, J., Wang, L. (1998): Improving the Interpretability of TSK Fuzzy Models by Combining Global Learning and Local Learning. IEEE Transactions on Fuzzy Systems, 6(4), 530–537
188. Yoshinari, Y., Pedrycz, W., Hirota, K. (1993): Construction of Fuzzy Models Through Clustering Techniques. Fuzzy Sets and Systems, 54(2), 157–165
189. Yoshinari, Y., Pedrycz, W., Hirota, K. (1993): Construction of Fuzzy Models through Clustering Techniques. Fuzzy Sets and Systems, 54(2), 157–165
190. Zadeh, L.A. (1965): Fuzzy Sets. Information and Control, 8, 338–353
191. Zadeh, L.A. (1975): The Concept of a Linguistic Variable and Its Application to Approximate Reasoning: Part I; Part II; Part III. 8, 199–249;, 8 301–357; 9, 43–80;
192. Zadeh, L.A., Kacprzyk, J. (1999): Computing with Words in Information/Intelligent Systems, Vol 1: Foundations, Vol 2: Applications
193. Zitzler, E., Deb, K., Thiele, L. (2000): Comparison of Multiobjective Evolutionary Algorithms: Empirical Results. Evolutionary Computation, 8(2), 173–195
194. Zitzler, E., Thiele, L. (1999): Multiobjective Evolutionary Algorithms: a Comparative Case Study and the Strength Pareto Approach. IEEE Transactions on Evolutionary Computation, 3(4), 257–271

Index